Introduction

This proceedings contains the papers presented at a workshop held at Cornell University in Ithaca, New York, during July 5-7, 1989. The workshop was sponsored by the Army Research Office through the Mathematical Sciences Institute.

The goal of the workshop was to present current research into formal methods for hardware design. Because of the complexity of VLSI circuits, assuring design validity before circuits are manufactured is imperative. The goal of research in this area is to develop methods of improving the design process and the quality of the resulting designs. The analytic tool of this research is logic; the fundamental problems are to develop ways of using logic to specify systems, model hardware, and verify designs; and to develop tools (for example, theorem provers) that simplify the application of logic to hardware specification and synthesis.

The workshop was attended by over 70 researchers from North America and Europe and papers were presented by 20 invited lecturers. In developing the workshop program, we tried to include representatives from a diverse set of hardware verification projects and geographical regions. We believe that this goal was achieved with one exception – continental Europe is not represented though there are several important projects that would have been appropriate. Funding constraints forced us to focus most of our program on research being performed in the United States. As a result, the workshop provided a forum for US researchers in formal methods for hardware to present their work in the United States. Previously they have had to travel to Europe or Canada to present their results.

The major trend apparent at the workshop is that researchers are rapidly moving away from *post hoc* proof techniques which have received considerable criticism for their great expense. A number of papers were presented that dealt with problems of synthesizing correct circuits and of designing with the goal of verification. In addition, researchers are beginning to deal with the difficult theoretical issues of reasoning about concurrent systems and asynchronous systems. The workshop also saw the introduction of constructive type theory and category theory into the hardware verification community thus providing new logical tools.

The area of formal methods encompasses three major issues: specification, verification, and synthesis. Each of these was addressed at the workshop.

There is no consensus on the best type of specification language to use for formal hardware tools. This is primarily due to the tradeoffs between expressiveness and ease of automated proof. Two types of specification languages have found the widest acceptance – functional programming languages and higher order logics –. with higher order logic being more expressive, and consequently more difficult to mechanize. Papers based upon the higher order logic (HOL) approach were presented by Brian Graham, Paul Loewenstein, Shiu-kai Chin, and Jeffrey Joyce. The functional programming view was supported by papers presented by Steven Johnson, Warren Hunt, and M. K. Srivas. Even more expressive than HOL is constructive type theory and, at the workshop, some of the first results by researchers using this form of logic were presented. These included papers presented by Miriam Leeser,

Peter Del Vecchio, and Keith Hanna. In addition a paper on category theory was presented by Mary Sheeran.

Several speakers presented results on the verification of actual systems. While *post hoc* proof is extremely time consuming, it serves the useful function of driving the development of specification languages and of developing our ability to reason about complex systems. The papers presented on verification considered quite complex systems such as processors (Brian Graham and Graham Birtwistle, M.K. Srivas) and vertically verified systems consisting of a compiler and an underlying processor (Joyce).

The issues of synthesis of correct circuits and design for verification were discussed by Chris Lengauer, George Milne, Miriam Leeser, Raul Camposano and Steve Johnson.

For many years asynchronous design has not been widely used, and the circuits designed have tended to be small. These circuits were simply too hard to design, and the available tools were inadequate. Recently, the application of formal design techniques has led to a revival of asynchronous circuits by making their design more tractable. Papers supporting this revival were presented by P.A. Subrahmanyam, David Dill, and Alain Martin.

Formal methods have been slow to find their way into standard engineering practice; however, it appears that this will soon change. Randy Bryant presented a paper demonstrating the use of formal techniques to speed up traditional hardware simulation tools.

We would like to thank Bob Constable for presenting the welcome address and the following people for chairing sessions: Bob Constable, Beth Levy, Jo Ebergen, Mike Fourman, Jim Caldwell, and Geraint Jones.

Miriam E. Leeser
Geoffrey M. Brown

Table of Contents

DESIGN FOR VERIFIABILITY

George J. Milne
HARDLAB
Department of Computer Science
University of Strathclyde
Glasgow, Scotland, UK.

Abstract. *The concept of Design for Verifiability is introduced as a means of attacking the complexity problem encountered when verifying the correctness of hardware designs using mathematical proof techniques. The inherent complexity of systems implemented as integrated circuits results in a comparable descriptive complexity when modelling them in any framework which supports formal verification. Performing formal verification then rapidly becomes intractable as a consequence of this descriptive complexity. In this paper we propose a strategy for dealing, at least in part, with this problem. We advocate the use of a particular design strategy involving the use of structural design rules which constrain the behaviour of a design resulting in a less complex design verification. The term Design for Verifiability is used to capture this concept in an analogous way to the term Design for Testability.*

1. INTRODUCTION

It is becoming increasingly accepted that *formal verification* has an important role in establishing the functional and temporal correctness of hardware designs. In formal verification mathematical proof techniques are used to demonstrate design correctness to overcome the limitations of the traditional simulation approach. Recent results in applying formal verification techniques to realistically sized examples such as microprocessors [Cohn 87] has revealed the difficulty of post-design verification. This is a consequence of the inherent complexity of integrated circuit hardware due to the number of primitive components from which it is constructed (transistor, gates etc.) and the large amount of interaction which occurs between them at any point in time. Complex hardware leads to complex description in any modelling framework which supports formal verification. This in turn leads to extremely large and complex verification proofs; while any part of the proof may be relatively straightforward, there are a large number of sub-proofs which each need to be performed to establish the complete result.

While most attention has focused to date on post-design verification, that of verifying design correctness as a subsequent procedure following completion of the design, the intractability of this approach must encourage a search for alternative verification strategies. Such alternatives include the integration of verification into the design process with both design and the verification of the last design step being closely coupled and proceeding step by step throughout the design process. This approach is advocated in [Milne 86] and [Davie 88b]. Another approach is to formally verify the correctness of automated design tools such as silicon compilers. This approach, described for a simple example in [Milne 83], has the advantage that the complete class of designs which can be produced mechanically from some high-level design language are all shown to be correct, in some fashion, by the use of a single verification of the translation function.

1.1. The Complexity of Verification

In this paper the concept of *Design for Verifiability* is introduced as a further contribution to the search for (partial) solutions to the complexity issue in hardware verification. Design for Verifiability reduces the verification effort required to establish the correctness of a design by *restricting* designers' freedom to well known *constructions* which are known to simplify the potential behaviour of the hardware being designed. This reduces the number of states the hardware can evolve into at any point in time, depending on the interaction which occurs with the environment, and so reduces the number of distinct "things", such as assertions, requiring proof. Reducing the potential number of states that a system may evolve into is central to this reduction in verification complexity. As is well known from a design perspective, the insertion of clocked latches between blocks of combinational logic reduces the distinct number of states which can be reached at any point in time compared to an unconstrained asynchronous design. This design restriction is then also of significance from a verification perspective and it is this concept which is captured by the phrase *Design for Verifiability*.

The intention in this paper is to introduce the concept of Design for Verifiability and to argue the case for it intuitively rather than formally. Before defining and discussing this concept in more detail, it should be pointed out that the all pervasive nature of design and verification complexity is such that no one approach to the complexity issue will in practice be sufficient. Design for Verifiability is just one approach and it will probably need to be used in conjunction with other complexity reducing techniques such as those mentioned above.

2. DESIGN FOR VERIFIABILITY

While Design for Verifiability is a concept which may have far reaching significance for hardware design in the future, it is not a strange concept. Some of the relevant ideas are prevalent today in current design practice.

2.1 Reducing Design Complexity

The classic application of managing design complexity is that of performing purely synchronous design as governed by an appropriately phased system clock rather than asynchronous design which is governed by the delays encountered in individual components. By constraining the design space by restricting a designer's freedom to an architecture involving interspersed clocked latches such as in Figure 1, a more easily understandable design results. In the absence of this synchronous *design template*, an asynchronous design with its attendant speed and area improvements may be attempted. However, it is well known that it is a difficult task to both design asynchronous hardware and to ensure that it works correctly.

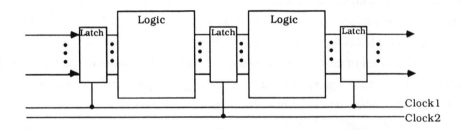

Fig. 1

Limiting designers freedom with the goal of aiding the formal verification of design correctness may require a price to be paid in terms of area and speed but this may be acceptable to achieve the goal. Adding in clocked latches as in Figure 1 may add extra components to a design, while slowing down the system clock driving the operation of the latches to that of the slowest functional unit in a datapath, for example, may seriously affect performance.

2.2   Reducing Verification Complexity

Formal verification requires that a *modelling framework* is used to describe the *behaviour* of a given design by creating a *model* of that particular design. Mathematical proof techniques are then used to establish whether the model satisfies certain required properties. These propeties capture the necessary features which determine that the hardware module will have the correct behaviour when manufactured, up to manufacturing errors. For this verification procedure to be of value requires that the intended physical behaviour of the design is described accurately in the model. A complex design will then be mirrored by an equally complex description in the model . If this is not the case then the description will probably be too much of an approximation and the value of any formal verification results which arise from using it must be questioned.

A prevalent property of hardware requiring verification is where a design described at a given level of detail is shown to satisfy a more abstract description of its required behaviour, its *specification*. The *implementation* and the specification both have their behaviour expressed in the model, the implementation or design behaviour usually being created *constuctively* from descriptions of its component parts. Whether a verification proof establishing the correctness of the design in terms of the relationship between the two descriptions is performed using an assertional model such as those based on various predicate logics [Eveking 86, Gordon 86, Hanna 85] or on an action/state process model [Milne 86], a form of case analysis is required. As the behaviour of the hardware being described evolves through various states depending on what external stimuli are input into it from its interconnected hardware environment, any properties of the implemented design which limit the possible state evolution under given inputs has obvious bearing on subsequent verification; the fewer the number of states which can be reached results in fewer distinct parts of the proof to be performed.

In Section 4 the advantages for verification of reducing the possible state space that a system may evolve into at any point in time are illustrated using an example. Before that, some ideas on limiting design freedom to achieve state space reduction are discussed.

3.   RESTRICTING DESIGNER FREEDOM

The key idea behind Design for Verifiability is the use of a particular way of limiting designers' freedom to make the subsequent verification procedure more tractable. Performing a design step, in going from a specification at one level of abstraction to an implementation at a lower level of abstraction, involves the designer making design choices. These alternative designs which the designer trusts will all satisfy the specified behaviour are what constitutes the design space. The purpose of formal verification is to rigorously demonstrate that the chosen implementation does in fact faithfully satisfy the specification. This scenario is pictured in Figure 2.

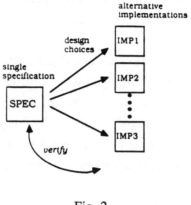

Fig. 2

3.1 Restricting the Structure of a Design

The principle approach to limiting the possible states which an implementation may evolve into at any point in time is to impose a particular *target architecture* on the designer. This restricts the design choices to those which are known by prior experimentation to produce an implementation which limits the possible states which the implementation evolves into. A particular architectural template will restrict the *structure* of the design and will involve restricting the designer to the use of a certain class of components to construct the implementation. This may involve the use of additional components to that of the "obvious" implementation, and it may restrict the designer to composing these components, that is constructing the implementation, in a particular way. An example of a particular microprocessor target architecture is that used by the MacPitts silicon compiler [Siskind 82] which because of the algorithmic nature of the automated design necessitates the production of a restrictive class of design. In this case it involves the regular placement of registers and functional units on the datapath of a microprocessor.

A target architecture may be used to *constrain* the designer into producing a particular class of designs which are known to simplify the verification procedure. The availability of additional clocked latches as illustrated in Figure 1 acts to constrain the potential behaviour of the combinational logic module by limiting when and how the inputs reach the logic. If we assume a propagation delay across *every* block of combinational logic which is less than the clock phase then no input changes can occur at the latch when it is on. This design constraint, consisting of the use of latches between logic modules together with assumptions as to the propagation delay across every module relative to the system clock period, is shown to simplify verification using the example in the following section. These constraining assumptions will need to be established at a subsequent design step and this is discussed in more detail in [Davie 88a, Davie 88b].

The restrictions used to limit the type of target architecture that an implementation should take can be enforced by the design language itself. A particular methodology for using a design language may also be required but it is thought that the enforcements of constraints may be achieved primarily at a language level. What may be proposed is a range of operators or constructs in the language which permit designs to be constructed in only that limited way which is known to satisfy a particular constraining strategy.

Essentially we use the design language to restrict the designer to creating particular design *structures* which are known to simplify the behaviour of the design. That is, the language restricts design choice to only those implementations in Figure 2 which have the desired structure; structure is being used to constrain behaviour.

This scenario is pictured in Figure 3.

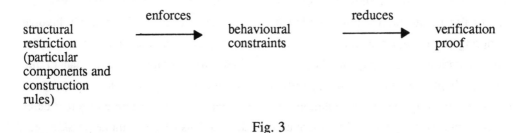

Fig. 3

3.2   Language Constructs for Structural Restriction

A design language can be used to assist the design process by using high-level language constructs to simplify the high-level representation of the design while at the same time restricting the designer to a particular design structure which leads to simplification of the verification procedure. This is analogous to the use of high-level programming languages to improve the chances of program correctness by restricting access to the total functionality of the host computer.

The advantages of using the rigorous latch/logic structure pictured in Figure 1, where the clock period is longer than the longest delay across any of the logic modules, was discussed above. Certain high-level language constructs can be created to ensure that only structures of this particular type can be produced. The "wire-up" language constructs introduced in [Davie 88b] can be used to illustrate this feature.

Two constructs called *wire-in-series* and *wire-in-parallel* may be the only construction rules given by a design language. The arguments for the wire-in-parallel operator would be the basic building-block gates available in a design library.

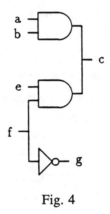

Fig. 4

The circuit pictured in Figure 4, taken from [Davie 88b], is expressed in the design language by:

block1 = wire-in-parallel (and (a,b,c), and (e,f,c),inv(f,g))

where the increasingly common concept of wiring together similarly named ports is used, as in VHDL. This language feature is constructive in that it constructs a larger block out of smaller parts. It may also generate an error signal if input and output ports are connected so indicating wiring in series rather than in parallel.

CIRCAL [Milne 86, Davie 88b] and HOL [Gordon 86] are two modelling frameworks used for hardware verification. They are both constructive with composition in CIRCAL being effected by the * operator while in HOL logical conjunction ^ is used. The CIRCAL and HOL definitions of the above use of the wire-in-parallel operator are given respectively by:

CIRCAL
>   block1 <= and [a,b,c] * and [e,f,c] * inv[f,g]

HOL
> ⊢ def block1 (a,b,c,e,f,g) = and (a,b,c) ^ and (e,f,c,) ^ inv(f,g)

The wire-in-series operator can be used to insert latches between some appropriate number of gates. The number n would be such that for a given maximum delay m across any of the component gates, mxn is a period of time less than a given clock period. The wire-in-series operator would then ensure this property by taking any number of arguments, either gates or parallel blocks, provided they did not exceed n. The convention that similarly named ports wire together would also be adopted by this language construct with all ports wired in series being *internalised*. In addition a single clocked latch would be attached to all remaining output ports, as pictured in Figure 5. Notice that the latch required on the input to the logic module would be created by a separate use of the wire-in-series operator, as used to create the preceeding logic module.

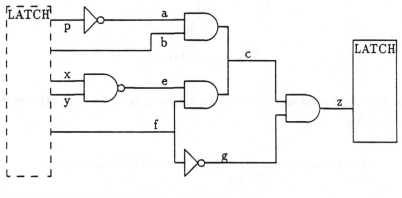

Fig. 5

The design pictured in Figure 5 would be constructed using the two language features as follows:

>   block 0 = wire-in-parallel (inv(p,a), nand (x,y,e))
>   block 1 = wire-in-parallel (and(a,b,c), and (e,f,c),inv(f,g))

>   big-block = wire-in-series (block0,block1,and(c,g,z))

These two language features, if provided as the sole structural construction mechanism in a design language, restrict the designer to producing clocked combinational logic which is consistent with the prescribed restrictive design strategy. In the next section we will use the same logic/latch structure to illustrate how structural design restrictions ensure constrained behaviour which in turn simplifies the verification procedure.

The above example and the two language features were used by Davie in [Davie 88b] to illustrate another advantage of using a design language to restrict a design. The above design strategy assists a novice designer by reducing the number of design choices (if any) that are made available. Furthermore, by using the two language features the user knows that the resulting design will always store the result of the combinational logic into the output latch before the latch is clocked, without the need for individual gate delay calculation.

4.   CONSTRAINING DESIGN BEHAVIOUR

The concept of using structure to constrain device behaviour was proposed in the previous section. It remains to be seen how this can be achieved and in this section the clocked latch/logic example is used to illustrate how the reduced behaviour assists the subsequent verification.

The form of verification pictured in Figure 2 consists of rigorously demonstrating that an implementation meets its specification. We are required to show that they have essentially the same behaviour according to some satisfaction relation, equivalence for example. Formal verification differs from simulation in that this property must hold for all possible input stimuli patterns. The role of additional components, such as clocked latches, in any Design for Verifiability methodology is to reduce the range of possible stimuli which may be input at any given point in time. This then reduces the possible states that the implementation may evolve into, so reducing the number of distinct cases which need to be proved.

4.1   An Outline Example

The amount of information contained in a specification and the amount described in an implementation, such as in Figure 2, will differ. The very nature of a design step from specification to implementation entails the addition of information. This then means that a certain amount of freedom exists in producing various distinct implementations; all that is required of them is that they are consistent with the more abstractly described specification.

In Figure 6 two possible implementations are shown for a particular specification. The specification essentially consists of a statement that a particular logic function is required but no indication is given as to how it should be constructed nor are any limits set on timing characteristics.

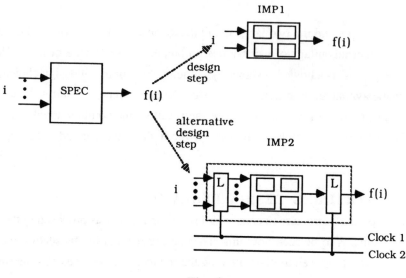

Fig. 6

It can be seen how implementation IMP1 is constructed from logic components such as gates. The alternative implementation IMP2 is constructed in an identical fashion to IMP1 but with the addition of an input and output latch which are driven from a suitable system clock; the language features described in Section 3 could have been used to produce IMP2 for example. Supposing that IMP1 and IMP2 are believed to satisfy SPEC in some way, that is the behaviour described by the specification is assumed to be achieved by both IMP1 and IMP2, then this property requires to be formally verified. A simple, informal argument can be given to show how the constrained behaviour imposed by the structure of IMP2 makes the proof of

IMP2 *satisfies* SPEC

simpler than that of

IMP1 *satisifes* SPEC.

The *satisfies* relation will exist in whichever formal modelling framework is being used to conduct the proof. For example, it can be defined in CIRCAL [Milne 85, Davie 88b] by:

IMP *satisfies* SPEC   iff   IMP*SPEC = SPEC

where IMP and SPEC are CIRCAL processes and = corresponds to CIRCAL equivalence.

Alternatively, it can be defined in HOL [Gordon 86] by:
$\qquad$ IMP *satisifes* SPEC   iff   IMP^SPEC is *true*

where IMP and SPEC are predicates.

4.2   State Reduction

Supposing the input vector to SPEC is of width n, that is the input consists of n bit lines say, and we intend the device to compute function f(i), a logical function of n arguments. Looking at IMP1, at any point-in-time any combination of the n input lines can change. If we assume that each distinct combination may cause the internal state of IMP1 to change, the implementation may evolve to one of 2^n-1 states. Each internal state will usually evolve through a number of other states at subsequent points-in-time before the input propagates through to the output. Unfortunately at each of the subsequent time points prior to the new output appearing there is no reason why the inputs cannot change yet again; it is the surrounding environment which determines this and not IMP1. This then means that a maximum of 2^n-1 new states may be reached from *every* internal state at *every* point-in-time and so the potential state space grows exponentially.

On the other hand IMP2 constrains *when* input changes appear at its combinational logic part, that which corresponds to the complete IMP1. If input changes can be restricted to occur only when latch L1 is off, then only one combination of changes on the n input lines will reach the logic during a complete cycle. The possible number of states which IMP2 may evolve into is then restricted to 2^n-1 and does not grow as IMP2 evolves through further internal states until the output appears.

To prove that either implementation *satisfies* the specification requires showing that under any input pattern both the specification and the implementation evolve into states where the new-state of the implementation again *satisfies* the new-state of the specification. In comparing the behaviour of IMP2 to SPEC the 2^n-1 potential states need to be examined by some form of case analysis; with IMP1 we need to examine all $(2^n-1)^m$ possible states, where m is the number of time units required to propagate the result through the logic! The reduced state-space that IMP2 may evolve into directly reduces the effort required to verify the correctness of the implementation against the specified behaviour. The consequences for verification of restricting design freedom by the use of restrictive language constucts such as those given in Section 3 are therefore significant.

5. CONCLUDING REMARKS

In this paper, a strategy for improving the tractability of hardware verification is proposed. As VLSI designs increase in size the need to consider the feasibility of formally validating them becomes even more pressing. This Design for Verifiability strategy is intended to restrict designers to using particular structures which are known to constrain the behaviour of the design and so reduce the verification effort required to establish design conrrectness. The intention of this design technique is not to restrict design to correct as opposed to incorrect implementations of a specification, but rather to design alternative architectures which, according to predefined architectural construction rules, are known to simplify the subsequent verification process.

The goal of this paper was to introduce this Design for Verifiability concept and to informally justify it. No concrete results are available since Design for Verifiability is just a concept and not a proven design methodology; one of the goals of an EEC Esprit research project known as "CHARME" is to develop the concept in more detail. The hope is that this discussion will stimulate researchers into delving further into the relationship between design and verification with the aim of making formal verification a *practical* alternative to simulation for future VLSI design. While the example involving latched combinational logic is known to simplify design and hence verification, the ultimate objective will be to synthetically generate design construction rules which may not at first appear as obvious as the inclusion of latches but which also simplify the verification procedure.

REFERENCES

[Cohn 87]   A. Cohn, "A Proof of Correctness of the Viper microprocessor: the First Level". Technical Report 104, Computer Laboratory, University of Cambridge, January 1987.

[Davie 88a]   B.S. Davie and G.J. Milne, "Contextual Constraints for Design and Verification". In VLSI Specification, Verification and Synthesis, Birtwistle and Subrahmanyam (Eds). Kluwer Academic Publishers, 1988.

[Davie 88b]   B.S. Davie, "A Formal, Hierarchical Design and Validation Methodology for VLSI", Ph.D. thesis CST-55-88, Department of Computer Science, University of Edinburgh.

[Eveking 86]   H. Eveking, "Formal Verification of Synchronous Systems". In Formal Aspects of VLSI Design, Milne and Subrahmanyam (eds). Elsevier North-Holland, 1986.

[Gordon 86]   M. Gordon, "Why Higher-Order Logic is a Good Formalism for Specifying and Verifying Hardware". In Formal Aspects of VLSI Design, Milne and Subrahmanyam (eds). Elsevier North-Holland, 1986.

[Hanna 85]   F.K. Hanna and N. Daeche, "Specification and Verification using Higher-Order Logic". Proc. 7th Int. Symp. on Computer Hardware Description Languages and their Applications (CHDL 85), Elsevier North-Holland, 1985.

[Milne 83]   G.J. Milne, "The Correctness of a Simple Silicon Compiler". Proc. 6th Int. Symp. on Computer Hardware Description Languages and their Applications (CHDL 83), Uehara and Barbacci (eds), Elsevier North-Holland, 1983.

[Milne 86]   G.J. Milne, "Towards Verifiably Correct VLSI Design". In Formal Apsects of VLSI Design, Milne and Subrahmanyam (eds), Elsevier North-Holland, 1986.

[Siskind 82]   J. Siskind, J. Southard and K. Crouch, "Generating Custom High-Performance VLSI Designs from Succinct Algorithmic Descriptions". In Proc. MIT Conference on Advanced Research in VLSI, MIT, 1982.

Verification of Synchronous Circuits by Symbolic Logic Simulation

Randal E. Bryant
Carnegie Mellon University

Abstract. *A logic simulator can prove the correctness of a digital circuit when it can be shown that only circuits implementing the system specification will produce a particular response to a sequence of simulation commands. By simulating a circuit symbolically, verification can avoid the combinatorial explosion that would normally occur when evaluating circuit operation over many combinations of input and initial state. In this paper, we describe our methodology for verifying synchronous circuits using the stack circuit of Mead and Conway as an illustrative example.*

1. Verification by Simulation

Logic simulators have long been used to test for errors in digital circuit designs. Typically, however, the user only simulates a limited set of test cases and assumes that the circuit is correct if the simulator yields the expected results for all cases. Unfortunately, this form of simulation provides no guarantee that all design errors have been eliminated. A successful simulation run can indicate either that the circuit design is correct, or that an insufficient set of test cases was tried. Conventional wisdom holds that simulators are incapable of more rigorous verification. They are viewed in the same class as program debuggers–useful tools for informal testing, but nothing more.

The conventional wisdom about logic simulation overlooks the capabilities provided by three-valued logic modeling, in which the state set $\{0, 1\}$ is augmented by a third value X indicating an unknown digital value. Most modern logic simulators provide this form of modeling, if for nothing more than to provide an initial value for the state variables at the start of simulation. Assuming the simulator obeys a relatively mild monotonicity property, a three-valued simulator can verify the circuit behavior for many possible input and initial state combinations simultaneously. That is, if the simulation of a pattern containing X's yields 0 or 1 on some node, the same result would occur if these X's were replaced by any combination of 0's and 1's. This technique is effective for cases where the behavior of the circuit for some operation is not supposed to depend on the values of some of the inputs or state variables.

Using a conventional simulator, a surprisingly large class of circuits can be verified in polynomial time (as measured in the circuit size). For example, an N-bit random access memory (RAM) can be verified by simulating just $O(N \log N)$ patterns with a switch-level simulator [6]. By this means, we have successfully verified a 4K static CMOS RAM. In this verification, we exploit the property that an operation on one memory location should not affect or be affected by the value at any other memory location. Thus many aspects of circuit operation can be verified by simulating the circuit with all, or all but one, bits set to X, covering a large number of circuit conditions with a single simulation operation.

Other classes of circuits cannot be verified by simulating a polynomial number of patterns. Many functions computed by logic circuits, such as addition and parity, depend on a large number of input or state variables. For these circuits, we propose *symbolic* simulation [2] as a feasible and straightforward approach to design verification. A symbolic simulator resembles a conventional logic simulator, except that the user may introduce symbolic Boolean variables to represent input and initial state values, and the simulator computes the behavior of the circuit as a function of these Boolean variables. Earlier attempts at symbolic simulation [7] had only limited success, because they did little more than trace the possible control sequences of the system. By endowing a symbolic simulator with a powerful Boolean manipulation capability [4], we derive canonical representations of the Boolean functions describing the value of every state variable and primary output in the circuit. These functions can then be compared with ones derived from the system specification.

Our first symbolic simulator MOSSYM [2] demonstrated the feasibility of symbolic switch-level simulation, verifying ALU circuits in minutes of CPU time that would have required centuries to verify by exhaustive simulation. Since that time, others have improved the efficiency of symbolic simulation significantly [9]. Most recently, we have added a symbolic capability to our switch-level simulator COSMOS [5]. On benchmarks for which MOSSYM required 10 minutes of CPU time, COSMOS requires only 11 seconds.

2. Verification Methodology

Verifying a combinational circuit by symbolic simulation is conceptually straightforward. Each circuit input is set to a different Boolean variable, and the circuit is simulated to derive representations of the Boolean functions for each primary output. These output functions are then compared to ones derived from the system specification. This technique even applies to some forms of clocked circuits, such as those using domino logic or precharged carry chains, where the outputs should only depend on the most recent inputs. Such a circuit is verified by simulating it over one complete clock cycle, with the clock inputs set to constants according to the clocking pattern, and with the remaining inputs set to Boolean variables. With the COSMOS symbolic simulator, we have verified a variety of such circuits including ALU's and an 80-bit priority encoder.

Sequential circuits, however, require a totally different verification methodology. We have shown [3] that, with only a limited set of exceptions, a sequential system cannot be verified by simply observing its output response to a set of simulation patterns. This result holds even when using three-valued simulation. Instead, verification requires specifying how the system state is represented in the circuit. Verification then involves proving that the state transition behavior of the circuit matches that of the system specification.

We have devised a methodology for verifying synchronous circuits that involves specifying the circuit at 4 levels of abstraction:

1. The desired functionality, expressed as a state machine operating on an abstracted system state.

2. The circuit interface, expressed in terms of the clocking patterns, as well as the times within a clock cycle at which the inputs are applied and the outputs sensed.

3. The mapping between the abstract system state and the internal circuit state.

4. A transistor-level description of the circuit.

The first two parts comprise the *external* specification of the system. That is, they define the desired input/output behavior. We find it convenient to divide the external specification into these two components. The first part defines the high level system behavior in a manner that is independent of any implementation. The second part defines the details of the input/output interface including the signalling and clocking conventions. The third part of the specification provides the details we require about the internal circuit state in order to make verification by simulation possible. This is far less information than most other approaches to formal verification require. From these first three parts, we can derive a set of symbolic patterns to be simulated.

The fourth part of the system specification is used by the COSMOS preprocessor to produce an executable symbolic simulation program. In effect, the preprocessor automatically converts the detailed representation of the circuit structure into an executable representation of the circuit behavior. If the simulator produces the desired response to the symbolic patterns, then the circuit is proved correct.

3. Specification Example

We illustrate our verification methodology by verifying the nMOS stack circuit presented in Mead and Conway [8]. This circuit is an interesting test case for formal verification for several reasons:

- It uses circuitry that cannot be represented at the gate level. Hence, switch-level modeling is imperative.

- Two stack control signals are multiplexed onto a single input. Consequently, the circuit timing is tricky.

- The circuit employs a small amount of pipelining. The stack command signals for clock cycle t are supplied during the last part of cycle $t-1$ and the first half of cycle t.

It is important that any approach to formal verification be able to handle subtleties such as these, because they are frequent sources of design errors. We cannot expect designers to simplify their circuits and interfaces simply to facilitate formal verification.

3.1. High Level Specification

Specifying the desired behavior of a stack is straightforward. We assume that the stack is 1 bit wide and k bits deep. When d elements are stored in the stack, the stack locations are numbered 1 (top) to d (bottom). We will define the desired behavior of the stack in terms of a set of predicates. The definitions of these predicates will later be formalized according to the detailed circuit interface and state representation. For now, we describe the predicates informally:

$push(t)$: The stack executes a Push operation on clock cycle t.

$pop(t)$: The stack executes a Pop operation on clock cycle t.

$hold(t)$: The stack executes a Hold operation on clock cycle t.

$Depth(d,t)$: There are d $(0 \leq d \leq k)$ items on the stack at end of cycle t.

$Stored(i,t,v)$: Value $v \in \{0,1\}$ is stored at stack location i $(1 \leq i \leq k)$ at end of cycle t.

$Input(t,v)$: Value $v \in \{0,1\}$ is supplied to the stack input during cycle t.

$Output(t,v)$: Value $v \in \{0,1\}$ appears on the stack output during cycle t.

With these predicates, we can define the effect of a push operation on a nonfull stack on cycle t in terms of the circuit state on cycle $t-1$ and the circuit input on cycle t. That is, a push operation should cause the input to be stored in stack location 1, and the value at each stack location i to move to location $i+1$. Thus, for any d such that $0 \le d < k$:

$$
\begin{aligned}
&Depth(t-1,d) \ \wedge \ \forall[1 \le i \le d]Stored(i,t-1,v_{i+1}) \\
&\wedge \ Input(t,v_1) \ \wedge \ push(t) \\
&\Rightarrow \\
&Depth(t,d+1) \ \wedge \ \forall[1 \le i \le d+1]Stored(i,t,v_i)
\end{aligned}
\tag{1}
$$

In this equation, the variables v_i for $1 \le i \le k$ are considered to be universally quantified over $\{0,1\}$.

Similarly, the effect of a pop operation on a nonempty stack should be to transfer the value at each stack location $i+1$ to location i, and for the output to equal the value popped off the top. Thus, for any d such that $1 \le d \le k$:

$$
\begin{aligned}
&Depth(t-1,d) \ \wedge \ \forall[1 \le i \le d]Stored(i,t-1,v_i) \ \wedge \ pop(t) \\
&\Rightarrow \\
&Depth(t,d-1) \ \wedge \ \forall[1 \le i < d]Stored(i,t,v_{i+1}) \ \wedge \ Output(t,v_1)
\end{aligned}
\tag{2}
$$

Finally, during a hold operation, the stack contents should not change. Thus, for any d such that $0 \le d \le k$:

$$
\begin{aligned}
&Depth(t-1,d) \ \wedge \ \forall[1 \le i \le d]Stored(i,t-1,v_i) \ \wedge \ hold(t) \\
&\Rightarrow \\
&Depth(t,d) \ \wedge \ \forall[1 \le i \le d]Stored(i,t,v_i)
\end{aligned}
\tag{3}
$$

The above specification should hold for any implementation of a stack. We have been careful not to overspecify its behavior. We have not specified the effect of a push operation on a full stack or a pop operation on an empty stack. We also have not specified the stack output for stack operations other than pop. Details such as these vary from one stack implementation to another. If a particular application requires a specific way of handling such boundary conditions, these could also be verified.

3.2. Interface Specification

Figure 1 gives a timing diagram of the stack circuit interface. The circuit operates with a two-phase nonoverlapping clock. The stack command is specified by a pair of signals, OP1 and OP2, according to the following table:

Operation	OP1	OP2
Push	1	0
Pop	0	1
Hold	0	0

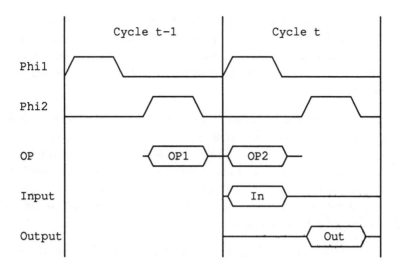

Figure 1: **Stack Circuit Timing Interface.** Control signal OP is pipelined 1/2 cycle ahead of the data signals In and Out.

As is shown in Figure 1, these two signals are multiplexed onto circuit input OP. That is, the stack command for clock cycle t is specified by supplying OP1 on the Phi2 phase of cycle $t-1$, and OP2 on the Phi1 phase of cycle t. The input data must be supplied during the Phi1 phase, and the output is valid during the Phi2 phase.

3.3. State Specification

Figure 2 shows a single cell of the stack circuit. The stack is created by composing these cells horizontally, numbered 1 to k from left to right. The control signals

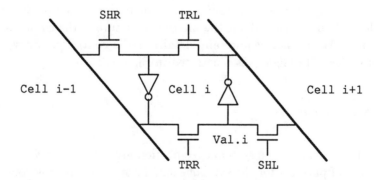

Figure 2: **Cell i of Stack.** Stack element i is stored on node Val.i.

SHR, TRL, TRR, and SHL are derived from the clocks and the OP input by the control circuitry [8, p. 73]. The charge on the node labeled Val.i is considered to represent the contents of stack location i in complemented form. That is, we will consider the predicate $Stored(i,t,v)$ as specifying that at the end of cycle t, node Val.i is charged to logic value $\neg v$.

This particular stack implementation does not keep track of the stack depth. Instead, on a push or pop operation, it shifts whatever data happen to be stored in the stack cells. Thus, we can handle the details how the stack operates for different depths by verifying a stronger set of conditions than is required to satisfy Equations 1, 2, and 3. The modified equations omit all explicit references to the stack depth. Instead, they place constraints on a range of stack locations that covers all possible depths. The effect of a push operations becomes:

$$Input(t,v_1) \;\wedge\; \forall[1 \leq i \leq k-1]Stored(i,t-1,v_{i+1}) \;\wedge\; push(t)$$
$$\Rightarrow \tag{4}$$
$$\forall[1 \leq i \leq k]Stored(i,t,v_i)$$

The effect of a pop operation becomes:

$$\forall[1 \leq i \leq k]Stored(i,t-1,v_i) \;\wedge\; pop(t)$$
$$\Rightarrow \tag{5}$$
$$\forall[1 \leq i < k]Stored(i,t,v_{i+1}) \;\wedge\; Output(t,v_1)$$

Finally, the effect of a hold operation becomes:

$$\forall[1 \leq i \leq k]Stored(i,t-1,v_i) \;\wedge\; hold(t)$$
$$\Rightarrow \tag{6}$$
$$\forall[1 \leq i \leq k]Stored(i,t,v_i)$$

Any circuit which satisfies these modified equations must also satisfy the original equations, since the modified equations place more stringent conditions on the circuit operation.

Given the modified verification conditions, a definition of the predicate $Stored$ is the only information we need about the internal structure of the circuit to carry out the verification. We do not require any details of the control circuitry, or even as much detail of the cell design as is illustrated in Figure 2.

4. Simulation Patterns

From the three parts of the system specification given in the previous section, we can derive a set of patterns for the symbolic simulator. The patterns consist of three sections, one for each stack command. Each section starts by resetting the circuit so that every node has state X. It then simulates 1 1/2 clock cycles: the last half of cycle $t-1$ and all of cycle t.

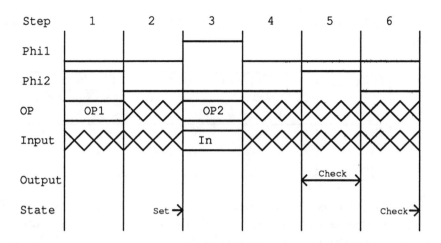

Figure 3: **General Form of Simulation Patterns**. Verifying 1 cycle of system operation requires simulating 1 1/2 cycles (6 steps) of circuit operation due to the pipelining of the control signals.

Each section has the general form illustrated in Figure 3. The patterns involve simulating 6 steps: 2 for cycle $t-1$ and 4 for cycle t. During each step, an input is set either to 0 (low horizontal line), 1 (high horizontal line), X (cross hatches), or to a case-specific value (annotated double line). Thus, the clocks are operated according to a two-phase, nonoverlapping discipline. During steps 1 and 3, input OP is set to the appropriate values for the operation being verified. On all other steps, OP is set to X, indicating that the value on this input should not matter during these times. During step 3, data input In is set to either a variable (push) or to X. It is set to X on all other steps. When verifying the pop operation, the circuit output is monitored during step 5. The states of the stack cells are set after step 2 and are checked after step 6.

Observe how these simulation patterns use the power of three-valued modeling to express the full generality of the circuit operation. By initializing all internal nodes to X, we cover all possible operations that could have occurred prior to the last half of cycle $t-1$. By setting OP to X on all steps other than 1 and 3, we cover all possible operations in which this signal either makes a transition or is set to some value during these other steps. In actual use, OP would be set either to 0 or to 1 during step 5 to specify the OP1 value for cycle $t+1$. By simulating the circuit with this value set to X, we cover both possibilities. Similarly, by setting the data input to X on all steps other than 3, we cover all possible times at which this signal may make a transition. Observe also that by setting and checking the internal state exactly one clock cycle apart, we maintain a consistent view of how data are stored.

The values of OP1 and OP2 for the three stack operations have already been specified. The following table shows the other values used for the 3 different sets of patterns:

Operation	Settings			Checks		
	In	val.i $1 \leq i < k$	val.k	Out	val.i $1 \leq i < k$	val.k
Push	v_1	$\neg v_{i+1}$	X	$-$	$\neg v_i$	$\neg v_k$
Pop	X	$\neg v_i$	$\neg v_k$	v_1	$\neg v_{i+1}$	$-$
Hold	X	$\neg v_i$	$\neg v_k$	$-$	$\neg v_i$	$\neg v_k$

The symbolic patterns involve k Boolean variables $v_1, \ldots, v_k$. Under the "Checks" section, '$-$' indicates that this value need not be checked. These patterns follow directly from our modified system specification (Equations 4, 5, and 6), the interface specification, and the state specification.

5. Experimental Results

We have successfully verified stacks of both $k = 4$ and $k = 16$. Running on a Digital Equipment Corporation Microvax-II, the symbolic simulations require only 1 and 2.3 seconds, respectively. In fact, the time complexity of the verification grows only linearly with the circuit size.

6. Observations

This example illustrates the power of symbolic simulation as a tool for formal verification. Although the verification uses a detailed, switch-level model, virtually all details of the internal circuit structure were handled automatically. We only needed to specify a mapping from the abstract system state to the state representation within the circuit. Furthermore, the simulation interface provides a natural means to specify operational details such as the clocking scheme, the input and output timing, etc. Using the power of three-valued modeling, we could verify circuit operation for cycle t in such a way that it would be compatible with any operations on cycles $t-1$ and $t+1$.

Verifying other implementations of stack circuits requires creating different simulation patterns according to their interface and state specifications. For example, in a stack implemented as a RAM plus a pointer to the top of stack, stack location i in the system specification would correspond to RAM address $d - i$, when the stack depth equals d. We could introduce Boolean variables $d_0, \ldots, d_k$, where $d_i = 1$ indicates that the stack depth equals i. The symbolic simulation patterns would then involve Boolean formulas over $v_1, \ldots, v_k$ and $d_0, \ldots, d_k$.

Whereas our approach involves defining a mapping from specification states to the circuit states, Bose and Fisher have developed a methodology where the mapping is made from the circuit state to the specification state [1]. They have verified circuits containing very subtle forms of pipelining. More experience is required to see how best to incorporate the detailed state representation.

In our example, we derived the symbolic simulation patterns manually. We hope to make this process more automated. Doing so requires a more formal notation to express the interface specification.

We feel we have just begun to tap the power of symbolic simulation in terms of both expressive power and performance. We hope to create a tool that can be used to verify a wide range of complex VLSI systems in a manner that circuit designers find intuitive.

7. Acknowledgements

Derek Beatty and Carl Seger have provided valuable assistance in this work. This research was supported by the Defense Advanced Research Projects Agency, ARPA Order Number 4976.

References

[1] S. Bose, and A. L. Fisher, "Verifying pipelined hardware using symbolic logic simulation," *International Conference on Computer Design*, IEEE, 1989.

[2] R. E. Bryant, "Symbolic verification of MOS circuits," *1985 Chapel Hill Conference on VLSI*, 1985, 419–438.

[3] R. E. Bryant, "Can a simulator verify a circuit?", in *Formal Aspects of VLSI Design*, G. J. Milne, and P. A. Subrahmanyam, *eds.*, North-Holland, 1986, 125–126.

[4] R. E. Bryant, "Graph-based algorithms for Boolean function manipulation", *IEEE Transactions on Computers*, Vol. C-35, No. 8 (August, 1986), 677–691.

[5] R. E. Bryant, D. Beatty, K. Brace, K. Cho, and T. Sheffler, "COSMOS: a compiled simulator for MOS circuits," *24th Design Automation Conference*, 1987, 9–16.

[6] R. E. Bryant, "Verifying a static RAM design by logic simulation," *Fifth MIT Conference on Advanced Research in VLSI*, 1988, 335–349.

[7] J. A. Darringer, "The application of program verification techniques to hardware verification," *16th Design Automation Conference*, 1979, 375–381.

[8] C. A. Mead, and L. Conway, *Introduction to VLSI Systems*, Addison-Wesley, 1980.

[9] D. S. Reeves, and M. J. Irwin, "Fast methods for switch-level verification of MOS circuits," *IEEE Transactions on Computer-Aided Design of Integrated Circuits and Systems*, Vol. CAD-6, No. 5 (Sept., 1987), 766–779.

Constraints, Abstraction, and Verification

Daniel Weise
Computer Systems Laboratory
Stanford University

Abstract *Circuits are not designed to work in all environments: a contract exists between a circuit and the environments in which it correctly operates. The contract is specified by constraints, predicates that must be satisfied by the inputs supplied to the circuit by its environment. A verifier employs constraints during verification to ignore behaviors that will not arise. This paper systematically investigates constraints. We show that: the standard verification condition needs to be revamped to avoid technical and philosophical problems; that there are two important classes of constraints; that one of these classes can be automatically generated; and that constraints arise from an interaction between models and abstractions.*

1 Introduction

Verification of digital circuits is concerned with *implementations,* which are structural descriptions, *behaviors,* which are the input/output relations that a circuit computes, and *constraints,* which are promises about the inputs a circuit will receive. These three items, as discussed in Section 2, appear in different guises in nearly every verification system. This paper investigates the purpose and role of constraints during verification, where they come from, and how they should be handled. We believe that constraints should be explicit to enable the verifier to reason about them.

In Section 3 we analyze *abstract behavioral specifications* and show that they weaken the force of specifications. The key to abstract behavioral specifications are *implicit* constraints that dictate when the specification is to hold. These implicit constraints allow for abstract behavioral specifications, but at the same time they prevent one from requiring that the implementation exhibit specific behaviors. Making constraints *explicit* allows for abstract behavioral specifications without losing the rigor of non-abstract specifications.

Data abstraction and verification is presented in Section 4. When the domain of the desired behavior is more abstract than the domain of the derived behavior — for example, boolean values versus analog values or integers versus booleans — abstraction functions are used to map the lower-level domain to the more abstract domain. Not all lower-level values abstract to higher level values; we call such values *invalid.* We use *abstraction constraints* to ensure that the invalid values will not arise.

Section 5 examines different circuit models and the abstraction constraints that are needed as the models become more detailed. It discusses models for resistances, threshold drops, capacitances, charge leakage, and for storing state either through capacitors or feedback loops. It presents the relevant abstraction constraints for each model.

The automatic generation of abstraction constraints is discussed in Section 6. The key idea is a representation that makes invalid values explicit. The conditions that yield the invalid values are then outlawed by issuing a constraint. Automatically generating abstraction constraints is very important, as it it very tedious for a designer to produce the constraints a verifier needs.

2 Nomenclature and Review

This section defines terminology and reviews circuit verification. The *implementation* of a circuit is defined as the structural composition of primitive elements and circuits. We let *Design* range over all possible structural descriptions of circuits. A given *Design* has a vector of ports $\vec{P}$ of length $|\vec{P}|$. These ports can assume different values from the *implementation domain,* denoted D_i. We denote the values on the ports as $\vec{p}$. When we consider circuits as having specific inputs and outputs we will refer to those ports of $\vec{P}$ which are inputs as $\vec{I}$, and those ports which are outputs as $\vec{O}$. The values on the input and output ports are denoted $\vec{\imath}$ and $\vec{o}$, respectively.

We calculate a circuit's *derived behavior* by applying circuit models to the implementation. A *compositional model* can derive an implementation's behavior from the behavior of its parts and the composition of the parts. A *non-compositional model* computes derived behavior considering the circuit as a collection of primitives regardless of the hierarchy used to describe the circuit. Coarse circuit models are usually compositional whereas detailed circuit models are usually non-compositional. Winskel [10] has developed the most complete formal compositional circuit model for verification. His model includes gross capacitive and resistive effects.

A circuit's *desired behavior* is the behavior we wish the circuit to exhibit. Often we want our specifications to be more abstract than the derived behavior. We investigate two different kinds of abstraction. The first is *behavioral abstraction,* where the desired behavior is a subset of the derived behavior. The second is *data abstraction*, where the domain of the desired behavior, denoted D_a, is an abstraction of the implementation domain. Other types of abstraction methods for verification are presented in [6].

Derived and desired behaviors are expressed either logically, as predicates on consistent values $\vec{p}$ can assume, or functionally, as an equality between a function of $\vec{\imath}$ and $\vec{o}$. For example, an AND-GATE's behavior is expressed logically as AND-RELATION(IN1, IN2, OUT) and functionally as OUT = AND-FUNCTION(IN1, IN2).

Constraints are predicates on the inputs a circuit will receive from its environment. Either by design or necessity, circuits do not operate in all possible environments. Constraints tell the verifier to only consider behaviors that will be exhibited by the implementation. Constraints that arise by design will be called *designer constraints*, necessary constraints will be called *abstraction constraints*. We elucidate the difference between these two classes below.

A *verification condition* is the predicate whose truth proves that the circuit will exhibit its desired behavior. The simplest verification condition requires that the derived behavior and the desired behavior be the same. This is expressed logically as

$$\forall_{\vec{p}} derived\text{-}b(Design)(\vec{p}) \equiv desired\text{-}b(Design)(\vec{p})$$

and functionally as

$$\forall_{\vec{i}} derived\text{-}b(Design)(\vec{i}) = desired\text{-}b(Design)(\vec{i}).$$

This is an extremely strong verification condition. It forces the derived behavior to be identical to the desired behavior. This type of verification condition is too strong for either complicated circuits, or for detailed circuit models.

3 Behavioral Abstraction

A behaviorally abstract specification leaves the behavior on certain inputs unspecified. A circuit may have an undefined (don't care) output for a given input either because the output isn't sampled when that input appears, or because that input won't arise. The two major ways of expressing don't-care conditions in verification systems are either to add explicit don't-care values into behavioral domains, or to add constraints to the verification condition to ignore inputs that don't arise. We show methods of achieving behavioral abstraction, and problems with abstraction that are remedied by making constraints explicit.

We consider the boolean domain (TRUE and FALSE) to present an example of making don't-care conditions explicit. We add a new element X to the domain along with the axioms that TRUE < X and FALSE < X. We then cast the functional style verification condition as

$$\forall_{\vec{i}} derived\text{-}b(Design)(\vec{i}) \leq desired\text{-}b(Design)(\vec{i}).$$

(Some verification systems also use X as a *don't know* condition that the implementation can generate. The same verification condition holds in such systems.)

When behavior is expressed logically, explicit don't-care values aren't used. Logically based verification conditions use implications of the form

$$valid\text{-}port\text{-}values(\vec{p}) \supset desired\text{-}b(Design)(\vec{p}).$$

The antecedent of the implication, *valid-port-values*$(\vec{p})$, indicates which inputs to consider. These are what we term designer constraints: they are constraints the designer is aware of and has designed into the circuit. The logically based verification condition for abstract behavioral specifications is

$$\forall_{\vec{p}} derived\text{-}b(Design)(\vec{p}) \supset (valid\text{-}port\text{-}value(\vec{p}) \supset desired\text{-}b(Design)(\vec{p})).$$

Where before there was logical equivalence between the derived and desired behaviors, there is now an implication. This implication allows the verification condition be true when the derived and desired behaviors don't agree on invalid inputs. For example, the verification condition for a clocked flip-flop that has setup and hold constraints is written

$$\forall_{\vec{p}} derived\text{-}b(FF)(\vec{p}) \supset (setup\text{-}and\text{-}hold\text{-}constraints(\vec{p}) \supset register\text{-}behavior(\vec{p})).$$

Introducing the implication to the verification condition has the intended effect, but, as a side effect, it prevents *requiring* that the implementation exhibits its desired behavior. For example, consider the following ALL-ONES circuit which has three terminals, each connected to VDD:

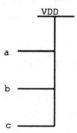

We can prove that this circuit is, for example, either an AND gate or an OR gate. We get this result because the only case when ALL-ONES(x, y, z) is true is for x = y = z = TRUE, and ALL-ONES matches the behavior of both an AND gate and OR gate for this particular input. A version of this difficulty, called the "False implies everything problem," was noted by Gordon [5]. He ascribed the problem to inadequate circuit models.

We claim that the problem is deeper than a modelling problem. A deeper philosophical question is "What is the status of a desired behavior (specification)?" If it is to act as a filter of illegal derived behavior then there is no problem. But if it is to be a requirement on derived behaviors, that is, something that they must match, then there is a problem.

As another example, consider the desired behavior TRUE. This behavior says that the derived behavior can be anything. But does it *require* that it be everything? Consider a three input terminator circuit whose purpose is to terminate each of its inputs. In the boolean domain this device imposes no structure on its inputs, all are possible. Therefore TRUE is the appropriate desired behavior. In fact, it is the only desired behavior that fully expresses the behavior of the terminator. Now consider proving that some circuit is a terminator. If implications are used, then every three port circuit is a three port terminator. This is clearly wrong.

We fix this problem by factoring out the designer constraints and subordinate the equality of the derived and desired behaviors to the constraints:

$$\forall_{\vec{p}} valid\text{-}port\text{-}values(\vec{p}) \supset (derived\text{-}b(Design)(\vec{p}) \equiv desired\text{-}b(Design)(\vec{p})).$$

Comparing the truth table of this formula to the truth table of the earlier formula (Table 1) shows only one discrepancy: when the derived behavior is FALSE and the constraints and desired behavior is TRUE. The verification condition based on implications yields TRUE in this instance where this verification condition yields FALSE.

Constraint Predicate	Derived Behavior	Desired Behavior	Previous Verification Condition	New Verification Condition
F	F	F	T	T
F	F	T	T	T
F	T	F	T	T
F	T	T	T	T
T	F	F	T	T
T	F	T	T	F
T	T	F	F	F
T	T	T	T	T

Table 1: Truth table for verification conditions

This is precisely the effect we want. For inputs when the constraints are met and the desired behavior is TRUE, then the implementation must also be TRUE.

This simple change still allows for behavioral abstraction while forcing the implementation to exhibit the desired behavior. For example, consider again our All-Ones circuit. To prove it is an OR gate we would have to prove

$$\forall_{i1,i2,i3}\text{All-Ones}(i1,i2,i3) \equiv OR(i1,i2,i3),$$

which is clearly false. Similarly, for the Terminator Circuit $\forall_{i1,i2,i3}OR(i1,i2,i3) \equiv$ TRUE will also be false.

We can also formulate the functional version of the verification condition that uses implications rather than don't-care values. This version of the verification condition is similar to the logical version:

$$\forall_{\vec{i}}\text{valid-port-values}(\vec{i}) \supset (derived\text{-}b(Design)(\vec{i}) = desired\text{-}b(Design)(\vec{i})).$$

This style of verification condition was used in the *Silica Pithecus* verifier [9].

4 Multilevel Verification (Data Abstraction)

Multilevel verification proves that some abstraction of the derived behavior meets some specification. For example, the derived behavior may be in terms of voltages but the desired behavior may be in terms of booleans, or the derived behavior may in terms of vectors of boolean values and the desired behavior in terms of integers. A function *abs* maps elements of the implementation domain into elements of the abstract behavioral domain D_a. Some elements of D_i do not correspond to useful elements of D_a, these values are mapped to the $\perp$ element of D_a.

The verification condition has a different form for multilevel verification. Let $\vec{abs}(\vec{p})$ be the vector obtained by applying *abs* to each element of $\vec{p}$. The verification condition is changed by applying the abstraction function to the inputs of the constraints and of the desired behavior as follows:

$$\forall_{\vec{p}} valid\text{-}port\text{-}values(abs(\vec{p})) \supset (derived\text{-}b(Design)(\vec{p}) \equiv desired\text{-}b(Design)(abs(\vec{p})))$$

The functional form of the verification condition is

$$\forall_{\vec{p}} valid\text{-}port\text{-}values(abs(\vec{\imath})) \supset abs(derived\text{-}b(Design)(\vec{\imath})) = desired\text{-}b(Design)(abs(\vec{\imath}))$$

Note that we have abstracted the inputs before applying the constraints to them. We do this because the designer constraints are expressed in the abstract behavioral domain.

Two major issues of multilevel verification are composing desired behaviors, and guaranteeing that no inputs or outputs map to $\perp$. We first present an example of multilevel verification, then show the difficulties of composing desired behaviors. We then introduce *abstraction constraints* which ensure abstraction to non-$\perp$ values. How abstraction constraints interact with the verification condition and with circuit models is then presented.

4.1   Example: An Adder Cell

As an example we show the verification of a full adder (Figure 1) using the functional form of the verification condition. The adder has three inputs A, B, and $Carryin$, and two outputs called $Carryout$ and Sum. Its output is a vector consisting of Sum and $Carryout$. The Adder Cell is composed of gates, the implementation domain consists of booleans and vectors of booleans. We wish to show the adder cell adds numbers, therefore the abstract domain consists of W, the whole numbers. Our abstraction function is

$ABS(true) = 1;$
$ABS(false) = 0;$
$ABS([b_0, \ldots, b_n]) = \sum_{0 \le i \le n} 2^i ABS(b_i).$

The Adder Cell's derived behavior is

$$\lambda \; a \; b \; c \; . \; [\mathrm{sum}(a, b, c), \mathrm{carry}(a, b, c)].$$

The Adder Cell's desired behavior is

$$\lambda \; a \; b \; c \; . \; a + b + c.$$

The Adder Cell's verification condition is

$$\forall_{i_1, i_2, i_3 \in \{\text{TRUE,FALSE}\}}$$

$$ABS((\lambda \; a \; b \; c \; . \; [\mathrm{sum}(a, b, c), \mathrm{carry}(a, b, c)])(i_1, i_2, i_3))$$
$$= (\lambda \; a \; b \; c \; . \; a + b + c)(ABS(i_1), ABS(i_2), ABS(i_3))\}.$$

Using beta-reduction, the above equation is simplified to

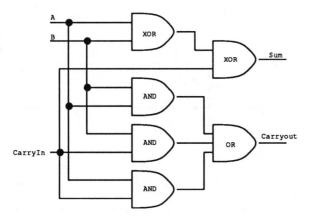

Figure 1: A Full Adder

$$\forall_{i_1,i_2,i_3\in\{\text{TRUE,FALSE}\}}$$
$$ABS(\text{sum}(i_1, i_2, i_3)) + 2ABS(\text{carry}(i_1, i_2, i_3))$$
$$= ABS(i_1) + ABS(i_2) + ABS(i_3)$$

This equation is shown to hold by exhaustively enumerating all combinations of the inputs, thereby verifying the design of the adder cell.

4.2 Compound Data

A major benefit of abstract desired behaviors is using them in subsequent verifications. Consider verifying a circuit composed of previously verified components. It would save much effort and time if the abstract behaviors of the components could be composed to derive the abstract behavior of the circuit, instead of composing the derived behaviors of the components and then abstracting. For circuits with ganged outputs, such as vectors of bits, a straightforward substitution of intended abstract behavior for concrete behavior fails.

For example, consider a 3-bit adder which returns a 4-bit result (Figure 2). This adder is constructed from three adder cells. Although we proved that

$$\forall_{i_1,i_2,i_3\in\{\text{TRUE,FALSE}\}}$$

$$ABS((\lambda \text{ a b c . } [\text{sum(a, b, c)}, \text{carry(a, b, c)}])(i_1, i_2, i_3))$$
$$= (\lambda \text{ a b c . a} + \text{b} + \text{c})(ABS(i_1), ABS(i_2), ABS(i_3))\},$$

it does no good to use the abstract behavior λ a b c . a + b + c when deriving the behavior of the 3-bit adder because neither *sum* nor *carry* can be replaced by some function solely of the abstracted inputs to the adder. Either must be replaced in terms of the other. However, we can use the equation as a lemma in the verification of the 3-bit adder.

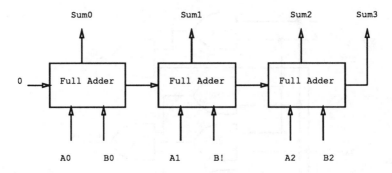

Figure 2: 3-Bit Adder

The desired behavior of the 3-bit adder is

$$desired\text{-}b(3\text{-bit Adder}) = \lambda \text{ a b} . a + b.$$

The derived behavior of the 3-bit adder, computed by composing the derived behavior of its parts, is

$derived\text{-}b(\text{Adder Cell}) =$
$\quad \lambda [A_0, A_1, A_2, A_3] [B_0, B_1, B_2, B_3] .$
$\quad [Sum(A_0, B_0, \text{FALSE}),$
$\quad Sum(A_1, B_1, Carry(A_0, B_0, \text{FALSE}))$
$\quad Sum(A_2, B_2, Carry(A_1, B_1, Carry(A_0, B_0, \text{FALSE})))$
$\quad Carry(A_2, B_2, Carry(A_1, B_1, Carry(A_0, B_0, \text{FALSE})))].$

(This example uses automatic destructuring of formal parameters. This function's inputs are two length four vectors. Destructuring names each bit in the input vectors.)

The abstraction of the adder's derived behavior is ˙

$2^3 abs(Carry(i_2, j_2, Carry(i_1, j_1, Carry(i_0, j_0, \text{FALSE}))))+$
$2^2 abs(Sum(i_2, j_2, Carry(i_1, j_1, Carry(i_0, j_0, \text{FALSE}))))+$
$2^1 abs(Sum(i_1, j_1, Carry(i_0, j_0, \text{FALSE})))+$
$2^0 abs(Sum(i_0, j_0, \text{FALSE})).$

This must be validated against the sum of the abstraction of the inputs, namely $(2^2 abs(i_2) + 2abs(i_1) + abs(i_0)) + (2^2 abs(j_2) + 2abs(j_1) + abs(j_0))$.

These elements are put together into the verification condition. There are three alternative methods to proving the verification condition holds. The first is to expand out the calls to *Sum* and *Carry* and use exhaustive methods to prove the equivalence. Although this strategy would work for the 3-bit adder, it fails as adders get larger. The second alternative is to replace the abstraction of the concrete behaviors of with the intended behavior of the outputs. But as mentioned earlier, this alternatives fails because the outputs are interrelated and are not eliminated by this approach. The third alternative is to be "intelligent" about which of *Sum* and *Carry* to eliminate.

We rewrite the verification condition of the adder cell as

$$abs(sum(i_1, i_2, i_3)) = abs(i_1) + abs(i_2) + abs(i_3) - 2abs(carry(i_1, i_2, i_3)).$$

This equation is used to eliminate the *Sums* from the verification condition. Once this is done the proof is very simple. Without this insight the proof would be much harder. Because of the thought required, not all verifiers do this proof algebraically. For example, Verify [1] does this proof structurally.[1]

5 Abstraction Constraints

As the models of components and circuit data values become more detailed, the abstraction function becomes more complex. In particular, the implementation domain contains elements that don't correspond to elements at the abstract level. Such values are mapped to special error indicators, or arbitrary fixed values [6]. For the verification to succeed, all values must abstract to known and valid abstract values. To guarantee this, *abstraction constraints* are used as part of the verification condition.

Let us call the set of abstraction constraints AC. We place these constraints on equal footing with the designer constraints in the verification condition:

$$\forall_{\vec{p}} \bigvee_{c \in AC} c(\vec{\imath}) \wedge \text{valid-input-ports}(abs(\vec{p})) \supset$$
$$abs(derived\text{-}b(Design)(\vec{\imath})) = desired\text{-}b(Design)(abs(\vec{\imath})).$$

The logical version of the verification condition is

$$\forall_{\vec{p}} \bigvee_{c \in AC} c(\vec{p}) \wedge \text{valid-input-ports}(abs(\vec{p})) \supset$$
$$derived\text{-}b(Design)(\vec{p}) \equiv desired\text{-}b(Design)(abs(\vec{p})).$$

The abstraction constraints depend on the circuit model. The more detailed the model, the more constraints that are needed. This section incrementally considers more and more detailed circuit models and the constraints needed to perform verification with them. We first review the simple decaying capacitor model of [6]. We then cover the modeling of threshold drops, charge sharing, and level sensitive register designs.

5.1 Simple Decaying Capacitor Model

We model the passage of time with *signals* which map time into a value such as a voltage or a boolean. The inputs and outputs of circuits are modeled as signals. In the decaying capacitor model, there are three values a signal can have at a given time: H, L, and Z. The value Z represents stored charge that can be either L or H. A node has the value Z when it is not connected (either directly or indirectly through conducting transistors) to either VDD or GND.

---

[1]Verify uses knowledge of the representation of numbers as vectors of booleans to effect the proof: it is hardwired to recognize predetermined structures as correct implementations of adders.

We model a transistor as being able to store a TRUE value on its gate node for one clock tick:

$$\text{Ntran}(g, s, d) \equiv$$
$$\forall t.g(t) = \text{H} \vee (g(t) = \text{Z} \wedge g(t-1) = \text{H}) \supset s(t) = d(t).$$

The model for a p-channel transistor is similar.

The abstract behavioral domain consists of signals that contain just TRUE and FALSE. Therefore the abstraction function is

$$\lambda i.\lambda t.(i(t) = H \Rightarrow \text{TRUE}, i(t) = L \Rightarrow \text{FALSE}, \bot)$$

where $\bot$ represents an error condition.

Consider a standard cMOS inverter:

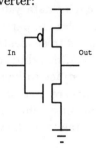

We would like to prove

$$\forall_{i,o}\, derived\text{-}b(inverter)(i, o) \equiv \text{NOT-signal}(abs(i), abs(o))$$

where NOT-signal produces a signal containing the elementwise logical negation of its input signal. Unfortunately, this formula is false because neither the input nor output signals are guaranteed to always abstract to signals that contain only TRUE or FALSE.

A sufficient method for ensuring that the input and output signals abstract to either TRUE or FALSE is to posit an abstraction constraint which promises the input signal will never contain Z. Let *Def* be such a constraint where

$$Def(i) \equiv \forall t.i(t) = \text{H} \vee i(t) = \text{L}.$$

This constraint says that i is never floating (has a Z value). For the inverter, this constraint is sufficient to ensure that output is also abstractable. There are circuits that will produce $\bot$ values even when the inputs never abstract to $\bot$. Such circuits require even more abstraction constraints, as shown below.

The verification condition which can be proved for the inverter is

$$\forall_{i,o} Def(i) \supset derived\text{-}b(inverter)(i, o) \equiv \text{NOT-signal}(abs(i), abs(o)).$$

We now investigate other circuit models and the abstraction constraints needed to perform verification with them. The next three models have no easy logical formulation, so we use a more circuit oriented approach that refers to *nets*. We view the conducting and non-conducting transistors of a circuit as partitioning a circuit into a number of disjoint nets. We say that two nodes belong to the same net if

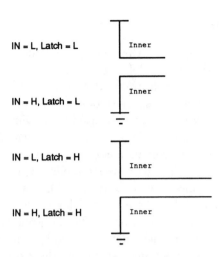

IN = L, Latch = L   Inner

IN = H, Latch = L   Inner

IN = L, Latch = H   Inner

IN = H, Latch = H   Inner

Figure 3: Nets of the Latched Inverter under a very simple circuit model.

there is a path through conducting transistors between the two nodes. We consider the *net behavior* of each node as the different nets a node can be a member of and the conditions that give rise to the nets. For example, consider the following simple circuit:

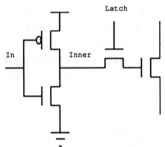

Given a circuit model with two values, TRUE and FALSE, and that models a conducting transistor (gate = TRUE) as a short circuit and a non-conducting transistor (gate = FALSE) as an open switch, the node INNER can be a member of 4 different nets. The net behavior of INNER consists of the four different conditions and the nets they generate (Figure refsimplenets). Within any given net the circuit model determines how to compute the voltages at the nodes.

What are the sources of constraints? Constraints will arise because not all components of nets are known. We will often want the abstraction of the voltage at a node to be TRUE or FALSE even though the entire net computing the voltage at the node isn't known. In such cases we issue constraints on what the remainder of the net must be like. Constraints also come from outlawing nets that yield invalid voltages.

5.2   Resistive Model

Resistive models are used to determine the voltages of nodes in a net that contains off-chip input nodes (charge sharing models are used for nets that don't contain input nodes). The two major resistive models are what we call the *gross resistive model* and the *fine resistive model*. In the gross resistive model a few values are used to rank the different resistances. These few ranks are then used to predict voltages. The appeal of the gross model is that it is compositional; simple rankings are sufficient to easily determine what happens when two signals merge at a join point.

We are more concerned with the fine resistive model, which uses Kirchoff's laws to determine voltages. This importance of this model has waned as cMOS replaces nMOS because cMOS designers don't use ratioed logic. A compounding factor is threshold drops. A simple ranking model won't suffice for accurate modeling of nMOS circuits. In the fine grain resistive model a net is formed by considering each conducting transistor as a resistor whose resistance depends on the geometry of the transistor. For example, the following net has 1 volt at A and 2 volts at B.

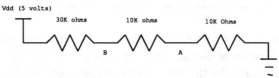

We would need an extremely contrived circuit to demonstrate abstraction constraints because circuits that need them aren't standard. Usually the nets for all the internal nodes of a real circuit are known, with only the nets for port nodes being incomplete. That is, VDD and GND are part of the circuit, and don't need to be externally supplied. Real circuits that need abstraction constraints because of resistive problems are shown below when we consider the resistive model together with a threshold drop model.

5.3   Threshold Drop Model

The threshold drop model correctly models threshold drops across transistors. Transistors are not perfect conductors when they are conducting. First, they have resistance. Second, they turn off before the voltages of the source and drain equalize: nMOS transistors cannot "transmit" high values, pMOS transistors cannot "transmit" low values.

To model threshold drops we introduce additional operating regions for transistors. Where before they only had two states, non-conducting and conducting with a given resistance, they now have 4 states: high conductance, one-drop conductance, unknown conductance, and non-conducting. In addition, part of the model consists of a "threshold drop" device that regulates how much voltage can build up on the driven side. A similar model can be used for pMOS transistors.

With this model there are now nets that produce invalid voltages because voltages on the gates of transistors suffer threshold drops. These invalid voltages can be avoided by posting constraints to prevent the threshold drops from occuring. For an example see [9].

5.4   Capacitive (Charge Sharing) Model

In custom MOS design, state is usually implemented via capacitors rather than by feedback, as it is for TTL. Any reasonable model of MOS includes capacitors and charge sharing. Given a net containing no input nodes, a capacitive (charge sharing) model is used to predict the voltages of the nodes in the net. As in the resistive model there can be either gross or fine approximations. Gross models use a set of ranks to predict final voltages. Finer models account for actual capacitance values. An additional issue is the time taken to achieve steady state, either an instantaneous or RC model can be used.

At least two types of constraints apply when a capacitive model is used. The first is similar to the type used for threshold models which outlaw conditions leading to nets that yield invalid voltages. The second type ensures that information flows in the correct direction. For example, consider a latched inverter:

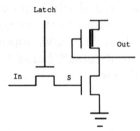

To ensure that the input is really an input, we issue a constraint that information must be flow from in to S.

5.5   Level-Sensitive Registers

State is tricky either for capacitive or feedback methods. The problems in either case are races and hazards. A sequential circuit has a race condition when its next state depends the relative speed of two signals; it has a hazard when a control signal goes through extra transistions.

In level-sensitive designs the circuit is in a critical state whenever the control signal letting information onto a storage capacitor is high. If a race develops between a change on the input line and the control line going low, then there are problems that need controlling. The constraints used to ensure proper operation put an ordering on the relative events within a circuit. For example, a constraint will require that one signal arrive at a point after another signal, or require that a given signal be stable during some interval. One can relate these issues to abstraction, for more information, see [9].

6   Abstraction Constraints Generation

Detailed models require detailed constraints. It is tedious and error prone for the designer to produce all the relevant constraints. For example, the simple Latched Inverter shown above requires four constraints:

1. That information flow be from In to S

2. If Latch is to fall, it must do so before In changes value.

3. Latch is a control signal and must not glitch.

4. Latch cannot suffer a threshold drop.

Requiring the designer to be aware of these constraints, and to declare them, is to require too much. Very often designers aren't even aware of constraints, which is why bugs occur. The automatic generation of abstraction constraints in necessary.

Some research has been performed on the automatic generation of abstraction constraints [9]. The basic idea is to have a representation that makes invalid values explicit. For example, for the more detailed circuit models, nets that produced invalid voltages were proscribed via constraints. Although we didn't mention it at the time, given the explicitness of net behavior, it should be possible to have the program that derives circuit behavior also generate constraints whenever it notices that it can use them to prevent invalid values. Then, if the environment satisfies the constraint, the circuit will work. If the environment doesn't satisfy the constraint, the circuit will not work and the verifier can tell us so.

Acknowledgements

This research was sponsored by Darpa contracts N00014-86-K-180 and N00014-85-K-0124.

References

[1] H. Barrow, "Proving the correctness of hardware designs," VLSI Design, pp. 64–77, July 1984.

[2] R. Bryant, "Symbolic Verification of MOS Circuits" Proceedings from the 1985 Chapel Hill Conference on VLSI, Edited by Henry Fuchs, Computer Science Press, pp. 419 – 438, 1985

[3] Randal Bryant, "Can a Simulator Verify a Circuit?" In *Formal Aspects of VLSI Design,* G.J. Milne, Editor, North–Holland, 1986

[4] Hans Eveking, "The verification of mutilevel hardware descriptions," Unpublished proceedings of the Darmstadt Workshop on the Verification of Hardware Designs.

[5] Michael Gordon, "Hardware verification using higher–order logic" Computer Laboratory Technical Report 91, University of Cambridge, 1986.

[6] Thomas F. Melham, "Abstraction mechanisms for hardware verification," in *VLSI Specification, Verification, and Synthesis*, Birtwistle and Subrahmanyam, Eds, pp. 267-291, Kluwer Academic Publishers, 1988.

[7] Ben Moszkowski, "A temporal logic for multilevelreasoning about hardware," *IEEE Computer* 18(2) pp. 10-19 (February 1985)

[8] C. J. Terman, *Simulation Tools for Digital Design,* MIT Laboratory for Computer Science Report TR-304 (PhD Thesis) 1983

[9] Daniel Weise, *Formal Multilevel Hierarchical Verification of Synchronous MOS VLSI Circuits,* PhD Thesis, MIT Artificial Intelligence Laboratory Technical Report 978, 1987.

[10] Glynn Winskel, "A compositional model of MOS Circuits," in *VLSI Specification, Verification, and Synthesis,* Birtwistle and Subrahmanyam, Eds, pp. 323-347, Kluwer Academic Publishers, 1988.

Formalising the Design of an SECD chip

Brian Graham and Graham Birtwistle,
University of Calgary, Canada

Abstract

We describe work completed on a custom SECD chip which is powerful enough to run a LispKit compiler. The 20,000 transistor design was fabricated in 1988 and is being interfaced to a workstation so that it can run downloaded programs. We discuss the evolution of the architecture from its abstract specification and abstraction issues that arose at key levels in the verification of the design. The verification is being undertaken in Cambridge HOL. One hard issue (garbage collection) has been left over for a second iteration of the specification and verification.

Introduction

The SECD effort we describe is the corner stone of a long term research program in verification at Calgary initiated in late 1986. Our immediate goal is to design, fabricate, and employ a verified SECD chip. SECD is an abstract machine invented by Landin to reduce lambda expressions. The variant we chose to implement is described in [Hen80]. It has eager evaluation, supports recursion directly, and possesses a reasonable set of built-in operators.

Our longer term goal is to verify a complete system based upon this chip – the compiler as well as the hardware. Since we believe that this endeavour will be much easier with a functional programming language, the choice of SECD was not accidental. Besides work on the SECD hardware, we have written a LispKit compiler ([Hen80], [SBGH89]) which emits SECD code and completed a hand proof (along the lines of [Plo75]) of the fact that SECD executes LispKit code correctly. What remains to be done in this area is to extend the ideas to a better (typed) programming language and machine-verify the correctness of that compiler.

In this paper we look at the way the initial definition of SECD given by Henderson evolved into concrete hardware and discuss the abstraction mechanisms used to effect the transitions across some key levels in the design hierarchy. Section 1 introduces the abstract machine and shows how it evolved into an interpreter and then microcode. Section 2 shows how timing, clocking, I/O signals and data representations were refined through various levels of abstraction. We conclude with remarks on the status of the SECD chip and plans for its successor.

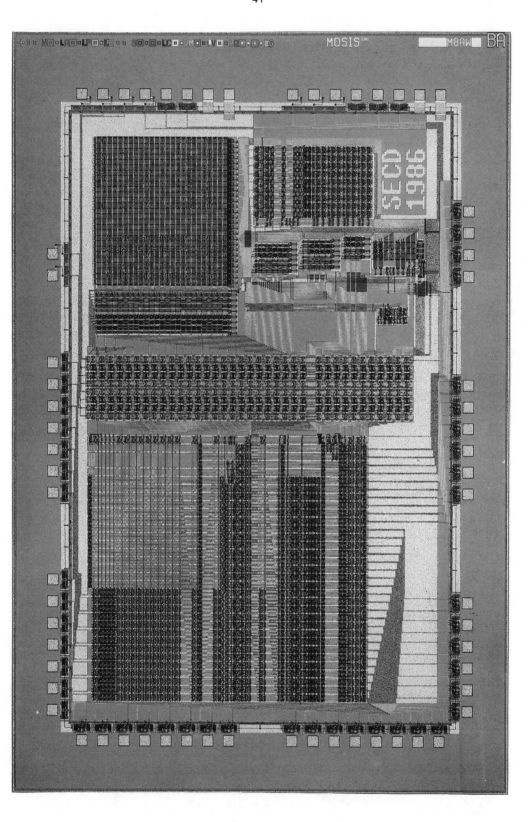

1 The abstract machine

Several abstract SECD machines can be found in the literature, for example [Bur75], [Hen80], [FH88]. Typically, an SECD machine is characterised by the four status registers (**S**tore, **E**nvironment, **C**ontrol, **D**ump) from which its name is taken.

1. Stack **S** is used to evaluate expressions, to build closures, and to hold the results returned from function calls. **S** is set to empty each time a function is entered, so that on return, **S** should contain one item only – the result of that call.

2. **E** points to an environment (a stack) of currently accessible bindings. **E** is reset on function entry and exit.

3. SECD code is generated in the form of a list (an S-expression). The control register **C** references the next instruction to be executed. **C** is usually incremented past the last instruction; but function calls and *IF–* expressions cause jumps to the function body definition, or to either the *THEN–* branch or the *ELSE–* branch, respectively.

4. **D** is used to save the state of the machine (a triple of the current **S**, **E**, and **C** values) on function entry; and the code 'rejoin' point on a *THEN–* or an *ELSE–* branch entry. Correct continuation points are restored from **D** on return from a function call or termination of an *IF–* expression.

		INITIAL STATE				TRANSFORMED STATE		
S	E	C	D	→	S'	E'	C'	D'
s	e	(LDF c'.c)	d	→	((c'.e).s)	e	c	d
((c'.e')v.s)	e	(AP.c)	d	→	NIL	(v.e')	c'	(s e c.d)
(x)	e'	(RTN)	(s e c.d)	→	(x.s)	e	c	d
s	e	(DUM .c)	d	→	s	(Ω.e)	c	d
((c'.e')v.s)	(Ω.e)	(RAP.c)	d	→	NIL	replcar(e',v)	c'	(s e c.d)
(x.s)	e	(SEL ct cf.c)	d	→	s		e	cx	(c.d)
		where cx = if (x=T) then ct else cf						
s	e	(JOIN)	(c.d)	→	s	e	c	d
s	e	(LD (m.n).c)	d	→	(x.s)	e	c	d
		where x = locate ((m.n),e)						
s	e	(LDC x.c)	d	→	(x.s)	e	c	d
(a b.s)	e	(OP.c)	d	→	(b op a.s)	e	c	d
		where (OP,op) = (EQ, =), (LEQ, ≤), (ADD, +), (SUB, -), (MUL, ×), (DIV, /), (REM, rem)						
((a.b).s)	e	(CAR.c)	d	→	(a.s)	e	c	d
((a.b).s)	e	(CDR.c)	d	→	(b.s)	e	c	d
(a.s)	e	(ATOM.c)	d	→	(t.s)	e	c	d
		where t = (a is an atom)						
(a b.s)	e	(CONS.c)	d	→	((a.b).s)	e	c	d
s	e	(STOP)	d	→	s	e	(STOP)	d

Table 1: SECD Instruction Definitions

Table 1 specifies the operation of Henderson's variant in terms of (**S**, **E**, **C**, **D**) transitions. For example, a non-recursive function call in LispKit, say **LET** $x = a$ **IN** *body* (a sugared version of *(λv.body)a*) uses **LDF**, **AP**, and **RTN**. First we place the evaluated argument on top of **S**. Then a closure consisting of the called environment *e* and the control list for the function body *c'* is placed on **S** by **LDF c'** where

$$s \ e \ (\textbf{LDF c'}).c \ d \rightarrow (c'.e).s \ e \ c \ d$$

Then the function is entered via a call on **AP**(ply) which takes the closure from the top of the stack. **AP** saves the calling state on **D**, completes the environment for evaluating the function by appending the values in the argument list *v* onto the environment for the call *e'*, sets **C** to the function entry point, and flushes **S**.

$$((c'.e') \ v.s) \ e \ \textbf{AP}.c \ d \rightarrow nil \ (v.e') \ c' \ (s \ e \ c.d)$$

Function exit is effected by executing **RTN** which restores the state triple (**S**, **E**, **C**) saved on **D** at function entry time and then pushes the result of the function call (x) onto **S**.

$$x \ e' \ \textbf{RTN}.c \ (s \ e \ c.d) \rightarrow (x.s) \ e \ c \ d$$

Definitions of recursive functions are signalled syntactically in LispKit by use of **LETREC** *defns* **IN** *call*. Recursion cannot be performed unless the recursively defined function definitions (*defns*) have access to each other. This SECD machine arranges that by constructing a circular environment for *defns*. An initial call on **DUM** places a marker *NIL* on top of the calling environment. Then the *defns* are compiled into closures on **S**. **RAP** clears away the old state onto the dump, and uses the *NIL* placed by **DUM** to create the required circular representation in **E**. The body of the **LETREC** will be an application and hence starts with an **AP**. **RAP** is misleadingly named – a better name would have been something like **MRC**, for *make recursive closure*. For gory detail see [Hen80] or [HBGS89].

The remaining transitions are obvious.

2 Refining the abstract specification

1	LD	8	SEL	15	ADD
2	LDC	9	JOIN	16	SUB
3	LDF	10	CAR	17	MUL
4	AP	11	CDR	18	DIV
5	RTN	12	ATOM	19	REM
6	DUM	13	CONS	20	LEQ
7	RAP	14	EQ	21	STOP

Table 2: SECD instruction codes

The machine code is designed so that when presented with compiled SECD code the control expression will always have the form *(opcode . . . .)*. Thus the control string is always a list and the next instruction is always to be found at its head, retrievable via a *CAR* operation. Thus the heart of an interpreter is a control loop of the form

```
LOOP:
    IR := (CAR C);
    case IR of
        LD: . . . .;
        LDC: . . . .;
            ⋮
        STOP: . . . .;
    end_case;
    goto LOOP;
```

The interpreter works by taking the next instruction from the code stream and switching on that key into one of 21 separate arms. Each arm contains appropriate actions for one specific instruction. The actions effect a specific transition from table 1 (updating S, E, C, and D), exits from the case statement and then (except for STOP) jumps back to the label LOOP.

2.1 The interpreter level view

As pointed out by Henderson *op. cit.*, it is possible to derive an interpreter for the SECD machine directly from its specification. We take the state of SECD as a 4-tuple (**S**, **E**, **C**, **D**) and derive the interpreter by noting how individual instructions update the state 4-tuple as they are executed. We show how this is done for the function call instructions. The remaining instructions are even easier to deal with.

$$\textbf{s e (LDF c'.c) d} \rightarrow \textbf{((c'.e).s) e c d}$$

The current instruction is found at the head of the code stream, i.e. as *car C*. Since it is a **LDF**, the program counter has to move past **(LDF c')** in the code stream, and the next instruction is found as *cdr (cdr C)*. **E** and **D** remain the same. The function closure *(c'.e)* – where *c'* references code for the function body and *e* the environment in which the body is to be executed – is to be pushed onto the stack **S**. By pattern matching *c'* is found as *car (cdr C)*. Thus we create the closure by *cons(car(cdr C), E)*, and then *cons* that onto **S**. Hence suitable interpreter code is:

S := cons (cons (car (cdr C), E), S);
E := E;
C := cdr (cdr C);
D := D;

Note that if we are to perform updates to the state 4-tuple, we must take some care about the order in which they are carried out. In this case, we must compute the new value for S before updating C. We can model this dependency by a partial ordering for each instruction. In this case we have:

which pictorially expresses the simple fact that we cannot overwrite the old value of C until it has been made available to the computation of the new S.

$$((c'.e')\ v.s)\ e\ (\mathbf{AP}.c)\ d \rightarrow nil\ (v.e')\ c'\ (s\ e\ c.d)$$

A new computation is entered when an **AP** instruction is carried out, The new computation has a function closure *(c'.e')* on top of **S**. We augment the environment of the closure by *v*, the argument to this call which lies on **S** directly below the closure. The function body *c'* becomes the new code sequence, and the old status is dumped onto **D**. Hence, by pattern matching

D := cons (cdr (cdr S), cons(E, cons(cdr C, D)));
E := cons (car (cdr S), cdr (car S));
C := car (car S);
S := nil;

Here is the partial order associated with **AP**[1]

$$x\ e'\ (\mathbf{RTN})\ (s\ e\ c.d) \rightarrow (x.s)\ e\ c\ d$$

RTN is executed when a function has run its course. The result, *x*, will be sitting on top of the stack **S** – it should be the only item there. The code stream

---

[1]This gets tedious. Dependencies for all the SECD instructions are gathered together in table 3.

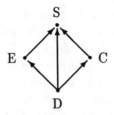

in the field **C** should also be just **RTN**. We restore **S, E, C** from the dump **D** and pop x onto the the restored **S**. Hence, by pattern matching

    S := cons(S, car D);
    E := car (cdr D);
    C := car (cdr (cdr D));
    D := cdr (cdr (cdr D));

$$\text{s e (DUM.c) d} \rightarrow \text{s (nil.e) c d}$$

DUM is executed prior to saving recursive function definitions in a **LETREC**. It leaves a marker in the environment and enables a circular environment to be constructed by the later call on **RAP**. **S** and **D** are not affected. Hence, by pattern matching

    S := S;
    E := cons (nil E);
    C := cdr C;
    D := D;

$$\text{((c'.e') v.s) (nil.e) (RAP.c) d} \rightarrow \text{nil replcar(v, e') c' (s e c.d)}$$

When used with **DUM**, **RAP** completes the circular environment required for recursive calls. The closure sitting on the stack **S** define the new code sequence and its environment. The old state is pushed onto **D**. Prior to entering the actual call (which inevitably will be an application prefixed by **AP**), the set of recursive definitions v is added to the environment e' of the closure in circular fashion to enable the lookup of recursive calls. We assume the existence of a built-in function *replcar* to carry out this task.

    D := cons(cdr(cdr S), cons(cdr E, cons(cdr C, D)));
    E := replcar(car (cdr S), cdr (car S));
    C := car (car S);
    S := nil;

	Register dependency			
Instruction	S	E	C	D
LD, LDC	C			
LDF	C, E			
AP, RAP		S	S	S, E,C
RTN	D	D	D	
SEL			S	C
JOIN			D	
DUM, others				

Table 3: Summary of the SECD instruction dependencies

2.2 The register-register view

Given some broad architectural decisions, the pattern matching technique devised by Henderson can be extended to generate code at more concrete levels in a systematic way. For ease of implementation and verification, we settled on a static design, with a single bus architecture and an external RAM memory. Access to the external memory **M** is via a register *MAR*. A *read* operation places *M[MAR]* on the bus; a *write* operation stores the value on the bus in *M[MAR]*. Given the Lispy flavour of the abstract language and the frequency of their occurrence in the register-register level view of the micro-code, support is provided for *car*, *cdr*, and *cons* operations on addresses in registers.

We decided to go for 32-bit words in this implementation. With type tags taking 2 bits and garbage collection flags another 2 bits per word, that leaves space for either a 28-bit two's complement number or a cons'ed word containing two 14-bit addressses. This is a sufficient address space for running the LispKit compiler on the SECD machine itself. Figure 1 provides a register-register level view of the chip design. We support two types of register: 14-bit address registers and 32-bit data registers. The bus is 32-bits wide. Roughly speaking, an address is passed using the 14 low order bits only, whereas all 32 bits are used when passing data values. Accordingly the 14-bit address registers are wired directly onto the 14 low order bits of the bus, and that takes care of *cdr*.

We handle *car* fields via the register *CAR* which is attached to the bus in a special way. Its write operation takes in bits (14–27) from a cons'ed word on the bus. Its read operation onto the bus is standard. We can thus extract the *car* field from a cons'ed word on the bus by filtering it through *CAR*.

The much used *cons* operation requires more thought. A call on *cons* requires the freeing of a fresh cell in memory (perhaps initiating a garbage collection) and the passing of two addresses to memory to fill out its fields. We chose to restrict *cons* to operating upon two specific registers which we call *X1* and *X2*. Our *consX1X2* operation locates a free cell in memory, fills out its two address fields from *X1* and *X2*, sets its type bits to indicate a cons'ed word, zeroes its garbage collection bits, writes it to the memory, and returns its address.

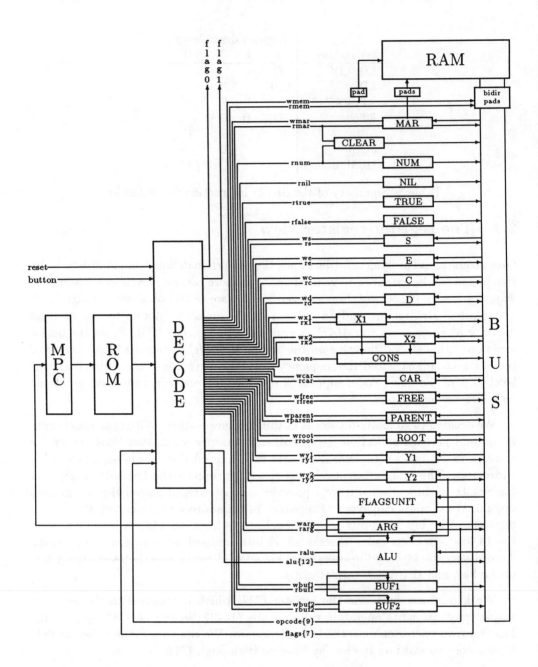

Figure 1: Register Transfer Level View of SECD Machine

Given these assumptions, here is an illustration of what emerges at the register-register level using **AP**. When carrying out the computation *cons A B*, we first build up the address for *B* in *X2* and the address for *A* in *X1*, then apply *consX1X2*.

d := cons(cdr(cdr s), cons(e, (cons(cdr c), d)))

x2	:=	d	*x2 := cons ((cdr c), d)*
x1	:=	cdr c	
x2	:=	consx1x2	
x1	:=	e	*x2 := cons (e, x2)*
x2	:=	consx1x2	
x1	:=	cdr s	*d := cons (cdr(cdr s), x2)*
x1	:=	cdr x1	
d	:=	consx1x2	

c := car(car s)

c	:=	car s
c	:=	car c

e := cons(car(cdr s), cdr(car s))

x2	:=	car s
x2	:=	cdr x2
x1	:=	cdr s
x1	:=	car x1
e	:=	consx1x2

s := nil

s	:=	nil

Table 4: ((c'.e') v.s) e AP.c d → nil v.e' c' (s e c.d)

We note that all the assignments in our register-register level description of the interpreter can be classified in one of four ways:

R	:=	S
R	:=	car S
R	:=	cdr S
R	:=	consX1X2

2.3   The micro-code level view

In the main, each register-register operation is split into a read onto the bus and a write from the bus at the bus level. Each register X has two control signals associated with it, systematically called rX and wX. When rX goes high, the contents of X are read onto the bus. The controller sees to it that only one register may be read onto the bus at a time. When wX goes high, the contents of the bus are written into X. All the bits of the bus if X is a 32-bit register; if X is a 14-bit register, the top 18-bits of the bus are ignored except for the special CAR register which is wired to accept bits 14-27 of the bus. For simplicity, only one register may be written from the bus at a time.

Bread and butter microcode can be generated directly from the register-register level description as soon as we supply a template for each class of assignment in the register-register level description.

- Copying the contents of register X to register Y is quite simply

$$rX \qquad wY$$

Movement involving *cdr*, *car* or *cons* require access to the external memory. The first two cases are have simple and short templates; *cons* is rather more involved and is implemented as a micro-code subroutine.

- To carry out the request $Y := cdr\ X$ we place the contents of X in MAR, read $M[MAR]$ onto the bus (all 32 bits), and then store its *cdr* field in Y.

$$
\begin{array}{ll}
rX & wmar \\
rmem & wY
\end{array}
$$

- To carry out the request $Y := car\ X$ we place the contents of X in MAR, read $M[MAR]$ onto the bus (all 32 bits), then filter out the *car* bits via the CAR register before passing the result to Y.

$$
\begin{array}{ll}
rX & wmar \\
rmem & wcar \\
rcar & wY
\end{array}
$$

- Calls to *consX1X2* occur so frequently in the code and are of such complexity that we inserted a sub-routine facility into the micro-code.

Table 5 gives the micro-code generated for the **D** and **C** segments of the **AP** instruction.

rfree		if nil then GCBegin()
rfree	wmar	
rmem	wfree	
rcons	wmem	

argument	register-register			micro-code	
d	x2	:=	d	rd	wx2
cdr c	x1	:=	cdr c	rc	wmar
				rmem	wx1
	x2	:=	consx1x2	call consx1x2	
				rmar	wx2
e	x1	:=	e	re	wx1
	x2	:=	consx1x2	call consx1x2	
				rmar	wx2
cdr(cdr s)	x1	:=	cdr s	rs	wmar
				rmem	wx1
	x1	:=	cdr x1	rx1	wmar
				rmem	wx1
	d	:=	consx1x2	call consx1x2	
				rmar	wd
car(car s)	c	:=	car s	rs	wmar
				rmar	wcar
				rcar	wc
	c	:=	car c	rc	wmar
				rmar	wcar
				rcar	wc

Table 5: **D and C calculations in AP** ·

3 The actual machine

The abstract SECD definition of table 1 contains no provisions for communicating with the outside world, and needs refinement. Our version of the SECD machine was designed to operate as a co-processor controlled from a workstation. Its mode of operation is: **1.** LispKit [Hen80] source programs are compiled down to SECD code on a workstation. **2.** The SECD object code is downloaded to the memory M. **3.** The SECD machine is initiated and executes the program in M. **4.** On completion, the SECD machine stops executing and signals the workstation. **5.** The program result is read back from M to the workstation. We have to be able to start SECD running, know when it has finished a computation, either successfully or through error, and be able to retrieve the result of a successful computation. Our new view of the top level specification is outlined in figure 2. It uses four major states – **Er-**

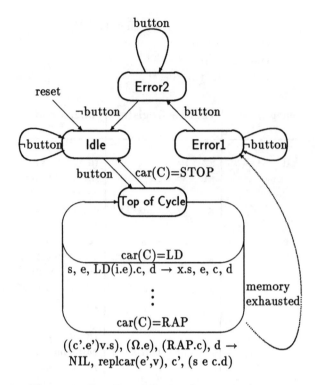

Figure 2: Top Level Finite State Machine

ror1, **Error2**, **Idle** and **Top of Cycle**; and two external signals **reset** and **button**. **reset** is used on the first clock cycle to ensure that the SECD system is correctly initialised and in state **Idle**. Thereafter, movement between states is controlled by **button**. Once a program has been loaded into memory, hitting button moves the machine into execution mode (state **Top of Cycle**). Exit from that state is made either by executing the **STOP** instruction or by running out of storage. Including the state **Error2** indicates that the button may be held on over several clock cycles. The state becomes **Idle** again on its release.

The SECD chip has 4 major functional components: the **control unit**, the **datapath**, the **shift registers** and the **pad frame** as depicted in Figure 3.

- The **control unit** interprets SECD machine instructions, breaking them up into a stream of micro-instructions to be effected one at a time by the **datapath** unit. It is conceived as a finite state machine whose state is held by a micro program counter (MPC) register which always refers to the current micro-control step. Inputs to the **control unit** include: external *reset* and *button* signals, status *flags*, and a 9-bit *opcode* (the code of the current machine instruction). Outputs include *read* and *write* signals for registers within the **datapath** and also for memory, *alu* control signals, the bi-directional pad control signal *bidir*, and the two state flags *flag0* and *flag1*.

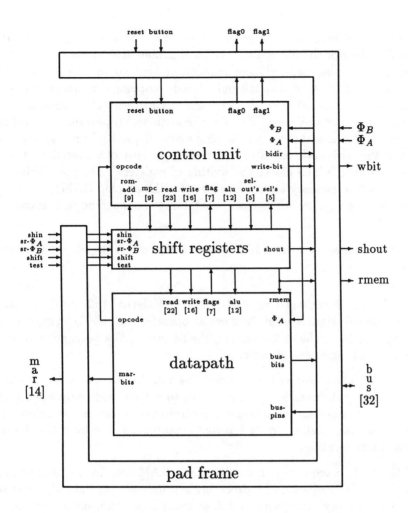

Figure 3: SECD Chip Major Subcomponents

- The **shift registers** provides a (rudimentary) means of entering test vectors and examining the state of the chip. In the absence of *designed testability*, this gives us a passable ability to test the chip in operation, and furthermore, permits independent testing of the **datapath** and **control unit** components. Most signals passing between the **control unit** and the **datapath** are routed through the **shift registers**. These include *read* and *write* signals, *alu* signals, and status *flags*. For observability and controllability, it also routes some signals which are functionally internal to the **control unit** (specifically the 5 select signals, and the **mpc** register contents). Thus all these signals may be read and/or altered, though in normal operation, signals pass through uninterrupted.

- The **datapath** executes simple micro-operations signalled by the **control unit**. The **datapath** unit is built as an ensemble of devices – registers, the arithmetic unit, and memory – communicating via a common *bus*. The operations performed by the **datapath** unit include: copying the value of a selected register onto a *bus*, storing a value from the *bus* into a selected register, the list manipulating functions cons, car, cdr, the arithmetic operations of addition, subtraction, decrementation, and setting status flags. Besides read and write lines and the arithmetic operator select lines, the only other input control line is the clock (Φ_A, which clocks the writing of registers). Outputs include the status *flags*, the memory address register (for the off chip RAM), the lower 9 bits of the **arg** register (the *opcode*, containing the machine instruction) and the 32 bit *bus*.

- The chip is framed by a set of **I/O pads** which connect the chip to the outside world.

The SECD chip is packaged in a 64-pin DIP. External (off chip) signals fall within three groups: signals used for normal operation of SECD, pwr/gnd, and SECD testing signals. To facilitate testing, the 64 pins in the package allow access to as many internal signals as possible.

Bidirectional i/o pads are used to connect the data bus to the external memory. The default mode for the pads is input, switching to output mode only when writing to memory. A set of busgates isolates the input from the datapath bus unless a read memory operation is signalled. A 14 bit *mar* exported off chip from the datapath selects the memory location.

Our SECD system requires a 16k x 32 Static RAM (ie. 14 bit addressing, 32 bit words). The SECD operates by executing a program with data that has been provided in the memory. Programs and data share a common list structure. The word configurations are

The bit assignments are shown in Table 6.

Four memory locations are reserved: TRUE, FALSE, NIL are built-in symbolic constants, and NUM is used for locating the problem and result. TRUE or FALSE will be loaded as a result of a LEQ machine instruction evaluation. The NIL constant is used in constructing user programs. NUM is used as a pointer to access the program loaded into memory (car NUM), as well as the free list of cells (cdr NUM). The free list consists of all unallocated and unreserved cells left in memory held as

bits	use	detail
31	field	used by mark routine to record if left or right subtree of a cons record is now being traversed.
30	mark	used to mark records already traversed in garbage collection.
29-28	type	00 - cons cell
		01 - * undefined *
		10 - symbol record, includes the built-in symbolic constants NIL, TRUE, and FALSE as well as any symbols defined by the symbol table of the software creating the memory image for the chip to use.
		11 - constant record, includes integers, but also things like machine code instructions, and the arguments to a LD instruction (m.n).
27 - 0	body	cons cell: bits 27–14 are the car field. bits 13–0 are the cdr field.
		symbol record: 28 bit symbol identifier.
		constant record: 28 bit 2's complement integer value

Table 6: Bit Assignments

a singly-linked list ending with a NIL value. The NUM memory location is also used to hold a pointer (cdr NUM) to the result upon completion of the program execution.

4   Formalizing the SECD Representation

This section concerns formalizing the implementation and specification of the SECD machine in HOL. We consider 3 levels of definition: the lowest level (implementation) definition, the intermediate (register transfer) level, and the top (abstract system) level. The discussion focuses on the representation of time, clocking and data types, and how they are used to specify the system behaviour. Abstraction mechanisms between levels of representation are described.

4.1   Time

The three levels each have a distinct granularity of time. The implementation level uses the finest grain, while the register transfer level grain is that of the clock cycle. The top level granularity relates to the time to execute individual SECD machine instructions.

4.1.1 Lowest Level

The finest granularity of time represented must permit the capture of the essential behaviour of every signal. Specifically, describing the signal using a finer sampling of time should not detect patterns that are not expressed at the chosen granularity of time. The choice of a fully static design determines that the essential behaviours of generated signals will be describable in terms of their settled values, assuming a clock rate that permits them to settle. The finest granularity needed is that which captures the behaviour of the clock signals. Further, we constrain all input signals appropriately to validate their abstraction to these discrete points in time.

The grain of time described bears no direct relation to real time, but instead corresponds to the changing of values on clock lines. Thus, if the clock is stopped for any interval, there are no points of fine grain time in that interval.

We use a 2 phase non-overlapping clock. This is abstracted to two boolean signals (referred to as phases), ϕ_A and ϕ_B, with values defined at 4 points of fine grain time per clock cycle: at 2 points one signal is asserted, alternating with points when neither is asserted:

We have used a second pair of clock phase lines for clocking the **shift register** unit. The intended mode of operation will not permit cycling of both clocks simultaneously. This unusual clock arrangement[2] obscures the simple relation of clocks to the granularity of time just described. The interesting point is that intervals of the finest grain of time must correspond to intervals for either system of clocks. We express the desired clocking behaviour in terms of predicates applied to both sets of clock phase lines, requiring that complete cycles will be executed when any clock is asserted. Further, advances in time correspond to cycling one of the clocks. This description of two independent clock pairs provides a logical expression of the system we have designed.

The behaviour of the 4 clock lines during any given clock cycle can be described using the following predicates:

$\forall$ (t_0:ftime) (f:fsig).
    CycleA t_0 f $\equiv$ (f (t_0)) $\wedge$ ($\neg$f ($t_0 + 1$)) $\wedge$ ($\neg$f ($t_0 + 2$)) $\wedge$ ($\neg$f ($t_0 + 3$))

$\forall$ (t_0:ftime) (f:fsig).
    CycleB t_0 f $\equiv$ ($\neg$f (t_0)) $\wedge$ ($\neg$f ($t_0 + 1$)) $\wedge$ (f ($t_0 + 2$)) $\wedge$ ($\neg$f ($t_0 + 3$))

---

[2]The use of distinct clocks for system and shift registers was chosen to simplify the logic design and improve the probability of obtaining working subcomponents on the chip by minimizing operational dependencies.

$\forall$ (t_0:ftime) (f:fsig).
   noCycle t_0 f $\equiv$ ($\neg$f (t_0)) $\wedge$ ($\neg$f ($t_0 + 1$)) $\wedge$ ($\neg$f ($t_0 + 2$)) $\wedge$ ($\neg$f ($t_0 + 3$))

$\forall$ ϕ_A ϕ_B:fsig (t:ftime).
   CYCLE_f ϕ_A ϕ_B t $\equiv$ CycleA t ϕ_A $\wedge$ CycleB t ϕ_B

$\forall$ ϕ_A ϕ_B:fsig (t:ftime).
   no_CYCLE_f ϕ_A ϕ_B t $\equiv$ noCycle t ϕ_A $\wedge$ noCycle t ϕ_B

$\forall$ ϕ_{A_1} ϕ_{B_1} ϕ_{A_2} ϕ_{B_2}:fsig (t:ftime).
   CLOCK_CYCLE_f ϕ_{A_1} ϕ_{B_1} ϕ_{A_2} ϕ_{B_2} t $\equiv$ CYCLE_f ϕ_{A_1} ϕ_{B_1} t $\wedge$ no_CYCLE_f ϕ_{A_2} ϕ_{B_2} t

In each clock cycle interval, we shall require that the following holds:

CLOCK_CYCLE_f ϕ_A ϕ_B sr-ϕ_A sr-ϕ_B t $\vee$ **CLOCK_CYCLE_f** sr-ϕ_A sr-ϕ_B ϕ_A ϕ_B t

4.1.2 Register Transfer Level

The time grain for the Register Transfer level corresponds to 4 intervals of finest grain time, or precisely one clock cycle (of either system or shift register clock). For the system clock, the cycle consists of the 4 points beginning with the point when ϕ_A is asserted. (A similar pattern applies to the shift register clock.) We map points in medium grain time to the first of these points.

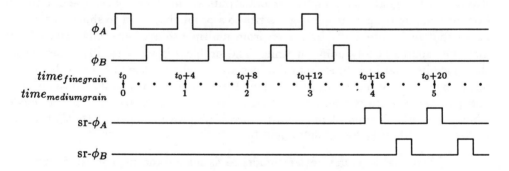

The existence of discrete clock phase lines is hidden entirely at this level. Normally, a register transfer view abstracts away the clock entirely, but the existence of two distinct clocks requires that we maintain signals at this level to indicate whether the system or shift register clock advances in any given clock cycle. Thus, registers must retain an actual clock input, rather than treating the clock as inherent in the time parameter. The correctness goal for the system will be constrained to the case where only the system clock advances.

4.1.3   Top Level

The most coarse grain of time used to describe the system corresponds to the points
when the system is in major states of the top-level FSM (*Idle, Error1, Error2,* and
Top_of_Cycle). We map from this coarse granularity to the medium grain points
of time when specific microcode addresses are in the **mpc** register. The mapping
is not a linear function as was the mapping from medium to fine grain time, since
the number of cycles needed to execute any machine instruction varies, and can
vary between executions of the same instruction. The latter differences arise due
to garbage collection calls during instruction execution, as well as varying search
distances required to load values from the environment. The method of defining
such mapping functions is well described in [Mel88].

4.2   Data Types

4.2.1   Lowest Level

We represent the clock phase lines as functions from the fine grain of time to boolean
values. Boolean values are used to model all signals, aside from pseudo-nmos regular structures where the modelling of pullup devices requires a tristate logic. The
validity of this abstraction relies upon several assumptions, including the ability
of all signals to settle within one time interval and that devices output acceptably
strong-valued signals. Floating values of outputs are modeled by the use of implication for defining behaviour. This gives rise to a proof obligation to show that circuit
nodes that may potentially be driven from multiple sources are only driven by at
most one source at any point in time. The problem is most readily observed for
the single internal bus. Since many values are gated onto the bus, the value of the
bus is expressed by the use of implication. If two devices are simultaneously driving
opposite values onto the bus, the situation arises in the abstracted circuit model
where "T = F". This problem is constrained if we prove independently that no two
devices ever drive the bus simultaneously.

Combinational logic devices are modelled as instantaneous, consistent with the
assumption that time intervals are sufficiently long to permit all signals to settle.
Memory devices (registers or latches), can be defined simply by giving the output
at (fine grain) time $(t + 1)$ in terms of input and clock signal at time (t).

latch wrt in out ≡
    ∀ t:time. out $(t + 1)$ = wrt t ⇒ in t | out t

This type of definition is appropriate where the circuit consists of sequences of memory elements clocked on alternating clock phases and separated by combinational
logic. The level-triggered latch devices used will actually produce the new output
at the start of the clock cycle, rather than at the end, although the value is latched

at the falling edge of the clock. An optimization in the fetch instruction microcode makes use of this observation, by utilizing the output of one latch (the **ARG** register) as an input of another (the **NEXTMPC** register), with both clocked on the same clock phase. This has required a redefinition of the latch.

latch wrt in out $\equiv$
$\qquad \forall$ t:time. out $(t + 1) =$ wrt $(t + 1) \Rightarrow$ in $(t + 1) \mid$ out t

This redefinition has the effect of shifting the output signal by one point in fine grain time: the new output appears one interval earlier that with the previous definition.

4.3 Register Transfer Level

Signals abstracted to this level are really a sampling of the signals described at the finer grain. This abstraction is certainly valid if the signals hold the same value at each of the 4 points of time that are abstracted to a single point at the medium grain. However, this property will not hold for signals arising from devices clocked on ϕ_B. Two sorts of stability are identified, which we shall label ϕ_A-stability and ϕ_B-stability, determined by the clocking of the memory device producing the signal. All registers in the datapath produce ϕ_A-stable signals, while the state registers in the control unit, namely the **mpc** and the stack registers, produce ϕ_B-stable signals.

It is clear that an output with ϕ_A-stability is suitable as in input to a device clocked on ϕ_B, and vice-versa. Further, with the definition of the latch behaviour above, devices clocked on the same clock line may feed each other *provided that there is no circular feedback path*[3]. Datapath registers are clocked on a signal dependent upon both ϕ_A and the write signal for the register, and thus will not change every clock cycle. Clearly then, such a datapath register which is not clocked in a cycle can feed any device latching on ϕ_A. These complete the set of constraint relations that arise between signals within the SECD chip at this level.

The definition of a control unit register at this level determined the point of fine grain time that was used to sample signals. Inputs to the controlunit state register include both ϕ_B-stable and ϕ_A-stable signals. When the current **mpc** contents are simply incremented to obtain the next **mpc** value, the next value is clearly dependent on values at the previous medium grain of time. For the case when the (lower 9 bits of the) ARG register feeds through into the state register, the point when we sample the fine grain signal determines whether we use the value at the last or present point of medium grain time. By selecting the point when ϕ_A is asserted, we can abstract both stability type signals from the same fine grain point in the cycle, and have a simple definition for the controlunit state register as follows.

---

[3]As described, the ARG register is the only component feeding another register clocked on the same phase, and the output of this second register, the NEXTMPC register, is an input to only one memory device, which is latched on ϕ_B. Thus no circular feedback path exists.

stateregister clocked reset in out ≡
   ∀ t:(medium_grain_time).
               out (t + 1) = clocked t ⇒
                           reset t ⇒ 000000000 | in t |
                           out t

An external *reset* input has been provided to permit a deterministic startup of the chip state. Asserting the *reset* input on a system clock cycle will force the **mpc** to 0 (the *idle* state). We require the reset line to be ϕ_A-stable, and asserted in the first clock cycle, and never reasserted at any later cycle. Further, the system clock must be advanced in the first medium grain time interval, in order for the reset to occur. The button input will be constrained to ϕ_B-stability, since it is an input to the **NEXTMPC** register latching on ϕ_A. ϕ_B-stability of the **mpc** and **flag** outputs is readily derived from clocking constraints. ϕ_A-stability of the datapath registers and memory is derivable from the clocking constraints, the ϕ_B-stability of the **mpc**, and the resulting ϕ_B-stability of the register control signals.

The behaviour of the system at this level is expressed in the composition of major components, whose behavioural specification is proven from the implementation level. The control unit is defined by 3 blocks: the **mpc** register and the 4 deep microcode stack, a **ROM**, and a **DECODE** component, consisting entirely of combinational logic. The datapath consists of registers and combinational logic devices (the **ALU**, **consunit**, **flagsunit**, and an array of transmission gates isolating the bus from memory output when not reading a memory location), with the bus modelled as the wiring together of these devices. The behaviour of the shift registers when disabled[4] is proved from the implementation, and we constrain the shift register controls and clock accordingly. Additionally, the logic of the padframe (the bidirectional pads particularly) is specified in terms of a mixture of wordn and discrete signals, once again proven from the implementation.

4.3.1   Top Level

At the most abstract level, the SECD machine is defined in terms of transformations to S-expressions in the 4 stacks, as shown in the first part of this report. A formal specification of the top level behaviour is ideally defined in terms of transformations to an S-expression data type, that closely resembles the elegant definition given by Henderson. The closer the resemblance the better assured are we that the HOL specification is equivalent.

The method of implementing recursive function definitions as closures with a circular environment component raises the complexity of the data representation problem considerably. Such circular S-expression lists, created by destructive operations, cannot be mapped to a simple recursive type. Further, structure is shared

---

[4]Shift registers are disabled when not being clocked and when the input values are passed directly through to output.

by S-expressions, particularly the environment component of closures. In defining mutually recursive functions originating within a LETREC in LispKit, each function closure references the same environment, which is also in the E "stack". When a destructive replace operation is performed to create the circular list structure, the change affects all those components simultaneously.

Thus, a much lower level of representation has been chosen to describe the top level specification. Rather than directly defining transformations to S-expression data type structures, we define an abstract memory type which can contain representations of S-expressions. Further, we define a set of primitive operations upon the memory which correspond to the operations on S-expressions, namely *cons, car, cdr, atom, replcar, dec, eq, leq, add, sub, mul, div*, and *rem*. The 4 state registers contain values that reference the appropriate S-expression representation. Finally, an additional **free** register containing a value to access the free list structure is needed to define the *cons* operation. The state of the machine is then defined by a tuple:

$$(S, E, C, D, Free, memory, FSM\ state)$$

where the FSM state is one of the 4 major states of the top level finite state machine view of the machine.

The implementation definition includes a memory function with simple read and write operations only. The task of the verification is to show that the sequence of operations performed on the real memory commutes with the specification transition of the abstract memory.

$$\begin{array}{ccc}
(\text{ s, e, c, d, free,} & \xrightarrow{\substack{\text{machine}\\\text{transition}}} & (\text{s', e', c', d', free',}\\
\text{memory imp, state)} & & \text{memory imp', state')}\\
\\
\text{abstraction} \downarrow & & \downarrow \text{abstraction}\\
\\
(\text{s, e, c, d, free,} & \xrightarrow{\substack{\text{specification}\\\text{transition}}} & (\text{ s', e', c', d', free',}\\
\text{abs memory, state)} & & \text{abs memory', state')}
\end{array}$$

The abstract memory type μ is basically a function :

$$\mu = \delta \rightarrow (\delta^2 \cup \alpha)$$

where δ is the domain of the function and α is the set of atoms:

$$\alpha = integers \cup symbols$$

The set of symbols includes the symbolic constants: T, F, and NIL. The domain of the function is chosen to be the type of 14 bit words, matching the type used by the implementation definition. We extend the definition of memory to incorporate garbage collection features, by adding mark and field bits to each cell:

$$\mu = \delta \rightarrow ((bool \times bool) \times (\delta^2 \cup \alpha))$$

Additionally, we include the *replcdr, setf,* and *setm* operators used by the garbage collector, as well as a *Garbage_collect* function, which is left undefined for the first proof attempt. Extractor functions *mark, field, Int_of,* and *Atom_of* are provided for the values returned by the μ function. The relevant built-in functions and their types are summarized in Table 7. Abstracting from the implementation memory to the abstract memory type maintains the mark and field bits unchanged, and maps the 28 bit field to the appropriate *cons, integer,* or *symbol* record based on the record type bits.

Operation	Type
Car, Cdr	$(\delta \times \mu \times \delta) \rightarrow (\delta)$
CAR, CDR	$(\delta \times \mu \times \delta) \rightarrow (\delta \times \mu \times \delta)$
Cons, Cons_tr	$(\delta \times \delta \times \mu \times \delta) \rightarrow (\delta \times \mu \times \delta)$
EQ, LEQ	$(\delta \times \delta \times \mu \times \delta) \rightarrow bool$
ADD, SUB, MUL, DIV, REM	$(\delta \times \delta \times \mu \times \delta) \rightarrow (\delta \times \mu \times \delta)$
Replcar, Replcdr	$(\delta \times \delta \times \mu \times \delta) \rightarrow (\delta \times \mu \times \delta)$
setm, setf	$(bool \times \delta \times \mu \times \delta) \rightarrow (\delta \times \mu \times \delta)$
mark, field	$\delta \rightarrow \mu \rightarrow bool$
Int_of	$(\delta \times \mu \times \delta) \rightarrow integer$
Atom_of	$(\delta \times \mu \times \delta) \rightarrow \alpha$
Atom	$(\delta \times \mu \times \delta) \rightarrow bool$
Is_int	$(\delta \times \mu \times \delta) \rightarrow bool$
Is_TRUE	$(\delta \times \mu \times \delta) \rightarrow bool$
Garbage_collect	$(\mu \times \delta) \rightarrow (\mu \times \delta)$

Table 7: Primitive Operations on Abstract Memory Data Type

As seen in the table, many of the functions return triples, consisting of a memory cell, a memory, and a second cell which represents a free list pointer. Operations such as *CAR, CDR, EQ, LEQ,* etc. do not alter memory, while *Cons, ADD, SUB, setm, setf, Replcar, Replcdr* do alter one cell in the memory, and thus must return the new memory. In order to permit composition of the primitive memory operations, we provide the *CAR* and *CDR* functions which return the unaltered memory and free pointer. For example, to access an argument to a *LD* command, we can write the following:

$$let \ m = Int\_of(CAR(CAR(CDR(c, MEM, free))))$$

In Table 8 we provide the top level transition specification for the *AP* instruction. Following this, in Table 9 the set of 21 such transitions are used to define the next state of the machine for each instruction, as well as the top level specification for the SECD.

We wish to verify the behaviour of the system only under very constrained conditions, representing the intended operating conditions of SECD. The major constraints include the following:

AP_trans $(s{:}\delta,e{:}\delta,c{:}\delta,d{:}\delta,\text{free}{:}\delta,\text{MEM}{:}\mu) \equiv$
        let cell_mem_free = Cons(e, Cons_tr(d,CDR(c,MEM,free))) in
        let d_mem_free = Cons_tr(cell_of cell_mem_free,
                                  CDR(CDR(s,mem_free_of cell_mem_free))) in
        let e_mem_free = Cons (Car (CDR (s,mem_free_of d_mem_free)),
                           CDR (CAR (s,mem_free_of d_mem_free))) in

(LK_NIL,	% S %
cell_of e_mem_free,	% E %
Car (CAR (s,mem_free_of e_mem_free)),	% C %
cell_of d_mem_free,	% D %
free_of e_mem_free,	% free %
mem_of e_mem_free,	% memory %
top_of_cycle)	% FSM state %

Table 8: Transition for AP Instruction

- Clock behaviour as described.

- The reset input is asserted at the start of machine operation and is never subsequently asserted.

- Input signal stability as mentioned earlier.

- The shift registers are disabled and the shift register clock does not advance.

- The free list pointer is never NIL. (i.e. No garbage collection is required.) This constraint will be eliminated in our next verification attemp.

- The control list represents a valid program. This constraint concerns the form of the control list, limits the instruction codes to the 21 machine instructions, and requires the appropriate argument and environment structure for the individual instructions. For example, the arguments to the LD instruction must reference a position within the environment list.

Conclusions

The first round of the SECD will be completed by Fall 1989. We have designed and fabricated the chip. We are now testing the chip which is also being interfaced to a workstation. The machine assisted specification and verification effort (in HOL) is almost finished and we have a hand proof (by Todd Simpson) that our SECD machine correctly reduces lambda expressions. We have also put in a considerable effort in documentation. The research project will continue with a second verification (accounting for garbage collection) the design of a second incarnation of the SECD chip.

NEXT $(s:\delta,e:\delta,c:\delta,d:\delta,\text{free}:\delta,\text{MEM}:\mu) \equiv$
let instr = Int_of (CAR (c, MEM, free)) in
(instr = LD) $\Rightarrow$ (LD_trans (s,e,c,d,free,MEM)) |
(instr = LDC) $\Rightarrow$ (LDC_trans (s,e,c,d,free,MEM)) |
(instr = LDF) $\Rightarrow$ (LDF_trans (s,e,c,d,free,MEM)) |
(instr = AP) $\Rightarrow$ (AP_trans (s,e,c,d,free,MEM)) |

$\vdots$

(instr = LEQ) $\Rightarrow$ (LEQ_trans (s,e,c,d,free,MEM)) |
(instr = STOP) $\Rightarrow$ (STOP_trans (s,e,c,d,free,MEM)))

SYS_spec (MEM:μ_csig)
  (s:δ_cvec) (e:δ_cvec) (c:δ_cvec) (d:δ_cvec)
  (free:δ_cvec)
  (reset:csig) (button:csig)
  (state:state_csig)
$\equiv \forall$ t:ctime.
 ((s (t+1), e (t+1), c (t+1), d (t+1), free (t+1), MEM (t+1), state (t+1)) =
 (reset t $\Rightarrow$ (s t, e t, c t, d t, free t, MEM t, idle) |
 (state t = idle) $\Rightarrow$
  (button t $\Rightarrow$ (Cdr (CAR (LK_NUM, MEM t, free t)),
      LK_NIL,
      Car (CDR (LK_NUM, MEM t, free t)),
      LK_NIL, LK_NIL, MEM t, top_of_cycle) |
     (s t, e t, c t, d t, free t, MEM t, idle)) |
 (state t = error0) $\Rightarrow$
  (button t $\Rightarrow$ (s t, e t, c t, d t, free t, MEM t, error1) |
     (s t, e t, c t, d t, free t, MEM t, error0)) |
 (state t = error1) $\Rightarrow$
  (button t $\Rightarrow$(s t, e t, c t, d t, free t, MEM t, error1) |
     (s t, e t, c t, d t, free t, MEM t, idle)) |
 (state = top_of_cycle) $\Rightarrow$
 (NEXT (s t, e t, c t, d t, free t, MEM t))))

Table 9: Top Level Specification

The first design opened our eyes to a number of problems which will be factored into the design process the next time. The clocking scheme is muddied considerably by the sequential registers latching on the same clock pulse. The control unit correctly uses the 2 clock phases, but the use of the same clock pulse in the datapath (and driving the memory control lines) to protect against undesired effects of write signals momentarily generated during state transitions, has been the focus of a lot of our attention. Adding an additional clock phase, or changing the control unit registers to edge triggered devices would clarify the timing considerably. Edge triggered devices add considerably to the real estate, and thus their use in the datapath, which consists of little besides registers, would be undesirable. The control unit, on the other hand, contains only storage for 45 bits in total (**mpc** plus the microcode stack). Clocked precharge of the ROM, using a semi-dynamic design proposed by Rick Schediwy, could also be explored, offering the advantage of a dramatic reduction in power dissipation as well.

We have been content with reliable rather than optimal microcode in this version of SECD. Table 3 displays the state $\rightarrow$ state dependencies instruction-group by instruction-group and was used to make sure that our microcode was correctly sequenced. Techniques for generating faster microcode will be investigated for SECD II, e.g. several busses, parallel evaluation of S, E, C, D, and extra registers (e.g. in **RAP** above, *car S* and *cdr S* are each evaluated twice).

Using the **alu** to decrement addresses for garbage collection required converting 14 bit addresses to 28 bit integers, and then back again, both conceptually in the specification as well as by padding with "0's" in the implementation. It would be preferable to have distinct functional components for operations on distinct data types.

We expect to broach the subject of efficiency, concentrating on a more efficient control and device speed. The microcode size alone is a constraint on the clocking speed, since the ROM is relatively large. Further, the control sequence for each instruction offers many opportunities for improvement, and the introduction of parallel computation, pipelining, etc. will keep our silicon hackers in ecstasy for months. It is also our desire to consider more "state of the art" designs as subjects for verification.

Acknowledgements

We wish to acknowledge the insight into representing LISP data structures gained from the work of (and conversations with) Ian Mason ([Mas86] and [Mas88]). We gratefully acknowledge the help and advice cheerfully given by team members at Calgary and by colleagues at Cambridge. To Mark Brinsmead, Inder Dhingra, Mike Gordon, Mike Hermann, Jeff Joyce, Mary Keefe, John Kendall, Wallace Kroeker, Breen Liblong, Tom Melham, Cameron Patterson, Rick Schediwy, Todd Simpson, Konrad Slind, Glen Stone, Walter Vollmerhaus, Mark Williams, Simon Williams, – many thanks.

The research described above is supported by Strategic, Operating, and Equipment Grants from the Natural Sciences and Engineering Research Council of Canada and The Canadian Microelectronics Corporation. The Strategic Grant is also supported by The Alberta Microelectronic Centre and LSI Canada Inc. The SECD verification effort is also suported by The Communication Research Establishment, Ottawa. We are also grateful to MOSIS (who built the chip) for their speedy, efficient and courteous service.

References

[Bur75]   W. Burge. *Recursive programming techniques.* Addison–Wesley, New York, 1975.

[FH88]   A. J. Field and P. G. Harrison. *Functional programming.* Addison–Wesley, New York, 1988.

[HBGS89]   M. J. Hermann, G. Birtwistle, B. Graham, and T. Simpson. The architecture of Henderson's SECD machine. Research Report 89/340/02, Computer Science Department, University of Calgary, 1989.

[Hen80]   P. Henderson. *Functional programming; applications and implementation.* Prentice Hall, London, 1980.

[Mas86]   I. A. Mason. *The Semantics of Destructive Lisp.* Center for the Study of Languange and Information, Stanford, 1986.

[Mas88]   I. A. Mason. Verification of Programs that Destructively Manipulate Data. *Science of Computer Programming*, 10:177–210, 1988.

[Mel88]   T. F. Melham. Abstraction mechanisms for hardware verification. In G. Birtwistle and P. A. Subrahmanyam, editors, *VLSI Specification, Verification and Synthesis*, pages 267–291, Norwell, Massachusetts, 1988. Kluwer.

[Plo75]   G. D. Plotkin. Call–by–name, call–by–value, and the lambda calculus. *Theoretical Computer Science*, 1(1):125–159, 1975.

[SBGH89]   T. Simpson, G. Birtwistle, B. Graham, and M. J. Hermann. A compiler for LispKit targetted at Henderson's SECD machine. Research Report 89/339/01, Computer Science Department, University of Calgary, 1989.

Reasoning about State Machines in Higher-Order Logic

Paul Loewenstein
Fairchild Research Center
National Semiconductor Corporation

Abstract

The promise of cost savings and guaranteed product reliability that have been claimed for formal verification of digital hardware have yet to be realised in practice. Largely, this is because it can be extraordinarily difficult and tedious verifying even a simple design. A large part of this difficulty is caused by the absence of much of real-world engineering theory in available theorem provers. The paper describes the formalisation of deterministic and non-deterministic state-machine theory in the HOL theorem prover. Proofs using the theory are not only shorter, but are much more tractable, and follow standard engineering reasoning much more closely than direct proofs without using the theory.

1 Introduction

The HOL theorem prover[10] has shown its power and versatility verifying many hardware designs, including microprocessors [6, 12], switch-level, gate-level and sequential circuits[5, 11]. Although successful, the verification proofs often do not follow real-world engineering reasoning very closely. This precludes design engineer guidance of the proof, and can make finding a proof very difficult and time-consuming.

1.1 Motivation

The immediate reason for the generation of this theory was failing to find an equivalence proof for the serial-parallel multiplier. This prompted the development of a deterministic state-machine theory[13]. Later, a theory of non-deterministic machines was developed. The deterministic theory was then derived from the non-deterministic theory.

The ability to represent non-deterministic machines renders systems such as inter-locked pipelines and multi-processor cache protocols to formal verification. It is in the design of this type of system that hard-to-find errors tend to creep in.

The use of general-purpose, extensible theorem provers such as HOL for engineering design allows the engineers to introduce theories of their own by defining concepts and proving theorems about them, without having to introduce any new axioms. This process is totally safe, no inconsistency can be introduced. This state machine theory is an example of such a definitional theory.

In contrast to languages specific to sequential systems[15, 4], the theory comes ready-integrated in a reasoning system which can deal with other aspects of the design, such as arithmetic properties. Only one verifier has to be integrated with the engineering design environment.

1.2   The general approach

The abstractions used in the specification of a state machine are usually not im-plementable directly in hardware. To ease the verification problems associated with translation of abstractions, it is possible to design a high-level state machine which uses the abstractions in the specification, and then proceed to refine that machine to use abstractions compatible with the models of the hardware components. Once the correctness of the high-level machine has been demonstrated, the design problem reduces to relating the behaviour of state machines with one another.

The theory is defined in the general-purpose typed lambda calculus used by the HOL theorem prover. The theory is not only applied using HOL; it is derived in it as well. This ensures the validity (but not the usefulness) of the theory. Polymorphic typing in the logic allows the theory to be totally independent of the representation of the input, output and state values of the machine.

Only behaviour is represented formally. No formal representation of the structure of a circuit, or semantic functions for mapping structure to behaviour is presented. This is a deliberate omission, since we are concerned primarily about verifying behaviour rather than verifying the relationship between behaviour and circuit structure.

The theory does not, as yet, explicitly address liveness. This is no problem for deterministic machines, as they are intrinsically live, but it does restrict the properties that can be expressed for non-deterministic machines.

At some point one has to exit the theorem prover and build some hardware. It is assumed that whatever translation system is employed, it will only be able to interpret terms of a restricted form, containing primitives which exist in some library. The theorem prover itself is used to express the design in this form, via the procedures outlined in section 6.

1.3 Relationship with other work

This work is unique in that not only can the theory be applied in a mechanical theorem prover, it has been formally derived in the theorem prover. It does not use any special language to represent sequential machines; they are defined directly in λ-calculus.

This paper is similar in approach to Gordon's paper[8], which treats the denotational semantics of fully initialised deterministic machines.

Bronstein and Talcott[3] have developed a string-functional semantics for sequential logic. This is a theory based on finite strings, which allows proofs to be performed in a first-order logic such as that of the Boyer-Moore theorem prover [2].

Browne and Clarke[4] developed a language to represent, and allow some reasoning about, deterministic Moore machines. This language guarantees through its semantics that it is describing a valid (logically consistent) machine. It also supports an interface to a temporal logic verifier.

Sheeran[15] has developed a special-purpose language to represent and manipulate deterministic sequential systems. Because of the doubly-infinite time model, initialisation behaviour cannot be modelled.

Abadi and Lamport[1] look at the existence of the refinement mappings between the states of machines at different levels of abstraction, and how to modify the machines to ensure their existence.

Devadas *et al.*[7] present an approach to the automatic verification of state machines with inputs, outputs and state represented as arrays of boolean values. The approach is by implicit enumeration of states and edges in the state-transition graph, and use of boolean logic analysis techniques to reduce the search space.

1.4 Notation and conventions

The logic used is that set out in [9]. Theorems and definitions are indicated by the symbol ⊢. These have been derived using the mechanical theorem prover, HOL[10], and should be correct apart from possible over-enthusiastic beautification. Defined constants are printed in sans serif typeface, and type operators and constants in *slanted* typeface.

2   Non-Deterministic Machines

Non-deterministic machines can have many possible next states for a given current state and external signal value. This is expressible by a relation, r, between the current state, the external signal, e, and the next state. Such a Relational Initialised State Machine may be represented in HOL by RISM $P\,r$, where:

$$\vdash \forall Pre.\ \mathsf{RISM}\ P\,r\,e = (\exists s.P(s\,0) \wedge (\forall t.r(e\,t)(s\,t)(s(\mathsf{Suc}\,t)))) \tag{1}$$

where P defines the possible initial states. e and s are both functions of time, which is represented by a natural number. e represents both inputs and outputs. RISM $P\,r$ can be considered as a predicate on e, defining a language accepted by the machine.

2.1   Relating two state machines

Machine 1 implements machine 2 if every e accepted by machine 1 is also accepted by machine 2.[1] This is true if we can find a relation between the state s_1 of machine 1, and the state s_2 of machine 2 such that:

- For every initial s_1, there exists a related initial s_2.

- For every possible external signal value, and for every s_1 related to s_2, and possible next state s_1', there must exist a next state, s_2', which is related to s_1'.

This can be expressed and proven in HOL as the theorem:

$$\vdash \forall P_1 P_2 r_1 r_2 r_e.$$
$$(\exists r.$$
$$(\forall s_1.P_1\,s_1 \supset (\exists s_2.P_2\,s_2 \wedge r\,s_1\,s_2)) \wedge \tag{2}$$
$$(\forall e s_1 s_1' s_2.r_1\,e\,s_1\,s_1' \wedge r\,s_1\,s_2 \supset (\exists s_2'.r\,s_1'\,s_2' \wedge r_2\,e\,s_2\,s_2'))) \supset$$
$$(\forall e.\ \mathsf{RISM}\ P_1\,r_1\,e \supset \mathsf{RISM}\ P_2\,r_2\,e)$$

Much of the theory of both deterministic and non-deterministic machines is derived from theorem 2. Its proof is presented in section 10, after the conclusion.

Many other theorems can be derived by appropriate specialisation and re-arranging. For instance, to compare two state machines with different representations for the

---

[1]Of course, if machine 1 accepts no e, it implements all other machines. One should show that an e exists, either directly, or via some implementation of machine 1.

external signal one can use:

$$\vdash \forall P_1 P_2 r_1 r_2 r_e.$$
$$(\exists r.$$
$$(\forall s_1.P_1 \, s_1 \supset (\exists s_2.P_2 \, s_2 \wedge r \, s_1 \, s_2)) \wedge$$
$$(\forall e_1 e_2 s_1 s_1' s_2.r_e \, e_1 \, e_2 \wedge r_1 \, e_1 \, s_1 \, s_1' \wedge r \, s_1 \, s_2 \supset$$
$$(\exists s_2'.r \, s_1' \, s_2' \wedge r_2 \, e_2 \, s_2 \, s_2'))) \supset$$
$$(\forall e_1 e_2.(\forall t.r_e(e_1 t)(e_2 t)) \supset \mathsf{RISM} \, P_1 \, r_1 \, e_1 \supset \mathsf{RISM} \, P_2 \, r_2 \, e_2)$$

(3)

or by combining implication in both directions we can derive an equivalence theorem, which also includes a constraint on the possible external signal values:

$$\vdash \forall P_1 P_2 P r_1 r_2.$$
$$(\exists r.$$
$$(\forall s_1.P_1 \, s_1 \supset (\exists s_2.P_2 \, s_2 \wedge r \, s_1 \, s_2)) \wedge$$
$$(\forall s_2.P_2 \, s_2 \supset (\exists s_1.P_1 \, s_1 \wedge r \, s_1 \, s_2)) \wedge$$
$$(\forall s_1 s_2 e.P \, e \wedge r \, s_1 \, s_2 \supset$$
$$(\forall s_1'.r_1 \, e \, s_1 \, s_1' \supset (\exists s_2'.r \, s_1' \, s_2' \wedge r_2 \, e \, s_2 \, s_2')) \wedge$$
$$(\forall s_2'.r_2 \, e \, s_2 \, s_2' \supset (\exists s_1'.r \, s_1' \, s_2' \wedge r_1 \, e \, s_1 \, s_1')))) \supset$$
$$(\forall e.(\forall t.P(e \, t)) \supset (\mathsf{RISM} \, P_1 \, r_1 \, e = \mathsf{RISM} \, P_2 \, r_2 \, e))$$

(4)

2.2 Introducing Invariants

It is sometimes useful to separate from the r of definition 1, a predicate which states properties of s which hold for all time. A definition of a machine with this separated from r is given by:

$$\vdash \forall P_0 P r e. \, \mathsf{PRISM} \, P_0 \, P \, r \, e =$$
$$(\exists s.P_0(s \, 0) \wedge (\forall t.P(s \, t)) \wedge (\forall t.r(e \, t)(s \, t)(s(\mathsf{Suc} \, t))))$$

(5)

It can easily be shown that:

$$\vdash \forall e P_0 P r. \, \mathsf{RISM} \, P_0(\lambda e' s s'.P \, s \wedge r \, e' \, s \, s')e = \mathsf{PRISM} \, P_0 \, P \, r \, e$$

(6)

thus demonstrating that the P argument is unnecessary.

Often, not all states represented by the type of s are reachable from the initial state. This can allow the derivation of an invariant which can be used in later proofs of properties of a machine. A theorem suitable for finding and including such an invariant is:

$$\vdash \forall P_0 P r.$$
$$(\exists r'.$$
$$(\forall s.P_0 \, s \supset P \, s \wedge r' \, s) \wedge$$
$$(\forall e s s'.r \, e \, s \, s' \wedge P \, s \wedge r' \, s \supset P \, s' \wedge r' \, s')) \supset$$
$$(\forall e. \, \mathsf{RISM} \, P_0 \, r \, e = \mathsf{PRISM} \, P_0 \, P \, r \, e)$$

(7)

P specifies the invariant we want to demonstrate. It is often necessary to supplement it with another invariant specified by r' to allow the proof. This theorem follows by specialisation of 2. It is the principal theorem used in proving the safety properties of Peterson's mutual exclusion algorithm in section 7.

Invariants can also be introduced while applying theorem 2 by including them as part of the relation r between the states of the two machines.

3 Dynamic Signals in Static Structure

A hardware implementation of a state machine consists of a static structure of registers and combinational circuits, through which flow dynamic signals. In this paper dynamic signals are represented as functions from time (a natural number) to values. For most digital technologies, signals are 2-valued, and can be represented as functions from *num* to *bool*.

Static structure can be represented in many ways, but here binary words are represented as boolean lists, and the pairing operator (,) is used to build tuples.

The sequence of values in a binary register could be represented using type $(num \rightarrow bool)$ *list*, where the list structure is static, and the elements dynamic.

Hardware primitives can be specified to operate on signals, for example, an And gate could be defined as:
$$\vdash \forall t.(x \text{ And } y) t = (x\, t) \wedge (y\, t) \tag{8}$$

We can define a static 1-bit $\times n$-bit binary multiplier:
$$\vdash (\forall x.\, \text{bin\_and } x\, [\,] = [\,]) \wedge \atop (\forall xyv.\, \text{bin\_and } x \text{ Cons } y\, v = \text{Cons}(x \wedge y)(\text{bin\_and } x\, v)) \tag{9}$$

or a version with dynamic values in a static structure:
$$\vdash (\forall x.\, \text{Bin\_And } x\, [\,] = [\,]) \wedge \atop (\forall xyv.\, \text{Bin\_And } x \text{ Cons } y\, v = \text{Cons}(x \text{ And } y)(\text{Bin\_And } x\, v)) \tag{10}$$

or with dynamic values and structure:
$$\vdash \forall t.\, \text{Bin\_AND}(x, v)t = \text{bin\_and}(x\, t)(v\, t) \tag{11}$$

It is the Bin_And formulation that is the cleanest for representing hardware with fixed-length words and time-varying signals. By contrast, bin_and is purely static, and the wordlengths in equation 11 can vary with time, which is not normally desired.

Unfortunately, the type polymorphism mechanism used in the development of the state-machine theory is unable to distinguish between the signal and structure components of the type. We are therefore forced to initially formulate the machine with potentially dynamic structure.

3.1 Converting between static and dynamic structure

Static structure can always be represented dynamically, but the converse is not true. For example, let us look at list structures. We can define a function, LFL for converting a list of functions to a function of a list:

$$\vdash (\forall x.\, \mathsf{LFL}[\,]x = [\,]) \wedge (\forall htx.\, \mathsf{LFL}(\mathsf{Cons}\, h\, t)x = \mathsf{Cons}(h\, x)(\mathsf{LFL}\, t\, x)) \qquad (12)$$

But the inverse operation, FLF, can only be performed when the length of the list is constant:

$$\vdash \forall un.(\forall x.\, \mathsf{Length}(u\, x) = n) \supset (u = \mathsf{LFL}(\mathsf{FLF}\, u)) \qquad (13)$$

Using:

$$\vdash \forall ux.\, \mathsf{Length}(\mathsf{LFL}\, u\, x) = \mathsf{Length}\, u \qquad (14)$$

we can also show:

$$\vdash \forall u.\, \mathsf{FLF}(\mathsf{LFL}\, u) = u \qquad (15)$$

In general, we can convert from a dynamic representation of structure to a static one, by:

- Identifying a property, or *metric*, of the representing type which corresponds to the structure (**Length** for lists).

- Showing that property to be time-independent.

For pairs (Cartesian products), we can always convert between dynamic and static structure. Converting from static to dynamic:

$$\vdash \forall xyz.\, \mathsf{PFP}(y, z)x = y\, x, z\, x \qquad (16)$$

and the inverse operator FPF can be defined such that:

$$\vdash \forall y.\, \mathsf{PFP}(\mathsf{FPF}\, y) = y \qquad (17)$$

and:

$$\vdash \forall s.\, \mathsf{FPF}(\mathsf{PFP}\, s) = s \qquad (18)$$

We can show similar properties for other structuring types, such as disjoint sum, which can be considered to have a boolean metric.

3.2 Ensuring Static Structure in State-Machine definitions

If the machine is to be hardware-buildable, the next-state relation should ensure that the relevant metrics, such as the lengths of binary words, remain constant. Even if this invariance is not needed to verify the specification of the machine, the expansion to a boolean register description (section 6) will fail if the metrics vary with time.

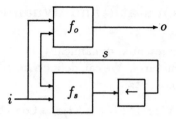

Figure 1: Mealy machine; ← indicates time delay

4 Deterministic Machines

A state-machine whose next state is uniquely determined by its current state and input is *deterministic*. It can be modelled as a Mealy Machine (fig 1).

All of these state machines can be represented by choosing appropriate P, f_s and f_o in ISM $P(f_s, f_o)$ where:

$$
\begin{aligned}
&\vdash \text{ISM } P(f_s, f_o)\, i\, o = \\
&\quad \exists s. P(s\, 0) \wedge (\forall t.(s(\text{Suc}\, t) = f_s(i\, t, s\, t)) \wedge (\forall t.(o\, t) = f_o(i\, t, s\, t))
\end{aligned}
\tag{19}
$$

Here the input and outputs are distinct, in contrast to definition 1.

4.1 Derivation of deterministic theorems

ISM is related to RISM by:

$$
\begin{aligned}
&\vdash \forall P f_s f_o i o. \\
&\quad \text{RISM } P(\lambda(i, o)s's''.(s'' = f_s(i, s')) \wedge (o = f_o(i, s')))(\text{PFP}(i, o)) = \\
&\quad \text{ISM } P(f_s, f_o)\, i\, o
\end{aligned}
\tag{20}
$$

So, by specialisation of theorem 2 we can derive an implementation theorem:

$$
\begin{aligned}
&\vdash \forall P_1 P_2 P f_{s1} f_{s2} f_{o1} f_{o2}. \\
&\quad (\exists r. \\
&\quad (\forall s_1. P_1\, s_1 \supset (\exists s_2. P_2\, s_2 \wedge r\, s_1\, s_2)) \wedge \\
&\quad (\forall i\, s_1\, s_2. P\, i \wedge r\, s_1\, s_2 \supset \\
&\quad\quad r(f_{s1}(i, s_1))(f_{s2}(i, s_2)) \wedge (f_{o1}(i, s_1) = f_{o2}(i, s_2)))) \supset \\
&\quad (\forall i o.(\forall t. P(i\, t))) \supset \text{ISM } P_1(f_{s1}, f_{o1})\, i\, o \supset \text{ISM } P_2(f_{s2}, f_{o2})\, i\, o)
\end{aligned}
\tag{21}
$$

and by specialisation of theorem 4 we obtain a machine equivalence theorem:

$$
\begin{aligned}
&\vdash \forall P_1 P_2 P f_{s1} f_{s2} f_{o1} f_{o2}. \\
&\quad (\exists r. \\
&\quad (\forall s_1. P_1\, s_1 \supset (\exists s_2. P_2\, s_2 \wedge r\, s_1\, s_2)) \wedge \\
&\quad (\forall s_2. P_2\, s_2 \supset (\exists s_1. P_1\, s_1 \wedge r\, s_1\, s_2)) \wedge \\
&\quad (\forall i\, s_1\, s_2. P\, i \wedge r\, s_1\, s_2 \supset \\
&\qquad r(f_{s1}(i, s_1))(f_{s2}(i, s_2)) \wedge (f_{o1}(i, s_1) = f_{o2}(i, s_2)))) \supset \\
&\quad (\forall io.(\forall t.P(i\,t)) \supset (\mathsf{ISM}\, P_1(f_{s1}, f_{o1})i\, o = \mathsf{ISM}\, P_2(f_{s2}, f_{o2})i\, o))
\end{aligned}
\tag{22}
$$

Note that for deterministic machines, the only extra requirement for equivalence concerns solely the initial states.

4.2   Uninitialised machines

Often synchronous hardware is initialised through its inputs, rather than by asynchronous initialisation circuitry. These machines "power up" uninitialised. They can be represented by:

$$
\vdash \mathsf{SM}(f_s, f_o)i\, o = \exists s.(\forall t.s(\mathsf{Suc}\, t) = f_s(i\, t, s\, t)) \wedge (\forall t.o\, t = f_o(i\, t, s\, t))
\tag{23}
$$

Although all possible state machines can be defined using SM, it requires the definition of a type which *exactly* models the possible values of the state. For example, if we wish to use a sub-range of the natural numbers to model the state, we would have to define that specific sub-range as a type, and define all the relevant arithmetic operators on that type. This is not only very tedious, but it precludes defining families of machines with different sub-ranges, as would be the case for implementations using different binary wordlengths.

Because of this, it is useful to use a definition of a state machine, FSM, which allows the set of possible state values to be a subset of that represented by the type of the state variable. This subset is represented by an invariant P:

$$
\begin{aligned}
&\vdash \mathsf{FSM}\, P(f_s, f_o)i\, o = \\
&\quad \exists s.(\forall t.P(s\, t)) \wedge (\forall t.s(t+1) = f_s(i\, t, s\, t)) \wedge (\forall t.o\, t = f_o(i\, t, s\, t))
\end{aligned}
\tag{24}
$$

By specialisation of theorem 7, FSM can be related to ISM:

$$
\begin{aligned}
&\vdash \forall P f_s f_o. \, (\exists s.P\, s) \wedge (\forall is.P\, s \supset P(f_s(i, s))) \supset \\
&\quad (\forall io.\, \mathsf{ISM}\, P(f_s, f_o)i\, o = \mathsf{FSM}\, P(f_s, f_o)i\, o)
\end{aligned}
\tag{25}
$$

When relating two machines, choosing a relation between their states of the form:

$$
\lambda s_1 s_2.(s_2 = f\, s_1) \wedge P_1\, s_1 \wedge P_2\, s_2
\tag{26}
$$

we can state that the initial state predicates P_1 and P_2 hold for all time, and also restrict the relation between the states to a function. Theorem 21 can be specialised with such a relation to give:

$$
\begin{aligned}
&\vdash \forall P P_1 P_2 f_{s1} f_{s2} f f_{o1} f_{o2}. \\
&\quad (\exists f. \\
&\quad\quad (\forall s.P_1 s \supset (P_2(f\,s)) \wedge \\
&\quad\quad (\forall i.P\,i \supset (f(f_{s1}(i,s)) = f_{s2}(i, f\,s)) \wedge (f_{o1}(i,s) = f_{o2}(i, fs))))) \supset \\
&\quad (\forall i.(\forall t.P(i\,t)) \supset (\forall o.\, \mathsf{FSM}\, P_1(f_{s1}, f_{o1})i\,o \supset \mathsf{FSM}\, P_2(f_{s2}, f_{o2})i\,o))
\end{aligned}
\tag{27}
$$

and theorem 22 gives:

$$
\begin{aligned}
&\vdash \forall P P_1 P_2 f_{s1} f_{s2} f f_{o1} f_{o2}. \\
&\quad (\exists f. \\
&\quad\quad (\forall s'.P_2 s' \supset (\exists s.P_1 s \wedge (fs = s'))) \wedge \\
&\quad\quad (\forall s.P_1 s \supset (P_2(f\,s)) \wedge \\
&\quad\quad (\forall i.P\,i \supset (P_1(f_{s1}(i,s))) \wedge \\
&\quad\quad (f(f_{s1}(i,s)) = f_{s2}(i, f\,s)) \wedge (f_{o1}(i,s) = f_{o2}(i, fs))))) \supset \\
&\quad (\forall i.(\forall t.P(i\,t)) \supset (\forall o.\, \mathsf{FSM}\, P_1(f_{s1}, f_{o1})i\,o = \mathsf{FSM}\, P_2(f_{s2}, f_{o2})i\,o))
\end{aligned}
\tag{28}
$$

Since these theorems impose the condition that the initial state condition holds for all time, they also hold when ISM is substituted for FSM.

5 Synchronous State-Machine Example

The circuit in figure 2 is the 3-bit member of a family of serial-parallel multipliers. It is redundantly encoded in order to avoid propagating the carry at each clock cycle. We shall show its equivalence to the more straightforward machine, HLM, of figure 3, which is described using natural-number representation.

The operation of SPM is as follows:

On each clock cycle the c (carry) bits are fed back through a unit delay into the same full adder, thus dividing their value by 2; the s (sum) bits are fed back one adder further down, also dividing their values by 2. At the same time the parallel input is conditionally added in. The bottom bit is output, and the rest of the sum is redundantly encoded in the s and c registers for dividing by two on the next cycle.

HLM achieves the division-by-2 directly, using the natural-number Div function. The "bottom bit" is extracted using the modulus function, Mod, and converted to boolean with Bit_Rep.

The equivalence of the two machines can be seen once the state-mapping function is determined. The value of s in HLM is equal to the sum of the binary values of the s and c registers in SPM. This mapping, provided by the designer, is key to a successful proof.

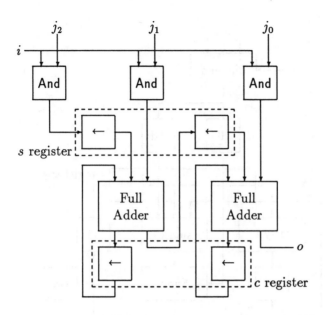

Figure 2: SPM, a redundantly encoded serial-parallel multplier

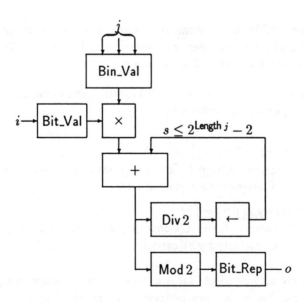

Figure 3: HLM, serial-parallel multiplier implemented with natural numbers

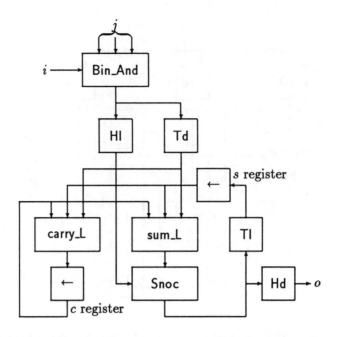

Figure 4: Alternative description of SPM

5.1 Definition of SPM

In order to express SPM in state-machine form it is useful to collect together the internal registers and represent them as boolean lists (figure 4). We shall convert the design back to the form of figure 2 in section 6.

We also collect the full adders as separate bit-wise sum (sum_L) and carry (carry_L) functions operating on three boolean lists:[2]

$$\vdash (\mathsf{sum\_L}[\,][\,][\,] = [\,] \wedge$$
$$\forall xuyvzw.(\mathsf{sum\_L}(\mathsf{Cons}\, x\, u)(\mathsf{Cons}\, y\, v)(\mathsf{Cons}\, z\, w) = \tag{29}$$
$$\mathsf{Cons}(\mathsf{sum}\, x\, y\, z)(\mathsf{sum\_L}\, u\, v\, w))$$

$$\vdash (\mathsf{carry\_L}[\,][\,][\,] = [\,] \wedge$$
$$\forall xuyvzw.(\mathsf{carry\_L}(\mathsf{Cons}\, x\, u)(\mathsf{Cons}\, y\, v)(\mathsf{Cons}\, z\, w) = \tag{30}$$
$$\mathsf{Cons}(\mathsf{carry}\, x\, y\, z)(\mathsf{carry\_L}\, u\, v\, w))$$

Because the top bit of j in SPM $i\,j\,o$ is a "special case", some juggling is needed to using Snoc, Hl and Td, which are defined to correspond to Cons, Hd and Tl, but operating on the other (msb) end of the list.

---

[2]These functions are defined to operate on three input lists of arbitary length; for the purposes of this paper only the part of the definition relating to equal-length inputs is presented.

We can now define the invariance (static structure) on the state of SPM:

$$\vdash \mathsf{SPP}\, n(s, c) = (\mathsf{Length}\, s = n - 1) \wedge (\mathsf{Length}\, c = n - 1) \tag{31}$$

the next state function:

$$\vdash \mathsf{SPFS}((i, j), s, c) = ((j = [\,]) \Rightarrow ([\,], [\,])|$$
$$\mathsf{let}\ x = \mathsf{bin\_and}\, i\, j\ \mathsf{in} \tag{32}$$
$$\mathsf{Tl}(\mathsf{Snoc}(\mathsf{Hl}\, x)(\mathsf{sum\_L}(\mathsf{Td}\, x)s\, c)), \mathsf{carry\_L}(\mathsf{Td}\, x)s\, c)$$

where $x \Rightarrow y|z$ is HOL syntax for "if x then y else z". The output function is defined as:

$$\vdash \mathsf{SPFO}((i, j), s, c) = ((j = [\,]) \Rightarrow \mathsf{F}|$$
$$\mathsf{let}\ x = \mathsf{bin\_and}\, i\, j\ \mathsf{in}\ \mathsf{Hd}(\mathsf{Snoc}(\mathsf{Hl}\, x)(\mathsf{sum\_L}(\mathsf{Td}\, x)s\, c))) \tag{33}$$

The definition of the serial-parallel multiplier is then:

$$\vdash \mathsf{SPM}\, i\, j\, o = \mathsf{FSM}(\mathsf{SPP}(\mathsf{Length}\, j))(\mathsf{SPFS}, \mathsf{SPFO})(\mathsf{PFP}(i, \mathsf{LFL}\, j))o \tag{34}$$

5.2 Definition of HLM

The state predicate, restricting the range of natural numbers is:

$$\vdash \mathsf{HLP}\, ns = s \leq (2^n - 2) \tag{35}$$

and the next-state function is:

$$\vdash \mathsf{HLFS}((i, j), s) = (((\mathsf{Bit\_Val}\, i) \times (\mathsf{Bin\_Val}\, j)) + s)\, \mathsf{Div}\, 2 \tag{36}$$

and the output function is defined as:

$$\vdash \mathsf{HLFO}((i, j), s) = \mathsf{Bit\_Rep}((((\mathsf{Bit\_Val}\, i) \times (\mathsf{Bin\_Val}\, j)) + s)\, \mathsf{Mod}\, 2) \tag{37}$$

giving the definition of HLM in figure 3:

$$\vdash \mathsf{HLM}\, i\, j\, o = \mathsf{FSM}(\mathsf{HLP}(\mathsf{Length}\, j))(\mathsf{HLFS}, \mathsf{HLFO})(\mathsf{PFP}(i, \mathsf{LFL}\, j))o \tag{38}$$

5.3 Outline of Equivalence Proof

Defining the static structure condition on the input:

$$\vdash \mathsf{PI}\, n(i, j) = (\mathsf{Length}\, j = n) \tag{39}$$

and the state mapping function:

$$\vdash \mathsf{SPHL}(x, y) = (\mathsf{Bin\_Val}\, x) + (\mathsf{Bin\_Val}\, y) \tag{40}$$

we can derive from theorems 28, 34 and 38:

$$\vdash (\forall s'.\,\mathsf{HLP}(\mathsf{Length}\,j)s' \supset (\exists s.\,\mathsf{SPP}(\mathsf{Length}\,j)s \wedge (\mathsf{SPHL}\,s = s')))\wedge$$
$$(\forall s.\,\mathsf{SPP}(\mathsf{Length}\,j)s \supset \mathsf{HLP}(\mathsf{Length}\,j)(\mathsf{SPHL}\,s))\wedge$$
$$(\forall s.\,\mathsf{SPP}(\mathsf{Length}\,j)s \supset (\forall i'.\,\mathsf{PI}(\mathsf{Length}\,j)i' \supset$$
$$\mathsf{SPP}(\mathsf{Length}\,j)(\mathsf{SPFS}(i',s))))\wedge$$
$$(\forall s.\,\mathsf{SPP}(\mathsf{Length}\,j)s \supset (\forall i'.\,\mathsf{PI}(\mathsf{Length}\,j)i' \supset \tag{41}$$
$$(\mathsf{SPHL}(\mathsf{SPFS}(i',s)) = \mathsf{HLFS}(i',\mathsf{SPHL}\,s))))\wedge$$
$$(\forall s.\,\mathsf{SPP}(\mathsf{Length}\,j)s \supset (\forall i'.\,\mathsf{PI}(\mathsf{Length}\,j)i' \supset$$
$$(\mathsf{SPFO}(i',s) = \mathsf{HLFO}(i',\mathsf{SPHL}\,s)))) \supset$$
$$(\forall t.\,\mathsf{PI}(\mathsf{Length}\,j)(\mathsf{PFP}(i,\mathsf{LFL}\,j)t)) \supset (\forall o.\,\mathsf{SPM}\,ijo = \mathsf{HLM}\,ijo)$$

giving 5 first-order sub-goals to prove the equivalence. The proofs of these sub-goals are not presented here. It can also be easily shown that:

$$\vdash \forall t.\,\mathsf{PI}(\mathsf{Length}\,j)(\mathsf{PFP}(i,\mathsf{LFL}\,j)t) \tag{42}$$

so that we can deduce:

$$\vdash \forall ijo.\,\mathsf{SPM}\,i\,j\,o = \mathsf{HLM}\,i\,j\,o \tag{43}$$

6 Synthesis of Hardware Designs from State Machine Descriptions

In order to interface a formal reasoning system such as HOL to the rest of the design environment we need some form of translator. Because HOL is much more expressive than more conventional design representations, it is only possible to translate certain forms of HOL terms.

It would be extremely tedious and dangerous to update the translation system every time new abstractions, such as state-machines, are introduced. It is much better to use the theorem prover to eliminate these abstractions before passing the design to the outside world.

This refinement of a behavioural description of a design to one which is directly translatable to hardware is known as behavioural synthesis. This can be performed in HOL by forward proof, thus producing guaranteed correct results.

6.1 Boolean Register Description

We shall produce a boolean register description of the design, using variables of type : $num \rightarrow bool$ representing digital signals.

A boolean register description having inputs i_i, state s_j and outputs o_k, can be represented by a term of the form:

$$
\begin{aligned}
&\exists s_1 s_2 \ldots s_n. \\
&\quad s_1 \leftarrow F_{s1}[i_1, \ldots, i_m, s_1, \ldots, s_n] \wedge \\
&\quad s_2 \leftarrow F_{s2}[i_1, \ldots, i_m, s_1, \ldots, s_n] \wedge \\
&\qquad \vdots \\
&\quad s_n \leftarrow F_{sn}[i_1, \ldots, i_m, s_1, \ldots, s_n] \wedge \\
&\quad o_1 = F_{o1}[i_1, \ldots, i_m, s_1, \ldots, s_n] \wedge \\
&\quad o_2 = F_{o2}[i_1, \ldots, i_m, s_1, \ldots, s_n] \wedge \\
&\qquad \vdots \\
&\quad o_p = F_{op}[i_1, \ldots, i_m, s_1, \ldots, s_n]
\end{aligned}
\tag{44}
$$

where $F_{xi}[i_1, \ldots, i_m, s_1, \ldots, s_n]$ denotes a time-independent function of the inputs and state, implemented as a combinational circuit, using dynamic signal primitives such as And, which are assumed to exist in a cell library.

The unit delay operator, $\leftarrow$, is defined as:

$$
\vdash \forall xy.x \leftarrow y = (\forall t.x(\mathsf{Suc}\, t) = y\, t)
\tag{45}
$$

and can be implemented with a clocked register element.

6.2   Generating the Boolean Register Description

The abstractions used to define state-machines, such as FSM, can be eliminated by rewriting with their definitions, such as theorem 24.

As mentioned in section 3 the state-machine formulations do not distinguish between static structure and dynamic signals; we therefore need to separate them.

The state in equation 1 is existentially quantified, so we use theorems of the form:

$$
\vdash \forall P.(\exists s.P\, s) = (\exists s_1 s_2.P(\mathsf{PFP}(s_1, s_2)))
\tag{46}
$$

to convert pairs to their static form, with dynamic components. Also by rewriting with equation 16 we can eliminate reference to PFP.

The equivalent theorem for lists is:

$$
\vdash \forall Pn.\, (\exists s.(\forall t.\, \mathsf{Length}(s\, t) = n) \wedge P\, s) = \\
(\exists s'.(\mathsf{Length}\, s' = n) \wedge P(\mathsf{LFL}\, s'))
\tag{47}
$$

which converts the existentially quantified dynamic list to a static one with dynamic elements.

LFL represents the boundary between signals represented as lists of functions and signals represented as functions of lists. After application of theorem 47, LFL occurs near the leaves of the term tree, and it can be propagated towards the root using theorems such as:

$$\vdash \forall txu.\, \text{bin\_and}(xt)(\text{LFL}\, u\, t) = \text{LFL}(\text{Bin\_And}\, x\, u)t \qquad (48)$$

while the static function bin_and is replaced with the dynamic-signal static-structure function Bin_And.

Eventually, one can apply theorems to eliminate LFL, such as:

$$\vdash \forall xt.\neg\, \text{Null}\, x \supset (\text{Hd}(\text{LFL}\, x\, t) = \text{Hd}\, x\, t) \qquad (49)$$

Also, lists can be expanded to their individual elements using theorem:

$$\vdash \forall P.(\exists l.(\text{Length}\, l = \text{Suc}\, n) \wedge P\, l) = (\exists xu.(\text{Length}\, u = n) \wedge P(\text{Cons}\, x\, u)) \qquad (50)$$

By applying the above, and other similar theorems, and expanding recursively defined functions such as Bin_And and Sum_L we obtain (for Length $j = 3$):

$$
\begin{aligned}
\vdash \text{SPM}\, &i[j_0; j_1; j_2]o = (\exists s_0 s_1 c_0 c_1. \\
&s_0 \leftarrow (\text{Sum}(i\,\text{And}\,j_1)s_1\, c_1) \wedge s_1 \leftarrow (i\,\text{And}\,j_2)\wedge \\
&c_0 \leftarrow (\text{Carry}(i\,\text{And}\,j_0)s_0\, c_0) \wedge c_1 \leftarrow (\text{Carry}(i\,\text{And}\,j_1)s_1\, c_1)\wedge \\
&(o = \text{Sum}(i\,\text{And}\,j_0)s_0\, c_0))
\end{aligned}
\qquad (51)
$$

which corresponds to the serial-parallel multiplier representation of figure 2, with its right-hand side in the form of equation 44. This procedure has been implemented to handle SPM $i\, j\, o$ for all wordlengths of j.

7 Non-Deterministic Example

Here the theory is used to prove the safety properties of Peterson's mutual exclusion algorithm, presented in imperative language form in figure 5, adapted from [14].

We start by defining a 4-valued type with values Rem,Setup,Loop and Crit for representing a program counter for each process. We define a successor function on this type:

$$
\begin{aligned}
\vdash &(\text{Suc\_p Rem} = \text{Setup}) \wedge (\text{Suc\_p Setup} = \text{Loop})\wedge \\
&(\text{Suc\_p Loop} = \text{Crit}) \wedge (\text{Suc\_p Crit} = \text{Rem})
\end{aligned}
\qquad (52)
$$

initially $f_0 = F$, $f_1 = F$;

Process 0:	*Process 1:*
repeat	**repeat**
$\quad f_0 := T$;	$\quad f_1 := T$;
$\quad w := T$;	$\quad w := F$;
$\quad$ **wait until not** f_1 **or** $w = F$;	$\quad$ **wait until not** f_0 **or** $w = T$;
$\quad$ *Critical Section*	$\quad$ *Critical Section*
$\quad f_0 := F$;	$\quad f_1 := F$;
$\quad$ *Remainder section*	$\quad$ *Remainder section*
until F;	**until** F;

Figure 5: Peterson's mutual exclusion algorithm

The code is translated to a next-state relation:

$$
\begin{aligned}
\vdash \mathsf{Pete\_r}\, & e(f_0, f_1, p_0, p_1, w)(f_0', f_1', p_0', p_1', w') = \\
& ((p_0' = p_0) \vee (p_0' = (\mathsf{Suc\_p}\, p_0))) \wedge \\
& ((p_1' = p_1) \vee (p_1' = (\mathsf{Suc\_p}\, p_1))) \wedge \\
& (((p_0 = \mathsf{Rem}) \wedge (p_0' = \mathsf{Setup})) \Rightarrow f_0' | \\
& \quad ((p_0 = \mathsf{Crit}) \wedge (p_0' = \mathsf{Rem})) \Rightarrow \neg f_0' | (f_0' = f_0)) \wedge \\
& (((p_1 = \mathsf{Rem}) \wedge (p_1' = \mathsf{Setup})) \Rightarrow f_1' | \\
& \quad ((p_1 = \mathsf{Crit}) \wedge (p_1' = \mathsf{Rem})) \Rightarrow \neg f_1' | (f_1' = f_1)) \wedge \\
& (((p_0 = \mathsf{Setup}) \wedge (p_0' = \mathsf{Loop})) \Rightarrow \\
& \quad (((p_1 = \mathsf{Setup}) \wedge (p_1' = \mathsf{Loop})) \Rightarrow T | w') | \\
& \quad ((p_1 = \mathsf{Setup}) \wedge (p_1' = \mathsf{Loop})) \Rightarrow \neg w' | (w' = w))) \wedge \\
& ((p_0 = \mathsf{Loop}) \supset (f_1 \wedge w) \supset (p_0' = \mathsf{Loop})) \wedge \\
& ((p_1 = \mathsf{Loop}) \supset (f_0 \wedge \neg w) \supset (p_1' = \mathsf{Loop})))
\end{aligned}
\tag{53}
$$

The initial state predicate is also derived from the code:

$$
\begin{aligned}
\vdash \mathsf{Pete\_I}(f_0, f_1, p_0, p_1, w) = \\
\neg f_0 \wedge \neg f_1 \wedge (p_0 = \mathsf{Rem}) \wedge (p_1 = \mathsf{Rem})
\end{aligned}
\tag{54}
$$

The safety property (invariance) that we wish to demonstrate is that both processes are not simultaneously in their critical region:

$$
\vdash \mathsf{Pete\_P}(f_0, f_1, p_0, p_1, w) = \neg((p_0 = \mathsf{Crit}) \wedge (p_1 = \mathsf{Crit}))
\tag{55}
$$

We shall need to also supplement the safety property with the invariance:

$$
\begin{aligned}
\vdash \mathsf{Pete\_R}(f_0, f_1, p_0, p_1, w) = \\
(p_0 = \mathsf{Rem}) \Rightarrow \neg f_0 | f_0 \wedge (p_1 = \mathsf{Rem}) \Rightarrow \neg f_1 | f_1 \wedge \\
((p_0 = \mathsf{Loop}) \wedge (p_1 = \mathsf{Crit}) \supset w) \wedge \\
((p_0 = \mathsf{Crit}) \wedge (p_1 = \mathsf{Loop}) \supset \neg w))
\end{aligned}
\tag{56}
$$

The f_0 and f_1 values are obvious. The w values was added after the proof failed, and the failed sub-goals were examined! Theorem 7 can be specialised with these constants to form:

$$\vdash (\forall f_0 f_1 p_0 p_1 w.$$
$$\text{Pete\_I}(f_0, f_1, p_0, p_1, w) \supset$$
$$\text{Pete\_R}(f_0, f_1, p_0, p_1, w) \land \text{Pete\_P}(f_0, f_1, p_0, p_1, w)) \land$$
$$(\forall c_0 c_1 f_0 f_1 p_0 p_1 w f_0' f_1' p_0' p_1' w'.$$
$$\text{Pete\_r}(c_0, c_1)(f_0, f_1, p_0, p_1, w)(f_0', f_1', p_0', p_1', w') \land \qquad (57)$$
$$\text{Pete\_R}(f_0, f_1, p_0, p_1, w) \land$$
$$\text{Pete\_P}(f_0, f_1, p_0, p_1, w) \supset$$
$$\text{Pete\_R}(f_0', f_1', p_0', p_1', w') \land \text{Pete\_P}(f_0', f_1', p_0', p_1', w')) \supset$$
$$(\forall e'. \text{ RISM Pete\_I Pete\_r } e' = \text{PRISM Pete\_I Pete\_P Pete\_r } e')$$

which gives two subgoals to show the equality of the two machines. After rewriting with definitions 55, 53, 54 and 56 the second subgoal gets rather large. The first (initial condition) sub-goal is trivial. The second is proven tediously by splitting into the possible values of p_0, p_1, p_0' and p_1'. A single proof procedure solves most of the 64 resulting sub-goals, leaving a few straightforward cases around the critical regions. With the introduction of more proof automation into HOL, the proof should be totally automatic after an appropriate definition of Pete_R has been found.

8 Conclusion

The derivation of state-machine theory in HOL has already shown its worth on non-trivial examples. Since virtually all digital systems can be modelled as state-machines, the applications should be diverse.

It is often simpler to derive proofs when the "essential truths" are not masked behind excessive detail. Proving the equivalence conditions of non-deterministic machines was much easier than for the special case of a deterministic machine. A "direct" equivalence proof of the serial-parallel multiplier was never found, although it was easy once the deterministic state-machine theorems had been derived.

Using general-purpose logic, rather than a language that is devoted to the representation of hardware, allows the reasoning to extend outside the direct representation of the hardware. This capability is essential if proofs of correctness are to be compatible with the engineer's line of reasoning.

This theory is intrinsically a higher-order theory, and is neither applicable nor derivable in a first-order logic. The ability to derive and use such a theory more than offsets the relative computational inefficiency of HOL.

The use of purely definitional theories is not only safe, it also facilitates the translation of designs for transfer to the outside world, as the definitions can be used for rewriting during the translation process.

9 Further Research

Work is continuing to tie up the loose ends as well as adding new features to the theory to handle composition, time abstraction and liveness properties.

9.1 Composition of state-machines

The composition of state machines is quite straightforward using the theorem:

$$\vdash \forall P_1 P_2 r r_1 r_2 e'.$$
$$(\exists e'_1 e'_2.$$
$$(\forall t. r(e' t)(e'_1 t)(e'_2 t)) \wedge \text{RISM } P_1 \, r_1 \, e'_1 \wedge \text{RISM } P_2 \, r_2 \, e'_2) =$$
$$\text{RISM}$$
$$(\lambda(s_1, s_2).P_1 \, s_1 \wedge P_2 \, s_2)$$
$$(\lambda e(s_1, s_2)(s'_1, s'_2).\exists e_1 e_2. r \, e \, e_1 \, e_2 \wedge r_1 \, e_1 \, s_1 \, s'_1 \wedge r_2 \, e_2 \, s_2 \, s'_2)$$
$$e'$$

This should allow SPM to be expressed as a recursively defined composition of smaller machines. The expansion of this composition should be much more straightforward than the propagation of LFL in section 6.

9.2 Time Abstraction

Time translation is trivial; machines which are initialised at some time t_0 are related simply to machines initialised at time 0.

It is possible to relate state-machines over differing time-steps by "exponentiating" the next-state relation by the size of the time step. This leads an equivalence relation between machines running at different speeds, or using different representations of time.

9.3 Further examples

- An inductive proof of a more complex n-process non-deterministic machine.

- Using time abstraction to relate HLM to a machine performing one multiplication per time step.

10   Proof of theorem 2

The proof here is presented as an informal, goal-directed proof. It is sufficiently complete to reproduce using HOL.

We are setting out to prove:

$$\forall P_1 P_2 r_1 r_2. \ (\exists r. $$
$$(\forall s_1. P_1 \, s_1 \supset (\exists s_2. P_2 \, s_2 \wedge r \, s_1 \, s_2)) \wedge$$
$$(\forall e s_1 s_1' s_2. \exists s_2'. r_1 \, e \, s_1 \, s_1' \wedge r \, s_1 \, s_2 \supset r \, s_1' \, s_2' \wedge r_2 \, e \, s_2 \, s_2')) \supset$$
$$(\forall e. \ \mathsf{RISM} \, P_1 \, r_1 \, e \supset \mathsf{RISM} \, P_2 \, r_2 \, e) \tag{58}$$

which is the same as theorem 2 apart from an immaterial placement of an existential quantifier.

Rewriting with definition 1, stripping the universal quantifiers and converting the antecedents to assumptions we obtain the goal:

$$\exists s. P_2(s0) \wedge (\forall t. r_2(et)(st)(s(\mathsf{Suc}\,t))) \tag{59}$$

and the assumptions:

$$\forall s_1. P_1 \, s_1 \supset (\exists s_2. P_2 \, s_2 \wedge r \, s_1 \, s_2) \tag{60}$$
$$\forall e s_1 s_1' s_2. \exists s_2'. r_1 \, e \, s_1 \, s_1' \wedge r \, s_1 \, s_2 \supset r \, s_1' \, s_2' \wedge r_2 \, e \, s_2 \, s_2' \tag{61}$$
$$P_1(s \, 0) \tag{62}$$
$$\forall t. r_1(e \, t)(s \, t)(s(\mathsf{Suc}\,t)) \tag{63}$$

Specialising assumption 60 and rewriting it with assumption 62 gives us two more assumptions:

$$P_2 \, s_2 \tag{64}$$
$$r(s \, 0)s_2 \tag{65}$$

Specialising assumption 61 with $e \, t, s \, t$ and $s(\mathsf{Suc}\,t)$, we obtain:

$$\forall t s_2. \exists s_2'.$$
$$r_1(e \, t)(s \, t)(s(\mathsf{Suc}\ t)) \wedge r(s \, t)s_2 \supset \tag{66}$$
$$r(s(\mathsf{Suc}\,t))s_2' \wedge r_2(e \, t)s_2 \, s_2'$$

Swapping the universal quantifiers and applying theorem:

$$\vdash \forall P. (\forall z. \exists x. P \, x \, z) = (\exists y. \forall z. P(y \, z)z) \tag{67}$$

twice, we obtain the assumption:

$$\forall s_2 t. \ r_1(e \, t)(s \, t)(s(\mathsf{Suc}\,t)) \wedge r(s \, t)s_2 \supset$$
$$r(s(\mathsf{Suc}\,t))(f_2 \, s_2 \, t) \wedge r_2(e \, t)s_2(f_2 \, s_2 \, t) \tag{68}$$

We can strengthen the goal 59 to:

$$\exists s'.\forall t. r(s(\operatorname{Suc} t))(s'(\operatorname{Suc} t)) \wedge P_2(s'\,0) \wedge r_2(e\,t)(s'\,t)(s'(\operatorname{Suc} t)) \tag{69}$$

and replace the existentially quantified s' with

$$\operatorname{Prim\_Rec} s_2\, f_2 \tag{70}$$

to yield:

$$\begin{aligned}
\forall t.\ &r(s(\operatorname{Suc} t))(\operatorname{Prim\_Rec} s_2\, f_2(\operatorname{Suc} t))\wedge\\
&P_2(\operatorname{Prim\_Rec} s_2\, f_2\, 0)\wedge\\
&r_2(e\,t)(\operatorname{Prim\_Rec} s_2\, f_2\, t)(\operatorname{Prim\_Rec} s_2\, f_2(\operatorname{Suc} t))
\end{aligned} \tag{71}$$

Prim_Rec is a constant already defined in HOL as part of the theory of primitive recursive functions; it satisfies the theorem:

$$\begin{aligned}
\vdash \forall x f.\ &(\operatorname{Prim\_Rec} x\, f\, 0 = x)\wedge\\
&(\forall m.\ \operatorname{Prim\_Rec} x\, f(\operatorname{Suc} m) = f(\operatorname{Prim\_Rec} x\, f\, m)m)
\end{aligned} \tag{72}$$

Performing induction on t we obtain a base goal and a step goal. The base goal is:

$$\begin{aligned}
&r(s(\operatorname{Suc} 0))(\operatorname{Prim\_Rec} s_2\, f_2(\operatorname{Suc} 0))\wedge\\
&P_2(\operatorname{Prim\_Rec} s_2\, f_2\, 0)\wedge\\
&r_2(e\, 0)(\operatorname{Prim\_Rec} s_2\, f_2\, 0)(\operatorname{Prim\_Rec} s_2\, f_2(\operatorname{Suc} 0))
\end{aligned} \tag{73}$$

which can be rewritten with 72 to yield:

$$r(s(\operatorname{Suc} 0))(f_2\, s_2\, 0) \wedge P_2\, s_2 \wedge r_2(e\, 0)s_2(f_2\, s_2\, 0) \tag{74}$$

which is satisfied by specialising assumption 68 with s_2 and 0, and then rewriting it with 65 and 63.

The step goal is:

$$\begin{aligned}
&r(s(\operatorname{Suc}(\operatorname{Suc} t)))(\operatorname{Prim\_Rec} s_2\, f_2(\operatorname{Suc}(\operatorname{Suc} t)))\wedge\\
&P_2(\operatorname{Prim\_Rec} s_2\, f_2\, 0)\wedge\\
&r_2(e(\operatorname{Suc} t))(\operatorname{Prim\_Rec} s_2\, f_2(\operatorname{Suc} t))(\operatorname{Prim\_Rec} s_2\, f_2(\operatorname{Suc}(\operatorname{Suc} t)))
\end{aligned} \tag{75}$$

with the additional assumptions formed by rewriting the induction hypothesis with theorem 72:

$$r(s(\operatorname{Suc} t))(f_2(\operatorname{Prim\_Rec} s_2\, f_2\, t)t) \tag{76}$$

$$r_2(e\,t)(\operatorname{Prim\_Rec} s_2\, f_2\, t)(f_2(\operatorname{Prim\_Rec} s_2\, f_2\, t)t) \tag{77}$$

Specialising assumption 68 with $\operatorname{Prim\_Rec} s_2\, f_2(\operatorname{Suc} t)$ and $\operatorname{Suc} t$ we obtain the assumption:

$$\begin{aligned}
&r_1(e(\operatorname{Suc} t))(s(\operatorname{Suc} t))(s(\operatorname{Suc}(\operatorname{Suc} t)))\wedge\\
&r(s(\operatorname{Suc} t))(f_2(\operatorname{Prim\_Rec} s_2\, f_2\, t)t) \supset\\
&r(s(\operatorname{Suc}(\operatorname{Suc} t)))(f_2(f_2(\operatorname{Prim\_Rec} s_2\, f_2\, t)t)(\operatorname{Suc} t))\wedge\\
&r_2\\
&(e(\operatorname{Suc} t))\\
&(f_2(\operatorname{Prim\_Rec} s_2\, f_2\, t)t)\\
&(f_2(f_2(\operatorname{Prim\_Rec} s_2\, f_2\, t)t)(\operatorname{Suc} t))
\end{aligned} \tag{78}$$

The antecedent of 78 is satisfied by 63 and 76, yielding:

$$r(s(\mathsf{Suc}(\mathsf{Suc}\,t)))(f_2(f_2(\mathsf{Prim\_Rec}\,s_2\,f_2\,t)t)(\mathsf{Suc}\,t))\wedge$$
$$r_2$$
$$(e(\mathsf{Suc}\,t)) \qquad\qquad (79)$$
$$(f_2(\mathsf{Prim\_Rec}\,s_2\,f_2\,t)t)$$
$$(f_2(f_2(\mathsf{Prim\_Rec}\,s_2\,f_2\,t)t)(\mathsf{Suc}\,t))$$

Rewriting the goal 75 with 72 we get:

$$r(s(\mathsf{Suc}(\mathsf{Suc}\,t)))(f_2(f_2(\mathsf{Prim\_Rec}\,s_2\,f_2\,t)t)(\mathsf{Suc}\,t))\wedge$$
$$P_2\,s_2\wedge \qquad\qquad (80)$$
$$r_2(e(\mathsf{Suc}\,t))(f_2(\mathsf{Prim\_Rec}\,s_2\,f_2\,t)t)(f_2(f_2(\mathsf{Prim\_Rec}\,s_2\,f_2\,t)t)(\mathsf{Suc}\,t))$$

which is satisfied by assumptions 64 and 79.

Q.E.D.

Acknowledgements

My thanks go to David Dill, of Stanford University, who helped me to get going with non-deterministic state-machines. I also appreciate the comments of Alex Bronstein, who stayed up into the small hours reviewing the manuscript.

References

[1] Martín Abadi and Leslie Lamport. *The Existence of Refinement Mappings*. SRC Report 29, Digital Equipment Corporation, 1988.

[2] Robert S. Boyer and J. Strother Moore. *A Computational Logic*. Academic Press, 1979.

[3] Alexandre Bronstein and Carolyn L. Talcott. *String-Functional Semantics for Formal Verification of Synchronous Circuits*. Report STAN-CS-88-1210, Stanford University Department of Computer Science, 1988.

[4] M. C. Browne and E. M. Clarke. SML - a high level language for the design and verification of finite state machines. In D. Borrione, editor, *IFIP International Working Conference: From HDL Descriptions to Guaranteed Circuit Designs*, Elsevier Science Publishers B. V. (North-Holland), 1987.

[5] Albert Camilleri, Mike Gordon, and Tom Melham. Hardware verification using higher-order logic. In D. Borrione, editor, *IFIP International Working Conference: From HDL Descriptions to Guaranteed Circuit Designs*, Elsevier Science Publishers B. V. (North-Holland), September 1987.

[6] Avra. J. Cohn. A proof of correctness of the viper microprocessor: the first level. In G. Birwistle and P. A. Subrahmanyam, editors, *VLSI Specification, Verification and Synthesis*, Kluwer Academic Publishers, 1988.

[7] Srinivas Devadas, Hi Keung Ma, and A. Richard Newton. *On the Verification of Sequential Machines at Differing Levels of Abstraction*. Memorandum UCB/ERL M86/93, University of California, Berkeley, 1986.

[8] Michael J.C. Gordon. The denotational semantics of sequential machines. *Information Processing Letters*, 10(1), February 1980.

[9] Mike Gordon. *HOL: A Machine Oriented Formulation of Higher-Order Logic*. Technical Report 68, University of Cambridge Computer Laboratory, 1985.

[10] Mike Gordon. HOL: a proof generating system for higher-order logic. In G. Birwistle and P. A. Subrahmanyam, editors, *VLSI Specification, Verification and Synthesis*, Kluwer Academic Publishers, 1988.

[11] Mike Gordon. Why higher-order logic is a good formalism for specifying and verifying hardware. In G. Milne and P. A. Subrahmanyam, editors, *Formal Aspects of VLSI Design*, North-Holland, 1986.

[12] J. J. Joyce, G. Birtwistle, and M. Gordon. Verification and implementation of a microprocessor. In G. Birwistle and P. A. Subrahmanyam, editors, *VLSI Specification, Verification and Synthesis*, Kluwer Academic Publishers, 1988.

[13] Paul Loewenstein. The formal verification of state-machines using higher-order logic. In *IEEE International Conference on Computer Design*, 1989.

[14] G. L. Peterson. Myths about the mutual exclusion problem. *Information Processing Letters*, 12(3):115–116, 1981.

[15] Mary Sheeran. *μFP - An Algebraic VLSI Design Language*. Technical Monograph PRG-39, Oxford University Computing Laboratory, 1983.

A MECHANICALLY DERIVED SYSTOLIC IMPLEMENTATION OF PYRAMID INITIALIZATION

Christian Lengauer[0]
Department of Computer Sciences

Bikash Sabata and Farshid Arman
Department of Electrical Engineering

The University of Texas at Austin
Austin, Texas 78712, U.S.A.

Abstract

Pyramidal algorithms manipulate hierarchical representations of data and are used in many image processing applications, for example, image segmentation and border extraction. We present a systolic network which performs the first phase of pyramidal algorithms: initialization. The derivation of the systolic solution is governed by a mechanical method whose input is a known Pascal-like pyramidal algorithm. After a few manual program transformations that prepare the algorithm for the method, parallelism is infused mechanically. A processor layout is selected, and the channel connections follow immediately.

1 Systolic Design

The concept of a *systolic array* [12] has received a lot of attention in the past decade. Systolic arrays are distributed networks of sequential processors that are linked together by channels in a particularly regular structure. Such networks can process large amounts of data quickly by accepting streams of inputs and producing streams of outputs. Many highly repetitive algorithms are candidates for a systolic implementation. Typical applications are image or signal processing.

More recently, mechanical methods for the design of systolic arrays have been developed (see [7, 16] for bibliographies). The starting point is, essentially, either an imperative program [7] or a functional program [14, 17]. The following program format is necessary but not sufficient for a systolic implementation:

---

[0]Supported in part by the National Science Foundation under Contract DCR-8610427.

> **for** x_0 **from** lb_0 **by** st_0 **to** rb_0 **do**
>> **for** x_1 **from** lb_1 **by** st_1 **to** rb_1 **do**
>>> $\vdots$
>>>> **for** x_{r-1} **from** lb_{r-1} **by** st_{r-1} **to** rb_{r-1} **do**
>>>> $x_0{:}x_1{:}\cdots{:}x_{r-1}$

where the *basic operation* $x_0{:}x_1{:}\cdots{:}x_{r-1}$ of the program is of the form:

$$x_0{:}x_1{:}\cdots{:}x_{r-1} \ :: \ \begin{array}{l} \text{\bf if } B_0(x_0, x_1, \cdots, x_{r-1}) \ \rightarrow \ S_0 \\ \text{\rlap{$\mathbb{I}$}} B_1(x_0, x_1, \cdots, x_{r-1}) \ \rightarrow \ S_1 \\ \qquad \vdots \\ \text{\rlap{$\mathbb{I}$}} B_{t-1}(x_0, x_1, \cdots, x_{r-1}) \ \rightarrow \ S_{t-1} \\ \text{\bf fi} \end{array}$$

The bounds lb_i and rb_i are expressions in the loop indices x_0 to x_{i-1} $(0 \le i < r)$; the steps st_i are constants; the B_j $(0 \le j < t)$ are Boolean expressions; the S_j $(0 \le j < t)$ are functional or imperative programs (depending on the method), possibly, with composition, alternation, or iteration but without non-local references.

Both the functional and the imperative method describe a systolic array by two functions. Let I denote the integers, and let Op be the set of basic operations of the imperative or functional program:

$step : Op \longrightarrow I$ specifies a temporal distribution of the program's operations. Operations that are performed in parallel are mapped to the same step number.

$place : Op \longrightarrow I^{r-1}$ specifies a spatial distribution of the program's operations. The dimension of the layout space is one less than the number of arguments of the operations.

The challenge is in the determination of optimal parallelism, i.e., of a step function with the fewest number of steps possible. Here the functional and the imperative method proceed differently. In the functional method, one employs techniques of integer programming [17]; in the imperative method one uses techniques of program transformation [7]. Both derivations are completely mechanical. After the derivation of *step*, the distribution in time, one chooses a compatible distribution in space by a search. The combination of *step* and *place* is consistent if *step* and every dimension of *place* are linearly independent [7]; if so, every processor of the array is required to execute at most one operation per step, i.e., the array processors may be sequential.

When *step* and *place* are linear, the flow direction and layout of the data can be computed. Let V be the set of program variables:

$flow : V \longrightarrow I^{r-1}$ specifies the direction and distance that variables travel at each step. It is defined as follows: if variable v is accessed by distinct basic operations s_0 and s_1 and by no basic operations in the steps between s_0 and s_1, then

$$flow(v) = (place(s_1) - place(s_0))/(step(s_1) - step(s_0))$$

Flow is only well-defined if the choice of the pair $\langle s_0, s_1 \rangle$ is immaterial. In other words, the variable may not change its flow direction or speed during the computation. This will become relevant in our application. $Flow(v)$ is well-defined if each subscript of v is a distinct argument of the basic operation, and v has either $r-1$ or r subscripts [7].[1]

$pattern : V \longrightarrow I^{r-1}$ specifies the location of variables in the layout space at the first step. It is defined as follows: if variable v is accessed by basic operation s and fs is the number of the first step, then

$$pattern(v) = place(s) - (step(s) - fs) * flow(v)$$

If *flow* is well-defined, so is *pattern* [7].

We present a new systolic array for the first phase of pyramidal algorithms, initialization, and sketch its derivation with the imperative method [7]. We have an implementation of the method and have used it in the derivation of the array.

2 Pyramidal Algorithms

Pyramids are hierarchical data structures with rectangular arrays of nodes in a bottom-to-top sequence of levels [1]. Image resolution decreases as we move from the bottom level (finest) to the top level (coarsest), as shown in Fig. 1. The input image is stored in the base level of the pyramid. Each pixel in the image represents a node. The values of the nodes can be the gray level, local standard deviation or an edge map, among others. The values of the nodes at the higher levels are computed by averaging the values of the nodes, in some neighborhood, at the level below. The node that is calculated this way is referred to as the *father* of the nodes in the neighborhood of the lower level, and the nodes of that neighborhood are called the *sons* of the node at the upper level. This averaging process is repeated until values for the four nodes at the top level have been determined. Assuming that the neighborhoods are square and overlap by 50% for neighboring fathers, each node has four fathers at the level above and sixteen sons at the level below. The nodes at the base level, the original image, have no sons, and the nodes at the top level have no fathers.

Next, in a bottom-to-top iterative process, the nodes are linked between levels, using information from the level above, the level below, and from the neighbor nodes at the same level, by calculating a weight for each son-father link. The goal is to select a single father for each node. This results in several trees with roots in the upper part of the pyramid and leaves at the bottom level, the original image. After

---

[1]The proofs of some theorems become more complex if the format of subscripted variables is relaxed as follows: they may be linear expressions in the x_i ($0 \leq i < r$), and their coefficient matrix is of rank $r-1$ or r [6]. This extended format covers, for example, convolution [13].

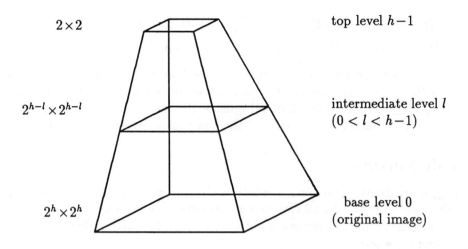

2×2

top level $h-1$

$2^{h-l} \times 2^{h-l}$

intermediate level l
$(0 < l < h-1)$

$2^h \times 2^h$

base level 0
(original image)

Figure 1: Structure of a pyramid. The base level contains the original image. The level number is given on the right, the size of each level in pixels on the left.

the iteration process has reached a steady state – it always does [10] – each node is assigned the value of its chosen father, top to bottom.

The three phases of pyramidal algorithms – initialization, node linking, and tree generation [1, 3, 4, 18] – are described more precisely in the following subsections.

2.1 Initialization

Assuming that the original image has $2^h \times 2^h$ pixels, where h is a non-zero natural number, an h-level pyramid, with levels numbered bottom to top 0 to $h-1$, is initialized by taking the averages of a $2c \times 2c$ area of level $l-1$ to generate a node at level l; the natural non-zero number c is called the *span factor* [3], and l $(0 < l < h)$ is the level being initialized. The span factor determines the amount of overlapping used in the averaging of the sons; in our case, $c=2$ results in 50% overlapping.

Let us denote the node at point (i, j) at level l by the triple $[i, j, l]$. If the property that we are interested in is $\mathcal{P}$, initialization is mathematically described as follows (assuming $c=2$):

$$\mathcal{P}([i,j,l]) \;=\; \frac{1}{numsons([i,j,l])} \left[\sum_{i'=2i-2}^{2i+1} \sum_{j'=2j-2}^{2j+1} \mathcal{P}([i',j',l-1]) \right] \tag{1}$$

$$0 < l < h, \; 0 \leq i,j < 2^{h-l}$$

The nodes indexed by $[i', j', l-1]$ are the sons of $[i, j, l]$, which is in turn used in determining the values of four nodes located at

$$[\lfloor(i-1)/2\rfloor, \lfloor(j-1)/2\rfloor, l+1], \quad [\lfloor(i-1)/2\rfloor, \lfloor(j+1)/2\rfloor, l+1], \qquad (2)$$
$$[\lfloor(i+1)/2\rfloor, \lfloor(j-1)/2\rfloor, l+1], \quad [\lfloor(i+1)/2\rfloor, \lfloor(j+1)/2\rfloor, l+1]$$

where $\lfloor x \rfloor$ designates the integer part of x. These four nodes are the fathers of the node $[i, j, l]$. In Equ. 1, $numsons([i, j, l])$ is the number of valid sons of $[i, j, l]$ ($numsons([i, j, l]) \leq (2c)^2$); nodes that fall outside the image's boundaries are not considered. Thus, the nodes on the edges of the image have fewer sons and fathers.

2.2 Node Linking

Node linking is an iterative process, in which each node *chooses* its best father [1]. This choosing process is based on a closeness measurement and is described in [1]: the *closeness*, in property value, between a node $[i', j', l-1]$ and its k-th father $[i_k, j_k, l]$ is evaluated using δ_k, where

$$\delta_k \;=\; \mid \mathcal{P}([i', j', l-1]) - \mathcal{P}([i_k, j_k, l]) \mid \qquad\qquad 0 \leq k \leq 3 \qquad (3)$$

A weight w between the node and its father is then assigned as follows:

$$w([i', j', l-1], [i_k, j_k, l]) \;=\; \begin{cases} 1 & \text{if } (\forall\, m : 0 \leq m \leq 3 \wedge m \neq k : \\ & \quad \delta_k \geq \delta_m \wedge (\delta_k = \delta_m \Rightarrow k < m)) \\ 0 & \text{otherwise} \end{cases} \qquad (4)$$

That is, we select the first closest father, with increasing k.

Once the weights between each node and its fathers have been determined, the property value of each node, at level l, is recalculated as follows:

$$\mathcal{P}([i, j, l]) \;=\; \frac{\displaystyle\sum_{i'=2i-2}^{2i+1} \sum_{j'=2j-2}^{2j+1} w([i', j', l-1], [i, j, l]) \cdot \mathcal{P}([i', j', l-1])}{\displaystyle\sum_{i'=2i-2}^{2i+1} \sum_{j'=2j-2}^{2j+1} w([i', j', l-1], [i, j, l])} \qquad (5)$$

It is possible that a node is not chosen as a father by any of its sons, namely, when the denominator of Equ. 5 is zero. In this situation, its $\mathcal{P}$-value remains undefined, until the next iteration, when all the weights are recalculated.

2.3 Tree Generation

The last phase of Pyramid Node Linking is tree generation. This phase uses the results of the linking phase and assigns a region label to each node. Nodes with matching labels define a region. Starting from a level H ($H < h$), a distinct label is assigned to all nodes with distinct property values at that level. Then, the nodes at level $H-1$ are assigned the labels of their chosen fathers (i.e., the fathers with weight one). This process is repeated for all the levels below, each son being assigned the label of its chosen father. At the end, the nodes at the base level are assigned one of the labels of the nodes at the chosen level H. The smallest maximum number of labels occurs when $H = h-1$; in this case, at most four labels are generated, segmenting the image into as many regions. As one decreases the value of H, the maximum number of possible labels increases, resulting in more segments in the image at the base level.

If one takes the property value of a node at level H to be its region label, tree generation is mathematically described as follows (assuming $c=2$):

$$\mathcal{P}([i,j,l]) \;=\; \sum_{i'=\lfloor(i-1)/2\rfloor,\lfloor(i+1)/2\rfloor} \;\; \sum_{j'=\lfloor(j-1)/2\rfloor,\lfloor(j+1)/2\rfloor} w([i,j,l],[i',j',l+1]) \cdot \mathcal{P}([i',j',l+1]) \quad (6)$$

Since only the weights of the closest fathers are one and all other weights are zero, the property value is propagated from father to son.

3   The Source Program

The following algorithm performs pyramid initialization:

$$\begin{aligned}
&\textbf{for } l \textbf{ from } 1 \textbf{ to } h{-}1 \textbf{ do}\\
&\quad \textbf{for } i \textbf{ from } 0 \textbf{ to } 2^{h-l}{-}1 \textbf{ do}\\
&\quad\quad \textbf{for } j \textbf{ from } 0 \textbf{ to } 2^{h-l}{-}1 \textbf{ do}\\
&\quad\quad\quad \textbf{for } i' \textbf{ from } 2i{-}2 \textbf{ to } 2i{+}1 \textbf{ do}\\
&\quad\quad\quad\quad \textbf{for } j' \textbf{ from } 2j{-}2 \textbf{ to } 2j{+}1 \textbf{ do}\\
&\quad\quad\quad\quad\quad l{:}i{:}j{:}i'{:}j'
\end{aligned}$$

Index l enumerates the levels of the pyramid, bottom to top; i and j enumerate the nodes at each level; i' and j' enumerate their sons. The basic operation $l{:}i{:}j{:}i'{:}j'$ is defined as follows:

$$l{:}i{:}j{:}i'{:}j' \;::\; node_{i,j,l} := node_{i,j,l} + f(node_{i',j',l-1})$$

The original image is assumed loaded into array elements $node_{i,j,0}$ ($0 \le i,j < 2^h$) at the start of the computation. The elements of $node$ at higher levels of the pyramid are initialized to zero. The cummulative computation of the fathers $node_{i,j,l}$ is defined, according to the problem description in the previous section (Equ. 1):

$$f(node_{i',j',l-1}) \;=\; node_{i',j',l-1}/16$$

We replaced variable $numsons$ by the constant 16, i.e., $(2c)^2$, ignoring border conditions to keep things simple.

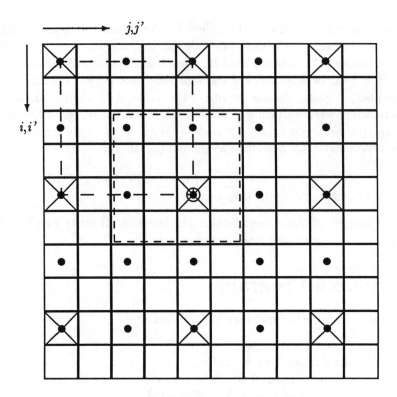

Figure 2: Father-son relationships in the two-dimensional systolic array. Nodes at level $l-1$ are depicted as solid boxes, nodes at level l as fat dots, and nodes at level $l+1$ as crosses. The sixteen sons of the node at level l that is highlighted with a circle (Equ. 1) are indicated by a box in small dashes. The four fathers of the same node (Equ. 2) are the four crosses that are linked by long dashed lines. Indices are scaled up by a factor of two when moving up a level, i.e., on level $l-1$ neighbors are adjacent, on level l they are two positions apart, and on level $l+1$ they are four positions apart.

4   Towards a Systolic Implementation

We have the following solution in mind (Fig. 2). The processor array consists of $2^h \times 2^h$ processors, one per pixel of the image. That is, each processor corresponds to a node at the base level of the pyramid. Initially, the property values of the image pixels are loaded into the array, each pixel at its respective node. The property values of all nodes at a fixed level of the pyramid are computed systolically and the same systolic array is reused iteratively for successive levels. Each computed property value is stored at its respective node. At the transition between levels, the node array is reduced: three quarters of the nodes are discarded – the respective processors become inactive;

the remaining active processors, which are evenly distributed throughout the array, are holding the input data for the computation at the next level. An even distribution of active processors, at every level, ensures that data communicated between levels are stationary, i.e., no channels need to be installed for them.

5 Adaptation of the Source Program

We need to modify the source program to reflect our specific ideas for a systolic solution. We will also need to make certain changes to make the program amenable to the systolic design method.

5.1 Fixing the Level

The five nested loops of the source program suggest a time-optimal systolic array of four dimensions – one less than the number of loops (see Sect. 1). We are aiming instead at a two-dimensional systolic array. Its benefits are an increased processor utilization, a simpler processor layout and fewer channels.

Our systolic array is specified for a fixed level. Consequently, we disregard the loop on levels in the systolic design and drop the corresponding argument of the basic statement (it becomes constant):

$$\textbf{for } i \textbf{ from } 0 \textbf{ to } 2^{h-l} - 1 \textbf{ do}$$
$$\textbf{for } j \textbf{ from } 0 \textbf{ to } 2^{h-l} - 1 \textbf{ do}$$
$$\textbf{for } i' \textbf{ from } 2i - 2 \textbf{ to } 2i + 1 \textbf{ do}$$
$$\textbf{for } j' \textbf{ from } 2j - 2 \textbf{ to } 2j + 1 \textbf{ do}$$
$$i{:}j{:}i'{:}j'$$

5.2 Scaling

Scaling yields an even distribution of active processors in the $2^h \times 2^h$ array, for any level. We scale the indices of every level by two with respect to the level below (as we do in Fig. 2). That is, our scaling factor for level l $(0 < l < h)$ is $u_l = 2^l$.

The standard semantics-preserving transformation for scaling the increments of a loop

$$\textbf{for } x \textbf{ from } rb \textbf{ by } st \textbf{ to } lb \textbf{ do } f(x)$$

by a factor fac is:

$$\textbf{for } x_{new} \textbf{ from } fac{\cdot}rb \textbf{ by } fac{\cdot}st \textbf{ to } fac{\cdot}lb \textbf{ do } f(x_{new}/fac)$$

We must scale the loops on i and j by u_l and the loop on i' and j' by u_{l-1}, since they access the level below. With simplification, the previous transformation scheme yields:

> **for** i **from** 0 **by** u_l **to** $2^h - u_l$ **do**
> **for** j **from** 0 **by** u_l **to** $2^h - u_l$ **do**
> **for** i' **from** $i - 2u_{l-1}$ **by** u_{l-1} **to** $i + u_{l-1}$ **do**
> **for** j' **from** $j - 2u_{l-1}$ **by** u_{l-1} **to** $j + u_{l-1}$ **do**
> $(i/u_l){:}(j/u_l){:}(i'/u_{l-1}){:}(j'/u_{l-1})$

This scales the loop increments; the following step actually scales the indices of array *node*, i.e., distributes array *node* over a $2^h \times 2^h$ range, for every level. *This step is the only transformation that does not preserve the semantics of the source program.*[2] We simply drop the fractions in the call of the basic operation again:

> **for** i **from** 0 **by** u_l **to** $2^h - u_l$ **do**
> **for** j **from** 0 **by** u_l **to** $2^h - u_l$ **do**
> **for** i' **from** $i - 2u_{l-1}$ **by** u_{l-1} **to** $i + u_{l-1}$ **do**
> **for** j' **from** $j - 2u_{l-1}$ **by** u_{l-1} **to** $j + u_{l-1}$ **do**
> $i{:}j{:}i'{:}j'$

For the limits of the outer two loops, we prefer the semantic equivalent $2^h - 1$, because it matches the size of the systolic array. For brevity, we introduce the new operators $\oplus$ and $\ominus$ to indicate addition and subtraction in units of u_{l-1}:

> **for** i **from** 0 **by** u_l **to** $2^h - 1$ **do**
> **for** j **from** 0 **by** u_l **to** $2^h - 1$ **do**
> **for** i' **from** $i \ominus 2$ **by** u_{l-1} **to** $i \oplus 1$ **do**
> **for** j' **from** $j \ominus 2$ **by** u_{l-1} **to** $j \oplus 1$ **do**
> $i{:}j{:}i'{:}j'$

5.3 Loop Elimination

We still have four loops – one too many for a two-dimensional array. We collapse the inner two loops, which iterate through the sons, to one:

> **for** i **from** 0 **by** u_l **to** $2^h - 1$ **do**
> **for** j **from** 0 **by** u_l **to** $2^h - 1$ **do**
> **for** k **from** 0 **to** 3 **do**
> $i{:}j{:}k$

---

[2]We could have specified the source program immediately with scaled indices and avoided this step, but we wanted to start with the specification provided in the literature.

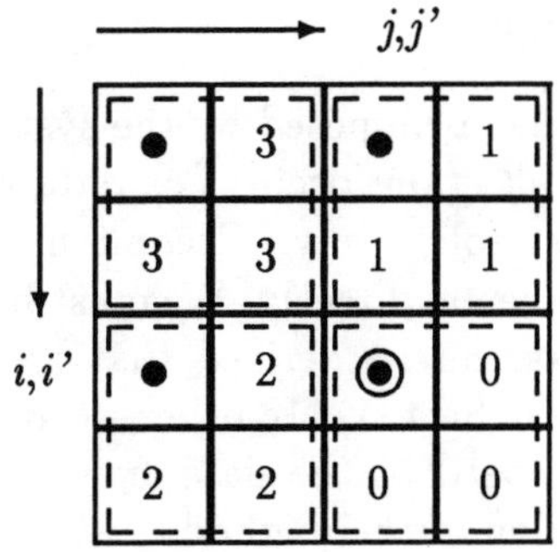

Figure 3: A father and its sixteen sons (compare Fig. 2). The father is the fat dot highlighted with a circle. Numbers indicate the value of k at which the sons are accumulated. The nodes of each quadrant have identical fathers. E.g., the four fathers in the picture are shared by the nodes of the upper left quadrant ($k=3$).

The previous loops on i' and j' each have four steps. The four steps of the vanishing loop are absorbed into the basic statement. We rearrange the additions that the two inner loops of the source program specify such that every step of the new loop accumulates one quadrant of the array of sixteen sons. We are justified in doing so, because addition is commutative. Case $k=0$ accumulates the lower right quadrant, $k=1$ the upper right, $k=2$ the lower left, and $k=3$ the upper left (Fig. 3). To access quadrants correctly, we modify indices i and j by a "hat function" to $\hat{i}$ and $\hat{j}$:

$$\hat{i} = i \ominus 2 \cdot (k \bmod 2)$$
$$\hat{j} = j \ominus 2 \cdot (k \operatorname{div} 2)$$

The new basic operation is defined as follows:

$$i{:}j{:}k \; :: \; node_{i,j,l} := node_{i,j,l} + f(node_{\hat{i},\hat{j},l-1}) \quad + f(node_{\hat{i},\hat{j}\oplus 1,l-1})$$
$$+ f(node_{\hat{i}\oplus 1,\hat{j},l-1}) + f(node_{\hat{i}\oplus 1,\hat{j}\oplus 1,l-1})$$

5.4 Commutation

At present, we step linearly through each of the two dimensions of the level. We can expect that the conflicts of neighbors caused by the 50% overlapping will reduce the potential for parallelism. Therefore, we break the linear progression by moving the loop on k to the outside (again, simply rearranging additions):

```
for k from 0 to 3 do
    for i from 0 by u_l to 2^h −1 do
        for j from 0 by u_l to 2^h −1 do
            i:j:k
```

5.5 Addition of Variables

The next change we make is one that is imposed by the systolic design method.

In many systolic arrays, data *reflections* occur, i.e., data change direction and/or speed on their way through the systolic array. Present mechanical systolic design methods cannot handle this phenomenon directly. We must bring the source program into a form from which data flows can be derived that are constant per program variable (see the definition of $flow$ in Sect. 1). In other words, we must add variables where breaks in the direction or speed of the data flow occur. These breaks are reported to us by our implementation of the method.

In our solution, the sixteen sons are stationary at the transition between levels but must travel during the systolic computation at a level. That is, we must create a new, moving variable for each son. The results of the computation are accumulated in the father node, which is stationary again and assumes the rôle of a son when the next level is processed. It will help us in the presentation of the systolic design, if we split the sixteen cases into four types of four variables each. We name the types A, B, C and D and number their four variables (with an infix period) 0 to 3. For each value of k, the basic computation accesses one variable of each type:

$$comp(i,j,k) \ :: \ node_{i,j,l} := node_{i,j,l} + f(a.k_{\hat{i},\hat{j},l-1}) \ + f(b.k_{\hat{i},\hat{j}\oplus 1,l-1})$$
$$+ f(c.k_{\hat{i}\oplus 1,\hat{j},l-1}) + f(d.k_{\hat{i}\oplus 1,\hat{j}\oplus 1,l-1})$$

We name this statement $comp(i,j,k)$. Before applying it, we must copy the respective sons into the variables $a.k_{\hat{i},\hat{j},l-1}$, $b.k_{\hat{i},\hat{j}\oplus 1,l-1}$, $c.k_{\hat{i}\oplus 1,\hat{j},l-1}$ and $d.k_{\hat{i}\oplus 1,\hat{j}\oplus 1,l-1}$. For copying, we use the operations:

$$cp.a(i,j,k) \ :: \ a.k_{i,j,l-1} := node_{i,j,l-1}$$
$$cp.b(i,j,k) \ :: \ b.k_{i,j,l-1} := node_{i,j,l-1}$$
$$cp.c(i,j,k) \ :: \ c.k_{i,j,l-1} := node_{i,j,l-1}$$
$$cp.d(i,j,k) \ :: \ d.k_{i,j,l-1} := node_{i,j,l-1}$$

The next and last step, the redefinition of basic operation $i{:}j{:}k$, is a big one. In systolic design, one may not manipulate compositions inside a basic statement – a basic statement is taken to be atomic. Because we would like to manipulate the compositions of cp and $comp$ operations when we add concurrency, we must combine cp and $comp$ in $i{:}j{:}k$ not by composition but with a choice construct, such that their compositions become external. We let i and j iterate through sons, not fathers, and use the evenness or oddness of i and j (before scaling) and the value of k, in combination, as a program counter. Since this accommodates, per value of k, only four choices of our five (four cps and one $comp$), we double the range of k.

The following program initializes every variable before it is read; this program has the same input-output behavior on array $node$ as the final program in the previous section:

$$\text{for } k \text{ from } 0 \text{ to } 7 \text{ do}$$
$$\text{for } i \text{ from } 0 \text{ by } u_{l-1} \text{ to } 2^h - 1 \text{ do}$$
$$\text{for } j \text{ from } 0 \text{ by } u_{l-1} \text{ to } 2^h - 1 \text{ do}$$
$$i{:}j{:}k$$

$i{:}j{:}k \quad :: \quad$ **if** k even $\wedge\ i/u_{l-1}$ even $\wedge\ j/u_{l-1}$ even $\rightarrow cp.a(\hat{\imath}, \hat{\jmath}, k \operatorname{div} 2)$
$\phantom{i{:}j{:}k \quad ::}$ ⫾ k even $\wedge\ i/u_{l-1}$ even $\wedge\ j/u_{l-1}$ odd $\ \rightarrow cp.b(\hat{\imath}, \hat{\jmath}, k \operatorname{div} 2)$
$\phantom{i{:}j{:}k \quad ::}$ ⫾ k even $\wedge\ i/u_{l-1}$ odd $\ \wedge\ j/u_{l-1}$ even $\rightarrow cp.c(\hat{\imath}, \hat{\jmath}, k \operatorname{div} 2)$
$\phantom{i{:}j{:}k \quad ::}$ ⫾ k even $\wedge\ i/u_{l-1}$ odd $\ \wedge\ j/u_{l-1}$ odd $\ \rightarrow cp.d(\hat{\imath}, \hat{\jmath}, k \operatorname{div} 2)$
$\phantom{i{:}j{:}k \quad ::}$ ⫾ k odd $\ \wedge\ i/u_{l-1}$ even $\wedge\ j/u_{l-1}$ even $\rightarrow comp(i, j, k \operatorname{div} 2)$
$\phantom{i{:}j{:}k \quad ::}$ ⫾ **else** $\rightarrow$ **skip**
$\phantom{i{:}j{:}k \quad ::}$ **fi**

6 Independence Declarations

The infusion of parallelism into the program exploits mutual independences of the program's operations. We must state these independences. The usual independence criterion for systolic design is the absence of shared variable accesses. This accounts for the stream processing and the lack of shared memory in systolic arrays [7].

The arguments of the basic operation are i, j and k. We must exclude any two basic operations with the same pair i and j. Some are dependent because they share a variable; in any case, in the layout that we have in mind, all will be mapped to the same processor and can therefore not be applied in parallel (or an inconsistency of *step* and *place* results; see Sect. 1). For varying i, j and fixed k, all operations are mutually independent. For varying i, j and varying k, there is some independence; declaring it complicates the step function but does not shorten the parallel execution (we tried). Consequently, we declare:

$$i_0 \neq i_1 \vee j_0 \neq j_1 \implies i_0{:}j_0{:}k \ \text{ind} \ i_1{:}j_1{:}k$$

7 The Systolic Array

7.1 For a Fixed Level

With the previous program and independence declaration, our method generates the following temporal distribution:

$$step(i{:}j{:}k) \ = \ k$$

We can choose a spatial distribution; the processor layout that we had in mind all along is:

$$place(i{:}j{:}k) \ = \ (i, j)$$

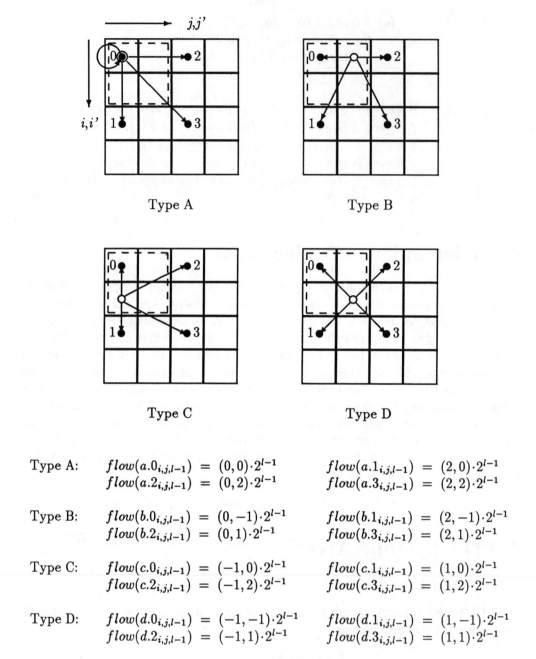

$$
\begin{aligned}
\text{Type A:} \quad & flow(a.0_{i,j,l-1}) = (0,0)\cdot 2^{l-1} & flow(a.1_{i,j,l-1}) = (2,0)\cdot 2^{l-1} \\
& flow(a.2_{i,j,l-1}) = (0,2)\cdot 2^{l-1} & flow(a.3_{i,j,l-1}) = (2,2)\cdot 2^{l-1} \\[6pt]
\text{Type B:} \quad & flow(b.0_{i,j,l-1}) = (0,-1)\cdot 2^{l-1} & flow(b.1_{i,j,l-1}) = (2,-1)\cdot 2^{l-1} \\
& flow(b.2_{i,j,l-1}) = (0,1)\cdot 2^{l-1} & flow(b.3_{i,j,l-1}) = (2,1)\cdot 2^{l-1} \\[6pt]
\text{Type C:} \quad & flow(c.0_{i,j,l-1}) = (-1,0)\cdot 2^{l-1} & flow(c.1_{i,j,l-1}) = (1,0)\cdot 2^{l-1} \\
& flow(c.2_{i,j,l-1}) = (-1,2)\cdot 2^{l-1} & flow(c.3_{i,j,l-1}) = (1,2)\cdot 2^{l-1} \\[6pt]
\text{Type D:} \quad & flow(d.0_{i,j,l-1}) = (-1,-1)\cdot 2^{l-1} & flow(d.1_{i,j,l-1}) = (1,-1)\cdot 2^{l-1} \\
& flow(d.2_{i,j,l-1}) = (-1,1)\cdot 2^{l-1} & flow(d.3_{i,j,l-1}) = (1,1)\cdot 2^{l-1}
\end{aligned}
$$

Figure 4: Data Flows

Functions *step* and *place* are consistent, if the determinant of their linear coefficients for the variable loop indices i, j and k is not zero [7]:

$$\begin{vmatrix} 0 & 0 & 1 \\ 1 & 0 & 0 \\ 0 & 1 & 0 \end{vmatrix} = 1 \neq 0$$

The sixteen flow directions for level l ($0 < l < h$), sorted by type, are given in Fig. 4. Each of the four diagrams follows the format of Fig. 3. The dashed box highlights the sons that share the four fathers in the diagram. This time, the circle represents a selected son. Arrows indicate that the son must be communicated to its four fathers.

To connect the whole processor array, cover it with dashed boxes, such that each father is in the upper left corner of a dashed box. Then match the relative position of a processor in its dashed box with that of the circle in the dashed box of one of the diagrams in Fig. 4. The processor must be connected as specified by that diagram. Remember that the borders of the array require further special consideration.

We mentioned already that *node* is stationary. Note that $a.0$ is also stationary; that is, the introduction of $a.0$ was unnecessary.

7.2 Composition of Levels

Levels are composed in sequence. Their systolic arrays are superimposed. The processor at point (i, j) has the following set of stationary variables: $\{node_{i,j,l} \mid 0 \le i,j < 2^h, \ 0 \le l < h\}$. We need not install separate channels for each level, even though, at first sight, the scaling factor seems to require it. The dormant processors that lie between neighboring active processors at level l can be used for routing.

8 Conclusions

This exercise was intended as a demonstration that mechanical systolic design methods can assist in the development of new systolic arrays in the application sector. Of the three authors, the latter two had previous knowledge of the application domain, pyramidal algorithms, and knew nothing about systolic design before they embarked on this project, which was part of a course on systolic design given by the first author. The first author advised them in the use of the imperative systolic design method, without any knowledge of pyramidal algorithms, helped simplify their solution and spear-headed the writing of the paper.

We wanted to make a particular processor layout work, which required specific modifications of the source program before the systolic design method could be applied. The last of these modifications was a bit tricky; we had the option of a more straight-forward development but, in the end, preferred the simple independence declaration and step function that we obtained the tricky way. We did not provide formal proofs of our transformations, but they should be no problem using well-known techniques of sequential program verification.

The implementation of our systolic design method helped deriving properties of the systolic array (parallelism and communication), kept the derivation simple and honest, and increased confidence in the correctness of the solution. The same method is even more useful when any systolic solution is welcome; see, for example, our treatment of Gauss-Jordan elimination [8]. There, given the most general independence declarations, the method provided additional guidance in the incorporation of reflections, and a search of all processor layouts quickly revealed the best solution.

It should be possible to derive, in the same fashion, systolic arrays for node linking and tree generation. Since their structure will be similar, we expect that the three arrays can be merged into one.

9 Acknowledgement

The first author thanks the members of PRG at Oxford University, particularly Michael Goldsmith, for useful comments during a presentation of this material.

10 References

[1] P. J. Burt, T. H. Hong and A. Rosenfeld, "Segmentation and Estimation of Image Region Properties through Cooperative Hierarchical Computation", *IEEE Trans. on Systems, Man and Cybernetics SMC-11*, 12 (Dec. 1981), 802–809.

[2] J. Cibulskis and C. R. Dyer, "Node Linking Strategies in Pyramids for Image Segmentation", in *Multiresolution Image Processing and Analysis*, A. Rosenfeld (ed.), Series in Information Sciences, Springer-Verlag, 1984, 109–120.

[3] W. I. Grosky and R. Jain, "A Pyramid-Based Approach to Segmentation Applied to Region Matching", *IEEE Trans. on Pattern Analysis and Machine Intelligence PAMI-8*, 5 (Sept. 1986), 639–650.

[4] T. H. Hong, K. A. Narayanan, S. Peleg, and A. Rosenfeld, "Image Smoothing and Segmentation by Multiresolution Pixel Linking: Further Experiments and Extensions", *IEEE Transactions on Systems, Man and Cybernetics SMC-12*, 5 (May 1982), 611–622.

[5] T. H. Hong and A. Rosenfeld, "Compact Region Extraction Using Weighted Pixel Linking in a Pyramid," *IEEE Trans. Pattern Analysis and Machine Intelligence PAMI-6*, 2 (Mar. 1984), 222–229.

[6] C.-H. Huang, "The Mechanically Certified Derivation of Concurrency and its Application to Systolic Design", Ph. D. Thesis, Department of Computer Sciences, The University of Texas at Austin, Aug. 1987.

[7] C.-H. Huang and C. Lengauer, "The Derivation of Systolic Implementations of Programs", *Acta Informatica 24*, 6 (Nov. 1987), 595–632.

[8] C.-H. Huang and C. Lengauer, "Mechanically Derived Systolic Solutions to the Algebraic Path Problem", in *VLSI and Computers (CompEuro 87)*, W. E. Proebster and H. Reiner (eds.), IEEE Computer Society Press, 1987, 307–310; full paper: TR-86-28, Department of Computer Sciences, The University of Texas at Austin, Dec. 1986.

[9] T. Ichikawa, "A Pyramid Representation of Images and its Feature Extraction Facility", *IEEE Trans. on Pattern Analysis and Machine Intelligence PAMI-3*, 3 (May 1981), 257–264.

[10] S. Kasif and A. Rosenfeld, "Pyramid Linking is a Special Case of ISODATA", *IEEE Trans. on Systems, Man and Cybernetics SMC-13*, 1 (Jan./Feb. 1983), 84–85.

[11] B. P. Kjell and C. R. Dyer, "Segmentation of Textured Images by Pyramid Linking", in *Pyramidal Systems for Computer Vision*, V. Cantoni and S. Levialdi (eds.), NATO ASI Series, Vol. F-25, Springer-Verlag, 1986, 273–288.

[12] H. T. Kung and C. E. Leiserson, "Algorithms for VLSI Processor Arrays", in *Introduction to VLSI Systems*, C. Mead and L. Conway (eds.), Addison-Wesley, 1980, Sect. 8.3.

[13] P. Quinton, "The Systematic Design of Systolic Arrays", Tech. Report 193, Publication Interne IRISA, Apr. 1983; also: TR84-11, The Microelectronics Center of North Carolina, May 1984.

[14] P. Quinton et al., "Designing Systolic Arrays with DIASTOL", in *VLSI Signal Processing II*, S.-Y. Kung, R. E. Owen, and J. G. Nash (eds.), IEEE Press, 1986, 93–105.

[15] P. Quinton et al., "Synthesizing Systolic Arrays Using DIASTOL", in *Systolic Arrays*, W. Moore, A. McCabe, and R. Urquart (eds.), Adam Hilger, 1987, 25–36.

[16] P. Quinton, "Mapping Recurrences on Parallel Architectures", in *Supercomputing '88 (ICS '88)*, Vol. III: *Supercomputer Design: Hardware & Software*, L. P. and S. I. Kartashev (eds.), Int. Supercomputing Institute, Inc., 1988, 1–8.

[17] S. K. Rao, "Regular Iterative Algorithms and their Implementations on Processor Arrays", Ph D. Thesis, Department of Electrical Engineering, Stanford University, Oct. 1985.

[18] A. Rosenfeld, "Some Useful Properties of Pyramids", *Multiresolution Image Processing and Analysis*, A. Rosenfeld (ed.), Series in Information Sciences, Springer-Verlag, 1984, 2–5.

[19] A. Rosenfeld, "Some Pyramid Techniques for Image Segmentation", in *Pyramidal Systems for Computer Vision*, V. Cantoni and S. Levialdi (eds.), NATO ASI Series, Vol. F-25, Springer-Verlag, 1986, 261–271.

BEHAVIOR-PRESERVING TRANSFORMATIONS FOR HIGH-LEVEL SYNTHESIS

R. Camposano

IBM Thomas J. Watson Research Center
Yorktown Heights, NY

Abstract. This paper addresses the synthesis of a circuit structure from a sequential behavioral specification. The problem is formally stated as a sequence of behavior-preserving transformations of a data- and control-flow graph. Behavior equivalence is defined strongly, so that it implies equal output sequences for equal input sequences and equal initial state. The transformations introduce the minimum number of control steps. The resulting structure includes both control and data-path. The combinational logic in this structure is passed to logic synthesis for further optimization. Several examples illustrate these techniques, giving results down to the logic level.

1. Introduction

High-Level synthesis, also called 'behavioral synthesis', is the synthesis of circuit structures from behavioral domain descriptions. A structure is described by a netlist of components such as logic gates, registers, ALU's, etc. Behavior is usually given in a formal procedural language such as C or behavioral VHDL. The atomic elements in a behavior are operations (such as addition, assignment, etc.) and variables. As outlined in [1] (earlier overviews can be found in [2, 3]), high-level synthesis can be decomposed into

* **Compiling** the formal language into an internal representation like control and data-flow graphs
* Optimizing the internal representation using **transformations** such as loop unfolding, constant propagation, code motion, etc.
* **Scheduling** the operations, i.e., assigning each operation to a so called control step (equivalent to a microprogram step, a machine cycle or a state in a control finite state machine)
* **Allocating** operations and variables to hardware (functional units, registers, communication paths)

This paper deals with scheduling and allocation, the two steps that essentially transform behavior into structure. Scheduling and allocation strongly depend on each other, hence they can be done in any order or they can be done together ("interleaved"). The method presented here allows to schedule first and then allocate, or to allocate and schedule interleaved. Unlike most approaches, control and data path are not separated but passed together to a global multi-level logic synthesizer for the optimization of the combinational part. These techniques were partly exercised in the Yorktown Silicon Compiler; a description on how they are integrated into the synthesis and design environments can be found in [4, 5].

The approach taken for synthesis consists of applying a series of transformations which can be proven to preserve behavior. Behavior equivalence is defined rather strongly implying equal output sequences for equal input sequences and equal initial state. The goal of the transformations is to meet certain hardware constraints (such as single assignment of registers during one control step) that allow a trivial conversion of behavior into structure. At the same time, the minimum number of control steps is introduced, so that the resulting control is optimal in the sense that it uses the minimum number of control steps for each possible execution sequence.

This paper presents the synthesis method in detail. Section 2 introduces the formal model for design representation, covering behavior representation, time representation, behavior equivalence and structural hardware constraints. The transformations for scheduling and allocation are developed in section 3, proving that they preserve behavior and showing that they introduce the minimum number of control steps. Section 4 gives some implementation details and results for two medium sized examples. The paper ends with conclusions and an outlook.

2. Design Representation

In most high-level synthesis approaches the design is represented internally by graphs. In particular, data-flow and control-flow are captured in one or two separated graphs [1]. Examples of internal representations are [6-10]. The representation used here is YIF (Yorktown Internal Form) [4, 5]. YIF is partly similar to the control-flow graphs used in data-flow analysis in software (e.g., [11]). It allows to represent behavior and structure to some extent. Time is represented with a granularity of control steps.

2.1 Behavior Representation

YIF allows the definition of operations, variables and their relations. A YIF description Y of a digital system is given by

$$Y = (V, S, type, \mathcal{P}, cond, \mathcal{I}, \mathcal{O})$$

- A set of operations V. Operations represent atomic computations, e.g., **and, addition, shift-left,** etc. One element $v_f \in V$ called the first operation must be indicated. The operations can be chosen according to the application and must be either described at the logic level in an operator library, or they are references to other YIF descriptions ("**module calls**"), thus allowing a hierarchical description of a design.

- A set of variables S. They are equivalent to variables in a program. A variable s in YIF has a *type*: $S \rightarrow \{port, net, register, constant, *\}$. The type indicates whether a variable represents a hardware element (port, net, register, constant) or whether its type is unknown (*). Ports and constants must be specified. Registers and nets might be specified. Variables in the sense of imperative programming languages with no specified type (*) are converted automatically during high-level synthesis into a register or a net.

- A precedence relation $\mathscr{P} \subseteq V \times V$, with $(v_1, v_2) \in \mathscr{P}$, (denoted $v_1 \mathscr{P} v_2$) iff v_1 is an immediate predecessor of v_2. $\mathscr{P}$ defines the control flow for the operations as implied by an imperative semantics, i.e., $v_1 \mathscr{P} v_2$ means that v_2 is executed after v_1. The relation $\mathscr{P}$ is irreflexive. The pair $(V, \mathscr{P})$ can be seen as a digraph, the so called **precedence** or **control-flow** graph. Node v_1 is said to be an (immediate) **predecessor** of node v_2 and, vice versa, v_2 is called an (immediate) **successor** of v_1. The first operation v_f must be such that $\nexists_{v \in V}[v \mathscr{P} v_f]$ and every operation must be reachable from it, i.e., $\forall_{v \in V} \exists_{n \in \mathbb{N}_0}[v_f \mathscr{P}^n v]$ ($\mathbb{N}_0$ denotes the natural numbers including 0, $\mathscr{P}^n$ denotes the n-th power of $\mathscr{P}$ and $\mathscr{P}^0$ denotes the identity relation).
  Conditional branches, i.e., the selection of exactly one among many possible successor operations, correspond to nodes with more than one successor, leading to a fork (figure 1). A particular branch is taken depending on the condition *cond*: $\mathscr{P} \rightarrow (f(value(S)) \rightarrow \{false, true\})$. Here f denotes a function on the values that the variables hold, usually of the form $(value(s) = c), s \in S, c$ a constant. Conditions are denoted in short by $(s = c)$, making no distinction between a variable an its value. $cond(v_1, v_2) = true$ (or false) means that the corresponding function evaluates to *true* (or false). If the result is *true*, that branch is taken, otherwise it is not taken. Conditions must make sure that all the successors of each operation are mutually exclusive, i.e.,

$$\forall_{v, s}[\,|\,\{v_1 \,|\, v \mathscr{P} v_1 \wedge cond(v, v_1) = true\}\,| \leq 1]$$

  Iterations or loops are represented by cycles in the graph.

- An input relation $\mathscr{I} \subseteq S \times V$, indicating the variables used as inputs (read) by each operation.

- An output relation $\mathcal{O} \subseteq V \times S$, indicating the variables produced as outputs (written) by each operation. The digraph defined by $(V \cup S, \mathscr{I} \cup \mathcal{O})$ represents the **data-flow**.

The operational semantics of YIF are defined as follows:

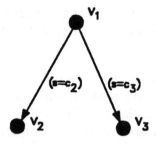

Figure 1. Representation of a conditional branch

Operations are executed one at a time, starting with the first operation v_f. The next operation is a successor of the executed operation. If there is more than one successor, exactly one of them is chosen depending on the conditions. An operation v writes a new value to all variables in $v\mathcal{O}$. It uses no value which is not in $\mathcal{I}v$. A variable retains its value until it is overwritten.

2.2 Time Representation

In synchronous systems a control step takes the time of a complete clock cycle. If control is implemented by a finite state machine, then one control step is equivalent to a state in this machine; if control is implemented by a microprogram, then one control step is equivalent to one microinstruction. Control steps impose certain constraints on the hardware (see section 2.4).

The notion of a control step will be represented in YIF as follows. Assume for this purpose that the precedence graph is acyclic. In section 3.1. we will see how an acyclic precedence graph can be constructed from one containing cycles. By definition there is a first node v_f. Since the graph is acyclic, there must be one or more nodes v_l that have no successors (sink). A control step starts with the execution of v_f. A certain path $v_f \not{h} v_l$ is taken, executing all operations on it ($v_1 \not{h} v_n$ denotes one path in the precedence graph $(V, \mathcal{P})$ from v_1 to v_n such that $\exists_{v_2, \ldots, v_{n-1}} [\forall_{1 \leq i < n-1} [v_i \mathcal{P} v_{i+1}]]$, a path is denoted in short $\not{h}$). The control step ends after v_l is executed. The next control step starts again with v_f.

We use a finite state machine to represent control. A control step corresponds to a state in the finite state machine. To identify control steps they must be represented symbolically: we number control steps consecutively starting with 1. The identification of the particular control step being executed (the state the finite state machine is in) will be held in a register called the state register. To sequence through control states a state decoder v_{stat} is introduced. The state decoder is the first operation. Its function is to take one of n possible conditional branches, n being the number of control steps (states). In general, the state register must be updated in each possible path $v_f \not{h} v_l$, i.e., the next control step (state) must be written into it. This is done by state update operations v_w which transfer new values to the control state register r_{stat}. The state update operations v_w are the sinks.

This is a rather unusual representation of a finite state machine, that is more easily derived from flow-graphs than the state-transition diagram. Also, it captures much more detail than a state diagram. It is suited for both Moore and Mealy automata. The example in figure 2 shows a YIF representation with two control steps and the corresponding state transition table.

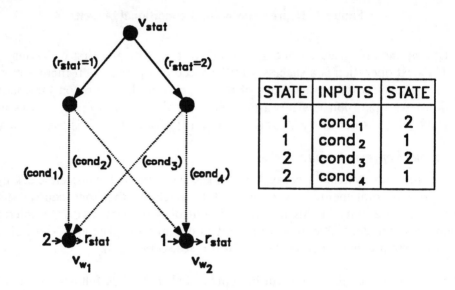

STATE	INPUTS	STATE
1	$cond_1$	2
1	$cond_2$	1
2	$cond_3$	2
2	$cond_4$	1

Figure 2. Control step representation in YIF

The notion of sequencing through control steps is captured in the definition of the precedence relation considering control steps:

$$\mathcal{P}_{ss} = \mathcal{P} \cup \{(v_w, v_{stat})\}$$

$$cond(v_w, v_{stat}) = clock$$

After the value of the state is updated in v_w, when the *clock* becomes true (meaning the clock edge or any other instantaneous event), the next control step is started. The precedence relation considering control steps $\mathcal{P}_{ss}$ is used in the definition of behavior equivalence.

If an initial specification already includes the total or partial assignment of operations to control steps, this can be represented as indicated above. For a YIF specification without control steps, the control state decoder is initially introduced decoding one unique state. At the end of each possible path we will add an operation writing precisely this state into the state register. We are assuming that all operation sequences can be executed during one control step (this does not mean that a hardware structure capable of performing each operation sequence in one control cycle can be found; we are still describing behavior).

Given a behavioral specification

$$Y = (V, S, type, \mathcal{P}, cond, \mathcal{I}, \mathcal{O})$$

without control step specification, the conditional branch operation v_{stat} to decode the control state register r_{stat} is added before the first operation v_f, yielding the new behavioral specification

$$Y' = (V', S', type', \mathcal{P}', cond', \mathcal{I}', \mathcal{O}') \text{ with}$$
$$V' = V \cup \{v_{stat}\}$$
$$S' = S \cup \{r_{stat}\} \text{ with } type'(r_{stat}) = register$$
$$\mathcal{P}' = \mathcal{P} \cup \{(v_{stat}, v_f)\} \text{ with } cond'(v_{stat}, v_f) = (r_{stat} = 1)$$
$$\mathcal{I}' = \mathcal{I}$$
$$\mathcal{O}' = \mathcal{O}$$

Additionally for all sink operations V_l

$$V_l = \{v_l \in V \mid \nexists_{v' \in V}[\, v_l \mathcal{P} v' \,]\}$$

a state update operation v_w writing "1" into the control state register r_{stat} is included following each v_l (here "1" is an arbitrary encoding of the state which may be changed if state encoding is optimized):

$$V' = V \cup \{v_w\}$$
$$S' = S \cup \{1\} \text{ with } type'(1) = constant$$
$$\mathcal{P}' = \mathcal{P} \cup \{(v_l, v_w)\} \text{ with } cond'(v_l, v_w) = true$$
$$\mathcal{I}' = \mathcal{I} \cup \{(1, v_w)\}$$
$$\mathcal{O}' = \mathcal{O} \cup \{(v_w, r_{stat})\}$$

We have chosen to write the initial state "1" at the end of each possible operation sequence, thus repeating infinitely the specified behavior. More sophisticated basic control schemes such as introducing a waiting state until a signal arrives to explicitly "reset" the initial state are possible (figure 3). The waiting state in this example is encoded as "0".

2.3 Behavior Equivalence

High-level synthesis will modify a given specification preserving the behavior. Generally two systems that can be modelled by finite state machines show equivalent behavior, if the output sequence is the same for equal input sequences and given initial states. To prove that the transformations involved in our synthesis algorithms are behavior-preserving, we will use a stronger definition of equivalence that implies the one above. It is based on the imperative semantics of our model of representation, keeping in mind that we don't want to modify the sequential algorithm given in a behavioral specification.

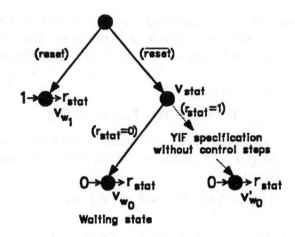

Figure 3. Introducing a waiting state and a reset signal

The behavior of two YIF representations is equivalent iff

1. The data flow operations are the same.
2. The data flow operations have the same inputs and outputs.
3. The data flow operations have the same precedence relation considering control steps.

Data flow operations are those which use variables as inputs that depend on input ports or that generate values as outputs on which output ports depend. Data flow operations are given by

$$V_{df} = \{ v \in V \mid \exists_{s \in S,\, n \in \mathbb{N}_0} [type(s) = port \wedge (s\mathcal{I}(\mathcal{OI})^n v \vee v\mathcal{O}(\mathcal{IO})^n s)] \}$$

Using V_{df} we now can define equivalence of behavior formally. The behavior of two YIF representations Y and Y' is equivalent iff

1. $V_{df} = V'_{df}$
2. $(\mathcal{I} \cap (S \times V_{df}) = \mathcal{I}' \cap (S' \times V'_{df})) \wedge (\mathcal{O} \cap (V_{df} \times S) = \mathcal{O}' \cap (V'_{df} \times S'))$
3. Let $\mathcal{D} = \mathcal{P}_{ss}|_{V_{df}} \cup (\mathcal{P}_{ss}(\mathcal{P}_{ss}|_{V - V_{df}})^n \mathcal{P}_{ss})|_{V_{df}}$ then
   $\mathcal{D} = \mathcal{D}' \wedge cond(\mathcal{D}) = cond'(\mathcal{D}')$
   Here
   $\mathcal{P}_{ss}|_{V_{df}}$ denotes $\mathcal{P}_{ss} \cap (V_{df} \times V_{df})$. $\mathcal{D}$ is the relation $\mathcal{P}_{ss}$ restricted to V_{df}, also including all those pairs that are "connected" by the transitive closure of $\mathcal{P}_{ss}$ in $V - V_{df}$ (V excluding V_{df}). These pairs represent an immediate predecessor-successor pair considering only operations in V_{df}. The condition $cond(v_1, v_2)$ for $(v_1, v_2) \in \mathcal{D}$ is obtained by *and-ing* the conditions along the paths $v_1 \wedge v_2$ in $\mathcal{P}_{ss}$ that fulfill the definition of $\mathcal{D}$, and *or-ing* them if more than one path exists.

Equivalence of behavior is an equivalence relation. Clearly the given equivalence definition implies that input/output behavior of two equivalent YIF descriptions is the same, in the sense that both the values and the sequences of the signals at the ports are identically equal.

2.4 Hardware Constraints

Real hardware imposes constraints on a structure. During high-level synthesis these hardware constraints, which do not necessarily apply to a behavioral description, must be ultimately met. We consider only general constraints that are not technology specific. Among these, the following two are sufficient for synchronous digital systems:

1. Values that are passed by nets must be generated before they are used in the same control step. Otherwise they are either constants, they are passed by a port (in that control step) or they were stored in a register in some previous control step.

   - 1. $\forall_s \left[\exists_{v \in s.\mathscr{I}} \exists_{v_{stat} \wedge v} [\mathscr{O}s \cap \mu = \phi] \Rightarrow type(s) \neq net \right]$

2. Hardware components can be used only once during one control step. Since each possible path $v_{stat} \wedge v_w$ is executed in one control step, each of them must meet the hardware constraints, e.g., in each path a register must be written only once, enough operators to execute all operations in each path must be provided, etc. In particular

   - A piece of combinational logic can perform its operation only once. This constraint is trivially met by allocating a distinct hardware module for each operation, which can be later changed during optimization.

   - Ports p can either receive or transmit only one value.
     2.1. $\forall_p \forall_{(v_{stat} \wedge v_w)} \left[|(\mathscr{O}p \cup p\mathscr{I}) \cap \mu| \leq 1 \right]$
     Notice that each port can only receive one *distinct* value in one control step. Of course this value can be used multiple times, e.g., a variable representing an input port can be used as a source multiple times if the same value is meant.

   - Nets q can have only one source (single assignment constraint).
     2.2. $\forall_q \forall_{(v_{stat} \wedge v_w)} \left[|\mathscr{O}q \cap \mu| \leq 1 \right]$
     In the case of a constant j this means that it is not the output of any operation (it is "sourced" with its constant value).
     2.3. $\forall_j \left[\mathscr{O}j = \phi \right]$

   - Registers r can be written only once (single assignment constraint).
     2.4. $\forall r \forall_{(v_{stat} \wedge v_w)} \left[|\mathscr{O}r \cap \mu| \leq 1 \right]$

The first constraint is met during high-level synthesis by introducing registers: variables written in one control step and read (used) in a different control steps will be mapped onto registers. The second constraint is met introducing control steps, i.e., by assigning the specified operations to control steps, providing enough hardware components to perform all operations needed in one control step.

If these constraints are met, then the behavior is trivially mapped onto a structure by replacing operations and variables in a one to one fashion by hardware and connecting them according to the input and output relation. The structure obtained in this way can then be further optimized.

3. Converting Behavior into Structure

Given a behavioral specification

$$Y = (V, S, type, \mathcal{P}, cond, \mathcal{I}, \mathcal{O})$$

a series of transformations is applied until a specification

$$Y' = (V', S', type', \mathcal{P}', cond', \mathcal{I}', \mathcal{O}')$$

is obtained that meets the hardware constraints and has equivalent behavior with respect to V. Since equivalence of behavior is transitive, it is enough to prove that each of the transformations is behavior-preserving.

3.1 Loops

A cycle (circuit) in the precedence graph $(V, \mathcal{P})$ represents a loop in the behavioral specification, e.g., a WHILE loop. Trivially, cycles within one control step violate the hardware constraints, e.g., by writing repeatedly to a port or register. To allow the repetition of the cycle, we introduce initially one control step to allow the repetition of the operations in the loop. Thus we eliminate the cycles in the precedence graph.

To eliminate the cycles we need to identify a set L of edges such that $(V, \mathcal{P} - L)$ is acyclic and still connected. The number of possible elementary cycles in a general directed graph with n nodes can be as large as $n!$ [12] . Finding a smallest set L that breaks all cycles is np hard. In our current system we do not attempt to find a minimum L for any possible graph. Since the initial YIF specification is derived from a high level language, it is trivial to identify a set L syntactically by looking at the looping control constructs and the "GOTO" statements. If the specification language is "structured", i.e., only allows properly nested loops and no "GOTO's", this set L is also minimum.

The elimination of the cycles in the graph is illustrated in figure 4. Instead of executing the next operation v_2 at the point where an edge in L is met, a new state n is written into the control state variable r_{stat}. In the next control step, the execution starts again at the first operation v_{stat} and, with the proper decoding provided, the next operation in the set of observed operations (remember we observe the operations in the initial YIF specification) will indeed be v_2.

The corresponding transformation introduces for each edge $(v_1, v_2) \in L$ a new control state n (n may be just the number that encodes the next available state).

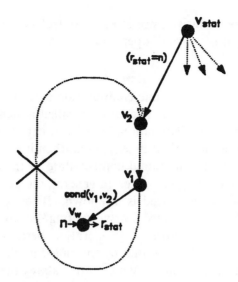

Figure 4. Making the precedence graph acyclic

$V' = V \cup \{v_w\}$
$S' = S \cup \{n\}$
$\mathscr{P}' = (\mathscr{P} - \{(v_1, v_2)\}) \cup \{(v_1, v_w)\,,\ (v_{stat}, v_2)\}$
    with $cond'(v_1, v_w) = cond(v_1, v_2)\,,\ cond'(v_{stat}, v_2) = (r_{stat} = n)$
$\mathscr{I}' = \mathscr{I} \cup \{n\mathscr{I}v_w\}$
$\mathscr{O}' = \mathscr{O} \cup \{v_w\mathscr{O}r_{stat}\}$

This transformation preserves the behavior.

Proof:

V_{df}, $\mathscr{I} \cap (S \times V_{df})$ and $\mathscr{O} \cap (V_{df} \times S)$ are clearly not changed (only the operation v_w is added, which obviously is not a data flow operation).

$\mathscr{D}$ is not changed: the only removed pair $v_1\mathscr{P}_{ss}v_2$ is still included in $\mathscr{P}'_{ss}$ by the path $(v_1, v_w, v_{stat}, v_2)$, $v_w, v_{stat} \notin V_{df}$. When $clock = true$, and since $r_{stat} = n$ is always true for this path,

$$cond'(v_1, v_2) = cond'(v_1, v_w) \wedge cond'(v_w, v_{stat}) \wedge cond'(v_{stat}, v_2)$$
$$= cond(v_1, v_2) \wedge clock \wedge (r_{stat} = n)$$
$$= cond(v_1, v_2)$$

No other pair is added to the relation $\mathscr{D}$. $\square$

The transitive closure $\mathscr{A}$ of $(V, \mathscr{P})$ is a partial order since the graph is now acyclic and $\mathscr{P}$ is irreflexive. If two operations are not ordered in $\mathscr{A}$ we will denote this

$$v_1 \| v_2 \equiv \neg(v_1 \mathscr{A} v_2 \vee v_2 \mathscr{A} v_1)$$

and call them **mutually exclusive** since in each control step either v_1 or v_2 or none of them is executed, but never both operations.

3.2 Module Calls

An operation can be either an atomic computation such as an addition or a reference to another YIF description. The latter is called a **module call**. If the called YIF description generates a combinational circuit, it can be treated as an atomic computation. If the resulting circuit is sequential, then it can not be treated as an atomic computation and an additional control state in the calling module must be introduced, splitting the original state. In general, the number of control states (cycles) that a module call will need is unknown. Therefore, for each of these sequential module calls we introduce a new "waiting" control state. This module call waiting state does not perform any operation besides enabling the called module, until a *ready* signal is generated by the called module. Ready signals can be generated automatically by identifying control states that contain final operations in a module.

For each sequential module call v_{call} with successors v_x , $(v_{call}, v_x) \in \mathscr{P}$, the YIF description is transformed by introducing a new waiting state n as follows (see also figure 5):

$$V' = V \cup \{v_{test}, v_w\}$$
$$S' = S \cup \{n\}$$
$$\mathscr{P}' = (\mathscr{P} - \{(v_{call}, v_x)\}) \cup \{(v_{call}, v_{test}) , (v_{test}, v_w) , (v_{test}, v_x) , (v_{stat}, v_{test})\}$$
$$\quad \text{with } cond'(v_{call}, v_{test}) = * , \ cond'(v_{test}, v_w) = \overline{ready} ,$$
$$\qquad cond'(v_{stat}, v_{test}) = (r_{stat} = n) , \ \text{and } cond'(v_{test}, v_x) = (ready \wedge cond(v_{call}, v_x))$$
$$\mathscr{I}' = \mathscr{I} \cup \{n \mathscr{I} v_w\}$$
$$\mathscr{O}' = \mathscr{O} \cup \{v_w \mathscr{O} r_{stat}\}$$

This transformation preserves the behavior.

Proof:

V_{df}, $\mathscr{I} \cap (S \times V_{df})$ and $\mathscr{O} \cap (V_{df} \times S)$ are clearly not changed (only the operations v_w, v_{test} are added, which obviously are not data flow operations). $\mathscr{D}$ is not changed: each removed pair $(v_{call}, v_x) \in \mathscr{P}_{ss}$ is still included in $\mathscr{P}'_{ss}$ by the paths $(v_{call}, v_{test}, v_x)$, $(v_{call}, v_{test}, v_w, v_{stat}, v_{test}, v_x)$, $(v_{call}, v_{test}, v_w, v_{stat}, v_{test}, v_w, v_{stat}, v_{test}, v_x)$, ... with $v_w, v_{stat}, v_{test} \in (V' - V_o)$. Since $r_{stat} = n$ is true for all but the first path,

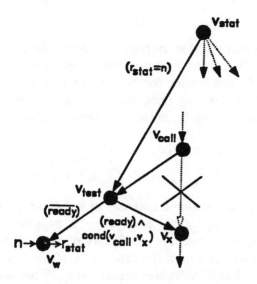

Figure 5. Control state due to a module call

$$
\begin{aligned}
cond'(v_{call}, v_x) = {} & cond'(v_{call}, v_{test}) \wedge cond'(v_{test}, v_x) \ \vee \\
& cond'(v_{call}, v_{test}) \wedge cond'(v_{test}, v_w) \wedge cond'(v_w, v_{stat}) \wedge \\
& cond'(v_{stat}, v_{test}) \wedge cond'(v_{test}, v_x) \ \vee \\
& cond'(v_{call}, v_{test}) \wedge cond'(v_{test}, v_w) \wedge cond'(v_w, v_{stat}) \wedge \\
& cond'(v_{stat}, v_{test}) \wedge cond'(v_{test}, v_w) \wedge cond'(v_w, v_{stat}) \wedge \\
& cond'(v_{stat}, v_{test}) \wedge cond'(v_{test}, v_x) \ \vee \\
& \ldots \\
= {} & ready_t \wedge cond(v_{call}, v_x) \ \vee \\
& \overline{ready_t} \wedge clock_t \wedge (r_{stat} = n) \wedge ready_{t+1} \wedge cond(v_{call}, v_x) \ \vee \\
& \overline{ready_t} \wedge clock_t \wedge (r_{stat} = n) \wedge \overline{ready_{t+1}} \wedge clock_{t+1} \wedge (r_{stat} = n) \wedge ready_{t+2} \wedge cond(v_{call}, v_x \\
& \ldots \\
= {} & cond(v_{call}, v_x) \wedge (ready_t \vee \overline{ready}_t \wedge ready_{t+1} \vee \overline{ready}_t \wedge \overline{ready_{t+1}} \wedge ready_{t+2} \vee \ldots) \\
= {} & cond(v_{call}, v_x)
\end{aligned}
$$

Notice that the condition *ready* which is an external signal for this module had to be considered in different control steps $t, t+1, t+2, \ldots$. If at some point in time *ready* becomes true, the above expression holds.
No other pair is added to the relation $\mathscr{D}$. □

The computational complexity of this transformation is proportional to the number of module calls and to the outdegree of the corresponding nodes in the precedence graph.

3.3 Cutting

Cutting is a transformation that introduces additional control steps to meet hardware constraints. It requires repeating the computation of the necessary registers (section 3.3.). We use cutting for hardware restrictions 2.1. and 2.4. (writing registers and using ports only once during a control step). Since both cases are analogous, cutting will only be shown for registers (2.4.).

Assume constraint 2.4. is not met, i.e.,

$$\exists_r \exists_{(v_{stat} \not h v_w)} [\, |\mathcal{O}r \cap \not h| > 1 \,]$$

If we "**cut**" the path $v_{stat} \not h v_w$ between two uses of r, $v_1 \mathcal{O} r$ and $v_2 \mathcal{O} r$ before an operation v_{cut}, such that $(v_{stat} \not h_1 v_1 \not h_1 \cdot v_{cut} \not h_2 v_2 \not h_2 \cdot v_w) = \not h$ assigning all operations on $\not h_2 \not h_2'$ to a new control step, then the cardinality of each of the sets $\mathcal{O}r \cap \not h_1 \not h_1'$ and $\mathcal{O}r \cap \not h_2 \not h_2'$ is clearly less than the cardinality of $\mathcal{O}r \cap \not h$. This transformation is repeated until the constraint is eventually met. Since we will cut the path between v_{cut} and its predecessor v_{pc} on the examined path $(v_{pc}, v_{cut}) \subseteq \not h$, we allow explicitly $v_{cut} = v_2$.

The transformation should also guarantee the minimum number of control steps for each path. Paths can certainly overlap, i.e., have operations in common. This means that a cut introduced in one path can affect other paths. To prevent this, only the path being examined should be cut. A path is identified uniquely by all the conditional branches in it, at each branch exactly one condition *cond* being true. The *and* of all the conditions on a path provides an exact path identification, i.e., the path is only taken if all these conditions are met. Let *pathid* be the condition $cond_1 \wedge cond_2 ... \wedge cond_m$ for all $cond_i$, $1 \le i \le m$ conditions of edges up to v_{pc} preceding the cutting point v_{cut} on the examined path $\not h$. To cut only the path being examined and thus indeed obtain a minimum number of steps for each path independent from the other paths, the path is only cut if the conditions *pathid* and $cond(v_{pc}, v_{cut})$ are met, otherwise the successor of v_{pc} is v_{cut}.

The transformation for cutting a path $v_{stat} \not h v_w$ with a path identification *pathid* at $(v_{pc}, v_{cut}) \in \not h$, introducing a new control step n is (see also figure 6):

$V' = V \bigcup \{v_w\}$

$S' = S \bigcup \{n\}$

$\mathcal{P}' = \mathcal{P} \bigcup \{(v_{pc}, v_w), (v_{stat}, v_{cut})\}$

    with $cond'(v_{stat}, v_{cut}) = (r_{stat} = n)$, $cond'(v_{pc}, v_w) = pathid \wedge cond(v_{pc}, v_{cut})$

    and $cond'(v_{pc}, v_{cut}) = \overline{pathid} \wedge cond(v_{pc}, v_{cut})$

$\mathcal{I}' = \mathcal{I} \bigcup \{n \mathcal{I} v_w\}$

$\mathcal{O}' = \mathcal{O} \bigcup \{v_w \mathcal{O} r_{stat}\}$

This transformation preserves the behavior.
    Proof:

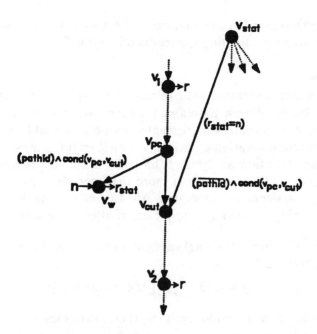

Figure 6. Control state due to the violation of single assignment of a register

V_{df}, $\mathcal{I} \cap (S \times V_{df})$ and $\mathcal{O} \cap (V_{df} \times S)$ are clearly not changed (only the operation v_w is added, which obviously is not a data flow operation).
$\mathcal{D}$ is not changed: The two paths (v_{pc}, v_{cut}) and $(v_{pc}, v_w, v_{stat}, v_{cut})$ in $\mathcal{P}'_{ss}$ yield the condition

$$cond'(v_{pc}, v_{cut}) \vee cond'(v_{pc}, v_w) \wedge cond'(v_w, v_{stat}) \wedge cond'(v_{stat}, v_{cut})$$
$$= \overline{pathid} \wedge cond(v_{pc}, v_{cut}) \vee pathid \wedge cond(v_{pc}, v_{cut}) \wedge clock \wedge (r_{stat} = n)$$
$$= cond(v_{pc}, v_{cut})$$

No other pair is added to the relation $\mathcal{D}$. □

The computational complexity of this transformation is proportional to the number of paths in the graph.

Each path is examined and cut individually, introducing with each cut a new sequential control step for just that path. If the minimum number of cuts for each path are introduced, then also the number of control steps for each path is minimal (but not for the whole graph!).

To guarantee the minimum number of cuts we have to examine all possibilities for v_{cut} on the examined path $v_{stat} \not\!\!\wedge v_w$ bounded by v_1 and v_2, for all hardware constraint violations. We implemented this in a straightforward fashion as a recursive backtracking which is equivalent in the extreme to examining all possibilities for each path (there are much better ways of solving this). To avoid excessive time consumption, the number of iterations that are considered is given by a system parameter, limiting the recursion depth.

3.4 Unfolding

Unfolding is a transformation used to meet hardware constraints by replicating hardware resources. We use unfolding for hardware restriction 2.2. to guarantee single assignment of variables implemented by nets. Variable unfolding basically consists of renaming a variable until single assignment is met. The algorithm is based on global data flow analysis. It basically introduces new nets for variables q with $type(q) = net$ that are written more than once in a path and thus do not meet the single assignment constraint. All uses of a variable as input must be identified, possibly introducing multiplexers if alternative sources exist.

The variables that violate the single assignment constraint are defined by the negation of constraint 2.2.:

$$Q = \{q | \exists_{(v_{stat} \wedge v_w)} [|\mathcal{O}q \cap \mathcal{A}| > 1]\}$$

Variable unfolding will unfold each of these variables $q \in Q$ replacing it by $m = | \{v | v\mathcal{O}q\} = \{v_1, v_2, ..., v_m\} |$ variables $q_1, q_2, ..., q_m$ of $type(q_i) = net$, $1 \le i \le m$.

$$V' = V$$
$$S' = S \cup \{q_i | 1 \le i \le m\}$$
$$\mathcal{P}' = \mathcal{P}$$
$$\mathcal{I}' = \mathcal{I}$$
$$\mathcal{O}' = (\mathcal{O} - \{v_i\mathcal{O}q | 1 \le i \le m\}) \cup \{v_i\mathcal{O}q_i | 1 \le i \le m\}$$

Before each operation v_r using q, $q\mathcal{I}v_r$, a multiplexer v_{mux} is inserted with output q_{mux} to select the correct q_i (figure 7). For each v_r with predecessors v_{pr}, $(v_{pr}, v_r) \in \mathcal{P}$ the multiplexer is added as follows:

$$V' = V \cup \{v_{mux}\}$$
$$S' = S \cup \{q_{mux}\}$$
$$\mathcal{P}' = (\mathcal{P} - \{(v_{pr}, v_r)\}) \cup \{(v_{pr}, v_{mux}), (v_{mux}, v_r)\}$$
$$\text{with } cond'(v_{pr}, v_{mux}) = cond(v_{pr}, v_r), \ cond'(v_{mux}, v_r) = true$$
$$\mathcal{I}' = (\mathcal{I} - \{q\mathcal{I}v_r\}) \cup \{q_{mux}\mathcal{I}v_r\} \cup \{q_x\mathcal{I}v_{mux}\}$$
$$\mathcal{O}' = \mathcal{O} \cup \{v_{mux}\mathcal{O}q_{mux}\}$$

The input variables q_x for the multiplexer are selected among all the unfolded output variables q_i finding all these, which are written by operations v_q that are the latest predecessors to v_r writing q

$$\left\{ q_x | \exists_{v_q, (v_q \wedge v_r)} \not\exists_{v_{qq}, (v_{qq} \wedge' v_r)} [v_q\mathcal{O}q_x \wedge v_{qq}\mathcal{O}q \wedge \mathcal{A}' \subseteq \mathcal{A}] \right\}$$

After the inputs of each v_r have been changed, the variable q is removed. The multiplexers introduced have no "select" inputs. The corresponding select inputs are given implicitly: whenever an operation writing one of the inputs of the

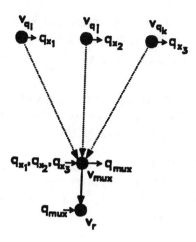

Figure 7. Variable unfolding

multiplexer is enabled and thus its output is valid, the corresponding data input of the multiplexer has to be selected. These are made explicit by generating *pathid* as done for cutting. Since by construction all the inputs q_x to the multiplexers are mutually exclusive, no conflicts in selecting two or more inputs at a time can arise.

The single assignment constraint for nets is now trivially met since each new net q_{mux} is written only by v_{mux} and each q_i is written by exactly one operation v_i.

To prove the equivalence of behavior for variable unfolding consider that the precedence relation has clearly not been changed, but the variables have. To prove that the data flow for all the observed operations is not changed by this transformation, it must be proved that the source operation generating each input q_x is the same as before unfolding. The construction given above obviously guarantees this.

Using the above transformation, the computational complexity of variable unfolding is, among other things, proportional to the number of paths in the precedence graph.

3.5 Registers

Hardware constraint 1 is trivially met for all variables which have *type ≠ net*. If the constraint does not hold for a variable of type net, this is a specification error.

Variables that have no type specified can be implemented either as nets or as registers (remember that ports and constants must be specified). Unless hardware constraint 1 is violated, we will implement these variables by nets. To compute the variables of unspecified type that must be implemented by registers we restrict hardware constraint 1 to these variables. Hence, the set R of variables of unknown type that have to be implemented by registers is given by

$$R = \{s \mid type(s) = * \wedge \exists_{v \in s \mathcal{S}} \exists_{v_{stat} \mathcal{S} v} [\mathcal{F} \cap \mathcal{O}s = \phi]\}$$

The precedence relation considering control steps of the observed variables is not affected in any way by changing the type of a variable. The data flow is also not changed, so the behavior is kept equivalent.

The computation of all s that must be registers can be done by searching for a path from v_{stat} to v in the graph $(V, \mathcal{P})$ after removing all nodes in $\mathcal{O}s$. Notice that implementing each of these variables in its own register is not necessary: lifetime analysis of variables can determine which ones can share registers (e.g., [13]).

3.6 Further Considerations

After applying the above transformations, hardware constraints are met (with the exception of constraint 2.3, writing to a constant, which is a specification error). Mapping YIF to a structure is now straightforward: registers, ports and functional units have been identified, and the connectivity is given by the input and output relations. The registers are hardware components known down to their layout and need no further processing. Input/output ports are kept as specified and are not modified. Constants produce constant inputs to operations and are taken into account by logic synthesis. Functional units are implemented by combinational logic. For each operation there is a logic specification described as a set of Boolean equations in a library (actually parameterized programs). The final logic is produced using logic synthesis.

The order in which the transformation are applied can be chosen. For the examples given below, path cutting and variable unfolding were used for variable constraints according to their type, i.e., registers and ports generate cuts, nets are unfolded. Functional units were unfolded.

It is equally possible to unfold any type of variable, replicating also ports and registers. We chose not to do so and to implement ports as well as registers (if they were specified) as specified initially, using cutting which modifies the control steps but not the ports or registers themselves. The cost of registers and ports (pins) is usually high.

It is also possible to generate cuts, instead of unfolding nets, at the cost of introducing more control steps and possibly more registers. In this case we chose to generate initially the minimum number of control steps at the cost of replicating nets, relying on later optimizations (control step splitting, see [5]) to optimize the used hardware resources.

Some optimizations are done during synthesis. For example, equal control steps are merged, whenever it is possible already existing control steps are used when cutting a path, trivial multiplexers with just one input are eliminated, etc. Conceptually this is not necessary, e.g., state minimization eliminates repeated control steps and logic synthesis eliminates multiplexers with just one input, but the complexity of the (intermediate) design is greatly reduced. Also, mutually exclusive operations (see section 3.1) can share functional units, and registers with non-overlapping lifetimes (see section 3.5) can be implemented by one register. The minimization of functional units and registers can be formulated as a clique covering problem [13].

4. Examples

To give an idea of the performance of the above algorithms, we include two examples. In figure 8., a V[14] description for the **EDIT** instruction of the IBM System/370 Extended Architecture [15] is given. The results of high-level and logic synthesis using YLL[4] are summarized in figure 9. All our examples were executed on an IBM 3090-200 computer with VM/SP HPO 4.2 under interpreted APL.

```
/*-------------- EDIT from E370 architecture --------------*/
MODULE E370DEC (PATTERN:IN,  SOURCE:IN,  LENGTH:IN,  CODE:IN,
                NEXTSRC:OUT, RESULT:OUT, DATAEX:OUT, CC:OUT);

EXTERNAL E370DEC;
 DCL PATTERN    BIT(8),
     SOURCE     BIT(8),
     LENGTH     BIT(8),
     CODE       BIT(8),
     NEXTSRC    BIT(1),      /* 1 if next source byte */
     RESULT     BIT(8),
     DATAEX     BIT(1),           /* Data exception */
     CC         BIT(2);           /* Condition code */

INTERNAL E370DEC;
 DCL L          BIT(8),      /* Length of pattern - 1 */
     FILL       BIT(8),      /* Fill byte, e.g., blank */
     SIGNIFIC   BIT(1),  /* 1 if digit is significant */
     RL         BIT(1),   /* 0 if left digit in byte */
     PLUS       BIT(1),  /* 1 if PLUS  sign in SOURCE */
     MINUS      BIT(1),  /* 1 if MINUS sign in SOURCE */
     ZERO       BIT(1),         /* 1 if DIGIT = 0 */
     DIGIT      BIT(4),           /* Source digit */
     DATAEXC    BIT(1),     /* 1 if data exception */
     COND       BIT(1),         /* 1 if CC not 0 */
     ZONE       BIT(4),          /* Zone is 1111 */
     MSIG       BIT(4),     /* Minus sign is 1101 */
     PSIG       BIT(4);     /* Plus  sign is 1100 */

BODY E370DEC;
 ZONE:=15 ; MSIG:=13; PSIG:=12;           /* Constants */
 DO INFINITE LOOP
  WHEN CODE
   CASE 222;                    /* 222 (Hex DE) is EDIT */
    RL       := 1;
    NEXTSRC := 1;
    SIGNIFIC:= 0;
    DATAEXC := 0;
    COND     := 0;
    L        := LENGTH + 1;
    FILL     := PATTERN;
    DO UNTIL (L = 0) | DATAEXC
     LOOP
            /* ((SOURCE::4,4) means bits 4,5,6 and 7   */
      PLUS := ((SOURCE::4,4)=10) | ((SOURCE::4,4)=12) |
              ((SOURCE::4,4)=14) | ((SOURCE::4,4)=15);
```

```
    MINUS:= ((SOURCE::4,4)=11) | ((SOURCE::4,4)=13) ;
    IF RL THEN DIGIT := (SOURCE::4,4);
          ELSE DIGIT := (SOURCE::0,4); ENDIF;
    ZERO    := DIGIT = 0;
    DATAEXC := (SOURCE::0,4) > 9;
    IF ¬DATAEXC THEN

    IF PATTERN = 32                 /* Digit selector */
      THEN
      WHEN SIGNIFIC || PLUS || MINUS || ZERO
        CASE 0,8,9;                 /* 0000-1000-1001 */
         RESULT:=ZONE || DIGIT; SIGNIFIC:=1; RL:=¬RL;
        CASE 2;                                 /* 0010 */
         RESULT:=MSIG || DIGIT; SIGNIFIC:=1; RL:= 1;
        CASE 4;                                 /* 0100 */
         RESULT:=PSIG || DIGIT; SIGNIFIC:=0; RL:= 1;
        CASE 1;                                 /* 0001 */
         RESULT:=FILL;          SIGNIFIC:=0; RL:=¬RL;
        CASE 3,5;                         /* 0011-0101 */
         RESULT:=FILL;          SIGNIFIC:=0; RL:= 1;
        CASE 10,11;                       /* 1010-1011 */
         RESULT:=MSIG || DIGIT; SIGNIFIC:=1; RL:= 1;
        CASE 12,13;                       /* 1100-1101 */
         RESULT:=PSIG || DIGIT; SIGNIFIC:=0; RL:= 1;
      ENDCASE;
      COND    := COND | ¬ZERO;
      NEXTSRC := RL;

    ELSE IF PATTERN = 33    /* Significance starter */
      THEN
      WHEN SIGNIFIC || PLUS || MINUS || ZERO
        CASE 0,8,9;                 /* 0000-1000-1001 */
         RESULT:=ZONE || DIGIT; SIGNIFIC:=1; RL:=¬RL;
        CASE 2;                                 /* 0010 */
         RESULT:=MSIG || DIGIT; SIGNIFIC:=1; RL:= 1;
        CASE 4;                                 /* 0100 */
         RESULT:=PSIG || DIGIT; SIGNIFIC:=0; RL:= 1;
        CASE 1;                                 /* 0001 */
         RESULT:=FILL;          SIGNIFIC:=1; RL:=¬RL;
        CASE 3;                                 /* 0011 */
         RESULT:=FILL;          SIGNIFIC:=1; RL:= 1;
        CASE 5;                                 /* 0101 */
         RESULT:=FILL;          SIGNIFIC:=0; RL:= 1;
        CASE 10,11;                       /* 1010-1011 */
         RESULT:=MSIG || DIGIT; SIGNIFIC:=1; RL:= 1;
        CASE 12,13;                       /* 1100-1101 */
         RESULT:=PSIG || DIGIT; SIGNIFIC:=0; RL:= 1;
      ENDCASE;
      COND    := COND | ¬ZERO;
      NEXTSRC := RL;

    ELSE IF PATTERN = 34            /* Field separator */
      THEN
      RESULT := FILL; SIGNIFIC := 0;
      COND    := 0;   NEXTSRC    := 0;

    ELSE                                 /* Message byte */
      IF SIGNIFIC THEN RESULT := PATTERN;
                  ELSE RESULT := FILL;   ENDIF;
      NEXTSRC := 0;

    ENDIF;ENDIF;ENDIF;
    ENDIF;
    DATAEX      := DATAEXC;
    (CC::0,1) := COND & (¬SIGNIFIC);
    (CC::1,1) := COND & SIGNIFIC;
    L           := L - 1;
   ENDDO;
  ENDCASE;
 ENDDO;

END E370DEC;
```

Figure 8. V program for the execution of the IBM System/370 EDIT instruction

	EDIT
V lines / statements	121 / 110
Compilation time	4.3 sec.
YIF lines / nodes Variable bits	995 / 149 245

High-level synthesis time
  Reading, writing, optimizing
  Synthesis
	62 sec.
	30 sec.
	32 sec.

Register bits Control states Combinational in-/outputs	21 2 52 / 31
YLL processing time	50 sec.
Functions Literals Levels	333 1886 21

	SCVS	CMOS
Logic synthesis (YLE) time	243 sec.	226 sec.
Gates Transistors Levels Estimated delay (ns)	55 384 7 12.0	74 370 9 -

Figure 9. Synthesis results for the EDIT instruction

The description given corresponds only to the execution of the instruction, assuming that the operands were fetched and present at the inputs. The instruction *CODE* is only decoded for code *222*. Adding more instructions consists basically in introducing more cases to the *WHEN CODE* statement.

High-level synthesis generated just 2 control steps, one for initialization and one for the loop. The necessary registers were *L* and *FILL* of 8 bits each, and *SIGNIFIC, RL, DATAIN, COND* and a *State Register* all of 1 bit. The example is small enough to generate just one combinational block specified in YLL. The initial processing of the logic specification produced by YLL generates 333 functions. The number of literals serves as an estimate for the number of transistors. Logic synthesis (YLE) reduces them by 80% in the example. Notice that the data path basically consists of one incrementer / decrementer for *L*, several decoders to identify all the possible cases and multiplexers to assign different values.

A larger example is the 16 bit FRISC microprocessor from McPitts used as an example in [16]. High-level synthesis was done in 340 CPU seconds, yielding 36 control states and 103 register bits. Logic synthesis of the whole unpartitioned microprocessor was done using LSS[17] and required around 6 CPU hours. The combinational logic was mapped onto a typical CMOS standard-cell library, resulting in 4535 cells.

5. Conclusions and Outlook

In this paper we described in detail the algorithms for converting behavior as specified with an imperative language into a circuit structure. We showed that these algorithms preserve the behavior and produce a design that meets given hardware constraints. The transformations do not change the specified sequential algorithm but minimize the number of control steps needed.

The algorithms presented involve several np-hard steps:

- The computation of all cycles in the precedence graph and a minimal covering of these cycles by edges to make the precedence graph acyclic. In the current implementation these edges are given explicitly in the behavioral specification by the looping control constructs. Using Johnson's algorithm [18] we can also find the cycles in a general precedence graph.

- The computation of all paths in the precedence graph is used in several transformations. In the current implementation we indeed compute all these paths. In practice the number of paths is a measure of how many different functions a system can perform. Our largest examples had several thousand paths, which is still manageable in practice. Pathological cases have been detected, but these could always be modified changing slightly the behavioral specification so that a reasonable number of paths resulted. A heuristic we have tried when there are too many paths consists in computing the paths one by one and cutting not only the path with a detected constraint violation but the whole graph at this point.

- Recursive backtracking is used to determine the optimal cutting points of a path. This problem was solved by limiting the recursion depth. In practice, limiting this depth to 2 or 3 (i.e., finding the optimal cutting point for the first two or three cuts) showed no difference with the exact solution in our examples.

The algorithms presented are based on global analysis. The exact solutions provide optimal results. Practical limits of the system are reached with problems of the order of 1000 nodes.

Our system has two other limitations. First, the specified sequential algorithm given by the precedence relation of the operations is preserved in the sense that operations ordered in the original specification will either be executed in the same control step or in different control steps maintaining the order. No attempt to reorder the operations is done. A few simple transformations of this type are well known, e.g., moving an operation up or down if the data dependencies are not violated (e.g., [14]), unrolling iterations of fixed limits or converting sequences of equal operations into iterations. Preserving the specified precedence relation has another important consequence: the sequence of signals at input/output ports can be easily specified by giving them the right order. This allows the specification of interfaces to a certain extent without the need of special constructs in the specification language.

The second limitation is the lack of automatic means to synchronize two concurrent parts of a design. This complicates, for example, the automatic synthesis of pipelines. If a design involves concurrent parts, they must be designed independently taking care manually of the communication and synchronization between them. There are many ways to do this; however, it seems difficult to provide a single efficient synchronization scheme for all possible design kinds.

Other avenues for future improvements are faster algorithms, and a more thorough investigation of optimization techniques and partitioning.

References

[1]   M.C. McFarland, A.C. Parker, R. Camposano, "Tutorial on High-Level Synthesis," *Proceedings of the 25th Design Automation Conference*, pp. 330-336, Anaheim, California, June 1988.

[2]   R. Camposano, "Synthesis Techniques for Digital Systems Design," *Proceedings of the 22nd Design Automation Conference*, pp. 475-480, Las Vegas, June 1985.

[3]   D.E. Thomas, "Automatic Data Path Synthesis," in S. Goto, editor, *Advances in CAD for VLSI*, vol. 6, Design Methodologies, pp. 401-439, North-Holland, 1986.

[4]   R.K. Brayton, R. Camposano, G. DeMicheli, R.H.J.M. Otten and J.T.J. van Eijndhoven, "The Yorktown Silicon Compiler System," in D. Gajski, editor, *Silicon Compilation*, Addison-Wesley, 1988.

[5]   R. Camposano, "Structural Synthesis in the Yorktown Silicon Compiler," in C.H. Sequin, editor, *VLSI'87, VLSI Design of Digital Systems*, pp. 61-72, Vancouver: North-Holland, 1988.

[6]   M.C. McFarland, The Value Trace: A Data Base for Automated Digital Design, Design Research Center, Carnegie-Mellon University, Report DRC-01-4-80, December 1978.

[7]   R. Camposano and R. Weber, Semantik und interne Form von DSL, Karlsruhe: Faculty of Computer Science, University of Karlsruhe, Research Report Nr.3.85, 1985.

[8]   D.W. Knapp and A.C. Parker, "A Unified Representation for Design Information," *7th International Symposium on Computer Hardware Description Languages and their Applications*, pp. 337-353, Tokyo, August 1985.

[9]   A. Orailoglu and D.D. Gajski, "Flow Graph Representation," *Proceedings of the 23rd Design Automation Conference*, pp. 503-509, Las Vegas, June 1986.

[10] R. Camposano, R.M. Tabet, "Design Representation for the Synthesis of Behavioral VHDL Models," *Proceedings CHDL'89*, Washington, DC, June 1989.

[11] B.G. Ryder, M.C. Paul, "Elimination Algorithms for Data Flow Analysis," *ACM Computing Surveys*, vol. 18, no. 3, pp. 277-316, September 1986.

[12] F. Harary and E. Palmer, *Graphical Enumeration* New York: Academic Press, 1973.

[13] C.-J. Tseng, D.P. Siewiorek, "Automated Synthesis of Data Paths in Digital Systems," *IEEE Transactions on Computer-Aided Design*, vol. CAD-5, no. 3, pp. 379-395, July 1986.

[14] V. Berstis, "The V Compiler: Automatic Hardware Design," *IEEE Design & Test of Computers*, pp. 8-17, April 1989.

[15] International Business Machines, IBM System/370 Extended Architecture - Principles of Operation, 1983. Publication Number SA22-7085-0.

[16] V. Berstis, D. Brand, R. Nair, "An Experiment in Silicon Compilation," *1985 ISCAS Proceedings*, pp. 655-658, Kyoto, June 1985.

[17] L. Trevillyan and C. L. Berman, "A Global Approach to Circuit Size Reduction," *Advanced Research in VLSI: Proceedings of the 5th MIT Conference on VLSI*, pp. 203-214., March 1988.

[18] D.B. Johnson, "Finding all the Elementary Circuits of a Directed Graph," *SIAM Journal on Computing*, vol. 4, no. 1, pp. 77-84, March 1975.

From Programs to Transistors: Verifying Hardware Synthesis Tools

Geoffrey M. Brown
Miriam E. Leeser*

Abstract

We describe a project for synthesizing circuits from a high-level language description. The aims of this project are to guarantee the correctness of the resulting designs while allowing the designer flexibility in interacting with the system. In this paper we discuss two components of the project. The first starts with a state transition system and generates a specification of a datapath and an implementation of a controller as a microcode ROM. The second generates correct CMOS implementations of boolean expressions. This component produces highly optimized circuits which contain transmission gates as well as series and parallel networks of transistors. These two components are part of a larger goal: to go from programs to transistors with a flexible, yet guaranteed correct system.

1 Introduction

We are accelerating the process of proving the correctness of hardware by moving this process into the design cycle. In this paper, we discuss our progress in developing a flexible framework for the design of complex VLSI circuits by formalizing design rules and developing synthesis procedures to generate circuits that satisfy these design

---

*School of Electrical Engineering, Cornell University

rules. Because the design process itself is being proven, the amount of proof required for each individual design will be minimized.

Our synthesis technique starts with a description of hardware as a simple computer program. A program is a powerful, concise way of describing the behavior which we wish to implement. Such programs are verified using software verification techniques, and realized by successively refining the description into intermediate levels of description of behavior, down to a transistor realization of the circuit. Each level of translation will be verified using formal techniques. Our approach is illustrated in Figure 1.

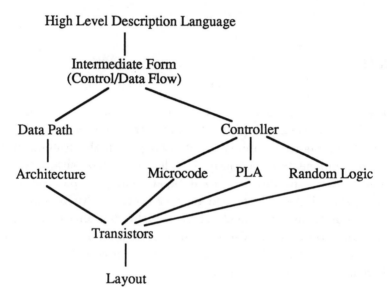

Figure 1: A Formal Synthesis System

We split the synthesis tasks into "high" and "low" levels. High-level tasks involve reasoning about programs, transforming these into state transition descriptions, and synthesizing register transfer level descriptions from the state transition systems. Low-level tasks involve transforming a circuit from a register transfer level description to a transistor level description.

This paper describes two components of this approach from programs to transistors. The first, an element of high-level synthesis, takes a circuit description in a conventional high-level language and produces a circuit implemented as a datapath and a controller. We assume the high-level language can be compiled into a state transition system and use the state transition system to generate a specification of the datapath and an implementation of the controller as a microcode ROM. We show how to use existing hardware verification techniques to ensure that the hardware correctly realizes the transition system.

The second component, part of low-level synthesis, concentrates on implementing hardware as networks of transistors. We generate transistor level implementations of boolean formulas in full complementary CMOS. Our component starts with boolean expressions, such as those output by logic synthesis systems, and applies synthesis rules to these expressions to realize them as networks of transistors. Currently, with only six rules our system generates highly optimized circuits which contain transmission gates as well as series and parallel networks. The system output can be implemented in silicon with a cell synthesis system [Mey88] or with sea-of-gates technology [Fuj88].

These two components are part of a larger project to go from programs to transistors in a formal yet flexible manner. Our synthesis procedures are being developed using the automated theorem prover Nuprl created at Cornell, thus assuring the correctness of our algorithms. The resulting system will allow the user to choose between different target implementations of the controller (e. g. microcode ROM vs. PLA), to choose between different target design styles (e. g. full complementary CMOS vs. domino logic), and to use handcrafted circuits in the synthesis system.

The remainder of this paper is organized as follows. We consider high-level synthesis in Section 2, where we present the approach to generating a datapath and a microcode ROM controller from a high-level description. In the section on low-level synthesis, Section 3, we present our algorithm for synthesizing combinational CMOS circuits. We conclude with a discussion of related research in Section 4.

2   High-level Synthesis

High-level synthesis is the activity of compiling hardware designs described in a high-level language into register transfer level descriptions. In this section we address the issue of validating such synthesis tools. In particular, we give an intermediate description language (state transition systems) and show how to prove hardware designs realized from such a description. In the remainder of this section we consider the following design process:

- The designer provides a high-level language description of the hardware to be synthesized.
- A compiler generates a state transition description of the hardware.
- The state transition description is used to synthesize a controller and datapath.

The state transition system referred to in this design process is an intermediate form in which all high-level control sequence primitives (e.g. while, if-then) have been replaced by explicit "goto's". The intermediate description is a convenient starting point for hardware realization because all state transitions, including changes to the "program counter," are expressed explicitly. However, its lack of structure makes reasoning about the implemented algorithm difficult at this level. A high-level language is better suited for design because its control structure admits formal reasoning about the hardware being developed.

Verifying the design process involves two major steps:

- Proving that the state transition systems compiled from the high-level language correctly implement the original program.
- Proving that the synthesized hardware correctly implements the state transition system.

In this section we discuss the second of these two steps through the development of an extended example. Previous work has addressed the verification of compilers [Pol81].

The remainder of this section is organized as follows. In Subsection 2.1 we present an example: the design of a multiplier. We begin with a program level description of such a circuit which is input by the designer. We then give a "compiled" state transition description and show how to realize this in hardware. In Subsection 2.2, we show how to verify that the synthesized hardware correctly implements the state transition description.

2.1 Design of a Multiplier

In this subsection, we develop a circuit to perform multiplication of two non-negative integers. The design begins with a program in an Algol-like language which describes the multiplication algorithm. We then present a "compiled" state transition description of the program and show how to realize the state transition description in hardware. The purpose of this example is to illustrate both the synthesis process and, in the next subsection, the process of verifying a high-level synthesis system.

The first step of the design process is to develop a program describing the algorithm to be implemented. The algorithm, illustrated in Figure 2, is the traditional shift-and-add implementation. (The notation "$\|$" is used to separate concurrently executed assignment statements.)

$$
\begin{aligned}
&\textbf{var } a, b, c : \textbf{ nat} \\
&a := A \parallel b := B \parallel c := 0; \\
&\textbf{while } a \neq 0 \quad \textbf{do} \\
&\qquad a := a \textbf{ div } 2 \parallel b := b * 2 \parallel c := c + b * (a \textbf{ mod } 2) \\
&\qquad \textbf{od}
\end{aligned}
$$

Figure 2: Multiplication Algorithm

The next step of the design process is to "compile" the program description of the multiplier into a state transition system. We use three types of state transitions: an assignment followed by an unconditional branch, a conditional branch, and a halt. The assignments in the transitions may be arbitrarily complex. In this example they correspond exactly to the assignments in the original program. The transition system for the multiplier is given in Figure 3.

$$
\begin{aligned}
&\textbf{begin} \\
&0: \ a := A \parallel b := B \parallel c := 0; \ \textbf{goto } 1; \\
&1: \ \textbf{if } a \neq 0 \textbf{ then goto } 2 \textbf{ else goto } 3 \textbf{ fi}; \\
&2: \ a := a \textbf{ div } 2 \parallel b := b * 2 \parallel c := c + b * (a \textbf{ mod } 2); \ \textbf{goto } 1; \\
&3: \ \textbf{halt} \\
&\textbf{end}
\end{aligned}
$$

Figure 3: Transition System for Multiplier

Finally, the state transition system is realized in hardware as a datapath and a controller. Our transition system requires that the datapath be capable of updating all three registers simultaneously. One such datapath is illustrated in Figure 4. Notice that each of the registers has two command inputs and a data input. The command inputs (e.g. *aload* and *aright*) are used by the controller to request state changes. For example, to perform the assignment of transition 0, the controller would hold the three command lines *aload*, *bload*, and *cclear* high for one clock cycle while holding the other command lines low. The datapath provides the state predicate required by the controller ($a = 0$) as output *azero*. The datapath can be formally specified as a set of recurrence equations describing the temporal behavior of the three registers and the output:

$$
\begin{aligned}
a(t+1) = \quad & \textbf{if } aload(t) \textbf{ then } A \textbf{ elsif } aright(t) \\
& \textbf{then } (a(t) \textbf{ div } 2) \textbf{ else } a(t) \textbf{ fi} \\
b(t+1) = \quad & \textbf{if } bload(t) \textbf{ then } B \textbf{ elsif } bleft(t) \textbf{ then} (b(t) * 2) \textbf{ else } b(t) \textbf{ fi} \\
c(t+1) = \quad & \textbf{if } cclear(t) \textbf{ then } 0 \textbf{ elsif } cload(t) \\
& \textbf{then } (c(t) + b(t) * (a(t) \textbf{ mod } 2)) \textbf{ else } c(t) \textbf{ fi} \\
azero(t) = \quad & (a(t) = 0)
\end{aligned}
$$

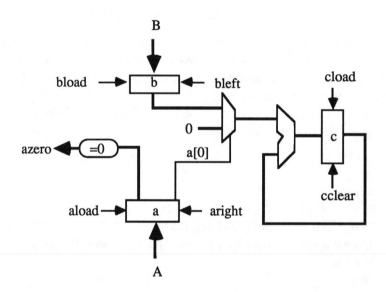

Figure 4: Multiplier Datapath

The controller provides the mechanism for sequencing between transitions and for issuing commands to the datapath. One possible realization of the controller for the multiplier is the microcode ROM illustrated in Figure 5. The current control state *pc* and the value of *azero* are used as addresses into the microcode ROM which produces as output the next control state and the current values of the command lines to the datapath. A complete multiplier consists of the datapath, ROM, and a register to hold the current control state. The behavior of the controller is described by a set of recurrence equations. The current microcode instruction at time t is $2 * pc(t) + azero(t)$. If we use the notation $rom[address].output$ to denote the value of *output* (e.g. *next*, *aload*) at ROM location *address*, then the value of the program counter at time $(t + 1)$ is:

$$pc(t + 1) = rom[2 * pc(t) + azero(t)].next$$

This equation assumes a delay of one clock period introduced by the program counter. The other outputs of the microcode ROM are defined by equations of the form:

$$aload(t) = rom[2 * pc(t) + azero(t)].aload$$

pc	azero	next	aload	aright	bload	bleft	cclear	cload
0	0	1	1	0	1	0	1	0
0	1	1	1	0	1	0	1	0
1	0	2	0	0	0	0	0	0
1	1	3	0	0	0	0	0	0
2	0	1	0	1	0	1	0	1
2	1	1	0	1	0	1	0	1
3	0	3	0	0	0	0	0	0
3	1	3	0	0	0	0	0	0

Figure 5: ROM Implementation of Controller

2.2 Correctness of the Multiplier Implementation

We presented the design of a simple multiplier from an initial program level description to a datapath and controller. The synthesis process involved two major steps – the compilation of the original program into a state transition system and the realization of the state transitions in hardware. In this subsection we show how to use existing hardware verification techniques to ensure that the hardware correctly realizes the transition system. We begin by giving a precise description of our transition language. In particular we give an operational semantics which describes the process of executing a transition system. The semantics is given as a set of transition rules of which we present a subset. Verifying the hardware realization consists of demonstrating that the values of the registers at times $(t+1)$ and (t) are related by one of the transition rules.

The transition rules define changes to the system state using notation of the form

$$\langle pc, \sigma \rangle \rightarrow \langle pc', \sigma' \rangle$$

where, pc and σ denote the control state and data state, respectively, before the transition is executed. Similarly pc' and σ' denote the control state and data state after the transition is executed. In Figure 6 we give the two transition rules for a conditional branch. Each rule has an enabling condition consisting of the transition corresponding to the current control state and a constraint on the data states in which the rule may be applied. The notation $\sigma(E)$ is used to denote the value of expression E in state σ; Γ_i denotes transition i of the transtion set Γ. The rules for the assignment and halt statements are similar. In all system states, exactly one transition rule applies.

$$\frac{\Gamma_i = \textbf{if E then goto } j \textbf{ else goto } k \textbf{ fi} \qquad \sigma(\text{E}) = true}{\langle i, \sigma \rangle \rightarrow \langle j, \sigma \rangle}$$

$$\frac{\Gamma_i = \textbf{if E then goto } j \textbf{ else goto } k \textbf{ fi} \qquad \sigma(\text{E}) = false}{\langle i, \sigma \rangle \rightarrow \langle k, \sigma \rangle}$$

Figure 6: Transition Rules

It remains to demonstrate that the datapath and controller presented in the preceding section correctly implement the transitions in Figure 3. There are two rows in the controller ROM of Figure 5 corresponding to each transition. Verifying the hardware realization consists of checking that the state change caused by "executing" the ROM row accessed by the current state is consistent with "executing" the transition rule enabled in that state. For example, assume that the system is in a state where $pc = 1$ and $a \neq 0$. The statement from the transition system to be executed is 1, and the enabled transition is:

$$\langle\, 1,\, \sigma \,\rangle \rightarrow \langle\, 2,\, \sigma \,\rangle$$

From the recurrence equations defining the controller and the datapath:

$$pc(t) = 1 \;\wedge\; azero(t) = 0 \;\Rightarrow$$
$$pc(t+1) = 2 \;\wedge\; a(t+1) = a(t) \;\wedge\; b(t+1) = b(t) \;\wedge\; c(t+1) = c(t)$$

we see that the transition is correctly realized. By checking the other rows of the ROM, we can completely verify the hardware.

3   Low-level Synthesis

Our work on low-level synthesis concentrates on implementing hardware as networks of transistors. This work interfaces with the work on high-level synthesis at the state transition system level. In the previous section we described how a program description of a hardware module can be compiled into a state transition system and shown how such a state transition system can be viewed as a specification of a datapath and a microcode implementation of a controller. Microcode ROM is, however, only one possible implementation of such a description. We may also wish to implement our controller with a programmable logic device or with random logic. The datapath must also be synthesized out of real hardware components.

At the low-level we are therefore interested in modeling hardware components and in proving the synthesis rules used for combining these components into hardware modules. To accomplish this for combinational hardware, we have developed a system which generates a transistor level implementation of a boolean formula in full complementary CMOS. Our system starts with boolean expressions, such as those output by logic synthesis systems, manipulates these expressions and realizes them as a network of transistors. This translation is driven by the syntax-directed application of synthesis rules. Currently, with only six basic rules, our system generates highly optimized circuits which contain transmission gates as well as series and parallel networks. The system output can be implemented in silicon with a cell synthesis system [Mey88] or with sea-of-gates technology [Fuj88].

Our algorithm has been formally verified and implemented within the Nuprl proof development system [C+86]. Within Nuprl a theory of combinational hardware has been developed, where the synthesis rules are represented as statements about the logical equivalence of CMOS representations. The rules are formally proved and are used, along with their correctness proofs, in a rewrite package which simultaneously applies the transformations and constructs a proof of correctness for each circuit it synthesizes. This synthesis process always terminates, and the synthesized circuit faithfully implements its logical specification.

Our correctness claim is with respect to an explicit model of transistor behavior. In addition to modeling boolean behavior, we also require that when the inputs are strongly driven so are the outputs, and that the circuit contains no short circuits. Just as each synthesis rule was formally proved to preserve logical meaning, each rule was also proved to preserve current drive.

Our methodology is quite flexible. New synthesis rules may be added to the system to allow the introduction of arbitrary circuits simply by proving that they preserve function and drive. Furthermore, our approach allows circuits that are not synthesized according to our algorithm to be connected to those which are, without compromising correctness. A hand-crafted circuit must simply be proven with respect to our model of behavior. Allowing synthesized components to be interfaced to hand-crafted ones gives the designer more flexibility than is available with many synthesis systems.

The remainder of this section is organized as follows. In the next subsection we discuss our hardware models. Then, in Subsection 3.2 we describe the algorithm. The algorithm and its implementation are discussed in more detail elsewhere [BBL89]. Finally, in Subsection 3.3 we present some examples.

3.1 Hardware Models

We can show, by formal proof, that our synthesis transformations preserve the required behavior of a circuit. Specifically we can show:

- The behavior of the circuit is preserved by the transformations.
- If the specification guarantees that the output is strongly driven, then the synthesized circuit also has its output strongly driven.

Our correctness guarantees are proven with respect to a formal transistor model. The transistor model is then used to prove, for each transformation, that the stated properties hold. We use mathematical logic to model circuits, and theorem proving techniques to assure their correctness. Our transistor models are based on those used by Gordon [CGM86] and Hoare [Hoa88].

A transistor is modeled as a switch. For example, consider an n-type transistor with gate, source and drain labeled g, s, and d respectively. We model its behavior as follows. When the gate is active, the switch is on and the source and drain nodes are connected. When the gate is inactive, the switch is off, and the source and drain nodes are isolated from one another. The behavior of a p-type transistor can be described similarly. At this level, no distinction is made between the behaviors of the source and the drain nodes. We express this behavior in predicate logic by defining relations ptrans and ntrans which are true when the gate, source, and drain nodes have the relationship defined above. We use predicate calculus to express this behavior. The logic operators *not* ($\neg$), *and* ($\wedge$), and *or* ($\vee$) should be familiar from boolean algebra. In addition we use *is defined by* ($\equiv$), *equivalence* ($\Leftrightarrow$), *implies* ($\Rightarrow$), *for all* ($\forall$) and *there exists* ($\exists$). The constant 1 stands for both logical true, and a high voltage. Similarly 0 stands for logical false, and a low voltage.

$$\text{ntrans}(g, s, d) \equiv (g \Leftrightarrow 1) \Rightarrow (s \Leftrightarrow d)$$
$$\text{ptrans}(g, s, d) \equiv (g \Leftrightarrow 0) \Rightarrow (s \Leftrightarrow d)$$

These formulas model the switching behavior of the transistors. We may also wish to model other aspects of transistor behavior, including drive, capacitance, and delay. We can model these behavioral aspects as projections of our basic switching model. For example, n-type transistors can only propagate logical 0's between source and drain without signal degradation. A signal is *strongly driven* if it is propagated without signal degradation; otherwise, it is *weakly driven*. The drive projection of ntrans is the predicate $\delta\text{ntrans}(g, s, d)$. δx is true of a signal x if x is strongly driven. δntrans is true of an n-type transistor if the following conditions hold: (i) its gate is high, (ii) it is transmitting a 0 (i. e. s and d are both low), (iii) its gate is strongly driven, and (iv) the drive on s and d are the same. We express this, as well as a similar relation δptrans, by the following formulas:

$$\delta\mathsf{ntrans}(g, s, d) \equiv g \wedge \neg s \wedge \neg d \wedge \delta g \quad \Rightarrow \quad (\delta s \Leftrightarrow \delta d)$$
$$\delta\mathsf{ptrans}(g, s, d) \equiv \neg g \wedge s \wedge d \wedge \delta g \quad \Rightarrow \quad (\delta s \Leftrightarrow \delta d)$$

A circuit's behavior is specified by an n-ary relation, $R(a_0, ..., a_n)$, and is built from logical connectives ($\wedge$, $\vee$, $\neg$, and others), quantifiers ($\exists$ and $\forall$), constants (0 and 1), and inputs (represented by the literals a_i). We represent CMOS by predicates built exclusively from the two relations **ptrans** and **ntrans**. Most of the circuits that we discuss have several inputs and one output. We assume that inputs and their negations are available. The variable z is used to designate the output. This approach is easily extended to describe circuits with multiple outputs; we simply specify the behavior of each output separately.

Any circuit may be characterized by one relation which specifies when the output of that circuit is high. Since we do not allow undefined outputs, we assume that whenever the output is not high it is low. Hence one relation totally specifies the output of the circuit. We will however use two relations: the first, R_1, specifies the conditions which make the output high, and the second, its complement R_2, specifies the conditions which make the output low. Our algorithm implements R_1 with p-type transistors and R_2 with n-type transistors. For CMOS, this guarantees that 0's are propagated through a network of n-type transistors, and that 1's are propagated through a network of p-type transistors. This two relation approach aids our optimization of synthesized CMOS circuits.

3.2   The Synthesis Algorithm

Our synthesis algorithm takes two complementary relations R_1 and R_2 as input and returns an equivalent transistor network and a proof of correctness. The algorithm is separated into five steps: boolean simplification, network realization, further boolean simplification, network expansion, and finally network simplification. A "network" is a set of transistors which may not yet represent a circuit, as the gates of the transistors may be connected to arbitrarily complex boolean expressions instead of inputs. Each of the five steps can be viewed as instances of term rewriting.

The first step, boolean simplification, consists of manipulating the behavioral specifications R_1 and R_2. Here, our goal is to produce two simpler propositional relations R_1' and R_2' that are logically equivalent to R_1 and R_2. At the end of step 1, R_1'

and R'_2 must contain only conjuncts, disjuncts, negation, the input variables, and the constants 0 and 1.

In the second step, we create a simple two node network, consisting of one p-type transistor and one n-type transistor. The p-type transistor has one channel node connected to power and the other connected to the output. The n-type transistor has one channel node connected to ground and the other connected to the output. We label the gate of the p-type transistor with the negation of R'_1, and the gate of the n-type transistor with R'_2.

In the third step, the relations labeling the two gates are again simplified. All negations are pushed down through the expression to the literals with DeMorgan's laws, and double negations are eliminated. The effect of these transformations is that the two gates are now labeled by simple propositional relations: those consisting of only conjuncts, disjuncts, literals, and their negations. The particularly simple form of these propositions reduces the number of synthesis rules needed in the remaining steps.

Note that up until this point our synthesis algorithm has consisted of manipulating boolean formulas. We do not manipulate circuit components, i.e. p-type and n-type transistors, until step four.

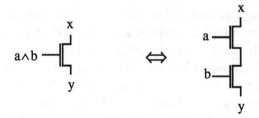

a) $\mathrm{ntrans}(a \wedge b, x, y) \Leftrightarrow \exists z.\ (\mathrm{ntrans}(a, x, z) \wedge \mathrm{ntrans}(b, z, y))$

Figure 7: A Transformation for Transistor Networks

The fourth step consists of expanding each transistor into a network of transistors whose gates are connected either to an input or to the negation of an input. One of these transformations is shown in Figure 7. These four transformation rules correspond to the two types of transistors and the two types of logical connectives. These rules are continually applied until each transistor is driven by an input or a negated input. As the relations R'_1 and R'_2 contain finitely many connectives and each transformation diminishes the number of gate connectives in the network, this expansion must terminate.

Although our foremost interest is in preserving circuit correctness with respect to behavior and drive, we cannot ignore the issue of optimization. Circuits may be optimized in the first step of our algorithm by minimizing the number of connectives in the relations R_1 and R_2. But we want to consider other simplifications that are not realizable as boolean simplifications. Such transformations are permitted provided they are proved correct with respect to our model.

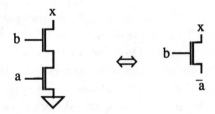

a) **if** $\bar{a} \wedge b \Rightarrow x$ **then** ntrans(a,0,y)$\wedge$ntrans(b,y,x) $\Leftrightarrow$ ntrans(b,$\bar{a}$,x)

Figure 8: A Restricted Transformation

The fifth step allows for direct circuit optimization by applying restricted, or conditional, transformations to our expanded CMOS network. The transformation shown in Figure 8 is an example of this and is valid only under certain circumstances. We have a similar transformation for p-type transistors. These transformations allow us to remove one transistor in a chain, by replacing a connection to power or ground with a connection to an input. This is a valid optimization only if the output of the chain would have always been strongly driven (either by the chain, or by its environment) before the optimization is made, and given that the transformation does not introduce a short. Note that the application of these restricted transformations results in pass transistor networks.

The application of all six of these transformations is deterministic. In other words, a boolean equation specifying when the output is high determines a unique p-type transistor network. Similarly, a boolean equation specifying when the output is low specifies a unique n-type transistor network. Note that the applicability of the conditional CMOS transformations depends upon the specific network synthesized by the first four steps. This in turn depends on the specification of R_1 and R_2 and the logical optimizations performed in step 1. Hence, by using two relations instead of one, we can separately customize the two networks and produce smaller circuits.

We have not yet explained how we produce proofs of correctness in addition to synthesizing CMOS circuits. However, the basic idea is simple. Each of the five steps consists of applying proven transformations. The transformation proofs of correctness are pieced together as each transformation is applied; the resulting proof states the correctness of the entire transformation. A similar proof of the drive of the output can also be generated. We have proved that each of our transformations preserves drive, i. e. that the output will be strongly driven if the inputs are strongly driven. We can piece together the proof that drive is preserved for each transformation to generate a proof that the output is strongly driven for the synthesized circuit, given that the inputs are strongly driven. This proof synthesis is an artifact of the rewrite package in which our algorithm is implemented.

The synthesis algorithm has been implemented within Nuprl, a proof development system designed and developed at Cornell. Nuprl's logic is a higher-order type theory, well suited for reasoning about mathematically formalizable objects such as boolean formulas and the switching behavior of transistors. The system itself features: sophisticated editors that support the interactive development of definitions and proofs; a high level meta-language, ML, that facilitates the development of tactics which are programs that automate theorem proving; and powerful decision procedures for arithmetic reasoning. A more detailed description of Nuprl and its application to formal methods in hardware is given elsewhere [BD89].

The implementation of the synthesis algorithm consists of a rewriting component and the rules that it applies. These rewrite rules state the transformations discussed above. The proof of each of these transformations was completely automated using tactics developed in Nuprl. In addition, the drive projection of each of the transistor transformation rules was also proved automatically. The implementation, discussed in [BBL89], requires only six lines of ML code: the first five lines of code correspond directly to the five steps of our algorithm, and the final line sequences them. Not only is the implementation concise, but the algorithm is also easy to extend. The user can add new rules by proving their correctness and adding the corresponding transformation to the appropriate rewrite step. As any new transformation must be associated with a theorem in the Nuprl library, extensions are guaranteed to be correct.

3.3 Experience

We have used our system to synthesize several CMOS circuits which have roughly the complexity of cells in a standard cell library. These circuits include standard logic components such as nands, nors, comparators, multiplexers, and adders.

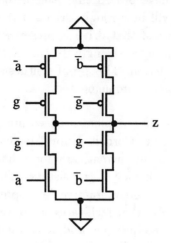

Figure 9: A Parallel/Serial 2-to-1 Multiplexer

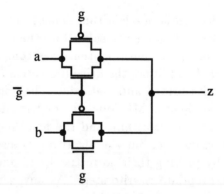

Figure 10: A Better Implementation of a 2-to-1 Multiplexer

Multiplexers

Consider a 2-to-1 multiplexer, whose behavior is specified by the formula:

$$z \equiv (\neg g \wedge a) \vee (g \wedge b)$$

If we map this into simple gates, this circuit requires two 2-input **and** gates, and one 2-input **or** gate, which in a full CMOS design style requires 12 transistors. If we implement the multiplexer in our system with the restricted rules turned off, we get a series/parallel implementation which employs 8 transistors. This implementation is shown in Figure 9. If we implement the multiplexer in our system using the restricted rules we get two transmission gates for the implementation, or 4 transistors, as shown in Figure 10. This simple example illustrates the flexibility and advantages of our approach.

Adder Circuits

We have used our system to synthesize several adder components, including the **sumpart** and **carrypart** of the adder shown in Figure 11 and in Weste and Eshraghian [WE85] Figure 8.4. This example illustrates our ability to synthesize circuits with multiple outputs by synthesizing each output and its related inputs as separate modules. In addition, it demonstrates how our system would interact with a boolean minimization system such as Espresso [BHMSV86]. We assume that $\overline{carry}$ has been factored out of the **sumpart** of the adder before the appropriate boolean formulas for *sum* and *carry* are input to our system.

We have described how a straightforward synthesis algorithm can be formally verified to guarantee that the generated circuits are correct. The major drawback of this approach is that not all correct CMOS networks can be generated with our algorithm. For example the highly optimized **sumpart** component, shown in Figure 12 cannot be derived in this manner. This implementation utilizes a **bridge** network which takes advantage of bidirectional transistors. This implementation makes better use of area than the **sumpart** we synthesized since it requires only 12 transistors. The one we synthesized required 14 transistors. We treat this and similar networks as special cases. They may be interfaced to our synthesized networks provided that the designer can prove, using the transistor models we have defined, that the required output conditions are met. We have proved that this circuit correctly implements the

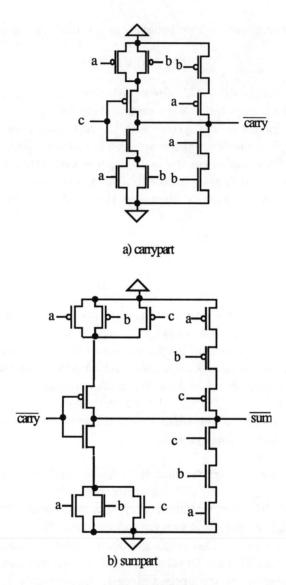

a) carrypart

b) sumpart

Figure 11: A CMOS adder

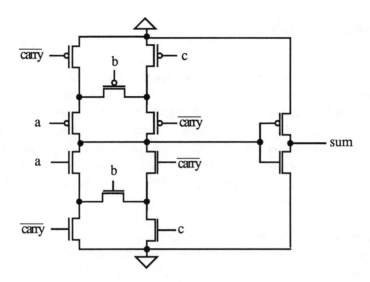

Figure 12: The sumpart of a CMOS adder

sumpart of an adder and that it meets its drive requirements; we can therefore use it as part of a larger adder circuit.

The synthesis of combinational CMOS illustrates our approach to low-level synthesis. We view the process as manipulating systems of boolean equations, and factoring these equations into components which can be synthesized with our techniques. We have successfully applied this approach to the synthesis of circuits which are expressed as networks of boolean formulas. The implementations produced by our synthesis system are highly optimized and make extensive use of pass transistors. We can extend this approach by specifying circuits recursively, and synthesizing them by unwinding the recursive specification. This allows us to take advantage of regular structures, and to synthesize only once components that will be used many times. This will allow our approach to easily scale to large circuits. An example of this is the inductive synthesis of an n-bit adder from 1-bit adder slices. Each adder slice is built out of a **sumpart** and **carrypart**.

4 Related Work

Our goal is to guarantee the correctness of hardware by proving the correctness of the software design tools used to develop that hardware. While many of the subproblems that must be solved to realize our methodology have been studied previously, no one has gone from programs to hardware with a verified approach. The most closely related ongoing research has explored the issue of correct execution of high-level programs by conventional processors. Other related research areas include synthesis of self-timed circuits, verifying asynchronous circuits, and formally proving low-level design tools for VLSI synthesis.

There have been a number of projects to verify compilers from high-level languages to the machine codes of specific processors [Pol81,Moo88,Joy89]. More recently, research projects at Computational Logic, Inc. [BHY87,Moo88,Hun86] and at Cambridge University Computer Laboratory [Coh88,Joy89] have begun developing "vertically verified computing systems." The goal in these projects is to develop computing systems in which each layer of the architectural hierarchy is proved to be correctly implemented by the lower levels. This hierarchy consists of an operating system, compiler, and processor. The processors in these projects were designed and then proved using traditional *post-hoc* methods. This work is impressive and important for the guaranteed correctness of software, especially in safety critical applications, and because it explores a wide range of system correctness issues. However, it does not address the problem that we propose to solve – the development of correct hardware design tools.

Martin and Burns have shown how to compile programs into self-timed circuits [BM88,Mar86]. They provide axiomatic descriptions of basic building blocks (e. g. and, or, arbiter, etc.) in terms of a simple programming language. They then design circuits as programs and compile these into primitive elements using program transformations. Recently they have used this approach to design an asynchronous microprocessor [MB+89]. Although their approach is similar to ours, their target design style is limited to self-timed circuits. Our approach, while geared to synchronous circuits, is more general purpose. In addition, the correctness of their approach is dependent upon the soundness of the programs describing their primitive elements. They do not provide a means for relating these programs to more sophisticated hardware models.

Mishra, Clarke, and Dill have used a computer program to automatically verify that an asynchronous circuit meets its temporal logic specification [BCDM86]. In this case, formal reasoning was performed at the level of primitive circuit elements rather than at the level of programming language descriptions of hardware. Our goal is to reason about hardware directly at the program level in order to build upon the existing work for verifying concurrent programs.

Johnson has used functional programming languages to develop verified digital designs to the register transfer level [Joh84]. The principal deficiency with this approach is that nondeterminism and hence concurrency is difficult to describe and reason about. Our goal is to directly reason about programs with concurrency that can be formally related to sophisticated hardware models.

Our work on low-level synthesis is directed at proving programs for producing hardware. While there exist programs for compiling low-level language descriptions of hardware directly into controllers described as PLAs (Programmable Logic Arrays) [DSV83] or into microcode [Hen81], these programs have not been verified. Milne [Mil83] describes proving the correctness of a simple silicon compiler which produces hardware from nor expressions. Although the silicon compiler is not very practical, it demonstrates how such a compiler could be proved. In a related work, Joyce has given a proof of the hardware to implement a generic PLA [Joy87]. Thus, given a correct PLA specification (in our case generated by a verified finite-state-machine synthesis program) we can generate correct hardware.

Acknowledgements

David Basin, a graduate student in Computer Science at Cornell University, implemented the CMOS synthesis algorithm with the Nuprl proof development system.

References

[BBL89]   David A. Basin, G. M. Brown, and M. E. Leeser. Formally verified synthesis of combinational CMOS circuits. Technical Report EE-CEG-89-7, Cornell University School of Electrical Engineering, April 1989.

[BCDM86]   M. C. Browne, E. M. Clarke, D. L. Dill, and B. Mishra. Automatic verification of sequential circuits using temporal logic. *IEEE Transactions on Computers*, C-35(12):1035–1043, December 1986.

[BD89]   David Basin and Peter DelVecchio. Verification of combinational logic in Nuprl. In these proceedings, July 1989.

[BHMSV86] R. K. Brayton, G. D. Hatchtel, C. T. McMullen, and A. L. Sangiovanni-Vincentelli. *Logic Minimization Algorithms for VLSI Synthesis*. Kluwer Academic Publishers, 1986.

[BHY87]   William R. Bevier, Warren A. Hunt, Jr., and William D. Young. Toward verified execution environments. In *Proceedings of the IEEE Symposium on Security and Privacy*, pages 106–115, April 1987.

[BM88]   S. Burns and A. Martin. Synthesis of self-timed circuits by program transformation. In G. Milne, editor, *International Working Conference on The Fusion of Hardware Design and Verification*, pages 97–115, 1988.

[C+86]   R. L. Constable et al. *Implementing Mathematics with the Nuprl Proof Development System*. Prentice Hall, 1986.

[CGM86]   A. J. Camillieri, M. J. C. Gordon, and T. F. Melham. Hardware verification using higher-order logic. In D. Borrione, editor, *From HDL Descriptions to Guaranteed Correct Circuit Designs*. North Holland, September 1986.

[Coh88]   Avra Cohn. A proof of correctness of the viper microprocessor: The first level. In *VLSI Specification, Verification, and Synthesis*, pages 27–71. Kluwer Academic Publishers, 1988.

[DSV83]   G. DeMicheli, A. Sangiovanni-Vincentelli, and T. Villa. Computer-aided synthesis of PLA-based finite state machines. In *IEEE International Conference on Computer Aided Design*, 1983.

[Fuj88]   Aki Fujimara. Automating the layout of very large gate arrays. *VLSI Systems Design*, pages 22–27, April 1988.

[Hen81]   J. Hennessy. SLIM: A simulation and implementation language for VLSI microcode. *Lambda*, pages 20–28, 1981. Second Quarter.

[Hoa88]   C. A. R. Hoare. A calculus for the derivation of C-MOS switching circuits. Draft, April 1988.

[Hun86]   W. A. Hunt, Jr. *FM8501: A Verified Microprocessor*. PhD thesis, Institute for Computing Science, The University of Texas at Austin, 1986.

[Joh84]   S. D. Johnson. *Synthesis of Digital Designs*. MIT Press, 1984. ACM Distinguished Dissertation.

[Joy87]   Jeffrey Joyce. Hardware verification of VLSI regular structures. Technical Report 109, Cambridge University Computer Laboratory, July 1987.

[Joy89]   Jeffrey Joyce. A verified compiler for a verified microprocessor. Technical Report 167, Cambridge University Computer Laboratory, March 1989.

[Mar86]   A. Martin. Compiling communicating processes into delay-insensitive VLSI circuits. *Distributed Computing*, 1(3), 1986.

[MB⁺89]   Alain J. Martin, Steven M. Burns, et al. The design of an asynchronous microprocessor. In *Advanced Research in VLSI*, pages 351–373. The MIT Press, 1989.

[Mey88]   Ernest Meyer. Cell synthesis in action. *VLSI Systems Design*, pages 52–60, May 1988.

[Mil83]   George J. Milne. The correctness of a simple silicon compiler. In T. Uehara and M. Barbacci, editors, *Computer Hardware Description Languages and Their Applications*, pages 1–12. North Holland, 1983.

[Moo88]   J. S. Moore. A mechanically verified language implementation. Technical Report 30, Computational Logic Incorporated, 1988.

[Pol81]   W. H. Polak. Compiler specification and verification. In *Lecture Notes in Computer Science No. 124*. Springer Verlag, 1981.

[WE85]   N. Weste and K. Eshraghian. *Principles of CMOS VLSI Design: A Systems Perspective*. Addison-Wesley Publishing Company, 1985.

COMBINING ENGINEERING VIGOR WITH MATHEMATICAL RIGOR§

Shiu-Kai Chin

Syracuse University, Syracuse, New York

"You always debug the simulation using the hardware."

- An anonymous designer

"The designer always picks the test vectors which work."

- An anonymous designer

"Every time I design another counter I get paid more money."

- Another anonymous designer

Abstract. *Higher order logic and a functional language are used to document and verify design procedures which correctly synthesize array multipliers of arbitrary size. The procedures work with general negabinary inputs and create design descriptions corresponding to practical designs which are correct-by-construction.*

1. INTRODUCTION

Hardware design has two identifiable phases: design synthesis and design verification [8]. The result of design synthesis is the creation of a network of hardware components. The result of design verification is demonstrating the function performed by the hardware is the same as the specified function. Often, synthesis methods or design heuristics are automated within a computer-aided design system or program. The methods and programs are not proved to be correct thus all designs produced by the programs must be verified using post-hoc methods. Typically, verification is done by *tautology checking*, i.e. showing that the relation $f_{hardware} = f_{specification}$ is a tautology. Conventional approaches to design verification rely on *boolean comparison*, i.e. exhaustive boolean case analysis or exhaustive simulation to show equivalence, [12,2]. Simulation-based and boolean comparison-based methods are

§This work was partially supported by NSF Grant MIP-8710826, IBM Contract 845, and RADC Contract F30602-87-C-0215

fundamentally limited by the potential for an exponential growth in representation size or computational effort with respect to hardware parameters like input word size. For example, [2] proves that directed acyclic graphs used to represent digital multiplier circuits grow exponentially with respect to input word size. Considering the increasingly large number of devices fabricated on very large scale integrated (VLSI) circuits, proving that an implementation meets its specification will become increasingly difficult if not practically impossible using conventional methods alone.

Several approaches have been suggested to address the increasing complexity of VLSI design and verification. [6] and [7] use predicate calculus as a hardware description and specification language. In both cases, *post-hoc* proof is employed to reconcile the implementation and specification descriptions. [5] uses the HOL proof assistant while [7] uses the Boyer-Moore theorem prover. Savings in design representation and verification relative to conventional approaches are obtained by capitalizing on the greater expressive power of predicate calculus relative to the propositional calculus on which conventional boolean comparison-based techniques rely. For example, recursive hardware descriptions and inductive proof exemplify this additional power. Unfortunately, the increased descriptive power complicates the proof procedures to such an extent that the post-hoc verification proofs are relatively inaccessible to design engineers unfamiliar with formal methods.

Special design languages with formal properties have also been proposed. [11] proposes a design language μFP based on Backus's FP language [1]. Like FP, μFP has an associated algebra which allows one circuit description to be equated with another.

The work presented here attempts to address the problems implied by the three quotes at the beginning of this paper: *1) inaccurate design descriptions, 2) incomplete design verification due to incomplete simulation, and 3) undocumented procedures used to create designs.* This paper formally documents *design procedures* or *design heuristics* which create the functional forms corresponding to hardware descriptions of adder arrays capable of summing arbitrarily sized arrays of *signed numbers.* These procedures are a subset of the procedures used to create *Pezaris* [9] multipliers. The functions which create the functional forms are called *hardware meta-functions.* The meta-functions are defined using higher order logic, formally verified using the HOL proof assistant, and implemented in SCHEME [10]. In contrast to [6] and [7], post-hoc proof is unnecessary to formally verify the hardware descriptions as all the design descriptions created by the meta-functions are *correct-by-construction.* In contrast to [11], machine usable correctness theorems are developed concurrently with the meta-functions along with *value functions* which relate one representation to another, e.g. ternary representations and integers. The correctness theorems show the validity of substituting a functional implementation for a functional specification. The value functions define the intended interpretation of input and output representations used by the synthesized hardware.

The *combination* of machine executable hardware meta-functions, theorems, and proofs of correctness makes the results of formal methods more accessible to design engineers who are not familiar with formal methods. While the verification of the meta-functions requires a knowledge of formal methods, once they have been verified the use of the meta-functions and theorems requires much less knowledge of formal methods. Specifically:

- Designs are created by applying the meta-functions to the appropriate inputs,
- Simple substitution of the meta-function input parameters into the correctness theorems immediately equates implementations to their specifications, and
- Machine executable proofs may be taken on faith or executed and observed to whatever detail is necessary to convince the observer of the validity of the correctness theorems.

2. OVERVIEW OF HIGHER ORDER LOGIC

The notation of higher order logic is summarized in this section. A complete description appears in [5].

Higher order logic uses the standard predicate calculus notation. Function applications and predicates have the form $F(x)$ or the more Lisp-like syntax *(F x)*; logical operators *not, and, or,* and *implies* are denoted by $\sim$, $\wedge$, $\vee$, and $\supset$; conditional expressions like *if c then e_1 else e_2* are denoted by $c \rightarrow e_1 / e_2$; universal and existential quantifiers are denoted by $\forall$ and $\exists$. Unlike first order logics (e.g. the logic underlying PROLOG), higher order logic allows the use of higher order variables.

2.1 Terms

There are four kinds of terms: variables, constants, function applications, and λ-abstractions. Variables and constants stand for values. Function applications have the form $t_1(t_2)$ or $(t_1 \; t_2)$ where t_1 and t_2 are terms. Functions can be higher order and are left-associative. λ-abstractions have the usual form $\lambda var.term$. Function applications also have the form *let x = term in expression* which is syntactic sugar for *($\lambda x.expression$)term*, i.e. replace *term* everywhere x appears free in *expression*.

2.2 Types

All terms have a type where types are expressions denoting sets of values. There are type constants, type variables, and compound types. Type constants denote sets of values like the booleans (*bool*) or natural numbers (*num*).

Type variables denote "any type" and typically are represented by α, β, etc. Type variables are convenient for describing functions which operate on terms of more than one type, e.g. the empty list predicate *NULL*.

Compound types are constructed from other types using type operators. Compound types have the form $(\sigma_1, \ldots, \sigma_n)op$ where σ_1 through σ_n are types and *op* in an n-ary type operator. Type operators include *list, fun* (also denoted by →), and *prod* (also denoted by ×). Thus, the list of natural numbers *[1;2;3;4]* is of type *(num)list*, the function $\lambda x.x+1$ is of type *num→num*, and the pair $(T,\lambda x.x*x)$ is of type *(bool×(num→num))*. The type operator → is right associative.

Terms are explicitly typed using the infix operator ":". For example, the variable x is specified to be a boolean, natural number, or arbitrary function by the corresponding expression: *x:bool, x:num, x:α→β*.

2.3 Tuples and Lists

The pair or cartesian product of terms t_1 and t_2 is denoted by t_1,t_2. "," is the infix constructor for pairs and is right associative. Pairs and tuples may contain elements of heteogeneous type.

Lists are similar to tuples except all list elements must be of the same type. The empty list is denoted by *NIL* or *[]*. Lists are constructed using *CONS* which has as arguments *head:α* and *tail:(α)list*, i.e. *CONS head:α tail:(α)list* denotes the list where the first element is *head* of type α and the remainder of the list is *tail*. Lists containing a finite number of elements $x_1, x_2, \ldots, x_n$ may also be represented as $[x_1;x_2; \ldots ;x_n]$ instead of *(CONS x_1 (CONS x_2 (... (CONS x_n NIL) ...)))*. The accessor functions for lists are *HD* and *TL*. *HD(CONS h t)* reduces to *h*, *TL(CONS h t)* reduces to *t*.

2.4 Sequents and Theorems

Sequents are expressions of the form $\Gamma \vdash t$. Γ denotes a set of HOL terms each of which evaluates to a boolean. t is also a HOL term which evaluates to a boolean. $\Gamma \vdash t$ states that t is a logical consequence or conclusion derivable from the assumptions Γ, i.e. t is true whenever all of the assumptions in Γ are true.

3. CONSTRUCTING A FORMAL FRAMEWORK

3.1 Theories of Design

A theory of design has design axioms defining hardware components, meta-functions which synthesize hardware descriptions, and correctness theorems for each meta-function. A theory of design serves to document a design process in much the same way a hardware description language is used to document a particular implementation. The advantage of documenting a design process as opposed to a single implementation is once a theory of design is verified, all designs produced by it are also verified, as opposed to just a single implementation.

3.2 Signed Boolean Terms and Integer Arithmetic

The theories of design described operate on signed boolean terms or *negabinary* terms, i.e. terms which are composed of ternary digits called *trits*. Trits are mapped to 0, 1, and -1. They are represented by the pair *(sign:bool,bit:bool)*.

Within the HOL88 Version 0 proof assistant, the built-in arithmetic operators like +, -, *, and EXP for addition, subtraction, multiplication, and exponentiation, respectively, are defined only for *natural* numbers. The corresponding integer operations are extensions to the built-in operators and are represented by *plus, minus, times,* and *neg,* for addition, subtraction, multiplication, and negation, respectively. Natural numbers are converted to integers by the *INT* function, e.g. *INT 0* represents the integer *0*.

3.3 Structure and Value Functions

Structure functions manipulate various data structures used to represent designs. The set of data structures includes atomic ternary terms, "columns" of equally weighted ternary terms represented by ternary lists, ternary words represented by ternary lists, and arrays of ternary columns and ternary words represented by lists of ternary lists. The functions which manipulate the data structures are called structure functions, e.g. *APPEND*.

Value functions are functions which map each ternary data structure to a numerical value. Value functions provide the basis for showing equivalence preservation. Two descriptions are the same or equivalent within a particular interpretation supplied by the value functions if they have the same numerical value, i.e. *description$_1$* is equivalent to *description$_2$* if *value_function$_1$(description$_1$) = value_function$_2$(description$_2$)*.

The value functions used in this paper are defined in Definitions 3.1 as axiomatic definitions. The functions *SUC* and *LENGTH* compute the successor of a natural number and the length of a list, respectively. *APPEND* has the usual meaning, e.g. *APPEND [1;2] [3;4;5]* reduces to *[1;2;3;4;5]*. The expression *m EXP n* denotes *m^n*.

Definitions 3.1: Value Functions

⊢ BV bit = (bit → 1 | 0)

⊢ INT_BV(SIGN,VAL) = (SIGN → neg(INT(BV VAL)) | INT(BV VAL))

⊢ (INT_COLVAL[] = INT 0) ∧
   (∀h t. INT_COLVAL(CONS h t) = (INT_BV h) plus (INT_COLVAL t))

⊢ (∀n. INT_WORDVAL n[] = INT 0) ∧
(∀n h t.
   INT_WORDVAL n(CONS h t) =
   ((INT(2 EXP n)) times (INT_BV h)) plus (INT_WORDVAL(SUC n)t))

⊢ (∀n. INT_ARRAYVAL n[] = INT 0) ∧
(∀n h t.
   INT_ARRAYVAL n(CONS h t) = ((INT(2 EXP n)) times (INT_COLVAL h)) plus
   (INT_ARRAYVAL(SUC n)t))

⊢ (INT_WORDARRAYVAL[] = INT 0) ∧
(∀h t. INT_WORDARRAYVAL(CONS h t) = (INT_WORDVAL(FST h)(SND h)) plus
      (INT_WORDARRAYVAL t))

⊢ INT_PAIRBITVAL x =
(INT_BV(FST x)) plus ((INT 2) times (INT_BV(SND x)))

⊢ INT_PAIRBITVAL_2 x = (INT_BV(FST x)) plus (INT_BV(SND x))

⊢ INT_PAIRARRAYVAL x = INT_ARRAYVAL 0(APPEND(FST x)(SND x))

⊢ INT_PAIRCOLVAL n col_pair =
(INT(2 EXP n)) times
((INT_COLVAL(FST col_pair)) plus
  ((INT 2) times (INT_COLVAL(SND col_pair))))

⊢ INT_COLPAIR_ARRAYVAL n colpair_array =
(INT_PAIRCOLVAL n(FST colpair_array)) plus
(INT_ARRAYVAL(SUC n)(SND colpair_array))

⊢ INT_TRIPLEVAL triple =
(let a1 = FST triple in
 let colpair_array = SND triple in
 let colpair = FST colpair_array in
 let a2 = SND colpair_array in
 let n1 = LENGTH a1 in
 let n2 = SUC n1 in
 (INT_ARRAYVAL 0 a1) plus
 ((INT_PAIRCOLVAL n1 colpair) plus (INT_ARRAYVAL n2 a2)))

3.4 Mechanizing the Meta-functions Using Functional Languages

The HOL meta-functions produce functional forms corresponding to interconnection lists of predefined hardware components. It is possible to produce the functional forms within the HOL theorem prover by expanding definitions of the meta-functions until only functions corresponding to predefined hardware components and inputs remain. However, this is a time consuming process as each rewrite is essentially a proof step. A more practical approach is to use a functional language with *partial evaluation* capability like SCHEME. SCHEME functions can be defined where evaluation is suspended unless otherwise specified. Functions corresponding to primitive hardware components are left unevaluated, all other functions are evaluated.

Usually an informal syntactic transformation exists between HOL and SCHEME functions, e.g. *FST* in HOL corresponds to *car* in SCHEME. Primitive recursive HOL expressions are implemented in SCHEME as conditional expressions selecting either the base case definition or the recursive definition.

4. A THEORY OF DESIGN FOR INTEGER ARRAY MULTIPLIERS

To illustrate how logic designs are created in a formal fashion, we outline the creation and verification of a set of meta-functions which synthesize array multipliers of arbitrary size with signed inputs in general and two's complement inputs in particular. The verification of a multiplier meta-function capable of synthesizing implementations of arbitrary size solves the important practical problem of exponential growth in representing the output product bits. [3] proves for $1 \leq i \leq n$ where n is the word size with outputs numbered from 0 (least significant) to 2n-1 (most significant), the number of vertices in an ordered binary decision diagram representing any output product bit i-1 or 2n-i-1 must have $\Omega(1.09^i)$ vertices.

The multiplier meta-function in Definition 4.1 has the property that all designs produced by it satisfy the relationship in Theorem 4.1, i.e. the INT_ARRAYVAL of the multiplier design equals the product of the INT_WORDVALs of the multiplier and multiplicand inputs where both inputs are of arbitrary size. Theorem 4.1 supports hierarchical design as it asserts the equivalence between a high level specification description and a lower level implementation. The proof of Theorem 4.1 is outlined below and appears as a machine executable HOL proof in [4].

INT_MULT_1 mirrors the process of long hand multiplication. First the array of partial products is formed by the function *INT_PPGEN* then each column of the partial product array *array* is summed by *INT_CARRY_SAVE_1* to form the result. What makes *INT_MULT_1* interesting is it incorporates knowledge about synthesizing adder arrays such that all bits except the most significant output bit have a positive interpretation. For carry-save adder arrays embedded within Pezaris [9] multipliers this is accomplished by sign-extending one of the middle product bits. This technique is representative of some design "tricks" used to obtain a particular array geometry while enforcing a particular arithmetic representation, i.e two's-complement.

Definition 4.1: INT_MULT_1

⊢ INT_MULT_1 n1 multiplier n2 multiplicand =
    (let prod_pair = INT_PPGEN n1 multiplier n2 multiplicand in
      let lsb_power = FST prod_pair in
      let array = SND prod_pair in

```
let limit = LENGTH multiplicand in
lsb_power,INT_CARRY_SAVE_1 array limit)
```

Theorem 4.1: INT_MULT_1_CORRECT

```
INT_MULT_1_CORRECT
⊢ ∀multiplier n1 multiplicand n2.
    (let mult_pair = INT_MULT_1 n1 multiplier n2 multiplicand in
    let power_of_2 = FST mult_pair in
    let array = SND mult_pair in
    INT_ARRAYVAL power_of_2 array) =
    (INT_WORDVAL n1 multiplier) times (INT_WORDVAL n2 multiplicand)
```

Proof: The proof depends upon the correctness of INT_PPGEN and INT_CARRY_SAVE_1 shown below.

```
INT_PPGEN_CORRECT
⊢ ∀mult m mcand n.
    INT_ARRAYVAL
    (FST(INT_PPGEN m mult n mcand))(SND(INT_PPGEN m mult n mcand)) =
    (INT_WORDVAL m mult) times (INT_WORDVAL n mcand)
```

```
INT_CARRY_SAVE_1_CORRECT_N
⊢ ∀array limit n.
    INT_ARRAYVAL n(INT_CARRY_SAVE_1 array limit) = INT_ARRAYVAL n array
```

Rewriting Theorem 4.1 by using the definition of *INT_MULT_1* and expanding all the *let* definitions followed by beta-conversion produces the following subgoal.

```
⊢ ∀multiplier n1 multiplicand n2.
    INT_ARRAYVAL
    (FST
     (FST(INT_PPGEN n1 multiplier n2 multiplicand),
      INT_CARRY_SAVE_1
      (SND(INT_PPGEN n1 multiplier n2 multiplicand))
      (LENGTH multiplicand)))
    (SND
     (FST(INT_PPGEN n1 multiplier n2 multiplicand),
      INT_CARRY_SAVE_1
      (SND(INT_PPGEN n1 multiplier n2 multiplicand))
      (LENGTH multiplicand))) =
    (INT_WORDVAL n1 multiplier) times (INT_WORDVAL n2 multiplicand)
```

The above subgoal is proved by rewriting using the correctness theorems for *INT_PPGEN* and *INT_CARRY_SAVE_1*. □

Figure 4.1 shows a 3-bit by 3-bit circuit synthesized by *INT_MULT_1*. Notice that the third output bit from the right is fed into the adder immediately to its left. This is a form of sign-extension used to insure that no intermediate product output bits have a negative interpretation. This is the type of detailed and specialized design knowledge necessary to produce practical designs.

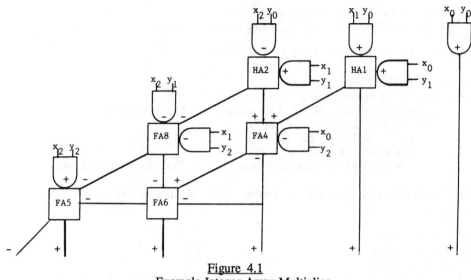

Figure 4.1
Example Integer Array Multiplier

5. A THEORY OF DESIGN FOR GENERATING PARTIAL PRODUCT ARRAYS

In this section we will briefly outline the justification for the INT_PPGEN meta-function which creates a column array of partial products. The creation of partial products mirrors long hand multiplication. First, the cartesian product of the trits of the multiplier and the trits of the multiplicand is performed in a word oriented manner, i.e. an array of ternary words is created where each word corresponds to the product of the multiplicand and a single multiplier bit. In a like manner to long hand multiplication, the word oriented array is transformed into an equivalent array of columns where the elements of each column have the same arithmetic weight. This column array of partial products is then passed to the adder array meta-function which reduces the array column by column to an equivalent form.

In all cases, the proofs of the lemmas and theorems follows the same pattern: induction is used on arguments of arbitrary size, case analysis is used for conditional expressions, and definitions are expanded using rewriting. As the same pattern is followed in all cases the proofs are omitted. All of the theorems and lemmas have been machine checked and are machine executable within the HOL proof assistant [4].

5.1 Product Generation Functions

The product generation functions build up the array of partial products in an incremental fashion. First, the product of two ternary terms is defined. Next, the product of a ternary word and a trit is defined followed by the definition of the product between two ternary words. The array of ternary words is then converted to an array of ternary columns.

The *INT_BITPROD* function defines the product between two ternary terms. The functions *INT_GET_SIGN* and *INT_GET_BIT* are accessor functions which extract the sign and bit components of a trit, respectively. The *AND* function takes the boolean product of its input pair.

Definition 5.1: INT_BITPROD

⊢ INT_BITPROD(x,y) =
  (let sign_x = INT_GET_SIGN x in
  let bit_x = INT_GET_BIT x in
  let sign_y = INT_GET_SIGN y in
  let bit_y = INT_GET_BIT y in
  (~sign_x ∧ sign_y ∨ sign_x ∧ ~sign_y),AND(bit_x,bit_y))

Lemma 5.1: BITPROD_CORRECT

⊢ ∀x y. (INT_BV x) times (INT_BV y) = INT_BV(INT_BITPROD(x,y))

The *INT_BITWORDPROD* function defines the product between a ternary term and a ternary word.

Definition 5.2: INT_BITWORDPROD

⊢ (∀b. INT_BITWORDPROD b[] = []) ∧
  (∀b h t.
  INT_BITWORDPROD b(CONS h t) =
  CONS(INT_BITPROD(h,b))(INT_BITWORDPROD b t))

Lemma 5.2: INT_BITWORDPROD_CORRECT

⊢ ∀word bit n.
  (INT_BV bit) times (INT_WORDVAL n word) =
  INT_WORDVAL n(INT_BITWORDPROD bit word)

The *INT_WORDCARTPROD* function produces an array of ternary words equal in value to the product of the values of the input words.

Definition 5.3: INT_WORDCARTPROD

⊢ (∀m n mcand. INT_WORDCARTPROD m[]n mcand = []) ∧
  (∀m h t n mcand.
  INT_WORDCARTPROD m(CONS h t)n mcand =
  CONS(m + n,INT_BITWORDPROD h mcand)
    (INT_WORDCARTPROD(SUC m)t n mcand))

Lemma 5.3: INT_WORDCARTPROD_CORRECT

⊢ ∀mult m mcand n.
  (INT_WORDVAL m mult) times (INT_WORDVAL n mcand) =
  INT_WORDARRAYVAL(INT_WORDCARTPROD m mult n mcand)

The *INT_PPGEN* function returns an array of columns equal in value to the product of the values of the input words. The *INT_CONV_WORDARRAY_COLARRAY* function transforms an array of words into an array of columns.

Definition 5.4: INT_PPGEN

> ⊢ INT_PPGEN n1 mult n2 mcand =
> INT_CONV_WORDARRAY_COLARRAY(INT_WORDCARTPROD n1 mult n2 mcand)

Theorem 5.1: INT_PPGEN_CORRECT

> ⊢ ∀mult m mcand n.
> INT_ARRAYVAL(FST(INT_PPGEN m mult n mcand))
> (SND(INT_PPGEN m mult n mcand)) =
> (INT_WORDVAL m mult) times (INT_WORDVAL n mcand)

6. A THEORY FOR SUMMING ARBITRARILY LONG TERNARY COLUMNS

We now consider the second part of the multiplier problem, namely summing each column of the partial product array created by *INT_PPGEN* to obtain the final product. Again, this process closely mirrors long hand multiplication. Each column of the array is rewritten into a *column pair*, i.e. a column of weight 2^n is transformed into a pair of columns where the first column has at most a single sum term of weight 2^n and the second column contains the carry output terms each with weight 2^{n+1}. The various adder interconnection patterns, e.g. carry-save arrays, Wallace-tree arrays, etc. are achieved by the order in which column elements are selected and summed together.

The equivalence preserving transformations developed in this section operate on and preserve the value of column pairs. A given column of ternary terms with weight 2^n is converted into a column pair where the sum column is the given column and the carry output column of weight 2^n is initially empty. The column pair transformation functions then sum the terms in the sum column to at most a single ternary term with their corresponding carry terms in the carry column. This process closely mirrors the manual process of adding columns of numbers together.

Four half adder types and eight full adder types are described for all sign combinations on the adder inputs. Also, a sign extension function is defined which correctly changes the sign of a negative ternary term into a positive one. By selective sign extension, a negabinary adder array can produce a sum in two's-complement form.

6.1 Adder Definitions

The hardware basis for summing columns into equivalent column pairs are half and full adders. Definitions 6.1 and 6.2 and Lemmas 6.1 and 6.2 describe the correct behavior of the adders. Since we are assuming that half and full adders are primitive components, for brevity we will not describe their component definitions but only describe their correct behavior.

Definitions 6.1: Example Half and Full Adder Functions

  ⊢ HA1(a,b) = HA1SUM(a,b),HA1CARRY(a,b)
  ⊢ FA1(a,b,c) = FA1SUM(a,b,c),FA1CARRY(a,b,c)

Definitions 6.2: Accessor Functions

  ⊢ So x = FST x
  ⊢ Co x = SND x

The accessor functions *Co* and *So* allow the behavior of the half and full adders to be described in terms of their sum and carry outputs as shown in Lemmas 6.1 and 6.2. Recall that if the sign component of a trit is F, then the trit is positive, otherwise it is negative.

Lemma 6.1: Half Adder Correctness Theorems

INT_HA1_CORRECT_1
  ⊢ (INT_BV(F,a)) plus (INT_BV(F,b)) = (INT_BV(F,So(HA1(a,b)))) plus
    ((INT 2) times (INT_BV(F,Co(HA1(a,b)))))

INT_HA2_CORRECT_1
  ⊢ (INT_BV(T,a)) plus (INT_BV(F,b)) = (INT_BV(F,So(HA2(a,b)))) plus
    ((INT 2) times (INT_BV(T,Co(HA2(a,b)))))

INT_HA3_CORRECT_1
  ⊢ (INT_BV(F,a)) plus (INT_BV(T,b)) = (INT_BV(F,So(HA3(a,b)))) plus
    ((INT 2) times (INT_BV(T,Co(HA3(a,b)))))

INT_HA4_CORRECT_1
  ⊢ (INT_BV(T,a)) plus (INT_BV(T,b)) = (INT_BV(T,So(HA4(a,b)))) plus
    ((INT 2) times (INT_BV(T,Co(HA4(a,b)))))

Lemmas 6.2: Full Adder Correctness Theorems

INT_FA1_CORRECT_1
  ⊢ (INT_BV(F,a)) plus ((INT_BV(F,b)) plus (INT_BV(F,c))) =
    (INT_BV(F,So(FA1(a,b,c)))) plus
    ((INT 2) times (INT_BV(F,Co(FA1(a,b,c)))))

INT_FA2_CORRECT_1
  ⊢ (INT_BV(T,a)) plus ((INT_BV(F,b)) plus (INT_BV(F,c))) =
    (INT_BV(T,So(FA2(a,b,c)))) plus
    ((INT 2) times (INT_BV(F,Co(FA2(a,b,c)))))

INT_FA3_CORRECT_1
  ⊢ (INT_BV(F,a)) plus ((INT_BV(T,b)) plus (INT_BV(F,c))) =
    (INT_BV(T,So(FA3(a,b,c)))) plus
    ((INT 2) times (INT_BV(F,Co(FA3(a,b,c)))))

INT_FA4_CORRECT_1
⊢ (INT_BV(F,a)) plus ((INT_BV(F,b)) plus (INT_BV(T,c))) =
(INT_BV(T,So(FA4(a,b,c)))) plus
((INT 2) times (INT_BV(F,Co(FA4(a,b,c)))))

INT_FA5_CORRECT_1
⊢ (INT_BV(F,a)) plus ((INT_BV(T,b)) plus (INT_BV(T,c))) =
(INT_BV(F,So(FA5(a,b,c)))) plus
((INT 2) times (INT_BV(T,Co(FA5(a,b,c)))))

INT_FA6_CORRECT_1
⊢ (INT_BV(T,a)) plus ((INT_BV(F,b)) plus (INT_BV(T,c))) =
(INT_BV(F,So(FA6(a,b,c)))) plus
((INT 2) times (INT_BV(T,Co(FA6(a,b,c)))))

INT_FA7_CORRECT_1
⊢ (INT_BV(T,a)) plus ((INT_BV(T,b)) plus (INT_BV(F,c))) =
(INT_BV(F,So(FA7(a,b,c)))) plus
((INT 2) times (INT_BV(T,Co(FA7(a,b,c)))))

INT_FA8_CORRECT_1
⊢ (INT_BV(T,a)) plus ((INT_BV(T,b)) plus (INT_BV(T,c))) =
(INT_BV(T,So(FA8(a,b,c)))) plus
((INT 2) times (INT_BV(T,Co(FA8(a,b,c)))))

6.2 Structure Functions

Structure functions are needed to extract elements from boolean columns to be used as inputs for half and full adders. These structure or accessor functions are defined in Definitions 6.3. In addition, a simple function for converting a boolean term to a boolean column is defined. Their properties appear in Lemmas 6.3. As before, since the individual proofs follow the same pattern, i.e. induction on elements of arbitrary size, case analyis for conditional expressions, and rewriting based on the definitions, the individual proofs are omitted.

Definitions 6.3: Structure Functions

⊢ INT_GETCOLPAIR col = HD col,HD(TL col)

⊢ INT_GETCOLTRIP col = HD col,HD(TL col),HD(TL(TL col))

⊢ (∀col. INT_STRIPCOL 0 col = col) ∧
(∀n col. INT_STRIPCOL(SUC n)col = INT_STRIPCOL n(TL col))

⊢ INT_BIT_TO_COL bit = [bit]

Lemmas 6.3: Structure Function Lemmas

INT_COLVAL_OF_APPEND
⊢ ∀l1 l2. INT_COLVAL(APPEND l1 l2) = (INT_COLVAL l1) plus (INT_COLVAL l2)

INT_GET_STRIP_EQUAL
⊢ ∀col.

~NULL col ∧ ~NULL(TL col) ⊃
    ((INT_PAIRBITVAL_2(INT_GETCOLPAIR col)) plus
    (INT_COLVAL(INT_STRIPCOL 2 col)) = INT_COLVAL col)

INT_GET_STRIP_3_EQUAL
    ⊢ ∀col.
        ~NULL col ∧ ~NULL(TL col) ∧ ~NULL(TL(TL col)) ⊃
        ((INT_BV(HD col)) plus
        ((INT_BV(HD(TL col))) plus
        ((INT_BV(HD(TL(TL col)))) plus
            (INT_COLVAL(INT_STRIPCOL 3 col)))) = INT_COLVAL col)

INT_BIT_TO_COL_CORRECT
    ⊢ ∀bit. INT_BV bit = INT_COLVAL(INT_BIT_TO_COL bit)

6.3 Basic Adder Transformations on Column Pairs

Two example adder transformations on column pairs appear in Definitions 6.4a. The remaining three half adder and seven full adder transformations are similar. They form the basis for the column reduction functions presented later. Assuming the existence of at least two or three terms in a column as appropriate, the first two or three elements in the first (sum) column of a column pair are stripped off from the first column, summed using a half or full adder as appropriate, and the resulting sum and carry bits are appended to the head and tail of the sum and carry columns respectively.

Two general half and full adder transformations are defined in Definitions 6.4b. The general transformations choose the appropriate adder transformation based on the number of elements in the column and the signs of the inputs.

Lemmas 6.4 assert the correctness of the adder transformations as they preserve the value of the input column pair. They are proved by case analysis and rewriting using the definitions and the correctness of the half and full adders.

Definitions 6.4a: INT_HA1TRANS_1 and INT_FA1TRANS_1

INT_HA1TRANS_1
    ⊢ INT_HA1TRANS_1 col_pair =
        (let col = FST col_pair in
        let carry_col = SND col_pair in
        let trit_pair = INT_GETCOLPAIR col in
        let Adder = HA1(INT_GET_BIT_PAIR trit_pair) in
        CONS(F,So Adder)(INT_STRIPCOL 2 col),
            APPEND carry_col(INT_BIT_TO_COL(F,Co Adder)))

INT_FA1TRANS_1
    ⊢ INT_FA1TRANS_1 col_pair =
        (let col = FST col_pair in
        let carry_col = SND col_pair in
        let trit_trip = INT_GETCOLTRIP col in
        let Adder = FA1(INT_GET_BIT_TRIP trit_trip) in
        CONS(F,So Adder)(INT_STRIPCOL 3 col),

APPEND carry_col(INT_BIT_TO_COL(F,Co Adder)))

Definitions 6.4b: INT_HATRANS_1 and INT_FATRANS_1

INT_HATRANS_1
  ⊢ INT_HATRANS_1 col_pair =
    (let col = FST col_pair in
     let sign_a = INT_GET_SIGN(HD col) in
     let sign_b = INT_GET_SIGN(HD(TL col)) in
    (NULL col →
     col_pair |
     (NULL(TL col) →
      col_pair |
      (sign_a →
       (sign_b → INT_HA4TRANS_1 col_pair | INT_HA2TRANS_1 col_pair) |
       (sign_b → INT_HA3TRANS_1 col_pair | INT_HA1TRANS_1 col_pair)))))

INT_FATRANS_1
  ⊢ INT_FATRANS_1 col_pair =
    (let col = FST col_pair in
     let sign_a = INT_GET_SIGN(HD col) in
     let sign_b = INT_GET_SIGN(HD(TL col)) in
     let sign_c = INT_GET_SIGN(HD(TL(TL col))) in
    (NULL col →
     col_pair |
     (NULL(TL col) →
      col_pair |
      (NULL(TL(TL col)) →
       INT_HATRANS_1 col_pair |
       (sign_a →
        (sign_b →
         (sign_c →
          INT_FA8TRANS_1 col_pair |
          INT_FA7TRANS_1 col_pair) |
         (sign_c →
          INT_FA6TRANS_1 col_pair |
          INT_FA2TRANS_1 col_pair)) |
        (sign_b →
         (sign_c →
          INT_FA5TRANS_1 col_pair |
          INT_FA3TRANS_1 col_pair) |
         (sign_c →
          INT_FA4TRANS_1 col_pair |
          INT_FA1TRANS_1 col_pair)))))))

Lemmas 6.4: HA1TRANS_1_CORRECT and FA1TRANS_1_CORRECT

INT_HATRANS_1_CORRECT
  ⊢ ∀col_pair n.
    INT_PAIRCOLVAL n(INT_HATRANS_1 col_pair) = INT_PAIRCOLVAL n col_pair

INT_FATRANS_1_CORRECT
  ⊢ ∀col_pair n.

INT_PAIRCOLVAL n(INT_FATRANS_1 col_pair) = INT_PAIRCOLVAL n col_pair

6.4 Basic Column Reduction

The basic half and full adder transformations in the previous section are repeated until the number of ternary terms in the first column of a column pair is one or fewer. This corresponds to summing completely the terms in a ternary column. The *INT_COLRED_1* function defined in Definition 6.5 operates on three inputs. The interpretation of *INT_COLRED_1 a b c* can be deduced from Lemma 6.5. Essentially, the first column of a column pair is split into two columns *a* and *b* such that *FST(colpair) = APPEND b a*. The second (carry) column of the column pair is represented by *c*. *INT_COLRED_1* will shift elements of *a* into *b* until *b* has three or more elements whereupon *INT_FATRANS_1* will be used to rewrite the column pair *(b,c)*. The process continues until *a* is empty.

Lemma 6.5 asserts the value of the input column pair is preserved.

Definition 6.5: INT_COLRED_1

⊢ (∀b c. INT_COLRED_1[]b c = INT_FATRANS_1(b,c)) ∧
(∀h t b c.
  INT_COLRED_1(CONS h t)b c =
  (let colpair = INT_FA1TRANS_1(APPEND b(INT_BIT_TO_COL h),c) in
  (NULL b →
    INT_COLRED_1 t(INT_BIT_TO_COL h)c |
  (NULL(TL b) →
    INT_COLRED_1 t(APPEND b(INT_BIT_TO_COL h))c |
    INT_COLRED_1 t(FST colpair)(SND colpair)))))

Lemma 6.5: INT_COLRED_1_CORRECT

⊢ ∀a b c.
  INT_PAIRCOLVAL 0(INT_COLRED_1 a b c) =
  ((INT_COLVAL b) plus (INT_COLVAL a)) plus
  ((INT 2) times (INT_COLVAL c))

The *INT_COLREDUCE_1* and *INT_COLREDUCE_2* functions defined below are the two primary functions used to produce a carry-save adder array structure. *INT_COLREDUCE_1* attempts to use a full adder each time to rewrite three terms into two terms. *INT_COLREDUCE_2* reduces a column which initially is rewritten using a half adder transformation.

Definitions 6.6: INT_COLREDUCE_1 and INT_COLREDUCE_2

⊢ INT_COLREDUCE_1 colpair = INT_COLRED_1(FST colpair)[](SND colpair)
⊢ INT_COLREDUCE_2 colpair = INT_COLREDUCE_1(INT_HATRANS_1 colpair)

Lemmas 6.6: INT_COLREDUCE_1_CORRECT and INT_COLREDUCE_2_CORRECT

INT_COLREDUCE_1_CORRECT
⊢ ∀colpair n.

INT_PAIRCOLVAL n(INT_COLREDUCE_1 colpair) = INT_PAIRCOLVAL n colpair

INT_COLREDUCE_2_CORRECT
⊢ ∀colpair n.
    INT_PAIRCOLVAL n(INT_COLREDUCE_2 colpair) = INT_PAIRCOLVAL n colpair

Clearly, *INT_COLRED_1*, *INT_COLREDUCE_1*, and *INT_COLREDUCE_2* are not the only column reduction functions which could be defined. Other functions which generate adder trees, for example, can easily be defined by altering the selection of input bits to be summed and the placement of the sum and carry bits within the column pairs.

6.5 Sign Extension

Selective sign extension is used to guarantee that the sum output of a column reduction is positive. The function *POSITIVE_SUM* is used to test the sum output after a column reduction. If the output is positive, then the column reduction results are unchanged. If the output is negative, then the sign of the sum output term is made positive and the original sum output term is appended to the end of the carry output column. *POSITIVE_SUM* is defined in Definition 6.7. Its correctness as stated in Lemmas 6.7 depends upon the correctness of sign extension which is also stated in Lemmas 6.7.

Definition 6.7: POSITIVE_SUM

POSITIVE_SUM
  ⊢ POSITIVE_SUM col_pair =
    (let sumcol = FST col_pair in
     let carrycol = SND col_pair in
     let sign = INT_GET_SIGN(HD sumcol) in
     let bit = INT_GET_BIT(HD sumcol) in
     (NULL sumcol →
      (CONS(F,F)sumcol,carrycol) |
      ((sign = F) →
       col_pair |
      (CONS(F,bit)(TL sumcol),APPEND carrycol(INT_BIT_TO_COL(T,bit)))))))

Lemmas 6.7: SIGN_EXTEND_BIT and POSITIVE_SUM_CORRECT

SIGN_EXTEND_BIT
  ⊢ ∀sign bit. INT_BV(sign,bit) =
    (INT_BV(sign,bit)) plus ((INT 2) times (INT_BV(sign,bit)))

POSITIVE_SUM_CORRECT
  ⊢ ∀col_pair n.
    INT_PAIRCOLVAL n(POSITIVE_SUM col_pair) = INT_PAIRCOLVAL n col_pair

POSITIVE_SUM_IS_POSITIVE
  ⊢ ∀col_pair. INT_GET_SIGN(HD(FST(POSITIVE_SUM col_pair))) = F

Column reductions based on *INT_COLREDUCE_1*, *INT_COLREDUCE_2*, and

POSITIVE_SUM are defined in Definitions 6.8 with their associated properties in Lemmas 6.8. Figure 6.1 show example applications of the reduction functions.

Definitions 6.8: POSITIVE_COLREDUCE_1 and POSITIVE_COLREDUCE_2

POSITIVE_COLREDUCE_1
⊢ POSITIVE_COLREDUCE_1 col_pair = POSITIVE_SUM(INT_COLREDUCE_1 col_pair)

POSITIVE_COLREDUCE_2
⊢ POSITIVE_COLREDUCE_2 col_pair = POSITIVE_SUM(INT_COLREDUCE_2 col_pair)

Lemmas 6.8: Correctness of POSITIVE_COLREDUCE_1 and POSITIVE_COLREDUCE_2

POSITIVE_COLREDUCE_1_CORRECT
⊢ ∀col_pair n.
    INT_PAIRCOLVAL n(POSITIVE_COLREDUCE_1 col_pair) =
    INT_PAIRCOLVAL n col_pair

POSITIVE_COLREDUCE_2_CORRECT
⊢ ∀col_pair n.
    INT_PAIRCOLVAL n(POSITIVE_COLREDUCE_2 col_pair) =
    INT_PAIRCOLVAL n col_pair

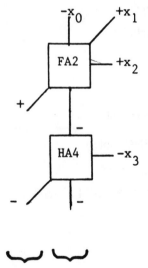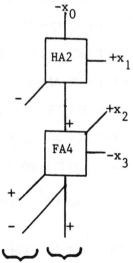

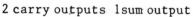

2 carry outputs 1 sum output   3 carry outputs 1 sum output

Figure 6.1
Application of *INT_COLREDUCE_1* and *POSITIVE_COLREDUCE_2* to ([x0;x1;x2;x3],[])

7. A THEORY FOR SUMMING ARRAYS OF COLUMNS OF ARBITRARY SIZE

Having defined functions which synthesize adder arrays which sum arbitrarily long columns of ternary terms, all that remains to be defined are several higher order composition functions which use the column reduction functions along with structure functions to manipulate column pairs and other data structures.

To facilitate the reduction of ternary arrays by successively reducing the component column pairs, a new data structure called a *triple* is used. The interpretation of the component structure of a triple is deduced from the definition of *INT_TRIPLEVAL* in Definitions 3.1. Essentially a triple has the form *(al,(colpair,a2))*. *al* contains the columns already reduced, *a2* contains the columns remaining to be reduced, and *colpair* is the column pair being reduced.

7.1 Structure Functions

Definitions 7.1 defines functions which convert column arrays into triples, and various accessor functions to extract the components of triples. Lemma 7.1 asserts the correctness of the conversion from arrays to triples.

Definitions 7.1: Structure Functions

    ⊢ INT_CONV_COLARRAY_TRIPLE array =
      (NULL array → ([],([],[]),[]) | ([],(HD array,[]),TL array))

    ⊢ INT_GET_PARTIAL_RESULT triple = FST triple

    ⊢ INT_GET_COLPAIR_ARRAY triple = SND triple

    ⊢ INT_GET_COLPAIR triple = FST(SND triple)

    ⊢ INT_GET_ARRAY triple = SND(SND triple)

    ⊢ INT_GET_1ST_COLPAIR triple = FST(FST(SND triple))

    ⊢ INT_GET_2ND_COLPAIR triple = SND(FST(SND triple))

Lemma 7.1: INT_CONV_COLARRAY_TRIPLE_CORRECT

    ⊢ ∀array. INT_TRIPLEVAL(INT_CONV_COLARRAY_TRIPLE array) =
      INT_ARRAYVAL 0 array

7.2 Merging Reduced Column Pairs into Arrays

Once a column pair has been reduced or transformed, it must be merged into the array of previously reduced columns such that the sum column is appended to the array of previously reduced columns and the carry column is combined with the head of the remaining unreduced columns by some user specified combining function. *INT_COL_COMBINE_MOVE* in

Definition 7.2 shows how this is done.

Definition 7.2: INT_COL_COMBINE_MOVE

⊢ INT_COL_COMBINE_MOVE f triple =
(let partial_result = INT_GET_PARTIAL_RESULT triple in
let array = INT_GET_ARRAY triple in
let c1 = INT_GET_1ST_COLPAIR triple in
let c2 = INT_GET_2ND_COLPAIR triple in
let next_col = (NULL array → [] | HD array) in
let rest_cols = (NULL array → [] | TL array) in
let new_results = APPEND partial_result(INT_COL_TO_COLARRAY c1) in
let new_col = f next_col c2 in
new_results,(new_col,[]),rest_cols)

INT_COL_COMBINE_MOVE is a higher order function which takes a column combining function *f* and a triple *triple* and produces a new triple such that the *INT_TRIPLEVAL* of the input *triple* is preserved. For example, *INT_COL_COMBINE_MOVE f (al,(c1,c2), CONS((HD a2)(TL a2)))* reduces to the triple *((APPEND al c1),((f (HD a2) c2),[]),(TL a2))*.

Lemma 7.2 asserts the correctness of *INT_COL_COMBINE_MOVE* in general if *f* preserves the *INT_COLVAL* of both arguments.

Lemma 7.2: INT_COL_COMBINE_MOVE_CORRECT

⊢ ∀f triple.
(∀c1 c2.
INT_COLVAL(f c1 c2) = (INT_COLVAL c1) plus (INT_COLVAL c2)) ⊃
(INT_TRIPLEVAL(INT_COL_COMBINE_MOVE f triple) = INT_TRIPLEVAL triple)

Here, we consider three ways to merge two columns of equal weight. First, they can be shuffled or zipped together. Second, the tail of one column can be zipped with the other column. Third, one can simply be appended to the other. Definitions 7.3 defines the two shuffling operations. Lemmas 7.3 asserts the correctness of the the methods. The correctness of each results directly since each function preserves the *INT_COLVAL* of its arguments.

Definitions 7.3: SHUFFLE and SHUFFLE_TAIL

⊢ (∀l1. SHUFFLE[]l1 = l1) ∧
(∀h t l1.
SHUFFLE(CONS h t)l1 =
(NULL l1 → CONS h t | CONS h(CONS(HD l1)(SHUFFLE t(TL l1))))))

⊢ SHUFFLE_TAIL l1 l2 =
(NULL l1 → l2 | CONS(HD l1)(SHUFFLE(TL l1)l2))

Lemmas 7.3: Column Combining Lemmas

INT_COL_SHUFFLE_MOVE_CORRECT
⊢ ∀triple.
INT_TRIPLEVAL(INT_COL_COMBINE_MOVE SHUFFLE triple) =
INT_TRIPLEVAL triple

INT_COL_SHUFFLE_TAIL_MOVE_CORRECT
⊢ ∀triple.
    INT_TRIPLEVAL(INT_COL_COMBINE_MOVE SHUFFLE_TAIL triple) =
    INT_TRIPLEVAL triple

INT_COL_APPEND_MOVE_CORRECT
⊢ ∀triple.
    INT_TRIPLEVAL(INT_COL_COMBINE_MOVE APPEND triple) =
    INT_TRIPLEVAL triple

7.3 Transforming Column Pairs within Triples

In a similar fashion to the previous section, we define a higher order function which applies a column pair transformation function f within a triple. The definition of *INT_COLPAIR_TRANSFORM* appears in Definition 7.4. Its correctness, based upon f preserving the *INT_PAIRCOLVAL* of the column pair, is stated in Lemmas 7.4. Several other theorems stating the correctness of the half and full adder and column reduction transformations also appear in Lemmas 7.4 since they are direct results of the correctness of *INT_COLPAIR_TRANSFORM*.

Definition 7.4: INT_COLPAIR_TRANSFORM

⊢ INT_COLPAIR_TRANSFORM f triple =
  (let partial_result = FST triple in
  let colpair_array = SND triple in
  let colpair = FST colpair_array in
  let array = SND colpair_array in
  partial_result,f colpair,array)

Lemmas 7.4: INT_COLPAIR_TRANSFORM_CORRECT

INT_COLPAIR_TRANSFORM_CORRECT
  ⊢ ∀f triple.
  ($\forall$cp n. INT_PAIRCOLVAL n(f cp) = INT_PAIRCOLVAL n cp) ⊃
  (INT_TRIPLEVAL(INT_COLPAIR_TRANSFORM f triple) = INT_TRIPLEVAL triple)
INT_COLPAIR_HATRANS_1_CORRECT
  ⊢ ∀triple.
    INT_TRIPLEVAL(INT_COLPAIR_TRANSFORM INT_HATRANS_1 triple) =
    INT_TRIPLEVAL triple

INT_COLPAIR_FATRANS_1_CORRECT
  ⊢ ∀triple.
    INT_TRIPLEVAL(INT_COLPAIR_TRANSFORM INT_FATRANS_1 triple) =
    INT_TRIPLEVAL triple

COLPAIR_COLREDUCE_1_CORRECT
  ⊢ ∀triple.
    INT_TRIPLEVAL(INT_COLPAIR_TRANSFORM INT_COLREDUCE_1 triple) =
    INT_TRIPLEVAL triple

COLPAIR_COLREDUCE_2_CORRECT
  ⊢ ∀triple.

INT_TRIPLEVAL(INT_COLPAIR_TRANSFORM INT_COLREDUCE_2 triple) =
INT_TRIPLEVAL triple

INT_COLPAIR_POSITIVE_COLREDUCE_1_CORRECT
⊢ ∀triple.
 INT_TRIPLEVAL(INT_COLPAIR_TRANSFORM POSITIVE_COLREDUCE_1 triple) =
 INT_TRIPLEVAL triple

INT_COLPAIR_POSITIVE_COLREDUCE_2_CORRECT
⊢ ∀triple.
 INT_TRIPLEVAL(INT_COLPAIR_TRANSFORM POSITIVE_COLREDUCE_2 triple) =
 INT_TRIPLEVAL triple

7.4 Array Transformation Functions

Using the column reduction functions and the column combining functions defined in previous sections, we define functions which compose the column reduction and combining functions to reduce arbitrarily large ternary arrays.

As the column reduction and column combining functions are defined for triples, we define in Definition 7.5 an additional structure function *INT_CONV_TRIPLE_COLARRAY* which converts triples into column arrays. Its correctness is asserted by Lemma 7.5. The arguments to *INT_CONV_TRIPLE_COLARRAY* are a column combining function f and a triple *triple*. If f preserves the value of the column pair, then the conversion to a column array will be correct.

Definition 7.5: INT_CONV_TRIPLE_COLARRAY

⊢ CONV_TRIPLE_COLARRAY f triple =
 (let new_triple = INT_COL_COMBINE_MOVE f triple in
  let partial_result = INT_GET_PARTIAL_RESULT new_triple in
  let array = INT_GET_ARRAY new_triple in
  let c1 = INT_GET_1ST_COLPAIR new_triple in
  APPEND partial_result(CONS c1 array))

Lemma 7.5: INT_CONV_TRIPLE_COLARRAY_CORRECT

⊢ ∀f triple.
 (∀c1 c2. INT_COLVAL(f c1 c2) = (INT_COLVAL c1) plus (INT_COLVAL c2)) ⊃
 (INT_ARRAYVAL 0(INT_CONV_TRIPLE_COLARRAY f triple) =
  INT_TRIPLEVAL triple)

The *INT_CSARED_1* function is defined in Definition 7.6. As it uses only formally verified column reduction and column combining functions, it is easily proved to be correct and its correctness is asserted by Lemma 7.6. *INT_CSARED_1* attempts to capture formally the heuristics used by logic designers to create carry-save adder arrays. For our multiplier example in Figure 4.1 there are two related design choices to be made. First, choosing between *INT_COLREDUCE_1, INT_COLREDUCE_2, POSITIVE_COLREDUCE_1,* and *POSITIVE_ COLREDUCE_2* to reduce columns, and second, when to use *SHUFFLE* instead of *SHUFFLE_TAIL* to combine carry outputs with partial products.

The expression *INT_CSARED_1 n index limit triple* captures the design decisions as follows: 1) *triple* is the triple being reduced, 2) *limit* specifies the arithmetic weight, i.e. $2^{lim\ it}$, at which all columns will be reduced by *INT_COLREDUCE_1* or *POSITIVE_COLREDUCE _1* instead of *INT_COLREDUCE_2* or *POSITIVE_COLREDUCE_2*, 3) *limit* also specifies when *SHUFFLE* instead of *SHUFFLE_TAIL* will be used to combine carry outputs with partial products, specifically carry outputs of weight $2^{lim\ it}$ and greater will use *SHUFFLE* instead of *SHUFFLE_TAIL*, 4) *index* specifies the arithmetic weight of the column in the column pair being reduced, and 5) *n* specifies how many more columns in the triple will be reduced.

Definition 7.6: INT_CSARED_1

```
⊢ (∀index limit triple.
    INT_CSARED_1 0 index limit triple =
    (limit ≤ index →
     INT_COLPAIR_TRANSFORM INT_COLREDUCE_1 triple |
     INT_COLPAIR_TRANSFORM INT_COLREDUCE_2 triple)) ∧
  (∀n index limit triple.
    INT_CSARED_1(SUC n)index limit triple =
    INT_CSARED_1
    n
    (SUC index)
    limit
    (limit ≤ index →
    INT_COL_COMBINE_MOVE SHUFFLE
    (COLPAIR_TRANSFORM POSITIVE_COLREDUCE_1 triple) |
    ((SUC index) < limit →
     INT_COL_COMBINE_MOVE
     SHUFFLE_TAIL
     (INT_COLPAIR_TRANSFORM POSITIVE_COLREDUCE_2 triple) |
     INT_COL_COMBINE_MOVE
     SHUFFLE
     (INT_COLPAIR_TRANSFORM POSITIVE_COLREDUCE_2 triple))))
```

Lemma 7.6: INT_CSARED_1_CORRECT

```
⊢ ∀n index limit triple.
    INT_TRIPLEVAL(INT_CSARED_1 n index limit triple) = INT_TRIPLEVAL triple
```

We finally arrive at Definition 7.7 which defines the *INT_CARRY_SAVE_1* function that creates carry-save adder arrays using *INT_CSARED_1*. Essentially, what *INT_ CARRY_SAVE_1* does is compute the arguments *n, index,* and *triple* in *INT_CSARED_1 n index limit triple*. The argument *limit* is passed to *INT_CARRY_SAVE_1* by *INT_MULT_1* in Definition 4.1 as the number of multiplicand bits. Theorem 7.1 asserts the correctness of

INT_CARRY_SAVE_1. As before, its proof is based on induction, case analysis, and rewriting based on previous definitions and lemmas.

Definition 7.7: INT_CARRY_SAVE_1

⊢ INT_CARRY_SAVE_1 array limit =
(let n = LENGTH array in
let f = ((SUC n) < limit → SHUFFLE_TAIL | SHUFFLE) in
INT_CONV_TRIPLE_COLARRAY
f
(INT_CSARED_1 n 0 limit(INT_ CONV_COLARRAY_TRIPLE array)))

Theorem 7.1: INT_CARRY_SAVE_1_CORRECT_N

⊢ ∀array limit n.
INT_ARRAYVAL n(INT_CARRY_SAVE_1 array limit) = INT_ARRAYVAL n array

8. CONCLUSIONS

Higher order logic, the HOL proof assistant, and SCHEME have been used to relate automatically synthesized functional forms corresponding to design implementations to design specifications. As the process of creating VLSI hardware becomes increasingly automated, i.e. increasingly dependent on synthesis software, the verification of synthesis methods underlying the software will become increasingly important. The synthesis functions and their associated correctness theorems are additional features which logically extend computer aided design systems for design synthesis and design verification.

Acknowledgements

Mike Gordon and Tom Melham of the University of Cambridge, U.K. made HOL88 version 0 available to me prior to its general release. The theory of integers and group theory on which my theories are partially based was given to me by Elsa Gunter of the University of Pennsylvania. I wish to thank them for their help.

References

1. Backus J., Can Programming Be Liberated from the von Neumann Style? A Functional Style and Its Algebra of Programs, *C. of the ACM Vol. 24 No. 8, 613-641, August 1978.*

2. Bryant R. E., Graph-Based Algorithms for Boolean Function Manipulation, *IEEE Trans. on Computers Vol. C-35 No. 8, 677-691, August 1986.*

3. Bryant R. E., On the Complexity of VLSI Implementations and Graph Representation of Boolean Functions with Application to Integer Multiplication, *Unpublished paper, Carnegie Mellon University, September 27, 1988.*

4. Chin S-K, Verified Hardware Synthesis Functions Using Higher Order Logic, To appear as a *CASE Center Technical Report, Syracuse University*

5. Gordon M. J. C., HOL - A Machine Oriented Formulation of Higher Order Logic, *University of Cambridge Computer Laboratory Technical Report No. 68, July 16, 1985.*

6. Gordon M. J. C., HOL - A Proof Generating System for Higher-Order Logic, *VLSI Specification, Verification and Synthesis*, Birtwistle and Subrahmanyam editors, Kluwer, 1988, 73-128.

7. Hunt W. A., The Mechanical Verification of a Microprocessor Design, *Proceedings of the IFIP Working Group 10.2 International Working Conference From H.D.L. Descriptions to Guaranteed Correct Circuit Designs, Grenoble, France, 85-114, September 9-11, 1986.*

8. Monachino M., Design Verification System for Large-Scale LSI Designs, *IBM J. Research Development Vol. 26 No. 1, 89-99, January 1982.*

9. Pezaris, S., A 40ns 17-bit-by-17-bit Array Multiplier, *IEEE Trans. Computers Vol. C-20 No. 4, 442-447, April 1971.*

10. Rees J., Clinger, W., Revised Report on the Algorithmic Language Scheme, *MIT Artificial Intelligence Laboratory, AI Memo 848A, September 1986.*

11. Sheeran M., Designing Regular Array Architectures Using Higher Order Functions, *Functional Programming Languages and Computer Architecture*, Lecture Notes in Computer Science 201, Springer-Verlag, New York, 1985, 220-237.

12. Smith G., Boolean Comparison of Hardware and Flowcharts, *IBM J. of Research Development Vol. 26 No. 1, 106-116, January 1982.*

Totally Verified Systems:
Linking Verified Software to Verified Hardware

Jeffrey J. Joyce

University of Cambridge

Abstract. We describe exploratory efforts to design and verify a compiler for a formally verified microprocessor as one aspect of the eventual goal of building *totally verified systems*. Together with a formal proof of correctness for the microprocessor, this yields a precise and rigorously established link between the semantics of the source language and the execution of compiled code by the fabricated microchip. We describe, in particular: (1) how the limitations of real hardware influenced this proof; and (2) how the general framework provided by higher-order logic was used to formalize the compiler correctness problem for a hierarchically structured language.

Keywords. compiler correctness, hardware verification, machine-assisted theorem proving, higher-order logic, safety-critical systems.

1. Introduction

Many safety-critical systems are implemented by a combination of hardware and software. The reliability of these systems depends not only on correct hardware and correct software, but also on the correctness of the compiler which provides the link between hardware and software levels. This paper describes exploratory efforts to design and verify a compiler for a formally verified microprocessor called 'Tamarack'. The source language is a very simple, hierarchically structured language with only a few basic constructs, e.g., expressions, assignment statements, while-loops, but this is enough to demonstrate how our approach could be applied to more realistic languages. We have used higher-order logic to formally specify this compiler and prove that it generates Tamarack machine code which executes correctly with respect to a denotational semantics for the source language.

The verification of this compiler builds upon an earlier proof of correctness showing that a transistor level model of the target machine satisfies a behavioural spec-

---

[1] Author's current address: Computer Laboratory, University of Cambridge, Pembroke Street, Cambridge CB2 3QG, England. After January 1, 1990: Department of Computer Science, University of British Columbia, 6356 Agricultural Road, Vancouver B.C., Canada V6T 1W5.

ification based on the semantics of the target machine instruction set [16]. The verification of both the compiler and the target machine in higher-order logic have been mechanically checked by the HOL system [13]. The HOL system has also been used to automatically generate substantial portions of these proofs.

The compiler correctness problem has a very long history beginning in the mid-1960's, but almost all of the previous work on this problem has been restricted to abstract, idealized target machines. These idealizations can include infinite word size and memory size, read-only code and symbolically addressed memory. By contrast, our target machine is not idealized hardware; indeed, an 8-bit version of the Tamarack microprocessor has been implemented as a CMOS microchip. Hence, our use of non-idealized hardware contributes to the more novel aspects of the work reported here.

Previous work has also generally relied upon specialized frameworks such as domain theory and algebraic concepts which are well-suited to the compiler correctness problem. But in the context of verifying both a compiler and the hardware of the target machine, a very general framework is needed to handle this many-sided problem. Such a framework is provided by the HOL system, a mechanization of higher-order logic, which has been used to reason about all kinds of computational systems.

Like most other examples of compiler verification, we ignore the problems of parsing and syntax analysis and use the abstract syntax of the source language as our starting point. The compiler is defined as a function which is applied to the parse tree of a program to generate code for the target machine. Semantic functions are applied in a similar way to the parse tree to generate the denotation of a program.

The work described here explores one aspect of the eventual goal of building *totally verified systems*. Assuming that our transistor level specification is an accurate model of the hardware, the compiler correctness proof combined with our earlier proof of correctness for the target machine results in a precise and rigorously established connection between the source language semantics and the execution of compiled code on the fabricated microchip. Hence, the semantics of the source language can be used to directly reason about the effect of running compiled programs on real hardware.

A detailed description of the Tamarack compiler and its formal verification is given in a separate report [17]. In this paper, we briefly outline the structure of this proof describing, in particular: (1) how the limitations of real hardware influenced this proof; and (2) how the general framework provided by higher-order logic was used to formalize the compiler correctness problem for a hierarchically structured language.

2. The Compiler Correctness Problem

The compiler correctness problem is easier to formulate than the general problem of program correctness. Unlike the general case, the compiler correctness problem has a built-in starting point for stating correctness, namely, the semantics of the source language. Intuitively, this problem is a question of whether the execution of compiled code agrees with the semantics of the source language. Compiler correctness is often expressed by the commutativity of a diagram similar to the one shown in Figure 1 where the two paths in the diagram from the source language programs to target language meanings (around opposite corners) are functionally identical.

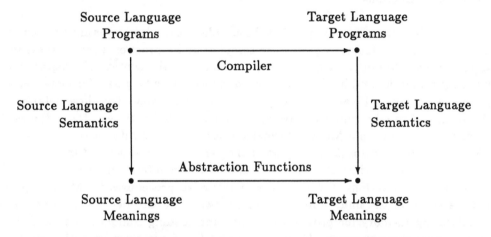

Figure 1: Compiler Correctness expressed by Commutativity.

The earliest example of compiler correctness (that we are aware of) was described more than twenty years ago by J. McCarthy and J. Painter [20]. They verified an algorithm for compiling arithmetic expressions into code for an abstract machine. This early work established a paradigm for subsequent work on compiler correctness (as summarized by A. Cohn [7]): (1) abstract syntax; (2) idealized hardware; (3) abstract specification of the compiler; (4) denotational source language semantics; (5) operational target machine semantics; (6) correctness stated as a relationship between the denotation of a program and the execution of its compiled form; and finally, (7) proofs by induction on the structure of source language expressions.

Subsequent developments include those described by: D. Kaplan [18]; R. Burstall and P. Landin [4]; R. Milner and R. Weyhrauch [23]; F. Morris [25,26]; L. Chirica [5]; R. Milne and C. Strachey [22]; J. Goguen et al. [11]; B. Russell [31]; A. Cohn [7]; W. Polak [29,30]; J. Thatcher et al. [33]; L. Chirica and D. Martin [6]; and P. Collier [9]. These developments include the use of algebraic methods and domain theory, more language features, verification by formal proof based on axioms and inference rules, mechanical assistance for proof-checking and proof-generation, and correctness proofs about parsing and syntax analysis.

However, all of the work mentioned above involves the use of a target machine with idealized features. Typically, the target machine has no finite limitations on word size or memory size. Another idealization is the use of read-only code, which avoids the problem of showing that a compiled program is not over-written during its execution. The target machine is occasionally provided with abstract mechanisms such as an infinite stack or display mechanism (admittedly, finite approximations of these mechanisms are available in real hardware). In some compiler verification examples, the memory of the target machine is addressed symbolically by program variables, dodging the problem of symbol table generation. Similarly, the target language may be block structured to avoid the complication of generating unique labels for instructions.

These idealizations, while simplifying the problem, can also be justified as reasonable strategies for structuring both the compiler and a proof of its correctness into several layers. Non-idealized aspects of hardware, in the context of programming language semantics and implementation, were recognized long ago; for instance, see papers by C. Hoare [15] and M. Newey [27]. But to our knowledge, these details and the attendant proof complexity have not been confronted until recently, in the work described here, and in J Moore's formal verification of the Piton assembler for the FM8502 microprocessor [24]. As part of the verified stack described by W. Bevier et al. [2], Piton provides considerable support as an intermediate language with stack-based instructions, typed data and recursive procedures [1]. Moore's proof takes account of the finite limitations of hardware; he also deals with issues such as allocating memory for program variables and loading compiled code and data into a single memory image. The semantics of Piton are given operationally by a formally defined interpreter expressed as a recursive function in the Lisp-like syntax of Boyer-Moore logic [3].

Our exploratory efforts with a simple 'toy' language are quite modest when compared to Moore's work on Piton. However, we have tackled a somewhat different problem by considering a hierarchically structured source language. We expect that methods similar to those described in this paper could be used to verify a compiler for a structured assembly language such as Vista [19] which is being used to write applications software for the (partially) verified Viper microprocessor [8,10,19]. Another important difference is the operational-style semantics of Piton in contrast to our denotational approach. We believe that the abstract and concise nature of a denotational semantics will be an advantage when compiler correctness results are used to relate conventional forms of reasoning about software (e.g., a verification condition generator based on Hoare logic) to the execution of compiled software on verified hardware.

---

[1] As another level in the verified stack described by Bevier et al. [2], W. Young has verified a code generator for a hierarchically structured source language with Piton as the target language [34].

3. The Source Language

Our source language is a very simple imperative language. It is not intended to be a useful programming language; it only provides a few basic constructs in order to demonstrate how our approach could be applied to more realistic languages. For instance, the only kind of compound arithmetic expression is a plus-expression. Conditional statements are not included because while-loops cover all the proof difficulties (and more) presented by conditional statements. We also simplify code generation by imposing an unusual restriction on plus-expressions and equal-expressions: the left-hand sides of these expressions must be atomic. An informal description of the abstract syntax for this language is shown below.

```
Aexp ::= {0,1,2,...} | Vars | Vars + Aexp
Bexp ::= Vars = Aexp | not Bexp
Cexp ::= skip | Vars := Aexp | Cexp ; Cexp | while Bexp do Cexp
```

There are three syntactic categories: arithmetic expressions, Boolean expressions and command expressions (or simply, commands). Vars is a set of string tokens which are used as variable names in programs, e.g., 'i' and 'sum' in the program shown in Figure 2. This program, called "SUM_0_to_9", computes the sum of the numbers 0 to 9 inclusive.

```
i := 0;
sum := 0;
while not (i = 10) do
   sum := sum + i;
   i := i + 1
```

Figure 2: The SUM_0_to_9 Program.

A denotational semantics for this simple language involves the definition of *semantic functions* for each syntactic category, namely, SemAexp, SemBexp and SemCexp. These functions map *syntactic objects* to their denotations as suggested by the type declarations,

$$\text{SemAexp}: \quad Aexp \rightarrow Asem$$
$$\text{SemBexp}: \quad Bexp \rightarrow Bsem$$
$$\text{SemCexp}: \quad Cexp \rightarrow Csem$$

where *Aexp*, *Bexp* and *Cexp* are syntactic domains and *Asem*, *Bsem* and *Csem* are the corresponding semantic domains.

These semantic functions can be described informally by a set of *semantic clauses* using the *emphatic brackets* ⟦ and ⟧ to surround syntactic objects when applying semantic functions to them [12]. *Semantic operators* on the right-hand sides of these clauses are used to construct denotations from variables, constants and denotations of sub-expressions.

```
SemAexp [v] = SemVar v
SemAexp [c] = SemConst c
SemAexp [v + aexp] = SemPlus (v,SemAexp [aexp])

SemBexp [v = aexp] = SemEq (v,SemAexp [aexp])
SemBexp [not bexp] = SemNot (SemBexp [bexp])

SemCexp [skip] = SemSkip
SemCexp [v := aexp] = SemAssign (v,SemAexp [aexp])
SemCexp [cexp1 ; cexp2] = SemThen (SemCexp [cexp1],SemCexp [cexp2])
SemCexp [while bexp do cexp] = SemWhile (SemBexp [bexp],SemCexp [cexp])
```

To formally define the functions SemAexp, SemBexp and SemCexp, we need a suitable representation for syntactic objects. This representation must allow SemAexp, SemBexp and SemCexp to be defined as functions which satisfy the above (sometimes recursive) semantic clauses. The next section of this paper describes how syntactic objects can be represented in logic as parse trees.

4. Representing Hierarchical Structure

Many of the specialized frameworks used in earlier work on compiler verification directly support the representation of syntactic objects. While a general framework does not necessarily provide this support, it is still possible to represent syntactic objects using only rudimentary data types. We have demonstrated how this can be done in higher-order logic using a relatively concrete model for the representation of syntactic objects as parse trees such as the one shown in Figure 3.

In a conventional programming language, a parse tree can be implemented by an indexed list of records. The structure of the tree would be represented by pointers (record indices) in each record to zero, one or two sub-expression(s). Such data structures can be modelled in higher-order logic [2] using: (1) n-tuples to represent records; and (2) functions from indices to n-tuples to represent indexed lists of records. Since the representing type does not restrict how records are structurally composed into parse trees, it is necessary to have *validity predicates*, ValidAexp, ValidBexp and ValidCexp, to check whether a parse tree conforms to the abstract syntax of the source language.

---

[2]The HOL formulation of higher-order logic associates a *type* with every term. Every type is a primitive type (e.g., Booleans, natural numbers, string tokens) or built up from existing types using type constructors. Cartesian product is expressed by $ty1 \times ty2$ while $ty1 \rightarrow ty2$ denotes the type of all total functions with arguments of type $ty1$ and results of type $ty2$.

Based on this representation for parse trees, we can define higher-order *mapping functions*, MapAexp, MapBexp and MapCexp, which allow a set of operations to be applied to the nodes of a parse tree in the same way that the Lisp function 'mapcar' allows an operation to be applied to the elements of a list. We use these mapping functions to define operations on parse trees by specifying operations for each kind of expression. These operations are applied recursively to the entire parse tree.

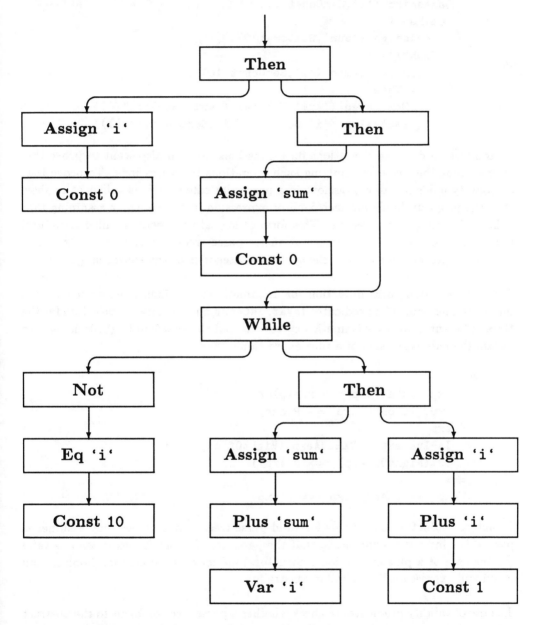

Figure 3: The Parse Tree for the SUM_0_to_9 Program.

For example, the definition of `SemCexp` (given in the next section) uses the mapping function `MapCexp` to recursively apply semantic operators to the parse tree of a command. This use of `MapCexp` is illustrated by the following term which denotes the result of applying `SemCexp` to the parse tree in Figure 3.

```
SemThen (
  SemAssign ('i',SemConst 0),
  SemThen (
    SemAssign ('sum',SemConst 0),
    SemWhile (
      SemNot (SemEq ('i',SemConst 10)),
      SemThen (
        SemAssign ('sum',SemPlus ('sum',SemVar 'i')),
        SemAssign ('i',SemPlus ('i',SemConst 1)))))))
```

In addition to defining operations on expressions, we will also want to prove theorems about the result of applying such operations to expressions. To prove that a property holds for all expressions in a particular category, it is sufficient to show that the property holds for each kind of expression in the category assuming that it holds for all sub-expressions. This form of logical argument is called structural induction. Based on our representation for parse trees, we can prove structural induction theorems for each of the syntactic categories of the source language.

For instance, structural induction for arithmetic expressions is expressed by the following theorem. The predicates `IsVar`, `IsConst` and `IsPlus` are selectors for the three different kinds of arithmetic expressions and the function `RightOf` is used to obtain the sub-expression of a plus-expression.

$$\vdash_{thm} \forall P.$$
$$(\forall exp.\ IsVar\ exp \implies P\ exp) \land$$
$$(\forall exp.\ IsConst\ exp \implies P\ exp) \land$$
$$(\forall exp.$$
$$IsPlus\ exp \land ValidAexp\ (RightOf\ exp) \implies$$
$$(P\ (RightOf\ exp) \implies P\ exp))$$
$$\implies$$
$$\forall exp.\ ValidAexp\ exp \implies P\ exp$$

Structural induction only holds for valid parse trees; however, we may assume, as part of the inductive hypothesis, that the parse tree for the sub-expression is valid (in the case of a plus-expression). Structural induction theorems for Boolean and command expression have similar constraints.

The use of validity predicates to check whether a parse tree conforms to the abstract syntax of the source language is slightly cumbersome. Validity predicates provide a simple way to represent structure in a generalized framework using only rudimentary data types. A more elegant approach avoids the use of validity predicates by formally introducing new types (as sub-types of the representing type) which contain (by definition) only valid syntactic objects.

We have used a relatively concrete representation for syntactic objects as collections of records organized into parse trees. The details of this representation are unimportant and are hidden at early point in our proof by the derivation of *abstract specifications* for the mapping functions MapAexp, MapBexp and MapCexp and the derivation of the above-mentioned structural induction theorems. In a more abstract approach, the unimportant details of a concrete representation can be entirely avoided by directly introducing a recursive type whose elements are (by definition) valid syntactic objects. This approach was taken by Cohn [7] working in LCF which is also a typed logic. This more abstract approach could also be followed in our higher-order logic framework - a task made easier by T. Melham's recent implementation of a recursive data types package for the HOL system [21].

To summarize this section, syntactic objects can be represented as parse trees which, in turn, can be represented by rudimentary data types in a generalized framework such as higher-order logic. Operations on parse trees can be defined in terms of a set of mapping functions; reasoning about parse trees is supported by a corresponding set of structural induction theorems. Full details on this representation, the mapping functions and the structural induction theorems are given in [17].

5. Semantics

A denotational semantics for the source language can be defined in higher-order logic using higher-order functions and relations as the denotations of expressions and commands respectively. This is a somewhat different framework than usual, i.e., Scott's logic for computable functions, but it is denotational in the sense that program constructs are mapped to abstract mathematical entities [12]. M. Gordon has also used higher-order logic to represent a denotational semantics in a similar manner [14].

The execution of a program is modelled by a sequence of states where each state is a mapping from variable names to their values. In this simple language only natural numbers can be assigned to variables. Hence, a state is represented by a function from string tokens to the natural numbers as shown by the following type abbreviation.

$$state = tok \rightarrow num$$

The execution of a source language program results in a sequence of updates to the current state. We use a standard model from denotational semantics for the effect of an update. The function Update creates a new state identical to the current state except for the updated variable which is assigned a new value. The following definition introduces some of our notation: Update is defined in terms of a function-denoting λ-expression and a conditional expression of the form "b $\Rightarrow$ t1 | t2".

$\vdash_{def}$ Update (s:*state*,x,y) = λz. (x = z) $\Rightarrow$ y | (s z)

The denotations for arithmetic and Boolean expressions are functions which specify the value of the expression in terms of the current state. The denotation of a command is a relation on pairs of initial and final states. The following type abbreviations summarize the types of denotations used for each of the three syntactic categories. These denotations are each parameterized by a number, namely, the word size of the target machine.

$$Asem = num{\rightarrow}state{\rightarrow}num$$
$$Bsem = num{\rightarrow}state{\rightarrow}bool$$
$$Csem = num{\rightarrow}(state{\times}state){\rightarrow}bool$$

We can now begin to define semantic operators for expressions and commands in the source language. The definition of SemVar states that the denotation of a variable is its value in the current state. This operator is a *curried* function which takes its arguments 'one at a time'. When SemVar is applied to the first of its arguments, i.e., SemVar v, the result is a term with the type given by the type abbreviation *Asem* (where ws is the word size of the target machine).

$\vdash_{def}$ SemVar (v:*tok*) = λws. λq. q v

The denotation of a constant is the value of the constant modulo the word size of the target machine. This use of the MOD function is due to our eventual goal of relating the semantics of the source language to the execution of compiled programs. Modular arithmetic is a convenient way of taking into account the finite word size of non-idealized hardware; an early example of this use of modular arithmetic appears in Hoare's seminal paper on axiomatic semantics [15].

$\vdash_{def}$ SemConst (c:*num*) = λws. λq. c MOD 2^{ws}

A plus-expression is an example of a compound expression; its denotation is obtained from its immediate constituents, in this case, from the sub-expression on the right-hand side of the '+'. Modular arithmetic is also used here to model the finite word size of the target machine.

$\vdash_{def}$ SemPlus (v:*tok*,s:*Asem*) = λws. λq. ((q v) + (s ws q)) MOD 2^{ws}

The semantic operator for equal-expressions is parameterized by the string token appearing on the left-hand side of the '=' and by the denotation of its arithmetic sub-expression. The semantic operator for not-expressions is parameterized by the denotation of its Boolean sub-expression.

$\vdash_{def}$ SemEq (v:tok,s:$Asem$) = λws. λq. (q v) = (s ws q)

$\vdash_{def}$ SemNot (s:$Bsem$) = λws. λq. $\neg$(s ws q)

The semantic operators for commands yield relations on pairs of states. The simplest case is the Skip command which has no effect on the state. Therefore, the initial and final states of a Skip command are related if they are identical [3].

$\vdash_{def}$ SemSkip = λws. λ(q1,q2). q1 = q2

In the case of an assignment statement, the final state is obtained from the initial state by the Update function.

$\vdash_{def}$ SemAssign (v:tok,s:$Asem$) =
     λws. λ(q1,q2). q2 = Update (q1,v,s ws q1)

In defining the semantics of a then-command (two commands in sequence), the two sub-commands must share a common intermediate state. Higher-order existential quantification is used to hide this intermediate state in the definition of SemThen. In a more standard framework, the denotation for a sequence of commands would be obtained by the functional composition of two partial functions. Partial functions allow for the possibility of non-terminating commands; however, all functions in higher-order logic are total. For this reason, we are using relations instead of partial functions. Our use of existential quantification for the denotation of a then-command is the analogue of functional composition for relations.

$\vdash_{def}$ SemThen (s1:$Csem$,s2:$Csem$) =
     λws. λ(q1,q2). $\exists$q3. s1 ws (q1,q3) $\wedge$ s2 ws (q3,q2)

The function Step is defined (by primitive recursion) to describe the condition where n iterations of a while-loop result in a final state, that is, a state in which the Boolean condition is false. Zero iterations of the while-loop is equivalent to the execution of a Skip command; otherwise, n iterations of the while-loop has the same effect as executing the body of the while-loop once followed by n-1 iterations of the while-loop. The semantic operators SemSkip and SemThen are used to define the zero and non-zero cases respectively. Since the actual number of iterations is not relevant to the semantics of a while-loop, this number is hidden by existential quantification in the definition of SemWhile.

---

[3] Predicates (including relations) in the HOL formulation of higher-order logic are simply functions which return Boolean values. Hence, the lambda expression, λ(q1,q2). q1 = q2 denotes the equality relation for pairs of states.

$\vdash_{def}$ Step n (s1:$Bsem$,s2:$Csem$) ws (q1,q2) =
    (n = 0) $\Rightarrow$ (((s1 ws q1) = F) $\wedge$ SemSkip ws (q1,q2)) |
     (((s1 ws q1) = T) $\wedge$
       SemThen (s2,Step (n-1) (s1,s2)) ws (q1,q2))

$\vdash_{def}$ SemWhile (s1:$Bsem$,s2:$Csem$) =
    λws. λ(q1,q2). $\exists$n. Step n (s1,s2) ws (q1,q2)

Although our use of higher-order logic is an unusual framework for denotational semantics, some familiar properties can be derived for the semantic operators from the definitions given in this section. For instance, assuming for a moment that our source language also includes conditional statements, the while-loop ,

$$\ulcorner\text{while bexp do cexp}\urcorner$$

should have the same meaning as,

$$\ulcorner\text{if bexp then (cexp ; while bexp do cexp) else skip}\urcorner$$

This property is expressed formally by the theorem,

$\vdash_{thm}$ $\forall$ s1 s2.
    SemWhile (s1,s2) =
      SemCond (s1,SemThen (s2,SemWhile (s1,s2)),SemSkip)

where SemCond is a semantic operator for conditional statements defined as:

$\vdash_{def}$ SemCond (s1:$Bsem$,s2:$Csem$,s3:$Csem$) =
    λws. λ(q1,q2).
      ((s1 ws q1) = T) $\Rightarrow$ (s2 ws (q1,q2)) | (s3 ws (q1,q2))

The operators, SemVar, SemConst, SemPlus, SemEq, SemNot, SemSkip, SemAssign, SemThen and SemWhile, describe how the denotation of an expression is obtained from its top-level form and the denotations of its sub-expressions. The denotation of a complete expression (including commands, and hence, complete programs) is obtained by using the mapping functions mentioned in Section 4 to recursively apply these operators to every node in a parse tree. From the *abstract specifications* for MapAexp, MapBexp and MapCexp given in [17], it is quite easy to show that the following definitions satisfy the semantic clauses given earlier in Section 3.

$\vdash_{def}$ SemAexp = MapAexp (SemVar,SemConst,SemPlus)

$\vdash_{def}$ SemBexp = MapBexp (SemAexp,SemEq,SemNot)

$\vdash_{def}$ SemCexp =
    MapCexp (SemAexp,SemBexp,SemSkip,SemAssign,SemThen,SemWhile)

Later in this paper we will show how the mapping functions are used in a similar way to compile a complete program by recursively applying *compilation operators* to every node in a parse tree.

6. Compiler Overview

The Tamarack compiler is implemented by two phases. The original motivation for splitting the compilation process into two phases was to control the complexity of the formal proof of correctness. However, the use of an intermediate form is common practice in compiler design for more conventional reasons. For instance, it may be possible to compile more than one source language into the intermediate form and/or compile the intermediate form into the machine code of more than one target machine. This also suggests certain opportunities for re-using correctness results.

The first phase compiles the hierarchically structured program into a flat intermediate form called SM code. In general, this is a process of compiling an expression by first compiling its sub-expressions (if any) and then using the result to generate code for the expression itself. The second phase of the compiler assembles SM code into executable Tamarack machine code called TM code. To generate TM code from the intermediate form, a symbol table is constructed to map symbols in the source program to memory addresses. Each SM instruction is mapped to a fragment of TM code where each TM instruction is a 3-bit opcode and an address field packed together into a single memory word. This second phase of the compilation process performs (very simple versions of) the tasks associated with the assembler and linking loader in a conventional programming environment. The two phases of the compilation process are shown in Figure 4 where the example SUM_0_to_9 program is first compiled into SM code and then assembled into TM code.

As an intermediate form, SM code shares some common features with the source language. In both cases, storage is addressed symbolically by variable names and 'program space' is separate from data and cannot be over-written. However, SM code also shares some common features with the target language, in particular, they are both linear sequences of accumulator-based instructions.

The semantics of SM code are described operationally by the specification of an abstract machine (called an SM machine) which directly executes this intermediate form. The SM machine consists of a fixed program, an infinite, symbolically addressed store, a program counter and an accumulator. For simplicity, we have designed the SM machine to operate exclusively on natural numbers where multiple data types might otherwise have been used. The Boolean values T and F are represented by the natural numbers 0 and 1 respectively. Modular arithmetic is used to model the finite word size of the target machine.

```
base:        (LD n (base+2))
             (JMP n (base+3))
             (0 MOD 2^(n+3))
base+3:      (ST n (symtab 'i'))
base+4:      (LD n (base+6))
             (JMP n (base+7))
             (0 MOD 2^(n+3))
base+7:      (ST n (symtab 'sum'))
base+8:      (LD n (base+10))
             (JMP n (base+11))
             (10 MOD 2^(n+3))
base+11:     (SUB n (symtab 'i'))
             (JZR n (base+16))
             (LD n (base+15))
             (JMP n (base+16))
             1
base+16:     (JZR n (base+20))
             (LD n (base+19))
             (JMP n (base+23))
             0
             (LD n (base+22))
             (JMP n (base+23))
             1
base+23:     (JZR n (base+27))
             (LD n (base+26))
             (JMP n (base+30))
             0
             (LD n (base+29))
             (JMP n (base+30))
             1
base+30:     (JZR n (base+40))
base+31:     (LD n (symtab 'i'))
base+32:     (ADD n (symtab 'sum'))
base+33:     (ST n (symtab 'sum'))
base+34:     (LD n (base+36))
             (JMP n (base+37))
             (1 MOD 2^(n+3))
base+37:     (ADD n (symtab 'i'))
base+38:     (ST n (symtab 'i'))
base+39:     (JMP n (base+8))
base+40:
```

```
i := 0;
sum := 0;
while not (i = 10) do
  sum := sum + i;
  i := i + 1
```

$\Downarrow$

```
base:        ('CONST',ARB,0)
             ('ST','i',ARB)
             ('CONST',ARB,0)
             ('ST','sum',ARB)
base+4:      ('CONST',ARB,10)
             ('EQ','i',ARB)
             ('NOT',ARB,ARB)
             ('NOT',ARB,ARB)
             ('JZR',ARB,base+16)
             ('LD','i',ARB)
             ('ADD','sum',ARB)
             ('ST','sum',ARB)
             ('CONST',ARB,1)
             ('ADD','i',ARB)
             ('ST','i',ARB)
             ('JMP',ARB,base+4)
base+16:
```

$\Rightarrow$

Figure 4.

7. Compiling Expressions and Commands

We begin to specify the compiler by defining a function for each kind of expression which compiles that expression into SM code. Each of these functions operates only on the top-level form of the expression; sub-expressions (if any) are compiled separately and the results supplied as arguments to the function. There is a close parallel between the role of these functions in compiling a hierarchically structured program and the semantic operators mentioned earlier in Section 5. For this reason, we call these functions *compilation operators*.

The intuitive sense in which the compilation operators for arithmetic and Boolean expressions are correct is fairly obvious. For instance, the compilation operator for plus-expressions is correct if and only if execution of the compiled code loads the sum of the sub-expression and the value of the program variable into the accumulator. In general, a compilation operator is correct if and only if the effect of executing the code generated for an expression or command agrees with its denotation generated by the corresponding semantic operator. In the case of an arithmetic expression, the value of the accumulator after executing the compiled code must be equal to the value given by its denotation in the current state. For a Boolean expression, the accumulator must contain either 0 or 1 depending on whether the denotation of the expression evaluates to true or false respectively.

Because commands do not necessarily terminate, the sense in which compilation operators for commands are correct is less obvious. By 'termination', we mean that the denotation of a command relates the initial state q1 to a final state q2, i.e., that there exists a final state q2.

$\vdash_{def}$ `Terminates p ws q1 = ∃q2. SemCexp p ws (q1,q2)`

Termination, in this sense, is a property of the abstract mathematical entities denoted by source language programs; the question of whether the SM machine halts when the compiled form of the program is executed is *prima facie* a different matter. For an SM machine 'to halt', means that it eventually reaches the end of the SM code.

Using these distinct notions of termination and halting, the correctness of a compilation operator for a command is expressed by separate conditions for the terminating and non-terminating cases. In the terminating case, the SM machine must halt and the final state of its store must agree with the final state given by the corresponding denotation. In the non-terminating case, the SM machine must not halt.

After formalizing these intuitive notions of correctness, we prove that the compilation operator for each kind of expression is correct with respect to the corresponding semantic operator. These correctness results are obtained by a sequence of inferences patterned on the *symbolic execution* of the compiled code for an expression. This use of the term 'symbolic execution' is purely descriptive; our proof technique is based entirely on the inference rules of higher-order logic.

This proof technique is straightforward for atomic expressions. Each step in the symbolic execution of the compiled code corresponds to the symbolic execution of a single SM instruction. A formal model of the SM machine is specified in terms of a *next state function* which is used to step through the code generated by the compilation operator for the atomic expression. After the appropriate number of steps, we show that the resulting state of the SM machine satisfies the correctness condition for this expression.

For compound expressions (including compound commands) symbolic execution involves steps corresponding to the execution of sub-expressions in addition to the execution of single SM instructions. We assume that the appropriate correctness conditions hold for the sub-expressions and use these assumptions to reason about the execution of each sub-expression as single steps in the symbolic execution of the compound expression. The remaining steps (steps corresponding to single SM instructions) are symbolically executed by an application of the next state function.

For example, the following theorem states that the top-level form of a plus-expression is compiled correctly by the compilation operator CmpPlus with respect to the denotation produced by the semantic operator SemPlus. The correctness condition for arithmetic expressions is expressed by the predicate AexpCorrect. The variables c and s are the compiled code and denotation respectively of the sub-expression on the right-hand side of the '+'.

$\vdash_{thm}$ ∀ c s v.
      AexpCorrect (c,s) $\implies$
      AexpCorrect (CmpPlus (v,c),SemPlus (v,s))

Similar results are obtained for every other kind of expression in the source language. For most expressions, symbolic execution corresponds to a fixed sequence of steps. However, correctness results for while-loops are more difficult and involve proofs by mathematical induction. The terminating case for while-loops is proved by mathematical induction on the number of iterations. The non-terminating case is even more difficult because there is more than one way that a while-loop can fail to terminate: at any point, the body of the while-loop may fail to terminate, or else the while-loop itself may continue to loop forever.

There are two essential ideas being used here to reason about compound expressions. One is the idea of using assumptions about the correctness of sub-expressions to prove correctness results for compound expressions. The other is the idea of 'mixed-mode' symbolic execution where single steps correspond to either single SM instructions or to sub-expressions.

8. Compiling Complete Programs

In section 4 we showed how semantic functions for each syntactic category can be defined by applying the mapping functions MapAexp, MapBexp and MapCexp to the semantic operators. In a similar manner, *compilation functions* for each syntactic category can be obtained by applying the mapping functions to the compilation operators.

$\vdash_{def}$ CmpAexp = MapAexp (CmpVar,CmpConst,CmpPlus)

$\vdash_{def}$ CmpBexp = MapBexp (CmpAexp,CmpEq,CmpNot)

$\vdash_{def}$ CmpCexp =
MapCexp (CmpAexp,CmpBexp,CmpSkip,CmpAssign,CmpThen,CmpWhile)

The correctness of these compilation functions is easily established from correctness results for each compilation operator using the structural induction theorems mentioned in Section 4.

These correctness results lead directly to the following theorem where the variable p denotes any source language program. The predicate SMHalts is defined directly in terms of the formally specified model of the SM machine. For a given SM program, SMHalts describes a relation on pairs of states (q1,q2) where the SM machine begins execution in state q1 and eventually halts in state q2. Hence, SMHalts is a semantic function for SM code.

$\vdash_{thm}$ $\forall$p. ValidCexp p $\implies$ (SemCexp p = SMHalts (CmpCexp p))

This theorem is the main result from the first part of our compiler correctness proof: it relates the denotational semantics of our source language to an operational semantics given by SMHalts applied to the compiled code generated by CmpCexp. We are using the term 'operational semantics' in a somewhat old-fashioned sense [4] where the semantics is given by an abstract machine and a translation from the source language into code for the abstract machine [32].

This result can also be expressed by the commutative diagram in Figure 5 which is similar to diagrams found in other discussions of the compiler correctness problem. In this case, there is no need for an abstraction function from source language meanings to target language meanings since they are identical. Consequently, the diagram has only three sides.

---

[4] A more recent form of operational semantics known as *Plotkin-style* or *natural* semantics has both structure and some denotational-style features [28].

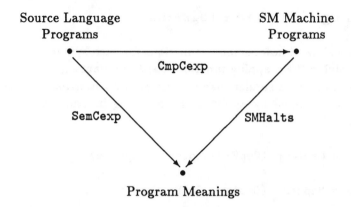

Figure 5: Compiler Correctness expressed by Commutativity.

The second part of our correctness proof considers the assembly of SM programs into TM code establishing a correspondence between the direct execution of an SM program and the execution of an assembled SM program by the target machine. Later, this result is combined with the above theorem to obtain a direct correspondence between the denotation of a source language program and the execution of its compiled form by the target machine.

9. Assembling Intermediate Code

The external architecture of the Tamarack microprocessor consists of three state components: the memory, program counter and accumulator. A single instruction word format is used by all Tamarack instructions: a 3-bit opcode followed by n address bits. The actual size of the address field is given by a parameter throughout the formal proof of correctness. The transistor level model of the Tamarack implementation is also parameterized by the size of the address field. The correctness of this implementation has been established for all possible sizes.

The assembly of SM code into TM code requires the generation of a *symbol table*, symtab, which maps string tokens appearing in SM instructions to memory addresses. Symbols (i.e., string tokens) are only added to the table when they appear on the left-hand side of an assignment statement in the source language program. Since each assignment statement corresponds to an ST instruction in the resulting SM code, symbols are only added to the table when they appear in the SM code as an operand in an ST instruction. The symbol table is generated by a single pass over the SM program. When a new symbol is added to the table, it is assigned the address of the next available location in the data area of memory.

The assembly of SM code into TM code also requires an *address table*, addrof, which maps locations in the SM code to corresponding locations in the TM code.

The location of the TM code generated for a particular SM instruction can be determined by adding up the sizes of the code fragments generated for all preceding SM instructions. This table can also be generated by a single pass over the SM program.

The symbol table, symtab, and address table, addrof, are used in a third pass over the SM program to generate the TM code. Most SM instructions are assembled into a single TM instruction. However, a CONST instruction, used to load a constant into the accumulator, is assembled into a three word fragment of TM code: an LD instruction; a JMP instruction; and the constant itself which is stored in a separate memory word (i.e., as an immediate constant). The JMP instruction prevents the constant from being executed as an instruction. The SM instructions EQ and NOT are also assembled into multiple words of TM code. This is because 0 and 1, representing true and false respectively, are stored as immediate constants [5].

For conceptual clarity, we have separated the assembly of SM code into three successive passes. However, there are well-known techniques, e.g., 'back-patching', which can be used to reduce the number of passes in a compiler [1].

Each of the three passes used to assemble SM code into TM code can be formally defined as an operation applied iteratively to a sequence of SM instructions; in concrete terms these functions can be defined by primitive recursion on the size of the SM code. As one might expect, correctness results for each of these passes over the SM code will involve proofs by induction on the size of the SM code.

Correctness results for symbol table generation show that the iteratively generated symbol table has several properties needed to prove that SM code is correctly assembled into TM code. For instance, we show that different symbols are mapped to different addresses. Several other less obvious properties are described in [17].

The rest of the proof is concerned with showing that SM code is correctly assembled into TM code. Intuitively, it is fairly obvious what conditions need to be satisfied: execution of the TM code must correspond to the execution of the SM program. There are several provisos, most of which arise from limitations of the finite word size and finite memory size of the target machine.

Earlier steps in the correctness proof have already been influenced by the finite limitations of the target machine: the finite word size of the target machine is a feature of both the denotational semantics of the source language and the operational semantics of SM code. However, correctness results for the first compiler phase place no bounds on the size of the SM code or the size of the store. Therefore, finite limitations of the target machine are more important in the second part of the

---

[5] The use of immediate constants was slightly easier (in the initial effort of developing this proof) than the more economical approach of storing a single instance of these constants in memory.

correctness proof when showing that SM code is correctly assembled into TM code. The size of addressable memory is limited by the number of bits in the address field of a target machine instruction. The memory area reserved for code must be large enough to accommodate the code generated by the assembler. Similarly, the area reserved for data must provide a separate memory word for each symbol in the symbol table. These two areas of memory must not overlap and cannot exceed the boundaries of addressable memory. We assume explicitly that these conditions are satisfied in proving that SM code is correctly assembled into TM code.

The sense in which the execution of TM code 'corresponds' to the execution of an SM program is, roughly speaking, the condition that updates to the memory state, program counter and accumulator of the target machine correspond to updates to the store, program counter and accumulator of the SM machine. There are three distinct steps in proving that execution of the assembled form of an SM program corresponds to its direct execution by the SM machine. These three steps are very briefly summarized in the next few paragraphs.

The first step establishes that the execution of the compiled form of individual SM instructions corresponds to their direct execution by the SM machine. This step in the proof is concerned with the fragments of TM code generated for each SM instruction. For each SM instruction, we prove that the symbolic execution of the TM code fragment by repeated applications of the next state function for the target machine corresponds to a single application of the next state function for the SM machine. This step also proves that execution of the code fragment does not over-write any part of the TM code.

The second step establishes that the fragments of TM code generated for each SM instruction are correctly composed into a single fragment of TM code for the entire SM program. This step is proved by mathematical induction on the size of the SM program.

The third step establishes that the execution of an assembled SM program corresponds to its direct execution by the SM machine for any number of execution steps (within the limitations of the target machine). This step is proved by mathematical induction on the number of execution steps.

The correctness result obtained from these three steps states precise details about the relationship between the execution of an assembled SM program and its direct execution by the SM machine. In very simple terms, there exists an SM machine which provides an abstract model of the target machine while executing the compiled SM program. Therefore, true statements about the direct execution of the SM program are also true statements about the execution of its compiled form by the target machine. This theorem is used in combination with earlier results to obtain a correctness result for the complete compilation process.

10. Combining Two Levels of Correctness Results

The final step in the verification of the Tamarack compiler combines correctness results for the two phases of the compilation process.

Earlier correctness results for the first compiler phase established that direct execution of the SM code generated from a terminating source language program will result in a final state which agrees with its denotation. In the case of a non-terminating program, the SM machine will not halt. For the second compiler phase, we have just seen that 'true statements about the direct execution of the SM program are also true statements about the execution of its assembled form by the target machine'.

The combination of these two results implies that a terminating source language program will be compiled into target machine code which will execute to completion and yield a final state which agrees with its denotation. This depends, of course, on whether the compiled program can be loaded into addressable memory. A precise statement of this result uses the symbol table generated by the compiler for this program to relate memory states of the target machine to the denotation of the source language program. In the case of a non-terminating program, the target machine will never complete execution of the compiled code. The correctness theorem for the terminating case is shown below.

```
⊢thm ∀ p n mem.
        ValidCexp p ∧
        CompiledAndLoaded n p (mem 0) ∧
        Terminates p (n+3) ((mem 0)∘(SymTab p))
        ⟹
        ∀ pc acc.
          TM n (mem,pc,acc) ∧
          (pc 0 = 0)
          ⟹
          ∃t.
            FirstReaches (pc,t,EndOfProg p) ∧
            SemCexp p (n+3) ((mem 0)∘(SymTab p),(mem t)∘(SymTab p))
```

To paraphrase this theorem: if the compiled code for a syntactically valid, terminating program is loaded into memory at location 0 and executed by the target machine (whose behaviour is given by the predicate TM) beginning at time 0, then the target machine will eventually reach the end of the code at some time t. When execution of this code is completed, an abstract view of the initial memory state will be related to an abstract view of the final memory state by the denotation of the program. An 'abstract view' of the memory state is obtained by using the symbol table to access the contents of the target machine memory; in the above theorem, this is expressed by use of the operator '∘' which denotes functional composition.

11. Summary

Our main correctness theorem provides a direct link between the semantics of the source language and the behavioural specification of the Tamarack microprocessor. When coupled with an earlier proof of correctness relating this behavioural specification to a transistor level model of the hardware, we obtain a precise and rigorously established connection between the denotation of a source language program and the effect of executing its compiled form on actual hardware.

A link between software and hardware levels provides a sound basis for using the semantics of the source language to reason about programs. In related work, Gordon [14] shows how Hoare logic can be embedded in higher-order logic by regarding the syntax of Hoare formulae as abbreviations for higher-order logic formulae. The axioms and inference rules of Hoare logic are then derived from semantic operators similar to the semantic operators defined in Section 5 of this paper. This means that theorems proved in Hoare logic using these axioms and rules are logical consequences of the underlying denotational semantics.

To relate this work to our correctness results for the Tamarack compiler, we would need to slightly re-formulate the axioms and rules of Hoare logic to take account of the finite size of memory words as we have done for the semantic operators in Section 5. It would then follow that theorems proved in Hoare logic about a particular program are true statements about the result of executing the compiled program on the fabricated microchip. This depends, of course, on both explicit conditions, e.g., whether the compiled code fits into addressable memory, and implicit assumptions, e.g., that the transistor level specification is an accurate model of the hardware.

In this exploratory effort, we have not ventured beyond a traditional view of formal semantics that the meaning of a program is either a partial function from initial states to final states or, as in our approach, a relation between initial and final states. However, we are interested in embedded systems where a 'batch processing' view of program behaviour is not entirely appropriate. These systems continuously interact with an environment; they are typically implemented by a fixed program compiled and loaded into the memory of one or more microprocessors. Unlike a batch job, execution of the compiled code is meant to execute forever, or at least, until the microprocessor is reset or switched off. Instead of a final outcome, we are interested in the on-going behaviour of the microprocessor while executing the compiled code. We are concerned, for instance, that the system responds correctly to external stimuli or that certain invariants are maintained. Therefore, an important direction of future work will be to investigate the relationship between suitable kinds of semantics for proving the correctness of a compiler and formalisms which can be used to reason about continuously-operating systems.

Acknowledgements

I am grateful to Juanito Camilleri, Avra Cohn, Mike Gordon, John Herbert, Miriam Leeser and Glynn Winskel who have helped in various ways with this work. This research has been funded by the Cambridge Commonwealth Trust, the Canada Centennial Scholarship Fund, the Government of Alberta Heritage Fund, the Natural Sciences and Engineering Research Council of Canada, Pembroke College, and the UK Overseas Research Student Awards Scheme.

[1] Alfred V. Aho and Jeffrey D. Ullman, Principles of Compiler Design, Addison-Wesley, Reading, MA., 1977.

[2] William R. Bevier, Warren A. Hunt, Jr., and William D. Young, in: Towards Verified Execution Environments, in: Procs. of the 1987 IEEE Symposium on Security and Privacy, 27-29 April 1987, Oakland, California Computer Society Press, Washington, D.C., 1987 pp. 106-115. Also Technical Report No. 5, Computational Logic, Inc., Austin, Texas, February 1987.

[3] R.S. Boyer and J S. Moore, A Computational Logic, Academic Press, New York, 1979.

[4] R.M. Burstall and P.J. Landin, Programs and their Proofs: an Algebraic Approach, in: B. Meltzer and D. Mitchie, eds., Machine Intelligence, Vol. 4, Edinburgh Univ. Press, Edinburgh, Scotland, 1969. pp. 17-43.

[5] L.M. Chirica, Contributions to Compiler Correctness, Ph.D. Thesis, Report UCLA-ENG-7697, Computer Science Dept., Univ. of California, Los Angeles, October 1976.

[6] Laurian M. Chirica and David F. Martin, Toward Compiler Implementation Correctness Proofs, ACM Transactions on Programming Languages and Systems, Vol. 8, No. 2, April 1986, pp. 185-214.

[7] Avra Jean Cohn, Machine Assisted Proofs of Recursion Implementation, Ph.D. Thesis, Technical Report CST-6-79, Dept. of Computer Science, Univ. of Edinburgh, April 1980.

[8] Avra Cohn, Correctness Properties of the Viper Block Model: The Second Level, in: G. Birtwistle and P. Subrahmanyam, eds., Current Trends in Hardware Verification and Automated Theorem Proving, Springer-Verlag, New York, 1989, pp. 1-91. Also Report No. 134, Computer Lab., Cambridge Univ., May 1988.

[9] P.A. Collier, Simple Compiler Correctness - A Tutorial on the Algebraic Approach, Australian Computer Journ., Vol. 18, No. 3, August 1986, pp. 128-135.

[10] W.J. Cullyer, High Integrity Computing, in: M. Joseph, ed., Formal Techniques in Real-Time and Fault-Tolerant Systems, Lecture Notes in Computer Science, No. 331, Springer-Verlag, Berlin, 1988. pp. 1-35.

[11] J.A. Goguen, J.W. Thatcher, E.G. Wagner, and J.B. Wright, Initial Algebra Semantics and Continuous Algebra, Journ. of the ACM, Vol. 24, No. 1, January 1977, pp. 68-95.

[12] Michael J. C. Gordon, The Denotational Description of Programming Languages, Spring-Verlag, Berlin, 1979.

[13] Mike Gordon, A Proof Generating System for Higher-Order Logic, in: G. Birtwistle and P. Subrahmanyam, eds., VLSI Specification, Verification and Synthesis, Kluwer Academic Publishers, Boston, 1988, pp. 73-128. Also Report No. 103, Computer Lab., Cambridge Univ., January 1987.

[14] Michael J. C. Gordon, Mechanizing Programming Logics in Higher Order Logic, in: G. Birtwistle and P. Subrahmanyam, eds., Current Trends in Hardware Verification and Automated Theorem Proving, Springer-Verlag, New York, 1989, pp. 387-439. Also Report No. 145, Computer Lab., Cambridge Univ., September 1988.

[15] C.A.R. Hoare, An Axiomatic Basis for Computer Programming, Communications of the ACM, Vol. 12, No. 10, October 1969, pp. 576-583.

[16] Jeffrey J. Joyce, Formal Specification and Verification of Microprocessor Systems, in: S. Winter and H. Schumny, eds., Euromicro 88, Procs. of the 14th Symposium on Microprocessing and Microprogramming, Zurich, Switzerland, 29 August - 1 September, 1988, North-Holland, Amsterdam, 1988, pp. 371-378. Also Report No. 147, Computer Lab., Cambridge Univ., September 1988.

[17] Jeffrey J. Joyce, A Verified Compiler for a Verified Microprocessor, Report No. 167, Computer Lab., Cambridge Univ., March 1989.

[18] Donald M. Kaplan, Correctness of a Compiler for Algol-like Programs, Stanford Artificial Intelligence Memo No. 48, Stanford Univ., July 1967.

[19] J. Kershaw, The VIPER Microprocessor, Report No. 87014, RSRE, Malvern, UK Ministry of Defence, November 1987.

[20] J. McCarthy and J. Painter, Correctness of a Compiler for Arithmetic Expressions, in: J. Schwartz, ed., Procs. of a Symposia on Applied Mathematics, American Mathematical Society, 1967, pp. 33-41.

[21] Thomas F. Melham, Automating Recursive Type Definitions in Higher Order Logic, in: G. Birtwistle and P. Subrahmanyam, eds., Current Trends in Hardware Verification and Automated Theorem Proving, Springer-Verlag, New York, 1989, pp. 341-386. Also Report No. 146, Computer Lab., Cambridge Univ., September 1988.

[22] Robert Milne and Christopher Strachey, A Theory of Programming Language Semantics, Chapman and Hall, London, 1976.

[23] R. Milner and R. Weyhrauch, Proving Compiler Correctness in a Mechanized Logic, in: B. Meltzer and D. Mitchie, eds., Machine Intelligence, Vol. 7, Edinburgh Univ. Press, Edinburgh, Scotland, 1972, pp. 51-70.

[24] J Strother Moore, A Mechanically Verified Language Implementation, Report No. 30, Computational Logic Inc., Austin, Texas, September 1988.

[25] F. Lockwood Morris, Correctness of Translations of Programming Languages, Ph.D. Thesis, Report STAN-CS-72-303, Computer Science Dept., Stanford Univ., August 1972.

[26] F. Lockwood Morris, Advice on Structuring Compilers and Proving Them Correct, in: Procs. of the ACM Symposium on Principles of Programming Languages, Boston, Mass., October 1973, pp. 144-152.

[27] Malcolm C. Newey, Proving Properties of Assembly Language Programs, in: B. Gilchrist, ed., Information Processing 77, North Holland, 1977, pp. 795-799.

[28] Gordon D. Plotkin, A Structured Approach to Operational Semantics, Technical Report DAIMI FN-19, Computer Science Dept., Aarhus Univ., September 1981.

[29] Wolfgang Heinz Polak, Theory of Compiler Specification and Verification, Ph.D. Thesis, Report No. STAN-CS-80-802, Dept. of Computer Science, Stanford Univ., May 1980.

[30] Wolfgang Heinz Polak, Compiler Specification and Verification, Lecture Notes in Computer Science, No. 124, Springer-Verlag, Berlin, 1981.

[31] Bruce D. Russell, Implementation Correctness involving a Language with goto Statements, SIAM Journ. of Computing, Vol. 6, No. 3, September 1977, pp. 403-415.

[32] Joseph E. Stoy, The Scott-Strachey Approach to Programming Language Theory, The MIT Press, Cambridge MA., 1977.

[33] J.W. Thatcher, E.G. Wagner, and J.B. Wright, More on Advice on Structuring Compilers and Proving Them Correct, Theoretical Computer Science, Vol. 15, September 1981, pp. 223-245.

[34] William D. Young, A Verified Code Generator for a Subset of Gypsy, Report No. 33, Computational Logic Inc., Austin, Texas, October 1988.

What's in a Timing Discipline?
Considerations in the Specification and Synthesis of Systems with Interacting Asynchronous and Synchronous Components

P. A. Subrahmanyam
Rm 4E530, AT&T Bell Laboratories Research, Holmdel, NJ 07733

Abstract

Many large scale circuits and systems contain a mixture of synchronous and asynchronous (self-timed) subsystems; examples include digital control units and sequencers, processing units that have asynchronous interfaces to busses or memories, and systems that contain modules that are clocked by independent, locally generated clocks. This paper addresses some of the formal issues that arise in the specification and synthesis of such "mixed-mode" systems. In particular, we outline a specification technique suitable for such systems, formalize the notion of timing disciplines in this context, and indicated how the introduction of timing disciplines into a design affect the associated specifications. We also outline the correlations between the semantic models underlying such specifications, called temporally annotated labeled event structures (abbreviated TALES) and timing diagrams that are commonly used for specifying some of the temporal characteristics of interfaces. Some experiments in prototyping some of the implementation strategies for asynchronous, self-timed and mixed-mode systems are summarized.

1 Introduction

A number of superficially different techniques have been suggested for the specification and synthesis of synchronous and asynchronous digital systems. Most earlier work on automated circuit synthesis techniques has been targeted predominantly at synchronous systems exploying simple clocking strategies[6], [2]. Typical starting points for synchronous circuit synthesis include state machine descriptions and programs in various languages[2], although many of the languages used in this context have an inadequate support for types when compared to languages such as OBJ[8] or ML. Concomitantly, there have been a few scattered attempts at automating asynchronous designs[1], [14], [5]. Typical starting points for such techniques have additionally included Petri nets, and signal transition graphs[5]. There appears to have been an idealogical split of the advocates of the synchronous and asynchronous disciplines; further, some of these techniques have only recently begun to mature. As a consequence, almost no effort has considered the issues involved in automatically synthesizing "mixed-mode" systems that contain a mixture of synchronous and asynchronous (self-timed) subsystems, and in coupling with pre-defined interfaces such as standardized bus interfaces[19]. Examples of such systems frequently arise when designing digital control units or sequencers, processing units that have asynchronous interfaces to busses or memories, and systems that contain modules that are clocked by independent, locally generated clocks.

In view of the prevalence of mixed-mode circuits and systems, we have been exploring techniques for their specification and automated synthesis[19]. The goal of this work is to enable a designer to synergistically exploit the advantages of both the synchronous and asynchronous (self-timed) design styles in a system and to support experimentation with trade-offs in granularity and implementation strategies. As a consequence, it is important to have a technique for the specification of a system that exhibits a desired behavior, but that does not necessarily have an embedded timing discipline i.e., whose implementation is not committed to any specific timing discipline. It is equally important to allow a smooth transition of such specifications into specifications of (sub)systems that have explicit timing disciplines, be they synchronous or asynchronous. This requires an appropriate formalization of the hitherto informal notion of a timing discipline. In addition, it requires an explicit correlation between some of the superficially unrelated models used by conventional synthesis techniques, such as state machines and petri nets. The formalization of such relations can provide a basis for the implementation of synthesis techniques for mixed-mode systems, allowing both the use of existing techniques and the development of new ones.

This paper focusses on some of the formal issues that arise in the specification and synthesis of mixed-mode systems. In particular, we delineate a specification technique suitable for such systems, and formalize the notion of timing disciplines in this context. We also indicate the correlations between (1) the semantic models underlying such specifications, called Temporally Annotated Labeled Event Structures (abbreviated TALES) and (2) timing diagrams commonly used for specifying some of the temporal characteristics of interfaces. Once a (set of) timing discipline(s) has been incorporated into a specification, and detailed representations for the actions chosen, then the resulting specification may be further mapped into synchronous, asynchronous, or self-timed circuits using both existing and newly developed synthesis techniques. We will illustrate some of the concepts via fragments of various designs, including that of a Processor Interface Board for a multiprocessor. We will summarize, but not discuss in detail, experiments in prototyping some of the implementation strategies for asynchronous/self-timed as well as mixed-mode systems.

2 System Specifications without explicit timing disciplines

We begin by discussing relevant aspects of a technique for the specification of systems that exhibit a desired behavior, but that do not necessarily have any commitment to a specific (set of) timing discipline(s). We will then discuss how the notion of timing disciplines can be introduced into such specifications.

For the purpose of our discussion, a *specification technique* consists of an abstract *syntax* that defines the textual (or graphical) form of the specification, along with an associated *semantics*. Two flavors of semantics are relevant in this context: the *abstract semantics* provides an interpretation of the syntactic specifications over some meaningful (semantic) domain, while the *operational semantics* provides a basis for the mechanical simulation or execution of a specification.

The input specification syntax we adopt here is a subset of a language based on a variant of a Calculus for Communicating Systems (CCS)[15]. As a result, such specifications resemble languages based on Hoare's Communicating Sequential Processes (CSP) [9] and Dijkstra's Guarded Commands, although there are some subtle distinctions. A system is viewed as a set of interacting processes, where a process may have internal concurrency i.e., it is not constrained to be sequential. Processes interact with each other by communicating over channels formed by connecting *typed ports*. Communication actions such as input and output are defined on the underlying port types. By generalizing the notion of port types from inputs, outputs and bidirectional ports to user defined (abstract) port types at the specificiation level, we preserve the flexibility for *implementations* of such port types to have varying communication protocols and to eventually use primitive input/output/bidirectional ports and signals. This enables a process to concurrently read and write values using such a typed port. Synchronization between processes is achieved by communication between these processes over a channel; some information may also be communicated during synchronization. Such a generalization makes it convenient to provide abstractions that support standard communication protocols, such as a full 4-cycle handshaking protocol and, in addition, be able to support application specific communication protocols, such as a VME Bus protocol.

A program in the language describes a set of interacting processes. Each process (synonymously, hardware module) has several attributes, including: its external interface and behavior; temporal aspects of its behavior including interface protocols that must be obeyed; and its internal structure.

We will next summarize the structure of process descriptions and their denotation. We will then augment the semantic domain to enable a richer set of temporal relations to be imposed on the events in a computation.

2.1 Process descriptions and their denotations

A process can execute a set of primitive actions A, where the execution instances of such actions are called events. A process description denotes a set of possible computations. We adopt a slight variant of *labelled event structures* [21] as our concrete model of hardware modules. These structures embody the distinct relations of causal dependence ($a \leq b$), potential concurrency (causal independence) ($a \simeq b$), and conflict (choice) ($a\#b$) amongst events. Corresponding to these relations, there are 3 operations —sequential composition (denoted ;), parallel composition (denoted $\|$), and choice (denoted +)— that provide a way of constructing event structures. This is done by juxtaposing two event structures and setting the corresponding relation between their events.

Let **1** denote a terminated computation (or a "nil" process). Let $T(A)$ be the set of finite terms, denoting processes, generated by $\{1 , A\}$ that are closed under $\{;, \|, +\}$. The actions in the set A may in general be quite complex and possess a rich type structure. However, we will not elaborate on the semantics of such actions in this paper except in so far as is necessary.

We will refer to the temporal relations of causal dependence, causal independence, or conflict on the events in a computation as being *abstract* temporal constraints. It is noteworthy that while two causally independent events are *potentially* concurrently executable, a specific implementation may choose not to exploit this opportunity (for varied reasons), and enforce a strict sequencing between these events.

In addition to the class of abstract temporal constraints, other constraints may be imposed on a process specification, e.g., concrete minimum and maximum bounds on the duration between two events. We will refer to such constraints as *concrete* temporal constraints, and consider them in greater detail in Section 3. Preparatory to doing this, we next formally define labeled event structures (the semantic domain), and then summarize the correlation between the process descriptions (syntactically denoted by terms in an algebra), event structures and computations. For the sake of completeness, we will first review some pertinent results relating to process descriptions.

2.2 Labelled Event Structures and their composition

Definition 2.1 (Labelled Event Structures) *Let A be a nonempty set (denoting the atomic actions performed in a system). An event structure labeled by A (synonymously, an A-labeled event structure) is a quintuple $(A, E, \leq, \#, L)$ where*

1. *$E \subseteq \{0,1\}^*$ is the set of events;*

2. *$\leq\; \subseteq E \times E$ is a partial order on E, denoting the causality relation;*

3. *$\# \subseteq E \times E$ $(\leq \cup \geq)$ is the symmetric "conflict" relation;*

4. *$L{:}E{\to}A$ is the labelling function that names events.*

Two events in E are *concurrent* (denoted a $\simeq$ b) if they are neither ordered nor in conflict. That is,

$$\simeq\; =_{def} E \times E - (\leq \cup \geq \cup \#)$$

This relation $\simeq$ is symmetric and irreflexive. By definition, the relations $\simeq$, $\leq$, $\geq$, $\#$ induce a partition on $E \times E$.

Event structures that are similar except for renaming of the actions are said to be *isomorphic*; we will denote this renaming isomorphism by $\sim_L$.

We denote the set of finite A-labelled event structures by $L(A)$, and the set of infinite A-labelled structures by $L(A)^\infty$. These sets have a natural algebraic structure arising from the 3 relations that can exist amongst primitive events, namely causal dependence, concurrency (causal independence) and conflict. The 3 corresponding ways of combining event structures correspond to 3 ways of combining processes, viz., via sequential composition (;), parallel composition ($\parallel$), and selection (+). Recall that it is intended that event structures represent all of the possible computations of a (concurrent) process.

Formally, the composition of event structures ES_0 and ES_1, where $ES_i = (A, E_i, \leq_i, \#_i, L_i)$ for $i \in \{0,1\}$ is defined as follows: ES_0 **op** $ES_1 = (A, E, \leq, \#, L)$, **op** $\in \{;, \parallel, +\}$, where

1. $E = \{iu | u \in E_i\}$

2. $ix \leq jy \Leftrightarrow i = j$ and $x \leq_i y$ or op $= \leq$ and $i = 0, j = 1$

3. $ix \# jy \Leftrightarrow i = j$ and $x \#_i y$ or op $= \#$ and $i = 1$

4. $L(ix) = L_i(x)$

2.3 Interpreting Finite Processes

Let **1** denote a terminated computation (or a "nil" process); we also used **1** to denote an empty event structure. The interpretation of a process p $\in$ T(A) is given by a map ES:T(A)$\rightarrow$L(A)/ $\sim_L$.

$$ES(\mathbf{1}) = (A, \emptyset, \emptyset, \emptyset, \emptyset)$$
$$ES(a) = (A, \{\epsilon\}, =, \emptyset, \lambda), \text{ with } L(\epsilon) = a$$
$$ES(p;q) = (ES(p); ES(q))$$
$$ES(p \parallel q) = (ES(p) \parallel ES(q))$$
$$ES(p+q) = (ES(p) + ES(q))$$

In other words, a process p described by a term in T(A) is viewed as denoting the (isomorphism class of) the event structure ES(p), written [ES(p)].

2.4 Interpreting recursive processes

Given a set of identifiers X, let $T^{rec}(A \cup Y)$ denote the set of terms formed by using $\{\mathbf{1}, A\}$, the set $Y \subset X$ of identifiers, and containing recursion (denoted by $\mu x.p$). A map $ES^\infty : T^{rec}(A \cup Y) \rightarrow L(A)^\infty / \sim_L$ is the interpretation of recursive terms that denote processes involving recursion.

2.4.1 A structure on $L(A)^\infty$

In the set $L(A)^\infty$, the operations $\{;, \parallel, +\}$ are associative, and have **1** as an identity. Further, the operations $\parallel$ and $+$ are commutative.

In particular, $L(A)^\infty$ obeys the following axioms characterizing a triple monoid structure. For all p,q,r$\in L(A)^\infty$,

1. $(L(A)^\infty, ;, \mathbf{1})$ is a monoid

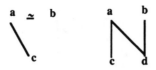

Figure 1: Excluded Event Structures ∇ and N.

A1: $(p;(q;r)) = ((p;q);r)$

I1: $(p;1\ ) = p = (1\ ;p)$

2. $(L(A)^\infty, \parallel, 1\ )$ is a commutative monoid

A2: $(p\parallel(q\parallel r)) = ((p\parallel q)\parallel r)$

I2: $(p\parallel 1\ ) = p = (1\ \parallel p)$

C2: $(p\parallel q) = (q\parallel p)$

3. $(L(A)^\infty, +, 1\ )$ is a commutative monoid

A3: $(p+(q+r)) = ((p+q)+r)$

I3: $(p+1\ ) = p = (1\ +p)$

C3: $(p+q) = (q+p)$

2.5   A subclass of A-labelled event structures

The set of A-labelled event structures is quite rich. It turns out that not all A-LES's correspond to processes that can be expressed using the operations ;, $\parallel$ and $+$. In particular, the fragment of event structures shown in Figure 1 below (labelled N and ∇ respectively because of their "geometric" appearance) cannot be expressed by means of the syntactic primitives defined earlier. Consequently, it is necessary to consider an appropriate subclass of event structures that can be used as a domain underlying processes that can be expressed using our syntactic primitives. This class of event structures is reasonably well understood in the context of net theory; for the sake of completeness, we include its definition next.

Let $R \subseteq E \times E$ be a relation on a set E.

1. $R^s = R \cup R^{-1}$, is the symmetric closure of R.

2. $R^c = R^s \cup R^0$, is the R-comparability relation.

3. $R^i = (E \times E)$- R^c is the R-incomparability relation.

Lemma 1 *An A-LES is N- and ∇- free if and only if $\forall\ U,\ V \in \{\leq, \#, \simeq\}$, $U \neq V$, and*

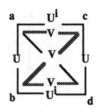

Figure 2: Condition obeyed by a subclass of Labeled Event Structures.

- *if e_0 U e_1 and e_0 U^i e_2, where $U^i = (E \times E) - (U \cup U^{-1} \cup U^0)$*
- *if e_2 U e_3 and e_1 U^i e_3*
- *then e_0 V e_3 $\Rightarrow$ { e_0, e_1 } $\times$ { e_2, e_3 } $\subseteq$ V .*

This condition is depicted in Figure 2, where solid lines indicate assumptions, and dotted (shaded) lines indicate the consequences implied by the assumptions.

The class of A-labeled event structures of interest is therefore those that are N-free and ∇-free. These are denoted $NG(A)$ and $NG(A)^\infty$ respectively.

2.6 A Characterization Theorem

We will denote by $=_{ES}$ the semantic equality induced over $T(A)$ and $T^{rec}(A \cup Y)$ by the equality of the corresponding event structures, and by $=_T$ the equality induced by the axioms of a triple monoid. The following theorem then formally characterizes the correspondence between processes described by terms in $T^{rec}(A \cup Y)$ and labeled event structures in $L(A)^\infty$.

Theorem 2 *The structure $(NG(A)/ \sim_L, ;, \|, +, 1)$ is the free triple monoid generated by A, i.e., it obeys the axioms A1-A3, I1-I3, C1-C2.*

1. *$s \in NG(A) \Leftrightarrow \exists\ p \in T(A)$, $ES(p) \sim_L s$, and $T(A) = NG(A)/ \sim_L$*
2. *$p =_{ES} q \Leftrightarrow p =_T q$.*

Further, $ES(T^{rec}(A)) \subseteq NG(A)^\infty/\simeq$.

2.7 Computations and operational semantics

Recall that a process description denotes a set of computations, and that we have used labeled event structures as a concrete model for this set of computations. Externally observable behavior is influenced only by specific computations, rather than a combination of all possible computations. Thus, it is desirable to be able to treat as equivalent, for example, the processes $a; (b + c)$ and $a; b + a; c$.

A *specific* (finite) computation is a *conflict-free* prefix of an event structure, i.e., one in which specific choices have been made amongst the competing alternatives.

For example, $a;b$ and $a;c$ are the two computations of the process $a;(b+c)$. We will here confine ourselves to NG(A), the subset of A-labeled event structures that are N- and ∇-free. This is trivially true of conflict-free (and therefore deterministic) structures, denoted D(A).

Thus, given an event structure S=(A, E, $\leq$, #, L) and a finite set E1$\subseteq$E of events, a computation is defined as a conflict-free restriction of S to E1, and denoted $S_{|E1}$. The part of S that remains after computation C is denoted S/C, and called the *quotient* or the *residual* of S modulo C. Formally, $S/C \equiv_{def} S_{|(E-E1\cup E1^{\#})}$ where $E1^{\#}$ =$\{e \mid \exists e' \in E1 \text{ and } e\#e'\}$.

Definition 2.2 *A labeled transition system Σ is a triple (S,C, Σ_S) where S is a set of states, C is a set of computations, and $\Sigma_S \subseteq S \times C \times S$ is a transition relation.*

The transition relation Σ_{ES} on A-LES's is given by $p \xrightarrow[\Sigma_{ES}]{u} p'$ iff u is a computation of p, and p' is the residual of the event structure after u has been executed.

Since we are primarily interested in the processes that are described by terms in $T^{rec}(A)$, a corresponding syntactic transition relation on the terms in $T^{rec}(A)$ can be defined that mirrors the semantic transition relation on A-LES's defined above. We will, however, not elaborate any further on this aspect of the operational semantics of such specifications.

3 Timing Disciplines

Many high level actions that are viewed as "atomic" events may actually have *finite durations* at a lower level, thereby permitting a richer set of interactions with other atomic or finite events than is possible otherwise. It is therefore necessary to have a way of identifying the duration that is associated with a high level atomic event. The paradigm that that enables such an identification when necessary is called a *timing discipline*. Examples of such timing disciplines include all of the commonly used synchronous and asynchronous disciplines. At one extreme, a single scheme may be used for all of the events in the system. This characterises *completely* synchronous and asynchronous circuits. At the other extreme, a different scheme may be used for each distinct event of concern. This is infrequently used because of the difficulty in coping with the complexity of the resulting implementation and/or the overhead involved. In *mixed-mode* systems, more than one scheme is used, under the assumption that a judicious mixture of schemes is either more efficient or more appropriate in a specific context.

A timing discipline may involve the introduction of new set of actions (and associated events) that serve to indicate the beginning and end points of finite events. A common example is the introduction of a clock signal; the associated events consist of *clock ticks*. Thus, given an initial set of actions $A1$, and an associated event structure $ES(A1)$, a timing discipline naturally leads to a new set of actions $A2$ and associated event structure $ES(A2)$. Further, there is a mapping from the events in original structure $ES(A1)$ to a pair of events in the new event structure $ES(A2)$ which indicate the start and finish of an event in $ES(A1)$ that has a finite duration. Such a mapping characterising a timing discipline has some important properties; one of immediate relevance here is that it "preserve" the partial order among events, where the partial order between events of finite duration is defined to be the partial order on the *beginning* of these events.

Stated more formally, given two event structures $ES1(A1)$ and $ES2(A2)$ where $A2$ is the set of actions introduced by a timing discipline, the map TD associated with a timing discipline has the form $TD : E1 \rightarrow E2 \times E2$ such that for all non-atomic actions $e \in E1 : TD(e) =< e_s, \ e_e > \Rightarrow e_s \leq e_e$ and for all atomic actions $e \in E1 : TD(e) = < e_s, \ e_e > \Rightarrow e_s = e_e$. Further, TD preserves the partial order on the *beginning* of events with finite duration. Thus if $e \leq e' \Rightarrow e_s \leq e'_s$ where $TD(e) =< e_s, e_e >, TD(e') =< e'_s, e'_e >$.

The choice of a timing discipline spawns additional temporal constraints on the events in a computation and intervals between them; such constraints must obtain to assure the correct operation of a system. For example, if an "input" action has finite duration, it is typically required that the input signals be stable during this duration. Such temporal constraints can be incorporated in an event structure by means of temporal annotations. A-labeled event structures that optionally have temporal assertions associated with the events will be referred to as *Temporally Annotated Labeled Event Structures* and abbreviated TALES(A). The temporal assertions can be in an appropriate temporal logic; we will not discuss further details of such annotations here.

Definition 3.1 (TALES) *Let A be a nonempty set (denoting the atomic actions performed in the system). An temporally annotated event structure labeled by A (synonymously, an TALES(A)) is a 6-tuple $(A, E, \leq, \#, L, TA)$ where*

1. $(A, E, \leq, \#, L)$ *is an A-labeled event-structure; and*

2. $TA : E \rightarrow TL(A)$ *is a partial function that associates a temporal assertion with some of the events in E. The assertions are in a temporal logic TL "parameterized" by A.*

It is interesting to note that such temporally annotated labeled event structures are closely related to the output that might be produced by a program that "simulates" the input-output behavior of the associated system, and to timing diagrams that are commonly used to graphically specify timing constraints of a system. We will shortly illustrate some aspects of this correspondence in the next section.

3.1 Examples of Timing Disciplines

Consider a module (synonymously, process) with inputs I, internal state S, and outputs O whose behavior is defined as follows:

```
M(S) = I?X; [O!F(S,X) || M(G(S,X)]
```

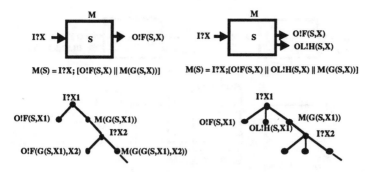

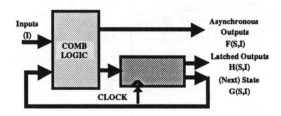

Figure 3: I/O and event structures.

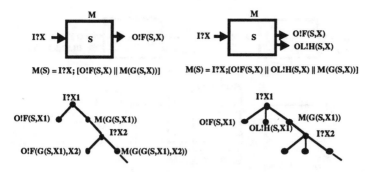

Figure 4: Circuit Structure for 1-phase clocking.

The functions F and G respectively yield the outputs and the modified state of the module M. Such a description may be written in a more familiar imperative form that does not involve recursion by using an explicit state variable S and using a loop (do-forever) construct to eliminate the tail recursion as follows:

```
process M
inputs I; output O; state S
do forever { I?X; [O!F(S,X) || S = G(S,X))] }
```

The input-output block-diagram and event structures for this module, are shown in the laft half Figure 3. A slight variant of this module, shown on the right half of Figure 3 has the behavior

$$M(S) = I?X; [O!F(S,X) \parallel OL!H(S,X) \parallel M(G(S,X)]$$

Synchronous 1-phase clocking Consider now the circuit structure shown in Figure 4 that corresponds to a circuit using a synchronous clocking discipline with edge-triggered latches. This circuit has inputs I, internal state S, asynchronous outputs F(S,I), next-state function G(S,I), and latched outputs H(S,I). Further, assuming that a negative-edge-triggered latch is used, the "timing diagram" associated with the circuit is shown in Figure 5.

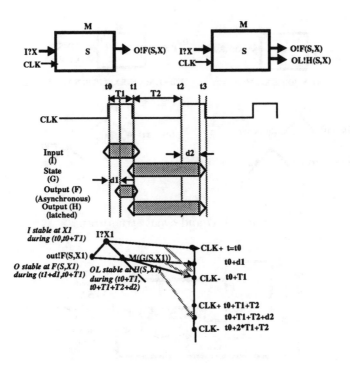

Figure 5: 1-phase clocking: I/O, timing diagram and event structure.

This timing discipline entails the introduction of a clock signal. Figure 5 also shows the mapping on event structures that characterises this timing discipline, and provides some examples of the temporal annotations associated with the events in the augmented event structure. Thus, the information embodied in the labeled event structure states that

- the "input event" I?X1 at port I has duration [t0, t0+T1], and consequently the input at port I must be stable at X1 during this period. Formally, the temporal assertion associated with this node, denoted TA(I?X), is `stable(I)(X1)(t0,t0+T1)` where stable is a predicate that takes 3 sets of arguments;

- the events O!F(S,X1) and M(G(S,X1)) proceed independently following (the beginning of) the input event;

- the output event O!F(S,X1) has a duration [t0+d1, t0+T1], i.e., that the asynchronous output at O is available after a delay d1 following the clock going high, and remains stable until the clock goes low;

- the latched output at OL is available from when the clock goes low, until shortly before the next time the clock falls (stated differently, for time d2 after CLOCK rises).

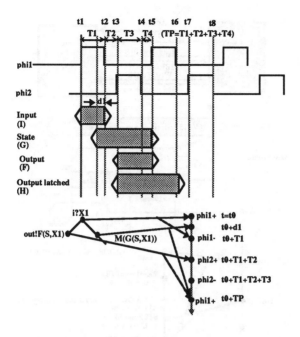

Figure 6: 2-phase clocking: I/O, timing diagram and event structure.

2-phase non-overlapping clocking.   A timing diagram corresponding to a timing discipline that employs a 2-phase non-overlapping clock is shown in Figure 6. The new signals introduced in this scheme are the two clock signals PHI1 and PHI2; the mapping associated with the timing discipline, as well as the correspondence between the temporally annotated labeled event structure and the timing diagram are also depicted in Figure 6.

Asynchronous protocols.   A timing diagram for an abstracted version of the read protocol between a Bus-Interface-Board and a Processor-Interface-Board is shown in Figure 7. The corresponding specification across the interface is shown below, and is obtained by augmenting the causal order amongst events with appropriate temporal operators that provide the ability to refer to events out of sequence. The statements within braces {...} are statements about the overall protocol.

```
establish ADDR;
raise ReadFromBIB at least 50ns after (establish ADDR);
     /* ''at least'' stipulates a mimimum bound */
     /* (establish ADDR) refers to the event */
{if ADDR=Status then (raise ReadFromBIB)
                guarantees BIBReadDone
                within 570ns
```

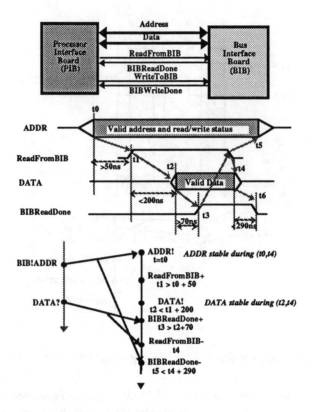

Figure 7: PIB-BIB Read Protocol: timing diagram and event structures.

```
                else (raise ReadFromBIB)
                    guarantees BIBReadDone
                    within 270ns
}
wait-for BIBReadDone; /* guaranteed by BIB protocol */
lower ReadFromBIB;
{(lower ReadFromBIB) guarantees
                (lower BIBReadDone) within 290ns;}
/* disestablish ADDR */
```

For readers familiar with temporal logic e.g.[16], the operators **A guarantees B** and **A guarantees B within D** can be defined using conventional temporal logic primitives (such as **eventually** and **next**) as follows:

A guarantees B $\equiv_{def}$ A $\Rightarrow$ eventually B
A guarantees B within D $\equiv_{def}$
            B or [next] (A guarantees B within D-1)

We will not discuss the detailed formal semantics of the internal representation in this paper.

Self-timed protocols. A completely self-timed protocol typically involves a full dual-rail encoding of the data paths and a 4-cycle handshake across each channel. The timing diagram for each handshake is analogous to that shown above for the BIB read protocol when restricted only to the signal pair `ReadFromBIB, BIBReadDone}`. More generally, small amounts of data can be exchanged across a channel during synchronization.

3.2 Timing diagrams and TALES

At a lower level, annotated timing diagrams provide a convenient and familiar technique for specifying interface protocols for standardized (sub)systems such as busses, processor and memory interfaces. As mentioned earlier, such diagrams have a close relation to temporally annotated labeled event structures, and therefore are very useful in complementing other specification techniques by providing a graphical perspective on the interface. It is of course possible to carry timing diagrams to the extreme and define a full-fledged language based on timing diagrams. This can sometimes be quite obfuscating, since the functionality of a complex system is often not obvious from examining a detailed timing diagram. We believe that it is better to combine textual and graphical specificatioñs as and when appropriate. Motivated by these observations, we have implemented an *object-based window-oriented* timing diagram editor that can be used for specifying system interface specifications.

3.3 Summary

So far, we have discussed a specification technique for systems that do not have an explicit timing discipline embedded in them. Such specifications describe a system as consisting of processes interacting by communicating over typed channels; the process descriptions embody both abstract and concrete temporal constraints on events. Computations are conflict free prefixes of event structures corresponding to a process.

We have also formalized the notion of a timing discipline in the context of such specifications. The introduction of a timing discipline introduces two components into the description of a system:

- additional actions (events) that are intended to mark the beginning and end of events that have finite durations;

- additional temporal assertions (constraints) associated with actions and events.

We have provided examples of how this notion may be applied to interpreting a few commonly used timing disciplines, namely synchronous disciplines employing one-phase and two-phase clocks, as well as asynchronous and self-timed disciplines. We will next briefly discuss some of the issues that pertain to the synthesis of mixed-mode systems.

4 Synthesis

The main motivation of this work is to investigate synthesis techniques for systems that are designed to have a *mixture* of the following different (but commonly occurring) kinds of subsystems:

- Asynchronous, self-timed subsystems that use signalling protocols to generate completion signals combinationally;

- Asynchronous, self-timed subsystems that use analog delays to generate completion signals;

- Synchronous subsystems.

Thus, our intent here is to enable a designer to synergistically exploit the advantages of some or all of these design styles in a system and to support experimentation with trade-offs in granularity and implementation strategies. It is not our primary intent to argue for the efficacy of one design style over another, except to note that no one style is ideal (or even feasible) in all situations. Additionally, the availability of appropriate automated design tools will clearly affect most such judgments.

The initial input consists of (1) the behavior and performance requirements; and (2) the interface protocol to be obeyed.

Given an initial specifiation, there are two tasks that are performed in designing a system. First, the overall system specification is decomposed into appropriate subspecifications for the constituent subsystems. The communication protocol across each channel and the timing discipline appropriate for each process is next determined. Criteria influencing such decompositions are discussed in Section 5.1. Second, once a (set of) timing discipline(s) has been incorporated into a specification, and detailed representations for the actions chosen, the resulting specification may be further mapped into synchronous, asynchronous, or self-timed circuits using both existing and newly developed synthesis techniques.

The intermediate output generated at this stage consists of a hierarchical structural description using primitives such as Muller C-elements, synchronizers, flip-flops and basic logic gates such as *nand* and *nor*. This hierarchical structural description is then converted into a physical layout using existing tools. This layout can either use a standard cell library or be a custom CMOS layout.

We first comment briefly on the synthesis models of relevance, and then elaborate on some of the issues that influence the decomposition of a system into interacting subsystems that are implemented as synchronous, self-timed or asynchronous modules.

4.1 Models used for synthesis

The synthesis task may be viewed as the application of a series of transformations on the initial specification that eventually yields a description that is suitable as a basis for fabrication. Such transformations typically either change the level of abstraction of the input description or improve the efficiency of the implementation according to some metric such as area, time, or testability. Each transformation tends to add increasing detail to the design, while perserving properties such as the externally observable behavior and the interface timing constraints. Each stage of such a transformation process may therefore be characterized by a triple $< Specification_i, Transformation_i, Specification_{i+1} >$. We will refer to such a triple as a "synthesis technique" because it locally accomplishes part of the overall synthesis task. As synthesis techniques mature, highly optimized sequences of transformations can be bundled together to yield new "macro" synthesis techniques, eventually serving to decrease the number of explicitly conceived transformation steps. Typical examples of this can be observed in the "scripts" that exist for logic optimization programs such as MISII.

We are interested in exploring the correlations that exist between some of the specification and synthesis techniques used for asynchronous, self-timed, and synchronous design. The formalization of such correlations enables appropriate sequences of transformations to be cascaded. Since some of the synthesis techniques are mature and automated, this can serve as the basis for constructing enhanced CAD tools. The synthesis models of interest include the following:

- *Temporally annotated labelled event structures.* Such structures provide a semantic domain for high level specifications discussed earlier.

- *Live-Safe Free Choice Petri-Nets* (and associated reductions into marked graphs components and state machine components). These models are often quite useful in synthesizing and analyzing some classes of asynchronous (self-timed) circuits at intermediate levels.

- *State machines.* These are used as a basis for the synthesis of synchronous systems and asynchronous systems at a lower level.

The details of these relations are discussed in a companion paper. We summarize the basic ideas here. Process descriptions are terms in an algebra generated by a set of actions A and the operations $\{;,\|,+\}$. Temporally annotated labeled event structures serve as a semantic model (domain) for processes. Unfoldings of processes give rise to computations; such computations are related to occurence nets obtained from executing a series of petri net transitions. When the transitions of such nets are interpreted as signal transitions, "complete" computations can be folded back to eventually yield graph representations from which equivalent state graph can be obtained. Existing techniques for logic optimizations and technology mapping can then be used at this stage to yield efficient structural descriptiosn that can serve as a starting point for layout.

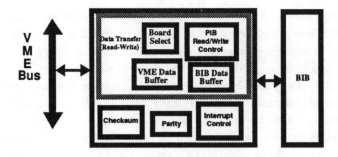

Figure 8: PIB Decomposition.

4.2 An Example — A Processor Interface Board

We will use fragments of the design of a Processor Interface Board (PIB) to illustrate some of the salient aspects of the techniques discussed. The PIB acts as an interface between a VMEBus[12] and a Bus Interface Board (BIB) in the S/NET[11], a prototype of the AT&T 3B4000 multiprocessor. It supports three categories of functions:

- Data transfer between the VME bus and the BIB.

- Parity and checksum logic to complement the data transfer between the VME bus and the BIB.

- Interrupt Control functions to handle interrupts arising during data transfer, as well as asynchronous interrupts from the VME Bus and BIB.

It is possible to decompose the PIB specifications into submodules that support the functions in each of these categories (Figure 8). The data transfer functions constitute the major function supported by the PIB, and we will restrict our attention in the rest of this paper to considering fragments of an implementation of this function.

Each instance of a PIB is required (i.e., is hard-wired) to respond to some subset of requests from the VME Bus, determined by some combination of the input signals Address[7..31] and AddressModifier[0..6] from the VME bus. When a read or write request is initiated by the VME Bus by virtue of the signal **AddressStrobeBar** going low (i.e., as specified by the VME Bus protocol), a particular PIB instance responds to this request only if it has been "selected" by the VME. The data transfer process may therefore be decomposed into a BoardSelect process that determines if a specific PIB instance should indeed respond to a read/write request, and a Read/Write Control process that handles the actual transaction. This Read/Write Control process is thus triggered by the BoardSelect process, and in turn orchestrates the actual data transfers into and out of the local data buffers that interface to the VME and the BIB.

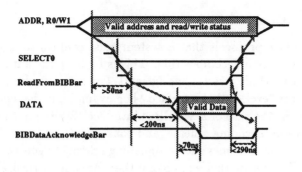

Figure 9: BIB Read Timing.

Interface timing specifications. To facilitate graphical display and editing of many of the temporal constraints in a familiar format, we use an editor for 2-dimensional timing diagrams (Figure 9). Internally, the constraints are represented as expressions using an appropriate set of primitives derived from temporal logic/algebra. This approach combines the benefits of (1) a familiar graphical specification and presentation technique and (2) the rigor associated with the use of description primitives having well-defined mathematical semantics.

As an example, consider the timing diagram in Figure 9 associated with a read operation on the bus interface board (BIB). The protocol to be followed by the master and slave processes may also be expressed formally; the overall transaction across the interface may also be described formally, and may in general be *inferred* from a specification of the independent protocols.

The formal representation of the behavior of the master process during a BIB-read operation is obtained by augmenting the causal order amongst events with appropriate temporal operators that provide the ability to refer to events out of sequence. Since it closely resembles the example outlined in Figure 7, we omit details for brevity.

5 Decomposition of systems into synchronous and self-timed components

5.1 Criteria Influencing System Decomposition

The synthesis techniques discussed here do not *a priori* restrict the manner in which a system may be decomposed into subsystems eventually implemented in an asynchronous, self-timed, or synchronous fashion. However, various criteria tend to play a significant role in influencing such a decomposition. We discuss some of these criteria below .

5.1.1 Interface Constraints

The external interface protocols that a system must confirm to are a major consideration influencing system decomposition. This is because the nature of the protocol may necessitate or preclude a certain design style (such as asynchronous, synchronous or self-timed) at the level of this interface. For example, if the signalling scheme is predetermined, as in the case of a VMEBus interface[12], it is not feasible to universally adopt a dual-rail encoding scheme, and consequently it is not feasible to design a self-timed system that assumes such a signalling scheme to generate completion signals combinationally. As another example, if there are any intrinsically asynchronous inputs in the external interface, then a completely synchronous design is not feasible.[1]

5.1.2 Area and Performance

The performance constraints that a system is designed to meet play an important role in the design style chosen. In general, asynchronous systems unrestricted by interface protocols tend to yield better performance. However, the complexity of analyzing large, *undisciplined* asynchronous designs and the hazards associated with such circuits constrain the unbridled use of asynchronous design, and motivate the introduction of self-timed designs. The area overhead associated with using analog delays to generate completion signals is relatively small, whereas the area overhead associated with dual-rail encoding can be significant if the cardinality of the data set involved is large. In particular, with a significant data path component in a circuit, dual-rail encoding may tend to roughly double the size of the circuit. In addition, the extra circuitry needed in generating completion signals tends to add to the area overhead; it may occasionally even degrade the performance. Synchronous designs alleviate the design problems associated with unrestricted asynchronous designs, but preclude the designer from taking advantage of data dependent performance improvements.

5.1.3 Portability

Self-timed designs that generate completion signals combinationally are the most robust in the sense of being portable across reductions in technology scales without the need for substantial redesign. This is because of their relative speed-independence, and consequent composability. Self-timed subsystems that use delays to produce completion signals involve the recomputation of these delays when the technology parameters are changed. The submodules will, however, retain their composability property at their interfaces. Synchronous systems using global clocks with fine-tuned clock distribution networks tend to involve the most redesign when moved across technologies. As a consequence, the subsystems of a synchronous design are typically not very portable.

---

[1] A completely asynchronous design is, in principle, always feasible, but is rarely adopted for complex systems because of the problems associated with such designs, including races, hazards, etc.

5.2 Example – Data Transfer Module Decomposition

The PIB Read/Write control module is concerned with handling the bulk of the communication protocol, and is mandated to communicate via channels associated with explicit request-acknowledge signals. These characteristics make this module a viable candidate for self-timed implementation. The Board Select process, on the other hand, involves a 32-bit wide data path with an asynchronous input and an asynchronous output. It is therefore well suited for being implemented as an asynchronous module. The processor itself, although not part of the subsystem we are considering here, is implemented using a synchronous discipline.

6 Synthesis Techniques

The synthesis method we adopt allows the implementation of individual processes to be either synchronous, asynchronous (self-timed), or combinational. Given a description of a module such as that illustrated earlier, we have explored three techniques for synthesizing self-timed circuits. The first technique consists of using a set of circuit structures that implement the basic linguistic primitives in the language, performing a syntax directed translation of the initial description to obtain an intermediate circuit description, and then improving the quality of the implementation by using local (peephole) and global (logic optimization) techniques. This technique uses combinational logic to generate the completion signals associated with the self-timed circuits and a "one-hot" state-assignment paradigm[10]. One flip-flop is used for each state in the state diagram; this is set upon entering the state, and reset upon exiting the state. The second technique consists of generating completion signals using analog delays instead of using combinational logic; the rest of the circuit generation process remains the same. The third technique consists of translating the initial description into an appropriate signal transition graph[5], generating a logic description of the circuit from this graph, and then optimizing this circuit using existing logic optimization techniques. The state assignment is derived from consistent live-safe markings of the intermediate signal transition graph. The rationale for exploring more than one strategy is that depending on the context of use, one of these strategies may yield a design that is superior to that generated by others. Such an option is useful, since a primary intent of this experiment was to provide architectural alternatives to the designer.

6.1 Mapping Structural Descriptions into Physical Layout

Once a structural description of the circuit is available, it is converted to a physical layout using existing tools. There are three alternatives that we have explored in this context. The first technique involves obtaining a layout using the Berkeley CAD tools, using the associated standard cell library. The second involves converting the hierarchical netlist synthesized into a layout that uses AT&T proprietary standard cells and associated layout tools. Transistor sizing and buffer introduction may also be performed during this process. A third alternative currently being explored the use a full-custom layout tool.

7 Summary

The overall goal of the research discussed here is to enable a designer to exploit asynchronous, self-timed and synchronous disciplines when and if appropriate. This paper has addressed some of the formal issues that arise in the specification and synthesis of mixed-mode systems. In particular, we have delineated a specification technique suitable for such systems, formalized the notion of timing disciplines in this context, and indicated how the introduction of timing disciplines into a design affect the associated specifications. We have also outlined the correlations between the semantic models underlying such specifications, called temporally annotated labeled event structures (abbreviated TALES) and timing diagrams that are commonly used for specifying some of the temporal characteristics of interfaces. Some experiments in prototyping some of the implementation strategies for asynchronous/self-timed as well as mixed-mode systems were described.

Acknowledgements. I wish to thank Bryan Ackland for valuable feedback on earlier drafts of this paper, David Horn for the many hours he devoted explaining me the intricacies of PIBs and BIBs, Mary Keefe for implementing a new version of the timing diagram editor, and Mark Yu for enlightening discussions.

References

[1] T. S. Balraj and M. J. Foster. Miss Manners: A specialized silicon compiler for synchronizers. In *Proc. 1986 MIT Conference on Advanced Research in VLSI*, pages 3–20, MIT Press, 1986.

[2] Brayton R. K. et al. *The Yorktown Silicon Compiler*. In *Silicon Compilation*, D. Gajski ed., pp. 204–311,Addison-Wesley, Reading, Mass., 1988.

[3] L. Cardelli and P. Wegner. On understanding types, data abstraction, and polymorphism. *ACM Computing Surveys*, 17(4):471–522, December 1985.

[4] T. J. Chaney and C. E. Molnar. Anomalous behavior of synchronizer and arbiter circuits. *IEEE Transaction on Computers*, 5C-22(4):421–422, April 1973.

[5] T.A. Chu. Synthesis of self-timed control circuits from graphs: an example. In *Proc. ICCD 1986*, pages 565–571, IEEE Press, 1986.

[6] R. A. Newton and B. Preas. *25 Years of Electronic Design Automation*. Association for Computing Machinery, 1988.

[7] Alan L. Davis. Generation of completion signals used in the design of the FAIM-II machine, personal communication. 1988.

[8] J. A. Goguen. Parameterized programming. *IEEE Trans. on Software Engg.*, SE-10:528–552, September 1984.

[9] C. A. R. Hoare. *Communicating Sequential Processes.* Prentice-Hall International Series in Computer Science, 1985.

[10] Hollaar, L. A. Direct Implementation of Asynchronous Control Units. In *IEEE Transactions on Computers*, pages 1133-1141, C-31(12), December 1982.

[11] David Horn. *A 32-bit Implementation of the S/NET Multiprocessor System.* Technical Report, AT&T Bell Laboratories, September 1986.

[12] IEEE. *IEEE Standard for a Versatile Backplane Bus: VMEBus.* IEEE Press, 1988.

[13] T. H.-Y.Meng et al. Asynchronous processor design for digital signal processing. In *Proc. IEEE ICASSP*, April 1988.

[14] A. Martin. The design of a self-timed circuit for distributed mutual exclusion. In *Proc. 1985 Chapel Hill Conference on VLSI*, Computer Science Press, 1985.

[15] R. Milner. *A Calculus of Communicating Systems.* Springer Verlag, LNCS 92, 1980.

[16] B. Moszkowski. A Temporal Logic for Multilevel Reasoning about Hardware. In *IEEE Computer*, Feb 1985, pp. 10-21.

[17] C. L. Seitz. Self-timed VLSI Systems. In *Proc. Caltech Conference on VLSI*, 1979.

[18] P. A. Subrahmanyam. Synthesizing VLSI circuits from behavioral specifications: a very high level silicon compiler and its theoretical basis. In F. Anceau, editor, *VLSI 83: VLSI Design of Digital Systems*, pages 195–210, North Holland, August 1983.

[19] P. A. Subrahmanyam. Automated Synthesis of Systems with Interating Asynchronous (Self-timed) and Synchronous Components. *Proceedings of ICCD 89*, IEEE Press, October 1989.

[20] T. E. M. Horowitz R. L. Alverson Williams and T. S. Yang. A self-timed chip for division. In *Advanced Research in VLSI, Proc. of 1987 Stanford Conference*, pages 75–96, MIT Press, March 1987.

[21] G. Winskel. Events in Computation PhD Thesis, Edinburgh University 1980.

Complete Trace Structures

David L. Dill
Computer Systems Laboratory
Stanford University
Stanford, CA 94061

1 Introduction

A speed-independent circuit is a sequential circuit that does not depend on the speeds of its components for correct operation. Speed-independent circuits are unclocked (asynchronous), because a clock inherently imposes timing constraints. This style of circuit design is of increasing interest to VLSI designers because it offers a solution to clock distribution problems that become more severe as circuits become more complex.

However, speed-independent design is more difficult because the circuits no longer have a global clock to rely on for synchronization. They are subject to the same subtle problems as all concurrent systems. Automatic verification of speed-independent circuit designs is of practical interest because it provides a potential way to cope with this difficulty. There have been several automatic verifiers for asynchronous circuits based on temporal logic model-checking [9], decision procedures for temporal logic [2], and trace theory [8, 7].

This paper presents an extension to trace theory that can handle general liveness properties, using sets of finite and infinite traces, while retaining the advantages trace theory: uniformity, integration of environmental assumptions, and decidability.

1.1 Background

In previous work, we defined *prefix-closed trace structures*, for formal semantics and specification of speed-independent circuits. The first idea behind this concept is that the set of *partial histories* of a system could describe its behaviors. Histories were assumed to be *sequences*, so this is a *linear-time* model, unlike tree-based models such as CCS [13]. Nevertheless, it is possible to define algebraic operations for composition, etc., on trace structures in the same style as CCS.

A unique feature of trace theory is a distinction between *successful traces*, which represent behaviors when the system is properly used, and *failure traces*, which represent undesirable behavior by the environment. Thus, a trace structure describes not only the circuit, but the environments with which it can properly be composed.

A binary relation between trace structures was defined, called *conformation*, which holds when the first can be substituted safely for the second in every context. We consider this to tbe the proper relation between an implementation and specification.

The conformation relation leads to a simple theory that supports modular verification very well, because the algebraic operations can be used on specifications as well as semantic descriptions. Also, the use of substitutability makes hierarchical verification very natural: a specification at one level of abstraction can be used as a description of a component at another level.

There is a decision procedure for conformation, which has been implemented. The resulting program has been applied to numerous speed-independent control circuits and has discovered bugs in several of them.

However, prefix-closed trace structures suffer from a deficiency: they can only capture (describe or specify) *safety properties*. Hence, circuits that have been verified may still suffer from potential deadlock or other failures of progress. An extreme example is the "universal do-nothing module" which accepts all inputs and produces no outputs — and implements every specification.

This limitation follows from the interpretation of a trace as a partial history. By re-interpreting traces to be *complete histories* and pursuing the consequences of that re-interpretation, we can formulate a theory that captures both safety and liveness properties. This paper is intended to be self-contained, so no prior knowledge of trace theory is assumed.

David Black [3] and Kevin Van Horn [12] have also looked into extending trace theory on complete traces. Their systems are based on earlier versions of trace theory, so they are more complicated and do not address the questions of conformation, receptiveness, and decision procedures to the same extent as this report.

2 Mathematical Preliminaries

Here we introduce our notation and terminology. We also summarize some results from the theory of regular languages of infinite sequences, for readers who are unfamiliar with it.

ω denotes the set of natural numbers (non-negative integers). An ω-*sequence over* A (or an *infinite sequence*) is a function from ω to A. The length of an ω-sequence x ($|x|$) is ω. $i \leq \omega$ means either $i \in \omega$ or $i = \omega$. Finite and infinite sequences can be concatenated, but only the last sequence in a concatenation can be infinite.

We use the function $\textbf{del}(D)(x)$, where D is a finite set of alphabetic symbols and x is a sequence, which deletes all of the D symbols from x. The image function $\textbf{del}(D)(X)$ (the natural extension of $\textbf{del}(D)$ to sets) and inverse image function $\textbf{del}(D)^{-1}(X)$ are of special interest. $\textbf{del}(D)^{-1}(X)$ is the set $\{x' \mid \textbf{del}(D)(x') \in X\}$; i.e., the set of all sequences that would be in X if all D symbols were deleted from them.

We define $\textbf{pref}(x)$ to be the set of all finite prefixes of the finite or infinite sequence x. This function is also naturally extended to sets of sequences. $\textbf{suf}(x, X)$ is defined to be the set $\{y \mid xy \in X\}$.

The set of all ω-sequences of type $\omega \rightarrow A$ is written A^ω. The set of all finite and infinite sequences over A is written A^∞ $(= A^* \cup A^\omega)$.

There is a theory of regular languages on infinite sequences, and there are finite-state automata that accept these languages. Most of the results for regular languages of finite sequences carry over to infinite sequences, as well, although the theory is somewhat more complicated. Regular sets of infinite sequences are called ω-*regular sets* [5, 10]. ω-regular sets are closed under union, intersection, and complementation; furthermore, if X is regular and Y is ω-regular, XY is ω-regular, too.

The ω-regular sets are defined as the sets described by ω-*regular expressions*, which are generated by adding an ω operator to regular expressions. If α is a regular expression and β is regular expression whose set does not contain ϵ, $\alpha \cdot (\beta^\omega)$ is an ω-regular expression; if γ_1 and γ_2 are both ω-regular expressions, so is $(\gamma_1 + \gamma_2)$. The set of ω-sequences $[\alpha \cdot (\beta^\omega)]$ is defined to be $[\alpha][\beta]^\omega$, and $[\gamma_1 + \gamma_2]$ is $[\gamma_1] \cup [\gamma_2]$. A set is ω-regular if and only if it can be written as an ω-regular expression.

We assume familiarity with regular sets and finite automata, but reiterate some of the definitions to introduce our particular notation. A *nondeterministic finite automaton*, $\mathcal{M}$, is a five-tuple $(A, Q, Q_F, \textbf{n}, Q_0)$, where A is a finite set of *symbols* (the *alphabet*), Q is a finite set of *states*, $\textbf{n}: Q \times A \rightarrow 2^Q$ is the *transition function*, $Q_0 \subseteq Q$ is the set of *initial states*, and $Q_F \subseteq Q$ is the set of *final states*. A *deterministic* finite automaton is a modified form of nondeterministic automaton: $\textbf{n}$ is defined to be a partial function in $Q \times A \rightarrow Q$, and there is a single initial state $q_0 \in Q$ instead of the set Q_0.

A *run*, p, of a nondeterministic automaton on a sequences $x \in A^*$ is a sequence on Q, such that $p(0) \in Q_0$ and for all $0 \leq i < n$, $p(i+1) \in \textbf{n}[p(i), x(i)]$ (for a deterministic automaton, $p(0) = q_0$ and $p(i+1) = \textbf{n}[p(i), x(i)]$). The run is *accepting* if $p(|x|) \in Q_F$. If there exists an accepting run on x, $\mathcal{M}$ *accepts* x. The *language* of an automaton $\mathcal{M}$, written $\mathcal{L}(\mathcal{M})$, is the set of all sequences accepted by $\mathcal{M}$.

A *Büchi automaton* has exactly the same structure as a nondeterministic finite automaton, but we call the set of accepting states Q_B instead of Q_F. The difference between a Büchi automaton and a finite automaton is the way it accepts a sequence. If p is a *run* of a nondeterministic Büchi automaton on an ω-sequence x, it is a sequence in Q^ω such that $p(0) \in Q_0$ and for all $i \in \omega$, $p(i+1) \in \mathbf{n}[p(i), x(i)]$ For any infinite sequence x, we define $\text{In}(x)$ to be the set of elements that appear infinitely often in x; formally, $\text{In}(x) = \{a \mid x^{-1}(a) \text{ is infinite}\}$. p is an *accepting run* if $\text{In}(p) \cap Q_B \neq \emptyset$ (at least one state in Q_B is repeated infinitely often). An automaton accepts x if there is some accepting run of the automaton on x.

Unlike finite automata on finite sequences, nondeterministic Büchi automata are more powerful than deterministic Büchi automata. Given two nondeterministic Büchi automata that have the same alphabet A and that accept ω-regular sets X and Y, there are effective procedures for finding automata that accept $X \cup Y$, $X \cap Y$ (in polynomial time), and $A^\omega - X$ (the complement of X) [19] (in single exponential time).

We will general use sets of both finite and infinite sequences. Given a set $X \subseteq A^\infty$, the set of all finite sequences in X is $X \cap A^*$, and the set of all ω-sequences is $X \cap A^\omega$. $X \subseteq A^\infty$ is a *mixed regular* set (or just *regular* when no confusion should result) when $X \cap A^*$ is regular and $X \cap A^\omega$ is ω-regular. Mixed regular sets are closed under union, intersection, complementation, deletion, and inverse deletion. The algorithm for deletion is similar to ϵ-closure in normal finite automata. The algorithm for inverse deletion first creates a non-final copy of each final state, then adds self-cycles on D symbols from the non-final states. Additionally, if X is regular and Y is mixed regular, XY is mixed regular.

Regular expressions can be extended to describe mixed regular sets by allowing $\alpha + \beta$ to be an expression if α is a regular expression and β is an ω-regular expression (but, in this case, $\alpha + \beta$ may not be embedded in another regular or ω-regular expression). These are called *mixed regular* expressions.

Mixed finite automata, which accept mixed regular languages, can be defined. A mixed automaton is a finite automaton $\mathcal{M}$ with two sets of accepting states: Q_F and Q_B. The states of Q_F are the *finitely accepting* states and those of Q_B are the *infinitely accepting* states. The language of a mixed automaton is the union of the language accepted by the finite automaton with accepting set Q_F and the language accepted by the Büchi automaton with accepting set Q_B. Union, intersection, complementation, deletion, and inverse deletion can all be performed on mixed automata at no greater expense than on Büchi automata.

3 Complete Trace Structures and Receptiveness

A *complete trace structure* $\mathcal{T}$ is a quadruple (I, O, S, F), where I and O are finite disjoint subsets of input and output wire names. S and F are mixed regular subsets of A^∞ (where $A = I \cup O$), representing "successful" and "failing" behaviors of the circuit. P, the set of "possible" traces, is defined to be $S \cup F$; it must be non-empty (even the circuit that "does nothing" has the empty sequence as its behavior).

There is one additional subtle property, called *receptiveness*, which ensures that a trace structure models all possible inputs. As a simple example of non-receptiveness, if $x \notin P$ but $xa \in P$ for some $a \in I$, the environment is *required* to send an a after the trace x. For receptiveness, the environment must be allowed to withhold inputs. As another example, suppose that **pref**$[(ab)^*]$ is subset of P, but $(ab)^\omega$ is not. Then the environment can send any *finite* number of inputs, but not an infinite number. Clearly, a definition of receptiveness cannot depend solely on the finite traces in P — the infinite traces must also be taken into account.

The circuit and its environment can be regarded as two entities that build up a trace by adding input and output symbols to it. This goes on forever (a finite trace is built if the circuit and environment only add ϵ to the trace after some finite time). No matter what input signals arrive there must be *something* that the output can do to cause the resulting trace to be in the P set of the trace structure; otherwise, those inputs will be forbidden by the trace structure, violating receptiveness.

In other words, the circuit and environment are engaged in an *infinite two-player game*. The circuit tries to cause the trace to be in the P set and the environment tries to cause it not to be in P. The circuit is receptive if there is a *winning strategy* for it.

What should each player's moves be? Since no assumptions are made about the relative speeds of components, we should assume that the environment can be arbitrarily fast. An arbitrarily fast environment is a worst-case adversary, since a fast environment can always act like a slow one, but a slow environment cannot act like a fast one. Hence, the environment should be allowed to add any number of inputs to the trace in a single turn. However, the environment cannot be *infinitely* faster than the circuit, so it should only be allowed to add a *finite* number of inputs in a move. In other words, the environment's moves should be the sequences in I^*. When the output gets a turn, it should be able to add at least one symbol to the trace. In fact, it should *only* be able to add one output since an arbitrarily fast environment might be able to slip an input between two successive outputs, no matter how close together the two outputs are. Of course, the output should be able to add ϵ to the trace, so the output moves should be $O \cup \{\epsilon\}$. The environment should get the first move; if it is arbitrarily fast, it can produce inputs before the circuit produces its first output.

If the circuit is receptive, it should be able to keep the resulting history (trace) in P no matter what the environment plays. In other words, the circuit must have a *winning strategy*. The strategy is a mapping from every finite sequence of input moves to an output move.

There is one remaining subtlety, which can be illustrated by an example. Consider a circuit having $I = \{a\}$ and $O = \{b, c\}$ with finite traces $[(a(b + c))^*]$ and infinite traces $[(ab)^\omega]$. If it receives a finite number of inputs, it can produce b's and c's arbitrarily, but if it receives an infinite number if inputs, it must produce only b's. This trace structure is either absurd or useless. In reality, the circuit has no way of knowing whether, after receiving the first a, it is going to get an infinite number of inputs. If it outputs a c, it constrains the input to be finite, in which case it is not receptive; if it only outputs b's, even for finite inputs, there is no point in including c's in the trace set. The finite traces $[(ab)^*]$ are the only ones that can really occur. The definition of receptiveness should require that the remainder of the P set after *any* finite prefix of P generates a game that can be won by the circuit.

It is now possible to give the full definition of receptiveness for complete trace structures: a complete trace structure T is receptive if and only if, for all $x \in \mathbf{pref}(P)$, there is a winning strategy for the circuit in the game in which the environment has moves from I^*, the circuit has moves from $O \cup \epsilon$, and the circuit wins when the resulting history is in $\mathbf{suf}(x, P)$.

Given an automaton provided by a user, it would be helpful to have an algorithm to check whether the language of the automaton is receptive. This is difficult, but possible: the first step is to transform the game into an equivalent game in which each turn is a pair of symbols, an input and output. This is made somewhat difficult because the infinite set of environment moves need to be partitioned into a finite set of equivalence classes. However, this step can be done in exponential time (for the detailed description, see Chapter 6 of the author's PhD thesis [8]).

The existence of a winning strategy for the resulting game is exactly the *solvability problem*, first proposed by Church [6] and first solved by Büchi and Landweber[4]. Since then, more efficient solutions have been proposed using automata on infinite trees [15, 17]. The basic idea behind the later methods is that a strategy is an infinite labeled tree. A Büchi automaton describing the winning history can be transformed into a tree automaton that accepts exactly the winning strategies. Hence, the language of the automaton is non-empty iff there is a winning strategy.

We must check that the game whose winning histories are $\mathbf{suf}(x, P)$ is winnable for each $x \in \mathbf{pref}(P)$. Fortunately, the usual subset construction for finite automata can be used to show that there are a finite number of these sets (one exponential in the number of states of the original automaton), and to enumerate them.

The essence of the receptiveness problem is a mismatch between relational specifications and more constrained implementations. Implementations cannot write every variable, and can only base their actions on events in the past. A trace set does not easily capture these constraints. Recently, Pnueli and Rosner in two papers [15, 16] and Abadi, Lamport, and Wolper in a third [1] have reported similar problems with finding implementations of specifications, when the implementations are restricted to a particular choice of input and output variables. Their problems is also to discover whether an there is a stategy (the implementation) that always wins an infinite game.

4 Algebraic Operations

Operations can be defined to build up trace structures from simpler trace structures. We define three: parallel composition, which models the effect of connecting circuits together; hiding, which conceals the signals on designated wires; and renaming, which changes the names of wires.

Parallel composition connects two circuits together by identifying the wire names they have in common. Let T and T' be two trace structures and let T'' be their parallel composition, $T'' = T \parallel T'$. This is defined only when the output wires of the T and T' are disjoint (i.e. output wires cannot be connected). Unlike some other models of concurrency, wires are not hidden when they are connected (this destroys associativity); instead, if an input is connected to an output, the result is an output wire which remains visible. Formally, $O'' = O' \cup O''$ and $I'' = (I \cup I') - O''$.

The definition of parallel composition is split into two steps: the first step expands the alphabets of T and T' so that they are the same. The second step (essentially) finds the intersections of success and possible sets.

The inverse of the **del** operation is used in the first step. Intuitively, if x is a trace not containing symbols from D, then $\mathbf{del}(D)^{-1}(x)$ is the set of all traces that can be generated by inserting members of D^* between consecutive symbols in x. Inverse deletion is extended to structures:

$$\mathbf{del}(D)^{-1}(T) = (I \cup D, O, \mathbf{del}(D)^{-1}(S), \mathbf{del}(D)^{-1}(F)).$$

The wires in D are the additional inputs, whose signals are unconstrained (ignored) by the trace structure. This is defined only when $D \cap A = \emptyset$.

For the second step, we want the sets of traces which are consistent with the component trace structures. Set intersection is extended to trace structures:

$$T \cap T' = [I \cap I', O \cup O', S \cap S', (F \cap P') \cup (P \cap F')],$$

which is defined when $A = A'$ and $O \cap O' = \emptyset$. According to this definition, a trace is a success in the composite if and only if it is a success in both components. A composite trace is a failure if and only if it is failure in either component. Note that the set of possible traces for the composite is $P \cap P'$.

Composition is defined using these two operations:

$$T \parallel T' = \mathbf{del}(A' - A)^{-1}(T) \cap \mathbf{del}(A - A')^{-1}(T').$$

It is illuminating to consider the effect of composition in two boundary cases: when the alphabets of the two traces are disjoint, and when they are the equal. In the first case, the trace set of the composition is the set of *shuffles* (interleavings) of traces from each component trace set. In the second, the trace set of the composite is the *intersection* of the trace sets of the components. Composition finds the set of traces that match at their common symbols and have arbitrary interleavings of the other symbols.

To illustrate the effect of the extended composition operation, consider the trace structures $(\emptyset, \{a\}, a^\omega, \emptyset)$ and $(\emptyset, \{b\}, b^\omega, \emptyset)$. Their composition is $(\emptyset, \{a, b\}, (a^+ b^+ + b^+ a^+)^\omega, \emptyset)$ (the traces in $(a + b)^\omega$ that have an infinite number of both a's and b's). This models the reality that both circuits run at a finite speed.

Although the definition of composition may seem unfamiliar, it is consistent with other composition operations for linear-time models (such as Hoare's trace model for CSP [11] or Rem, Snepscheut, and Udding's trace theory for VLSI [18]). There are two major differences: the most important is the distinction between successes and failures — only the P set was considered in previous work; the second difference is the division of the alphabet into inputs and outputs.

This composition operation is very similar to taking the conjunction of temporal logic formulas representing process behaviors (P sets, to be exact). Pnueli has noted that when processes communicate by *distributed variables* (there is at most one process that can write any variable), temporal logic specifications of the individual processes can be conjoined to yield a specification that is valid for the parallel composition of the processes [14]. The "inverse deletion" operation is not explicitly used because temporal logic formulas do not have explicit alphabets.

The hiding operation makes signals on output wires invisible. Only outputs may be hidden. Formally, $\mathbf{hide}(D)(I, O, S, F)$ is defined to be $(I, O - D, \mathbf{del}(D)(S), \mathbf{del}(D)(F))$. The renaming operation takes a bijective *renaming function* which maps old wire names to new wire names. Formally, $\mathbf{rename}(\mathbf{r})(\mathcal{T})$ is defined when r is a bijection in $[A \rightarrow A']$. It is $(\mathbf{r}(I), \mathbf{r}(O), \mathbf{r}(S), \mathbf{r}(F))$, where $\mathbf{r}$ is extended pointwise to sequences and naturally to sets.

It can be proved that trace structures are closed under each of these operations [8]. One interesting aspect of the proof of closure under composition is that receptiveness of the composed trace structures is used to show that the result is non-empty (in fact, this is how the author first discovered the need for receptiveness).

5 Verification

We have an unusual concept of verification based on safe substitution that allows trace theory to be used both as a formal semantics for circuits and for specification[1]. The basic principle is that circuits are ultimately used for the construction of *failure-free* systems; that is, systems whose trace structures have the empty set of failures. A trace structure $\mathcal{T}'$

---

[1] The definition of conformation here is identical to the definition for prefix-closed trace structures. It is repeated to make the presentation self-contained.

conforms to another T if substituting T' for T never introduces failures in a failure-free system. We write this relation more briefly as $T' \preceq T$.

This concept is highly advantageous: it allows the same formalism to be used both for program semantics and for specification. This facilitates hierarchical verification, because a trace structure that is a specification at one level of abstraction can be a description of a component at a higher level. Also, specifications can be composed just as models of components can be: If $T_1 \preceq T_1'$ and $T_2 \preceq T_2'$, then $T_1 \parallel T_2 \preceq T_1' \parallel T_2'$. In the temporal logic world, this is called modular verification (although in that context, T_1 and T_2 would be programs and T_1' and T_2' would be temporal logic formulas).

To define conformation formally, we first define an *expression context*, which is an expression with a single free variable. The variable has designated input and output wire sets. An expression context is written $\mathcal{E}[\,]$ and the trace structure that results when T is substituted for the free variable is written $\mathcal{E}[T]$ (the input and output wires of T must be the same as for the free variable in $\mathcal{E}[\,]$). T' conforms to T when, for every expression context $\mathcal{E}$, $E[T']$ is failure-free whenever $\mathcal{E}[T]$ is. T and T' must have the same alphabets in order for the substitution to be defined in all contexts.

It is very easy to prove (using the properties of set intersection and inclusion) that there is a simple sufficient condition for conformation:

Lemma 1 $T \preceq T'$ if $I = I'$, $O = O'$, $F \subseteq F'$, and $P \subseteq P'$.

However, this is not a necessary condition. As it turns out, it can be made into a necessary and sufficient condition by grouping complete trace structures into equivalence classes (with easily computed canonical representatives) based on the conformation relation.

6 Conformation equivalence

Conformation is reflexive and transitive, as is clear from the use of implication in the definition. However, it is not antisymmetric — it is a *pre-order*, not a partial order. Hence, conformation induces a nontrivial equivalence relation on trace structures. T is *conformation equivalent* to T' ($T \sim_C T'$) when $T \preceq T'$ and $T' \preceq T$. $T \sim_C T'$ does not necessarily imply that $T' = T$. Intuitively, trace structures have more information in them than is really necessary to determine conformation. For example, one may be able to tell from a trace structure that after it receives an illegal input, it produces no more than five output signals. But all we *need* to know to determine conformance are the exact circumstances under which the first failure occurs — the details of the circuit behavior after this failure are completely irrelevant. The topic of this section is how to remove irrelevant information from a trace structure.

Intuitively, if the environment of the circuit cannot *guarantee* failure-free execution of a circuit after a particular partial trace x, x is an autofailure (even if x itself is a success). If x is the prefix of a possible behavior in the composition of the circuit with any environment, that composition will have failures — and for verification, further information about the nature of those failures is irrelevant. This phenomenon is called *autofailure*.

Autofailures can be defined by considering an infinite game in which the circuit tries to fail and the environment tries to force the circuit to succeed. In this game, the environment cannot control the speed at which the circuit runs, so the circuit moves can be any finite sequence of output symbols (members of O^*), and the environment moves can be members of $I \cup \{\epsilon\}$. The environment loses this game if the circuit fails (the concatenation of the infinite history is a member of F). Equivalently, the environment wins if the history is a success (in S) or if the circuit "cheats" by playing a history that is not possible according to its specification (in $A^\infty - P$). Formally, a finite trace x in $\mathbf{pref}(P)$ is an autofailure if there is no winning strategy for the environment in the infinite game in which the circuit moves are O^*, the environment moves are $I \cup \{\epsilon\}$, and the winning histories for the environment are in $A^\infty - \mathbf{suf}(x, F)$.

The most difficult step in simplifying a complete trace structure is to convert autofailures into failures (this is called "autofailure manifestation"). We define $\mathbf{af}(T)$ to be the set of autofailures of T, according to the definition above. Call the result of applying autofailure manifestation T'; then $I' = I$, $O' = O$, $S' = S$, and $F' = F \cup \mathbf{af}(T) \cdot A^\infty$.

Autofailure manifestation can be implemented. As with receptiveness, the prefixes of P can be grouped into a finite number of classes by suffix equivalence, using the subset construction. Each one of these classes can be checked to see if it is an autofailure using the decision procedure for winnability of infinite games. If so, the regular set corresponding to the class can be added to the set of failures.

There is a second (easier) simplification, called *failure exclusion*: the successes of the transformed structure are set to $S - F$; none of the other parts of the trace structure are changed. The simplifications produce complete trace structures that are conformation-equivalent to the originals. After simplification, the result is a canonical representative of all of the conformation-equivalent trace structures: two trace structures simplify to the same thing exactly when they are conformation equivalent.

Conformation equivalence and canonical trace structures lead to a decision procedure for conformation, because the condition in Lemma 1 is both sufficient and necessary when applied to canonical trace structures. Therefore, it is possible to check conformation by reducing the trace structures to canonical form and then checking for inclusion of the F and P sets, using algorithms on mixed automata.

There is another way of looking at this procedure. Define the mirror T^M of a canonical trace structure T to be $(O, I, S, A^\infty - F)$. The mirror is the *maximum* trace structure (under the conformation ordering) that can be composed with the original to yield a failure-free result (except in one special case, when S is empty, in which no composition is failure-free). So to test whether $T \preceq T'$, first reduce T' to canonical form (T does not have to be canonical), then check whether $T \parallel T'^M$ is failure-free. Intuitively, the mirror is a conceptual "tester" derived from the specification.

7 Examples of Complete Trace Structures

This section shows how complete trace structures can be used to describe some speed-independent circuits.

7.1 Boolean Gates

Considered as a speed-independent circuit, a boolean gate has sequential behavior. It is *stable* when the value on the output is the same as that computed from the input values by its associated boolean function. If the boolean function and output disagree, the gate is *unstable*. If it stays unstable, after an arbitrary but finite time the output will change to agree with the boolean function again. However, if an input change causes the gate to go from unstable to stable before the output changes, the results are unpredictable: there may be a pulse on the output, or a partial pulse (to an a voltage level between the logic threshholds), or no change at all. This is called a *hazard*. Hazards are generally undesirable in speed-independent circuits, so we would like inputs that cause them to be classified as failures.

The description of a boolean gate should express that (1) the output does not change when the gate is stable; (2) the output eventually changes if the gate is unstable and stays unstable; and (3) an input change that takes the gate from an unstable to a stable state is a failure.

Figure 1 shows an automaton that accepts the success or failure sets of a NOR gate. The transitions that lead to the failure state are exactly those that would otherwise go from an unstable state to a stable state (so any input change that could cause a hazard is classified as a failure). Input transitions from a stable state to any other state are allowed, as are input transitions to an unstable state from any other state. There is an output transition from a state exactly when it is unstable. Finally, if the gate is continuously unstable, there must eventually be an output transition: no finite trace can end in an unstable state (because the unstable states are not marked with ∗) and no infinite trace can remain unstable forever (because the unstable states are not marked with ∞).

To be receptive, the circuit must have a strategy that keeps every infinite trace in P, no matter what inputs the environment sends. A winning strategy in this case is to change the output whenever the current state is unstable, and to do nothing (play ϵ) when it is stable. If the current state is the failure state, any output move will suffice. This is a winning strategy, because each time the circuit gets a turn, it can force the automaton into

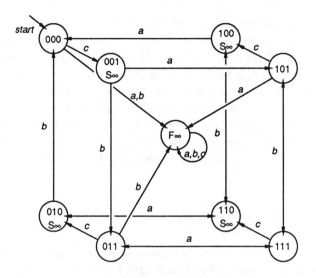

Figure 1: Live NOR Gate

a finitely and infinitely accepting state (for the P set). If the trace is finite, the strategy makes sure that it ends up in a stable state, which is finitely accepting.

This trace structure is also canonical. For this to be true, the environment must have a strategy that keeps every trace in $A^\infty - F$, no matter what the circuit does. A winning strategy for the environment is to make ϵ moves whenever the current state is unstable (essentially, waiting for the output to respond before sending another input). No history of a game played according to this strategy can reach the failure state.

7.2 Ring Oscillator

Figure 2 shows an automaton for a live buffer or inverter. The initial state of the automaton depends on the initial wire values. For a buffer or inverter starting in a stable state, the set of successful traces is $(ab)^* + (ab)^\omega$. The failure traces are $(ab)^* aa A^\infty$ (the gate receives two inputs without an intervening output). Traces of the form $(ab)^* a$ are *impossible*, even though they are prefixes of possible traces. This models the inevitability of a b transition once an a has been received.

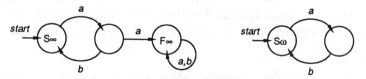

Figure 2: Live Buffer or Inverter and Ring Oscillator

The trace structure for a ring oscillator can be constructed by composing this structure with an inverter with input b and output a. The success set for such an inverter is $(ab)^*a + (ab)^\omega$, and the failure set is $(ab)^*abbA^\infty$. Since the alphabets match, the success set of the composition of these two trace structures is the intersection of the two success sets, which is $(ab)^\omega$. The failure set is empty. The two components have no *finite* traces in common, because all the buffer traces end with b and all the inverter traces end with a. The only remaining trace is $(ab)^\omega$, which represents infinite oscillation. This correctly models the non-terminating behavior of a ring oscillator. Intuitively, none of the finite traces is possible because one of the components always insists on adding another output.

7.3 Mutual Exclusion Element

A mutual exclusion element (ME element) ensures that no more than one of two users ever has access to a shared resource. The environment consists of the two "users". Each has a *request* (*r1* or *r2*) and *acknowledge* wire (*a1* or *a2*). To request mutually-exclusive access to the resource, a user raises its request line. The ME element grants the request by raising the acknowledge line; it guarantees mutual exclusion by making sure that there is never more than one acknowledge line high at a time. The user releases the resource by lowering its request wire. The ME element acknowledges the release by lowering the acknowledge wire, at which time the protocol is in the same state in which it began.

There are at least two different interesting descriptions of mutual exclusion elements using complete traces, which have the same finite behaviors but different infinite behaviors. The first requires liveness in the same sense as the description of boolean gates — the element eventually grants the resource to some client, and eventually acknowledges when the resource is released. The second requires, in addition, *fairness*: if a client requests, *that same client* is eventually granted the resource.

The first description can be obtained by starting with the obvious state graph, then choosing the accepting states to make it *impossible* for the automaton to wait forever in a state in which there are one or more outstanding requests, but none have been acknowledged. Similarly, it can be made impossible to wait forever in a state in which a release has been received but not acknowledged. Call these states unstable. If all but the unstable states are made finitely and infinitely accepting, the trace structure will have the desired properties. A state diagram is shown in Figure 3. The failures are not shown, to reduce clutter. The reader should imagine a single additional state marked "$F\infty$" with a self-loop transition on all symbols, as in the previous examples. Whenever there is no transition from a state on an input symbol, there is an implicit transition on that symbol to the failure state. The arguments for why this structure is receptive and canonical are similar to those for Boolean gates.

The first description of the mutual exclusion element allows starvation: if there are infinitely many requests on one input, it is possible that a request on the other input will never be granted. We would like to specify additionally that a request pending on one of

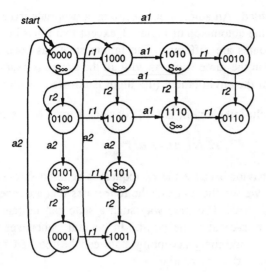

Figure 3: Live Mutual Exclusion Element

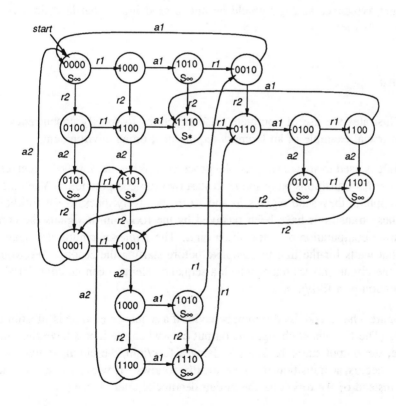

Figure 4: Fair Mutual Exclusion Element

the inputs is eventually granted. An automaton accepting appropriate trace sets is shown in Figure 4. It is similar to the automaton of Figure 3, except that it has been "unwound", and the sets of accepting states are different. The failure state has been omitted, as in Figure 3, and can be added in the same way. As with all the previous examples, there are no liveness requirements on the environment (the input is allowed to stop at that state).

To see why this mutual exclusion element is fair, consider a trace of the form

$$r2 \; (r1 \; a1 \; r1 \; a1)^{\omega},$$

which represents unfair behavior because the $r2$ request is ignored forever. Tracing the run through the automaton, we see that none of the four states that are repeated infinitely often is marked with $S\omega$ or $S\infty$. The only way such a state can be reached is for the symbol $a2$ to appear in the trace at some point. In general, whenever an $r2$ request occurs, the only way that an infinitely accepting state can be reached is for an $a2$ to occur. The situation with $r1$ and $a1$ is similar.

This trace structure is also both receptive and canonical. A receptiveness strategy would be for the output always to grant to the the earliest request that has not already been granted. A failure-avoidance strategy would be not to send inputs that lead directly to the failure state, as before.

7.4 Fork/Join

This example illustrates the use of complete trace structures to specify concurrency. It also gives a non-trivial example of an liveness requirement on an environment.

A *fork/join* module is used to spawn two parallel processes. When the fork/join receives a transition on r, it sends transitions on lr and rr to start two sub-computations. When these computations complete, they send signals la and ra, respectively, back to the fork/join. When both of these transitions have been received by the fork/join, it signals the completion of the entire computation by a transition on a. The *sequence* circuit also spawns two processes, but waits for the first to complete before starting the second. We would like to consider the circumstances under which a sequence element can be considered to be an implementation of a fork/join.

The circuit of Figure 5 has markedly different behavior if a sequence module is substituted for the fork/join. (The *C element* changes its output only when the inputs have the same value; otherwise, the output stays the same.) Using a fork/join, the circuit is live — if a transition on r occurs, a transition on a eventually follows. However, if a sequence module is used instead of the fork/join, the circuit deadlocks after sending lr.

Complete trace structures can be used to require a concurrent implementation of the fork/join. The automata of Figures 6 and 7 describe the behaviors of fork/join and sequence modules, with reasonable liveness assumptions. Using these trace structures,

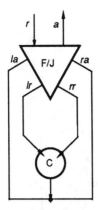

Figure 5: A Circuit that Distinguishes Fork/Join and Sequence

the sequence *does not* conform to the fork/join: the trace *r;lr* is *possible* in the sequence, but *impossible* in the fork/join (see Lemma 1). This accounts for the difference in deadlock behavior in the example of the previous paragraph.

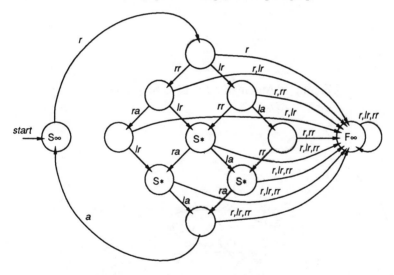

Figure 6: Automaton for Live Fork/Join

However, with some additional environmental assumptions, a sequence module *can* implement a fork/join. For example, if each of the request and acknowledge pairs for the left and right halves of the environment were required to be live even in the absence of a request on the other pair, it would be impossible for the sequence module to deadlock (the circuit of Figure 5 would violate this assumption). The trace structure of Figure 6 can be modified to include this assumption, as in Figure 8 (in which the newly forbidden environmental traces have been made into failures). The trace structure for the sequence module is similarly modified in Figure 9.

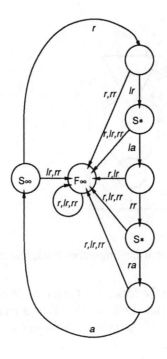

Figure 7: Automaton for Live Sequence

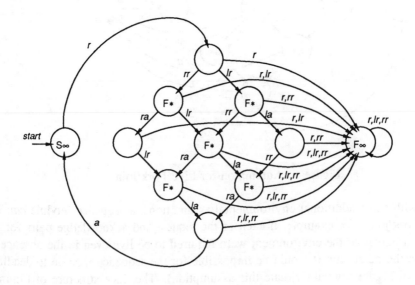

Figure 8: Fork/Join with Live Environment

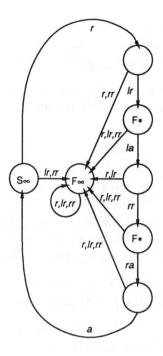

Figure 9: Sequence with Live Environment

It is easy to see that the modified sequence module conforms to the modified fork/join, since the sets of failures and possible traces of the first are included in the sets of failures and possible traces of the second.

8 Practical Considerations

A simpler formalism, based on prefix-closed regular sets of finite traces, has been implemented and used to verify a moderate number of non-trivial speed-independent control circuits. We would like to be able to implement complete trace structures, also. This section discusses some of the remaining difficulties in doing so.

First, Büchi automata are somewhat more difficult to work with than finite automata on finite sequences. Although the worst-case complexity of the basic constructions and decision procedures have the same number of exponentials as for finite automata, there are some potentially large factors (constant and $\log(n)$) to contend with. The implementations are also more complicated.

The most complicated part of the implementation would be the decision procedure for receptiveness and the algorithm for autofailure manifestation. The best known algorithms require involve finite automata on infinite trees, which are yet more difficult than automata on infinite sequences. Perhaps these problems can be circumvented by limiting the capabilities of the program or adding special cases; however, we feel that this nullifies some major virtues of trace theory: generality and uniformity.

However, there continue to be significant advances in relevant automata theory, so it is quite possible that a practical implementation of complete traces will be possible within the next few years.

References

[1] Martin Abadi, Leslie Lamport, and Pierre Wolper. Realizable and Unrealizable Specifications of Reactive Systems. In *Proceedings of the 16th International Colloquium on Automata, Languages, and Programming.* Springer-Verlag, 1989.

[2] Mark Bennett. *Proving Correctness of Asynchronous Circuits Using Temporal Logic.* PhD thesis, University of California, Los Angeles, 1986.

[3] David L. Black. On the existence of delay-insensitive fair arbiters: Trace theory and its limitations. *Distributed Computing*, 1(4):205–225, 1986.

[4] J. Richard Büchiand Lawrence H. Landweber. Solving Sequential Conditions by Finite-state Strategies. *Transactions of the American Mathematical Society*, 138:295–311, April 1969.

[5] Yaacov Choueka. Theories of Automata on ω-Tapes: A Simplified Approach. *Journal of Computer and System Sciences*, 8(2):117–141, April 1974.

[6] Alonzo Church. *Logic, Arithmetic, and Automata*, pages 23–35. Institut Mittag-Leffler, 1963.

[7] David L. Dill. Trace Theory for Automatic Hierarchical Verification of Speed-Independent Circuits. In Jonathan Allen and F. Thomson Leighton, editor, *Advanced Research in VLSI: Proceedings of the Fifth MIT Conference.* MIT Press, 1988.

[8] David L. Dill. *Trace Theory for Automatic Hierarchical Verification of Speed-independent Circuits.* MIT Press, 1989.

[9] David L. Dill and Edmund M. Clarke. Automatic Verification of Asynchronous Circuits Using Temporal Logic. *IEE Proceedings, Pt. E*, 133(5):276–282, September 1986.

[10] Samuel Eilenberg. *Automata, Languages, and Machines, Vol. A.* Academic Press, 1974.

[11] C.A.R. Hoare. A Model for Communicating Sequential Processes. Technical Report PRG-22, Programming Research Group, Oxford University Computing Laboratory, 1981.

[12] Kevin S. Van Horn. An Approach to Concurrent Semantics Using Complete Traces. Technical Report Technical Report 5236:TR:86, Computer Science Department, California Institute of Technology, 1986.

[13] Robin Milner. *A Calculus of Communicating Systems*, volume 92 of *Lecture Notes in Computer Science*. Springer-Verlag, 1980.

[14] Amir Pnueli. In Transition from Global to Modular Temporal Reasoning about Programs. In Kzysztof Apt, editor, *Logics and Models of Concurrent Systems*, volume 13 of *NATO ASI Series F: Computer and System Sciences*, pages 123–144. Springer-Verlag, 1985.

[15] Amir Pnueli and Roni Rosner. On the Synthesis of a Reactive Module. In *16th ACM Symposium on Principles of Programming Languages*, pages 179–190. ACM, 1989.

[16] Amir Pnueli and Roni Rosner. On the Synthesis of an Asynchronous Reactive Module. In *Proceedings of the 16th International Colloquium on Automata, Languages, and Programming*. Springer-Verlag, 1989.

[17] Michael O. Rabin. *Automata on Infinite Objects and Church's Problem*, volume 13 of *Regional Conference Series in Mathematics*. American Mathematical Society, 1972.

[18] Martin Rem, Jan L.A. van de Snepscheut, and Jan Tijmen Udding. Trace Theory and the Definition of Hierarchical Components. In Randal Bryant, editor, *Third CalTech Conference on Very Large Scale Integration*, pages 225–239. Computer Science Press, Inc., 1983.

[19] Shmuel Safra. On the Complexity of ω-Automata. In *29th IEEE Symposium on Foundations of Computer Science*, pages 319–327. IEEE, 1988.

The Design of a Delay-Insensitive Microprocessor: An Example of Circuit Synthesis by Program Transformation

Alain J. Martin

Department of Computer Science

California Institute of Technology

Pasadena CA 91125, USA

Abstract *We have designed the first delay-insensitive microprocessor. It is a 16-bit, RISC-like architecture. The version implemented in 1.6 micron SCMOS runs at 18 MIPS. The chips were found functional on "first silicon."*

The processor was first specified as a sequential program, which was then transformed into a concurrent program so as to pipeline instruction execution. The circuits were derived from the concurrent program by semantics-preserving program transformation.

1. Introduction

My students and I have designed the first entirely asynchronous microprocessor. The design was undertaken as a large-scale application of a high-level synthesis method for asynchronous VLSI that we have developed at Caltech during the last five years. The circuit is first described as a concurrent program—a set of communicating processes. A network of digital gates is then derived from the program by applying a series of *semantics-preserving program transformations*. Hence, the circuit obtained is correct by construction.

Since most efforts in formal techniques for circuit design are directed towards *verification*, we will emphasize our preference for a *synthesis* approach to provably correct design. All circuits we have designed so far according to this method have been found to be correct "on first silicon." They are also surprisingly robust and efficient. Undoubtedly, this processor experiment is a convincing illustration of the advantages of the method because of the performances achieved on this entirely

The research described in this paper was sponsored by the Defense Advanced Research Projects Agency, DARPA Order numbers 3771 & 6202, and monitored by the Office of Naval Research under contract numbers N00014-79-C-0597 & N00014-87-K-0745.

new architecture and because of the simplicity of the design—the whole project took five persons less than five months. The purpose of this paper is to present the processor design as a case in favor of delay-insensitive design techniques and of high-level synthesis.

The results of the experiment can be summarized as follows. First, it is possible and advantageous to describe circuits, even of the size and complexity of a microprocessor, in a high-level program notation. With the exception of the ALU function, the complete program takes less less than two pages—let us say that a complete description including all functions would take approximately three pages. The transformations performed on the initial sequential program to introduce pipelining show that the notation is appropriate for a designer to work with efficiently, since all important design decisions can be made at the level of source code.

Second, it is possible to derive the circuit from the program by applying systematic semantics-preserving transformations, and to obtain a circuit that is correct on first silicon. The compilation procedure is not described here, but can be found in several papers, in particular [6].

Third, the results of the experiment demonstrate that the often accepted "fatalities," that formal design methods and asynchronous techniques lead to inefficient solutions, are simply myths fueled by the natural resistance to change. Not only is the processor surprisingly small and fast for a first design, but it also exhibits a robustness to parameter variations that goes beyond our expectations and almost beyond our understanding: One of the two versions seems still to function with a voltage value of 0.35V for the VDD! Maybe the biggest surprise is the very low power consumption of the chips, which makes this design style ideally suited for use in highly concurrent architectures where a large number of chips are tightly packed.

2. The Processor: The Test Results

The processor has a 16-bit, RISC-like instruction set. It has sixteen registers, four buses, an ALU, and two adders. Instruction and data memories are separate. The chip size is about 20,000 transistors. Two versions have been fabricated: one in $2\,\mu m$ MOSIS SCMOS, and one in $1.6\,\mu m$ MOSIS SCMOS. (The dimension refers to the minimal width of a wire.) On the $2\,\mu m$ version, only twelve registers were implemented in order to fit the chip on the 84-pin $6600\,\mu m \times 4600\mu m$ pad frame.

With the exception of *isochronic forks* (see Section 4), the chips are entirely delay-insensitive; i.e., their correct operation is independent of any assumption on

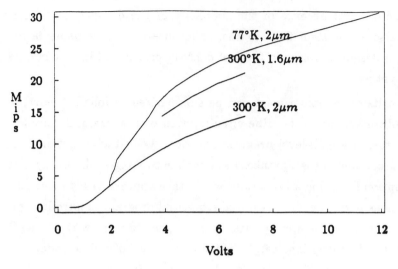

Figure 0: MIPS as a function of VDD

delays in operators and wires except that the delays are finite. The circuits use neither clocks nor knowledge about delays.

The only exception to the design method is the interface with the memories. In the absence of available memories with asynchronous interfaces, we have simulated the completion signal from the memories with an external delay. For testing purposes, the delay on the instruction memory interface is variable.

In spite of the presence of several floating n-wells, the $2\,\mu m$ version runs at 12 MIPS. The $1.6\,\mu m$ version runs at 18 MIPS. (Those performance figures are based on measurements from sequences of ALU instructions without carry. They do not take advantage of the overlap between ALU and memory instructions.) Those performances are quite encouraging given that the design is very conservative: It uses static gates, dual-rail encoding of data, completion trees, *etc.*

Only two of the 12 $2\,\mu m$ chips passed all tests, but 34 of the 50 $1.6\,\mu m$ chips were found to be functional. (However, within a certain range of values for the instruction memory delay, the $1.6\,\mu m$ version malfunctions. We will return to this phenomenon, which is related to the implementation of isochronic forks.) It takes less than 700 instructions to test the processors for stuck-at faults. The program counter is the only part that was not tested exhaustively because the memory used for the test did not contain the address required for testing the most significant bit of the program counter.

We have tested the chips under a wide range of *VDD* voltage values. At room temperature, the $2\,\mu m$ version is functional in a voltage range from 7V down to

0.35V! And it reaches 15 MIPS at 7V. We have also tested the chips cooled in liquid nitrogen. The $2\,\mu m$ version reaches 20 MIPS at 5V and 30 MIPS at 12V. The $1.6\,\mu m$ version reaches 30 MIPS at 5V. Of course, the measurements are made without adjusting any clocks (there are none), but simply by connecting the processor to a memory containing a test program and observing the rate of instruction execution. The results are summarized in Figure 0. The power consumption is 145mW at 5V and 6.7mW at 2V.

3. The Design Method

The general method—a complete description of which can be found in the referenced papers [1], [3], [4], [5], [6]—is based on program transformations. The circuit is first designed as a set of concurrent programs. Each program is then compiled (manually or automatically) into a circuit by applying a series of program transformations. Control and data path are first designed separately and then combined in a mechanical way. This important *divide-and-conquer* technique is a main innovation of the method.

The Source Notation

The program notation, which is inspired by C.A.R. Hoare's CSP [2], is briefly described. It is based on assignment and message-passing.

$b\uparrow$ stands for $b := \textbf{true}$, $b\downarrow$ stands for $b := \textbf{false}$.

Control Structures: The two control structures are *selection* and *repetition*. The execution of the selection command $[G_1 \rightarrow S_1 \| \ldots \| G_n \rightarrow S_n]$, where G_1 through G_n are boolean expressions, and S_1 through S_n are program parts, (G_i is called a "guard," and $G_i \rightarrow S_i$ a "guarded command") amounts to the execution of an arbitrary S_i for which G_i holds. If $\neg(G_1 \vee \ldots \vee G_n)$ holds, the execution of the command is suspended until $(G_1 \vee \ldots \vee G_n)$ holds.

The execution of the repetition command $*[G_1 \rightarrow S_1 \| \ldots \| G_n \rightarrow S_n]$, where G_1 through G_n are boolean expressions, and S_1 through S_n are program parts, amounts to repeatedly selecting an arbitrary S_i for which G_i holds and executing S_i. If $\neg(G_1 \vee \ldots \vee G_n)$ holds, the repetition terminates.

$[G]$, where G is a boolean expression, stands for $[G \rightarrow \textbf{skip}]$, and thus for "wait until G holds." (Hence, "$[G]; S$" and $[G \rightarrow S]$ are equivalent.)

$*[S]$ stands for $*[\textbf{true} \rightarrow S]$ and, thus, for "repeat S forever."

From (iii) and (iv), the operational description of the statement $*[[G_1 \to S_1] \ldots [G_n \to S_n]]$ is "repeat forever: wait until some G_i holds; execute an S_i for which G_i holds."

Sequencing: Besides the usual semicolon operator to denote the sequential composition of two arbitrary actions, we have two other composition operators.

For x and y both atomic, "x, y" is the execution of x and y in any order.

For X and Y both non-atomic, "$X \bullet Y$" stands for the coincident execution of X and Y, i.e., the completions of the two actions coincide. (For instance X and Y can be communication actions.)

As we shall see, the bullet operator, which is the main addition to the language we have used previously, plays a very important role in the description of the processor, both for reasons of efficiency and to realize certain synchronization requirements between processes.

In order to avoid simultaneous read and write actions on the same variable, we restrict the use of the bullet to actions that operate on disjoint set of variables.

Communication commands: Let two processes, $p1$ and $p2$, share a channel with port X in $p1$ and port Y in $p2$. (In the processes of Figure 3, the same name is used for all the ports of the same channel.) If the channel is used only for synchronization between the processes, the name of the port is sufficient to identify a commnication on this port. If the communication is used for input and output of messages, the CSP notation is used: $X!u$ outputs message u, and $X?v$ inputs message v.

At any time, the number of completed X-actions in $p1$ equals the number of completed Y-actions in $p2$. In other words, the completion of the nth X-action "coincides" with the completion of the n-th Y-action. If, for example, $p1$ reaches the nth X-action before $p2$ reaches the nth Y-action, the completion of X is suspended until $p2$ reaches Y. The X-action is then said to be *pending*. When, thereafter, $p2$ reaches Y, both X and Y are completed. It is possible (and even advantageous) to define communication actions as coincident and yet implement the actions in completely asynchronous ways. For an explanation, see [8].

Probe: Since we need a mechanism to select a set of pending communication actions for execution, we provide a general boolean command on ports called the *probe*. In process $p1$, the probe command $\overline{X}$ has the same value as the predicate "Y is pending in $p2$."

4. Delay-Insensitivity and Isochronic Forks

A circuit is delay-insensitive when its correct operation is independent of any assumption on delays in operators and wires except that the delays are finite. Such circuits do not use a clock signal or knowledge about delays.

The class of entirely delay-insensitive circuits is very limited. Different asynchronous techniques distinguish themselves in the choice of the compromises to delay-insensitivity. *Speed-independent* techniques assume that delays in gates are arbitrary, but there are no delays in wires. *Self-timed* techniques assume that a circuit can be decomposed into *equipotential* regions inside which delays in wires are negligible [9].

In our method, certain local forks are introduced to distribute a variable as the input of several gates. In order to be able to consider the different outputs of such a fork as representing the same variable, we must implement the fork in such a way that the differences between the delays in the branches of the fork are small compared to delays in other gates. We call such forks *isochronic* [4], [6].

The malfunctioning of the 1.6 μm chip for certain values of the instruction memory delay is caused by an implementation of an isochronic fork that does not always fulfill the delay requirement because of the unusually large capacitance of the fork node and because of large discrepancies in the switching thresholds of the gates to which the fork is connected.

5. Specification of the processor as a sequential program

The instruction set is deliberately not innovative. It is a conventional 16-bit-word instruction set of the *load-store* type. The processor uses two separate memories for instructions and data. There are three types of instructions: ALU, memory, and program-counter (*pc*). All ALU instructions operate on registers; memory instructions involve a register and a data memory word. Certain instructions use the following word as *offset*. The only important omissions, those of an interrupt mechanism and communication ports, are ones we found to be unnecessary distractions in a first design.

The sequential program describing the processor is a non-terminating loop, each step of which is a *FETCH* phase followed by an *EXECUTE* phase. The complete sequential program for the processor is shown in Figure 1. Variable i, which contains the instruction currently being executed, is described in the PASCAL record notation as a structured variable consisting of several fields. All instructions

$*[FETCH : i, pc := imem[pc], pc + 1;$

$[offset(i.op) \rightarrow offset, pc := imem[pc], pc + 1;$

$[\![\neg offset(i.op) \rightarrow skip$

$];$

$EXECUTE : [alu(i.op) \rightarrow \langle reg[i.z], f \rangle := aluf(reg[i.x], reg[i.y], i.op, f)$

$[\![ld(i.op) \rightarrow reg[i.z] := dmem[reg[i.x] + reg[i.y]]$

$[\![st(i.op) \rightarrow dmem[reg[i.x] + reg[i.y]] := reg[i.z]$

$[\![ldx(i.op) \rightarrow reg[i.z] := dmem[offset + reg[i.y]]$

$[\![stx(i.op) \rightarrow dmem[offset + reg[i.y]] := reg[i.z]$

$[\![lda(i.op) \rightarrow reg[i.z] := offset + reg[i.y]$

$[\![stpc(i.op) \rightarrow reg[i.z] := pc + reg[i.y]$

$[\![jmp(i.op) \rightarrow pc := reg[i.y]$

$[\![brch(i.op) \rightarrow [cond(f, i.cc) \rightarrow pc := pc + offset$

$[\![\neg cond(f, i.cc) \rightarrow skip$

$]$

$]$

$].$

Figure 1: Sequential program describing the processor

contain an *op* field for the *opcode*. The parameter fields depend on the types of the instructions. The most common ones, those for ALU, load, and store instructions, consist of the three fields, x, y, and z, which are the indices of the registers to be used as parameters of the instruction. Variable cc is the condition code field of the branch instruction, and f contains the *flags* generated by the execution of an *alu* instruction.

The two memories are the arrays *imem* and *dmem*. The index to *imem* is the program-counter variable, pc. The general-purpose registers are described as the array $reg[0 \ldots 15]$. (Only twelve registers are implemented in the first chip.) Register $reg[0]$ is special: It always contains the value zero.

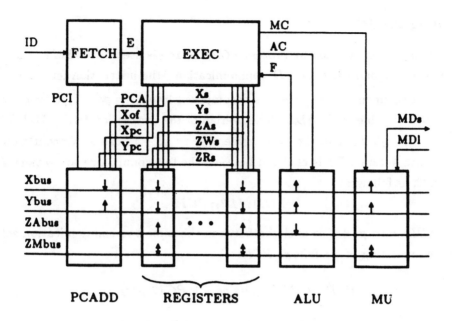

Figure 2: Process and channel structure

6. Decomposition into Concurrent Processes

We decompose the previous program into a set of concurrent processes that communicate and synchronize using communication commands on channels. A restricted form of shared variables is allowed. The control channels Xs, Ys, ZAs, ZWs, ZRs, and the bus ZA are one-to-many; the buses X, Y, ZM are many-to-many; the other channels are one-to-one. But all channels are used by only two processes at a time. The structure of processes and channels is shown in Figure 2. The final program is shown in Figures 3 and 4.

Process $FETCH$ fetches the instructions from the instruction memory, and transmits them to process $EXEC$ which decodes them. Process $PCADD$ updates the address pc of the next instruction concurrently with the instruction fetch, and controls the *offset* register. The execution of an ALU instruction by process ALU can overlap with the execution of a memory instruction by process MU. The *jump* and *branch* instructions are executed by $EXEC$; *store-pc* is executed by the ALU as the instruction "add the content of register r to the pc and store it." The array $REG[k]$ of processes implements the register file. Both MU and $PCADD$ contain their own adder. Processes $IMEM$ and $DMEM$ describe the instruction memory and data memory, respectively.

Updating the PC

The variable *pc* is updated by process *PCADD*, and is used by *IMEM* as the index of the array *imem* during the *ID* communication—the instruction fetch.

The assignment $pc := pc + 1$ is decomposed into $y := pc + 1; pc := y$, where y is a local variable of *PCADD*. The overlap of the instruction fetch, *ID?* (either *ID?i* or *ID?offset*), and the pc increment, $y := pc + 1$, can now occur while *pc* is constant. Action *ID?* is enclosed between the two communication actions *PCI1* and *PCI2*, as follows:

$$PCI1; ID?i; PCI2 .$$

In *PCADD*, $y := pc + 1$ is enclosed between the same two communication actions while the updating of *pc* follows *PCI2*:

$$\overline{PCII} \rightarrow PCI1; y := pc + 1; PCI2; pc := y .$$

Since the completions of *PCI1* and *PCI2* in *FETCH* coincide with the completion of *PCI1* and *PCI2* in *PCADD*, respectively, the execution of *ID?i* in *FETCH* overlaps the execution of $y := pc + 1$ in *PCADD*. *PCI1* and *PCI2* are implemented as the two halves of the same communication handshaking to minimize the overhead.

In order to concentrate all increments of *pc* inside *PCADD*, we use the same technique to delegate the assignment $pc := pc + offset$ (executed by the *EXEC* part in the sequential program) to *PCADD*.

The guarded command $\overline{Xof} \rightarrow X!offset \bullet Xof$ in *PCADD* has been transformed into a concurrent process since it needs only be mutually exclusive with assignment $y := pc + offset$, and this mutual exclusion is enforced by the sequencing between *PCA1; PCA2* and *Xof* within *EXEC*.

7. Stalling the Pipeline

When the pc is modified by *EXEC* as part of the execution of a *pc* instruction, (*store-pc*, *jump* or *branch*), fetching the next instruction by *FETCH* is postponed until the correct value of the pc is assigned to *PCADD.pc*.

When the offset is reserved for *MU* by *EXEC*, as part of the execution of some memory instructions, fetching the next instruction, which might be a new offset, is postponed until *MU* has received the value of the current offset. In the second design, we have refined the protocol to block *FETCH* only when the next instruction is a new offset.

$IMEM \equiv *[ID!imem[pc]]$

$FETCH \equiv *[PCI1; ID?i; PCI2;$

$\qquad [offset(i.op) \rightarrow PCI1; ID?offset; PCI2$

$\qquad \llbracket \neg offset(i.op) \rightarrow skip$

$\qquad]; E1!i; E2$

$\qquad]$

$PCADD \equiv (*[\llbracket \overline{PCI1} \rightarrow PCI1; y := pc + 1; PCI2; pc := y$

$\qquad\qquad \llbracket \overline{PCA1} \rightarrow PCA1; y := pc + offset; PCA2; pc := y$

$\qquad\qquad \llbracket \overline{Xpc} \rightarrow X!pc \bullet Xpc$

$\qquad\qquad \llbracket \overline{Ypc} \rightarrow Y?pc \bullet Ypc$

$\qquad\qquad]]$

$\qquad \| * [[\overline{Xof} \rightarrow X!offset \bullet Xof]]$

$\qquad)$

$EXEC \equiv *[E1?j;$

$\qquad [alu(j.op) \rightarrow E2; Xs \bullet Ys \bullet AC!j.op \bullet ZAs$

$\qquad \llbracket ld(j.op) \rightarrow E2; Xs \bullet Ys \bullet MC1 \bullet ZRs$

$\qquad \llbracket st(j.op) \rightarrow E2; Xs \bullet Ys \bullet MC2 \bullet ZWs$

$\qquad \llbracket ldx(j.op) \rightarrow Xof \bullet Ys \bullet MC1 \bullet ZRs; E2$

$\qquad \llbracket stx(j.op) \rightarrow Xof \bullet Ys \bullet MC2 \bullet ZWs; E2$

$\qquad \llbracket lda(j.op) \rightarrow Xof \bullet Ys \bullet MC3 \bullet ZRs; E2$

$\qquad \llbracket stpc(j.op) \rightarrow Xpc \bullet Ys \bullet AC!add \bullet ZAs; E2$

$\qquad \llbracket jmp(j.op) \rightarrow Ypc \bullet Ys; E2$

$\qquad \llbracket brch(j.op) \rightarrow F?f; [cond(f, j.cc) \rightarrow PCA1; PCA2$

$\qquad\qquad\qquad \llbracket \neg cond(f, j.cc) \rightarrow skip$

$\qquad\qquad\qquad]; E2$

$\qquad]$

Figure 3: The final program, first part

$$ALU \equiv *[[\overline{AC} \rightarrow AC?op \bullet X?x \bullet Y?y;$$

$$\langle z, f \rangle := aluf(x, y, op, f); ZA!z$$

$$[\overline{F} \rightarrow F!f$$

$$]]$$

$$MU \equiv *[[\overline{MC1} \rightarrow X?x \bullet Y?y \bullet MC1; ma := x + y; MDl?w; ZM!w$$

$$[\overline{MC2} \rightarrow X?x \bullet Y?y \bullet MC2 \bullet ZM?w; ma := x + y; MDs!w$$

$$[\overline{MC3} \rightarrow X?x \bullet Y?y \bullet MC3; ma := x + y; ZM!ma$$

$$]]$$

$$DMEM \equiv *[[\overline{MDl} \rightarrow MDl!dmem[ma]$$

$$[\overline{MDs} \rightarrow MDs?dmem[ma]$$

$$]]$$

$$REG[k] \equiv (* [[\neg bk \wedge k = j.x \wedge \overline{Xs} \rightarrow X!r \bullet Xs]]$$

$$\| * [[\neg bk \wedge k = j.y \wedge \overline{Ys} \rightarrow Y!r \bullet Ys]]$$

$$\| * [[\neg bk \wedge k = j.z \wedge \overline{ZWs} \rightarrow ZM!r \bullet ZWs]]$$

$$\| * [[\neg bk \wedge k = j.z \wedge \overline{ZAs} \rightarrow bk\uparrow; ZAs; ZA?r; bk\downarrow]]$$

$$\| * [[\neg bk \wedge k = j.z \wedge \overline{ZRs} \rightarrow bk\uparrow; ZRs; ZM?r; bk\downarrow]]$$

$$)$$

Figure 4: The final program, second part

Postponing the start of the next cycle in *FETCH* is achieved by postponing the completion of the previous cycle, i.e., by postponing the completion of the communication action on channel E. As in the case of the *PCI* communication, E is decomposed into two communications, $E1$ and $E2$. Again, $E1$ and $E2$ are implemented as the two halves of the same handshaking protocol.

In *FETCH*, $E!i$ is replaced with $E1!i; E2$. In *EXEC*, $E2$ is postponed until after either $Xof?offset$ or a complete execution of a pc instruction has occurred.

8. Sharing Registers and Buses

A bus is used by two processes at a time, one of which is a register and the other is *EXEC*, *MU*, *ALU*, or *PCADD*. We therefore decided to introduce enough buses so as not to restrict the concurrent access to different registers. For instance, *ALU* writing a result into a register should not prevent *MU* from using another register at the same time.

The four buses correspond to the four main concurrent activities involving the registers.

The X bus and the Y bus are used to send the parameters of an ALU operation to the ALU, and to send the parameters of address calculation to the memory unit. We also make opportunistic use of them to transmit the pc and the offset to and from *PCADD*.

The ZA bus is used to transmit the result of an ALU operation to the registers. The ZM bus is used by the memory unit to transmit data between the data memory and the registers.

We make a virtue out of necessity by turning the restriction that registers can be accessed only through those four buses into a convenient abstraction mechanism. The ALU uses only the X, Y, and ZA ports without having to reference the particular registers that are used in the communications. It is the task of *EXEC* to reserve the X, Y, and ZA bus for the proper registers before the ALU uses them.

The same holds for the *MU* process, which references only X, Y, and ZM. An additional abstraction is that the X bus is used to send the offset to *MU*, so that the cases for which the first parameter is *i.x* or *offset* are now identical, since both parameters are sent via the X bus.

Exclusive Use of a Bus

Commands *Xpc*, *Ypc*, and *Xof* are used by *EXEC* to select the X and Y buses for communication of *pc* and *offset*. Commands *Xs*, *Ys*, and *ZAs* are used by *EXEC* to select the X, Y, and ZA buses, respectively, for a register that has to communicate with the ALU as part of the execution of an ALU instruction.

Two commands are needed to select the ZM bus: *ZWs* if the bus is to be used for writing to the data memory, and *ZRs* if the bus is to be used for reading from the data memory.

Let us first solve the problem of the mutual exclusion among the different uses of a bus. As long as we have only one ALU and one memory unit, no conflict is possible on the ZA and ZM buses, since only the ALU uses the ZA bus, and only the memory unit uses the ZM bus. But the X and Y buses are used concurrently by the ALU, the memory unit, and the pc unit.

We achieve mutual exclusion on different uses of the X bus as follows. (The same argument holds for Y.) The completion of an X communication is made to coincide with the completion of one of the selection actions Xs, Xof, Xpc; and the occurrences of these selection actions exclude each other in time inside $EXEC$ since they appear in different guarded commands.

This coincidence is implemented by the *bullet* command: We recall that, for arbitrary communication commands U and V inside the same process, $U \bullet V$ guarantees that the two actions are completed at the same time. We then say that the two actions coincide. The use of the bullets $X!pc \bullet Xpc$ and $X!offset \bullet Xof$ inside $PCADD$, and $X!r \bullet Xs$ inside the registers enforces the coincidence of X with Xpc, Xof, and Xs, respectively. The bullets in $EXEC$, ALU, and MU have been introduced for reasons of efficiency: Sequencing is avoided.

9. Register Selection

Command Xs in $EXEC$ selects the X bus for the particular register whose index k is equal to the field $i.x$ of the instruction i being decoded by $EXEC$, and analogously for commands Ys, ZAs, ZRs, and ZWs.

Each register process $REG[k]$, for $0 \leq k < 16$, consists of five elementary processes, one for each selection command. The register that is selected by command Xs is the one that passes the test $k = i.x$. This implementation requires that the variable $i.x$ be shared by all registers and $EXEC$. An alternative solution that does not require shared variables uses demultiplexer processes. (The implementations of the two solutions are almost identical.)

The semicolons in the last two guarded commands of $REG[k]$ are introduced to pipeline the computation of the result of an ALU instruction or memory instruction with the decoding of the next instruction.

Mutual Exclusion on Registers

A register may be used in several arguments (x, y, or z) of the same instruction, and also as an argument in two successive instructions whose executions may overlap. We therefore have to address the issue of the concurrent uses of the same register. Two concurrent actions on the same register are allowed when they are both read actions.

Concurrency within an instruction is not a problem: X and Y communications on the same register may overlap, since they are both read actions, and Z cannot overlap with either X or Y because of the sequencing inside ALU and MU.

Concurrency in the access to a register during two consecutive overlapping instructions (one instruction is an ALU and the other is a memory instruction) can be a problem: Writing a result into a register (a ZA or a ZR action) in the first instruction can overlap with another action on the same register in the second instruction. But, because the selection of the z register for the first instruction takes place before the selection of the registers for the second instruction, we can use this ordering to impose the same ordering on the different accesses to the same register when a ZA or ZR is involved.

This ordering is implemented as follows: In $REG[k]$, variable bk (initially false) is set to true before the register is selected for ZA or ZR, and it is set back to false only after the register has been actually used. All uses of the register are guarded with the condition $\neg bk$. Hence, all subsequent selections of the register are postponed until the current ZA or ZR is completed.

We must ensure that bk is not set to true before the register is selected for an X or a Y action *inside the same instruction*, since this would lead to deadlock. We omit this refinement which does not appear in the program of Figures 3 and 4.

10. Conclusion

Instruction pipelining has been approached as a concurrent programming problem: Starting with a sequential program for the processor, concurrency is introduced through a series of program transformations. However, although the transformations are guided by the intent to overlap the important phases—fetch, decode, execute—of instruction execution, they are neither mechanical nor unique. The designer decides how to decompose a program into several concurrent ones. We do not claim that our solution in this first design is in any way optimal.

Since the choice of an instruction set was not part of the experiment, our design should be judged in two ways: the choice of the concurrent program of Figures 3 and 4, and its implementation. The implementation, which is described in [7], is satisfactory, but not optimal. The sizing of transistors can be improved and the number of transitions can be decreased, mainly by a better placement of inverters. For instance, the delays due to the control for a buffer are both about twice their theoretical minimum.

The program represents the choice of a pipeline, and of synchronization techniques to implement it. We have deliberately chosen a simple pipeline. In particular, the mechanism for stalling, which places part of the decoding in series with the fetch on the critical path, sacrifices efficiency for simplicity. However, performance evaluations show that the pipeline is well-balanced since the different stages have comparable average delays. Improving the critical path by overlapping fetch and decode requires improving the ALU and memory instruction execution stages by pipelining parts of these stages.

The practicality of overlapping ALU and memory instruction executions remains an open issue. It is not clear whether the gain in performance is worth the complexity of the synchronization involved and the requirement of two separate Z buses.

We find the synchronization techniques used to implement the concurrent activities between the different stages of the pipeline particularly elegant and efficient, since the delays incurred in a synchronization can be of arbitrary length and vary from instruction to instruction.

We foresee excellent performances for asynchronous processors as the feature size keeps decreasing. But the designer must be ready to use new methods based on concurrent programmming, in order to exploit asynchronous techniques to their fullest.

11. Acknowledgment

I am indebted to my students Steve Burns, Tony Lee, Drazen Borkovic, and Pieter Hazewindus for their contribution to the research and the design of the processor.

12. References

[1] Steven M. Burns and Alain J. Martin, Syntax-directed Translation of Concurrent Programs into Self-timed Circuits. In J. Allen and F. Leighton (ed), *Fifth MIT Conference on Advanced Research in VLSI*, pp 35-40, MIT Press, 1988.

[2] C.A.R. Hoare, Communicating Sequential Processes. *Comm. ACM* 21,8, pp 666-677, August, 1978.

[3] Alain J. Martin, The Design of a Self-timed Circuit for Distributed Mutual Exclusion. In Henry Fuchs (ed), *1985 Chapel Hill Conf. VLSI*, Computer Science Press, pp 247-260, 1985.

[4] Alain J. Martin, Compiling Communicating Processes into Delay-insensitive VLSI Circuits. *Distributed Computing*, 1,(4), Springer-Verlag, pp 226-234 1986.

[5] Alain J. Martin, A Synthesis Method for Self-timed VLSI Circuits. *ICCD 87: 1987 IEEE International Conference on Computer Design*, IEEE Computer Society Press, pp 224-229, 1987.

[6] Alain J. Martin, Programming in VLSI: From Communicating Processes to Delay-insensitive Circuits. In C.A.R. Hoare (ed), *UT Year of Programming Institute on Concurrent Programming*, Addison-Wesley, Reading MA, 1989.

[7] Alain J. Martin, Steve Burns, Tony Lee, Drazen Borkovic, and Pieter Hazewindus, The Design of an Asynchronus Microprocessor. In C.L. Seitz (ed), *Decennial Caltech Conference on VLSI*, MIT Press, 1989.

[8] Carver Mead and Lynn Conway, *Introduction to VLSI Systems*, Addison-Wesley, Reading MA, 1980.

[9] Charles L. Seitz, System Timing, Chapter 7 in Mead & Conway, *Introduction to VLSI Systems*, Addison-Wesley, Reading MA, 1980.

Manipulating Logical Organization
with System Factorizations*

Steven D. Johnson
Indiana University

ABSTRACT   *Logical organization refers to a system's decomposition into functional units, processes, and so on; it is sometimes called the 'structural' aspect of system description. In an approach to digital synthesis based on functional algebra, logical organization is developed using a class of transformations called system factorizations. These transformations isolate subsystems and encapsulate them as applicative combinators. Factorizations have a variety of uses, ranging from the refinement of actual architecture to the synthesis of certain kinds of verification conditions. This paper outlines the foundations for this algebra and presents several examples.*

1. Introduction

It is conventional wisdom in hardware design—as in every other branch of programming—to defer decisions about architecture until the control is understood. While design surely begins with an idea of the building blocks needed, engineering should focus first on an algorithm. It is usually a mistake to center a design around some device that seems to solve the problem. Ideally, the final details of architecture are developed once an acceptable algorithm has been designed; components are chosen to serve the needs of control (See [21], p. 166, for a discussion.).

In an algebraic approach to synthesis, this aspect of engineering gives rise to a family of transformations called *system factorizations*. Their purpose is to introduce a conceptual organization analogous to that of a functional block diagram, consisting of a hierarchy of communicating functional units, modules and processes.

*This research was supported, in part, by NSF grants MIP8707067 and DCR8521497.

This paper defines basic laws from which factorizations are composed and illustrates tactical issues with a series of examples.

The characterization of synthesis is founded on functional algebra. A sequence of transformations is applied to an initial expression, resulting in a target expression closer to a physical realization. The process is called a *derivation* to emphasize that source and target expressions are really dialects of a single modeling language of higher order functions. Following current terminology [3], source expressions correspond to 'specifications' and target expressions to 'implementations.' However, it is more accurate to say that an implementation is specified by the source expression *together with* a derivation sequence, since the latter expresses much of the design intent.

One purpose here is to consolidate previous observations about, and experiences with, the structural aspect of digital design derivation. Earlier work established a connection between functional descriptions of control flow and synchronous network descriptions [12, 10, 11]. *Abstract component factorizations* were introduced as a treatment for encapsulation and information hiding. These transformations isolated complex data abstractions, such as stack and memory, from their more directly implementable parameters, such as item and address. Subsequent experimentation revealed that essentially the same transformations are useful in developing other aspects of architecture. Slightly generalized factorizations were used to allocate operations to units, and to manipulate communication ports [13].

Ideally, individual transformations preserve a behavioral interpretation of notation. Derived implementations are, therefore, correct under that notion of equivalence. Derivation is a form of proof. In practice, however, correctness is relative to side conditions, such as the ubiquitous assumption that electronics can model the logic used. Transformations can also generate verification conditions, which become antecedents to correctness claims (See [20, 4, 22] for related discussions.). In a preliminary exploration of interplay between mechanical derivation and mechanical verification, factorizations play a role in isolating such conditions [14].

The importance of factorization is partly a consequence of the approach taken to description. A strength of functional modeling is the use of abstraction to gain representation independence—it is natural to manipulate complex entities as values. Hence, encapsulation mechanisms are needed to impose modularity. Although object oriented styles are prevalent in hardware description languages ([16] and [6] are examples), a more open view of type structures is justified. As discussed in the opening paragraph, it is often better to specify in terms of arithmetic rather than in terms of ALUs; and it is often easier to reason about storage abstractions than about of RAM processes. Under this thesis it is necessary to have algebra for introducing modularity; and this is the basic effect of a system factorization.

Section 2 defines a first order language of *system descriptions*, which depict synchronized networks in a simple language of applicative terms. The presentation follows the treatment in [12], but with refinements for multioutput operations. Multiple output combinations are so often seen in hardware that it is better to include them in the metalanguage. Sheeran builds a similar foundation for μFP [19]. Boute proposes an 'open semantics' approach in the same notational framework [1]. Harmond and Tucker adapt the formal-algebraic theory to get the model of sequential behavior used here [8]. Some of the vocabulary comes from a text book by Loeckx and Sieber [15].

The restriction to first order is temporary. Higher order description has an established role in hardware description. The most successful exploitation has been Sheeran's algebra for structural manipulation [18]. O'Donnell develops several useful interpretations using functionals [17]. In both cases, there is a restricted structural framework which is not necessarily assumed in this work. First order restrictions will be eliminated as the details are worked out.

Section 3 states fundamental transformation laws for system descriptions. It is claimed, but not proved, that the coarser grained factorizations illustrated in Section 4 reduce to these laws. The more basic transformations correspond to the inference mechanisms of a theorem prover, and factorizations correspond to tactical lemmas. This relationship is discussed further in Section 5, where experience with the use of mechanized factorizations is briefly reviewed.

2. Terms, Combinations and System Descriptions

In the definitions that follow, the language of terms for a many sorted algebra of multioutput functions is extended by a delay operator to form a language of *signal expressions*. A *system description* is a simultaneous system of signal expressions. The central fact established in this section is that the use of closed *combinations*, or parameterized expressions, commutes with a behavioral interpretation of the language of signals.

A *basis* describes a family of value sets, A_1, ..., A_n, together with a collection of total and strict functions, f_1, ..., f_m, on these sets. These functions are called *operations* in order to distinguish them from defined functions. With each set A_i is associated a type symbol, τ_i, a distinct set of constant symbols, and a distinct set of variable symbols. The notation $v : \tau_i$, sometimes phrased, "v is a τ_i," asserts that the variable v ranges over values in A_i. The *signature*, of an operation describes its domain and range, which in general are nested products. The formula $f : (\tau_1, (\tau_2, \tau_3)) \to (\tau_4, \tau_5, \tau_6)$ asserts that the operation f maps the product $A_1 \times (A_2 \times A_3)$ to the product $A_4 \times A_5 \times A_6$. Since product formation is not considered associative, parentheses are significant in signatures. The signatures $(\tau) \to \tau'$ and $\tau \to \tau'$ are distinct (although mathematical parentheses in some discussions may cloud the distinction).

Certain properties of the basis are always assumed. There must be a set of truth values, of type *Bool*, which includes constants true and false. Operations with range *Bool* are called *tests*. Each value set has an *unspecified element* called "don't care" and designated by a '#'. Other possible metaconstants, such as "don't know" and "undefined," do not arise in this paper.

For each type τ, there is a strict *selection operation*, $sel : (Bool, \tau, \tau) \to \tau$. A partial definition is

$$sel(b, v_1, v_2) = \begin{cases} v_1 & \text{if } b \text{ is true} \\ v_2 & \text{if } b \text{ is false} \end{cases}$$

There are several possibilities for $sel(\#, v_1, v_2)$, but this case is excluded from consideration in this paper. Finite product and projection operations are assumed. Projections are denoted by sans seriff adjectives, 1st, 2nd, 3rd, 4th, 5th ..., ith, ... Finally, it is assumed that arbitrary finite ordered sets of *tokens* can be represented in the basis; furthermore, tokens can be tested for equality. A concrete binary representation can be constructed using *Bool*.

The language of applicative *terms* is built from the base vocabulary. The usual treatment of terms is extended for multioutput operations.

Definition 1 A *simple term* is either a constant, a variable, or expresses the application, $f(T_1, \ldots, T_n)$, of an operation f to the terms T_i according to the f's signature. An application without an operation symbol, $(t_1, \ldots, t_n)$, forms of an n-tuple denoting an element of a product.

Take the semantics of this language to be an initial algebra, represented by the terms of the language itself [7]. Terms are partitioned by equivalence relation, written $S \equiv T$, according to equational laws of the basis. The equations of specific bases are not considered in this paper, but certain laws hold in universally. For instance,

$$ith(T_1, \ldots, T_i, \ldots T_n) \equiv T_i$$

Additional equations are discussed in Section 3.

The definition of substitution on terms is adapted for multioutput operations by allowing nested lists of variables to serve as substitution patterns. Such a list is called an *identifier*.

Definition 2 An *identifier* is either a variable or a nested list, $(X_1, \ldots, X_n)$, of *distinct* identifiers, meaning that they share no common variables.

Definition 3 The formula $T[R/X]$ denotes a *substitution* of the term R for the identifier X in the term T. The formula $T[R_1/X_1, \ldots, R_n/X_n]$ denotes the simultaneous and respective substitutions of terms R_i for identifiers X_i, $i \in \{1 .. n\}$. Substitution is defined by induction on the language of terms. In the base cases, constants are unchanged and for a variable symbol u,

$$u[R/X] = \begin{cases} R & \text{if } X = u \\ u & \text{if } X \neq v \end{cases}$$

For applications and n-tuples,

$$f(T_1, \ldots, T_n)[R/X] = f(T_1', \ldots, T_n')$$

where $T_i' = T_i[R/X]$ for $i \in \{1 .. n\}$ For nested identifiers, a simultaneous substitution is done on the constituents:

$$T[R/(X_1, \ldots, X_n)] = T[1\text{st}(R)/X_1, \ldots n\text{th}(R)/X_n]$$

In the last case, substitution of an n-tuple for an n-element identifier simplifies to

$$T[(R_1, \ldots, R_n)/(X_1, \ldots, X_n)] = T[R_1/X_1, \ldots R_n/X_n]$$

Hierarchic decomposition is expressed by the formation of closed combinations.

Definition 4 A *combination* is a fully parameterized term, written $\lambda X . T$ where each variable of the term T is also found in the identifier X. An *instance* of a combination is a term, $T[R/X]$, where R is a term.

Combinations may be nested, but may not be recursive. Where combinations are given names, it is customary to write $Name(X) \overset{\text{def}}{=} T$ rather than $Name = \lambda X . T$. The language of terms is extended to include applications of named combinations, such as $Name(R)$.

A *selection combination* encapsulates the decision structure of a nested selection. That is, selection combinations contain only constants, variables, and *sel* operations. A *case expression* is a selection combination associated with a set of tokens. If $A = \{c_1, \ldots, c_n\}$ is a token set, then the form

$$case \ R \ of \ c_1 \colon T_1$$
$$\vdots$$
$$c_n \colon T_n$$

abbreviates a combination that selects T_i where R is (or reduces to) the token c_i.

A *system description* is a collection of equations describing a network. The defining expressions are composed of terms over a given basis plus a notation of delay, expressed by the infix symbol, '!'.

Definition 5 A *signal expression* is either a term or has the form $v \ ! \ S$, where v is a simple term—usually a constant or a variable—and S is a signal expression. A *system description* is a set of equations

$$X_1 = S_1$$
$$\vdots$$
$$X_n = S_n$$

in which each X_i is a distinct identifier and each S_i is a signal expression over the variables in $X_1, \ldots, X_n$.

No interpretation of system descriptions may depend on the textual order of the equations; hence, a system description may be considered as an indexed collection of equations $\{X_i = S_i\}_{i \in I}$, for finite index set I. Two interpretations are used in this paper.

Under a *schematic interpretation*, each occurrence of a term is associated with a drawing. Operations are shown as boxes connected to their arguments by lines. The signal identifiers name some of these lines, and feedback cycles are allowed. A delay element, sometimes figuratively called a 'register,' is associated with every delay-expression. Figures 1 and 2 contain schematics for several of the partial system descriptions discussed in Section 4. Schematics are in a class of interpretations that Boute calls *structural semantics* [1]. Meaning is in close correspondence to syntax and any transformation applied to a description changes its interpretation.

Under a *sequential interpretation*, each signal expression S denotes a uniformly typed sequence of values, $\langle S^0, S^1, \ldots \rangle$. This is a *behavioral semantics* in Boute's terminology. A constant c denotes the constant sequence, $\langle c, c, \ldots \rangle$. The expression $v \ ! \ S$ denotes the sequence $\langle v, S^0, S^1, \ldots \rangle$. Operations are applied element-by-element. If f has signature $f \colon (\sigma_1, \ldots, \sigma_m) \to (\tau_1, \ldots, \tau_n)$, then $f(S_1, \ldots, S_m)$

denotes an n-tuple of sequences, $(T_1, \ldots, T_n)$, such that for all natural numbers i, $f(S_1^i, \ldots, S_m^i) = (T_1^i, \ldots, T_m^i)$. The signal equations of a system description are simultaneously defined; that is, for $k \in \{1 .. n\}$, and for all $i \geq 0$, $X_k^i = S_k^i$ when X_k is a simple variable. A nested variable is bound to the corresponding projection of its identifier's defining expression.

For the sequential interpretation of a system description to be well defined, it is sufficient for each feedback cycle to contain a delay element. For instance, in the system consisting of the single equation, $X = f(X)$, the sequence X is nowhere defined, while in $X = v \; ! \; f(X)$, X^i is, by induction, defined for all i. A system description is said to be *well formed* when it has this no-combinational-feedback property. Well formedness is assumed in most digital design disciplines (e.g. clocked sequential circuitry [9]). The synthesis method developed in [12] guarantees well formedness and the algebra to be discussed preserves it.

The use of combinations freely commutes with the sequential interpretation; hence, invocations of named combinations are allowed in signal definitions. Let $\mathcal{S}[\![T]\!]$ denote the sequential interpretation of a simple term; and let $\mathcal{D}[\![T]\!]$ denote its interpretation as a value. Then for any terms T, R, for any identifier X, and for all $i \geq 0$, $\mathcal{S}[\![T[R/X]]\!]^i = \mathcal{D}[\![T[\mathcal{S}[\![R]\!]^i/X]]\!]$. In [12] this fact is proved by reducing the language of terms to a set of combining functionals for composition, construction, and projection and showing that each of these functionals commutes the formation of sequences.

With extensions for substitution, subsystems with delay elements may be incorporated in *sequential combinations*. A parameterized system typically has the form

$$Name(v, V) \stackrel{\text{def}}{=} Z$$
$$where$$
$$X_1 = S_1$$
$$\vdots$$
$$X_n = S_n$$

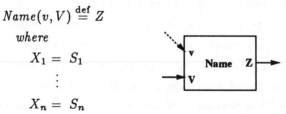

The syntax reflects the fact that system descriptions are just a dialect of recursive binding expression [10]. A parameterized system with no delay elements is reducible to a multiple output term combination, since there can be no feedback. The parameter typically includes an identifier for initial register values (v) and an identifier for input signals (V). In addition, there is an output identifier (Z) telling which signals are observable. Since this is a functional notation, all signals have direction. Combinations and parameterized systems are depicted in schematics as boxes, as above, containing the name of the combination and labeled input and output ports. Where possible, the flow in schematics is left-to-right, top-to-bottom.

3. Elementary Laws of Behavior

The derivation algebra manipulates system descriptions in ways that preserve behavior while improving some structural aspect. It has already been stipulated that the equations of a system may be written down in any order. Hence, the laws are presented as local transformations on the affected signals. The symbol $\stackrel{C}{\Longleftrightarrow}$ indicates that a transformation is subject to condition C. The first law states that signals can be added or removed provided the well formedness conditions and observable behavior are preserved.

SIGNAL INTRODUCTION AND ELIMINATION. *The signal equation $Y = R$ may be added to (deleted from) a system description under conditions for signal introduction (elimination).*

$$
\begin{array}{c}
SD(v, V) \stackrel{\text{def}}{=} Z \ where \\
X_1 = S_1 \\
\vdots \\
X_n = S_n
\end{array}
\qquad
\begin{array}{c}
\stackrel{(1)}{\Longrightarrow} \\
\stackrel{(2)}{\Longleftarrow}
\end{array}
\qquad
\begin{array}{c}
SD(v, V) \stackrel{\text{def}}{=} Z \ where \\
X_1 = S_1 \\
\vdots \\
X_n = S_n \\
Y = T
\end{array}
$$

For signal introduction (1), Y must be distinct from $\{Z, X_1, \ldots X_n\}$ and must introduce no combinational feed back. For signal elimination (2), the variables in Y must not occur in any defining expression other than T.

Condition (2) is stronger than necessary: intuitively, a signal can be eliminated if it does not contribute to observable output. For practical purposes however, this possibility can be dealt with using other laws. The next law has to do with the manipulation of common expressions.

IDENTIFICATION. *Signal identifiers can be exchanged with their defining expressions wherever these occur.*

$$
\begin{array}{c}
\vdots \\
X = S \\
Y = T \\
\vdots
\end{array}
\qquad \Longleftrightarrow \qquad
\begin{array}{c}
\vdots \\
X = S[T/Y] \\
Y = T \\
\vdots
\end{array}
$$

Using introduction, elimination, and identification, we can replace an expression that occurs several places by a name, whose definition is the common expression. The structural effect is to reduce the number of replicated components. A tactical step in many transformations is to form signals into groups. For example, grouping may be a prelude to simultaneously eliminating a collection of unused signals. Grouping is also a first step toward forming multioutput combinations.

> GROUPING. *A subsystem is grouped by nesting its identifiers and forming a tuple of their defining expressions.*

$$
\begin{array}{c}
\vdots \\
X_i = S_i \\
X_{i+1} = S_{i+1} \\
\vdots \\
X_{i+m} = Si + m \\
\vdots
\end{array}
\qquad \Longleftrightarrow \qquad
\begin{array}{c}
\vdots \\
(X_i, \ldots, X_{i+m}) = (S_i, \ldots, S_{i+m}) \\
\vdots
\end{array}
$$

In applying this transformation from right to left, if the defining expression is not an n-tuple, it may be rewritten as a product of projections, $(1st(S), \ldots, mth(S))$, according to the Replacement Law:

> REPLACEMENT   *Any term may be replaced by an equivalent one.*

$$
\begin{array}{c}
\vdots \\
X = R[S/X] \\
\vdots
\end{array}
\quad \overset{S \equiv T}{\Longleftrightarrow} \quad
\begin{array}{c}
\vdots \\
X = R[T/X] \\
\vdots
\end{array}
$$

Two signal expressions are equivalent if they are composed of equivalent terms. Therefore, replacement applies to signal expressions as well as terms. Of central interest are rewritings under the universal base laws, and in particular, manipulation of selection terms. First, the *sel* operation obeys a distributive law for strict operations:

$$
sel(P, f(S), f(T)) \quad \equiv \quad f(sel(P, S, T))
$$

Expressed with schematics, selections "push through" operations:

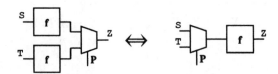

Since *sel* also distributes over products, this equation is sufficient to characterize distribution over complicated signatures. This form of optimization is commonly used in in silicon compilation [5]. However, an uncommon variation is more fundamental to factorization. In functional algebra, *sel* distributes over operations and combinations as well as over arguments:

$$sel(P, f(S), g(T)) \cong (sel(P, f, g))(sel(P, S, T))$$

Under first-order restrictions, "$sel(P, f, g)$" is not permitted; however, an implementation of this expression is always possible. Define a combination that is capable of doing either f or g, depending on an *instruction token*, $i \in \{f, g\}$:

$$FG(i, x) \stackrel{\text{def}}{=} case\ i\ of\ \textsf{f}: f(x)$$
$$\textsf{g}: g(x)$$

The second order identity can be represented as,

$$sel(P, f(S), g(T)) \equiv FG(sel(P, \textsf{f}, \textsf{g}), sel(P, S, T))$$

The aim is to encapsulate a collection of operations in a single module for which instructions are generated. This form of distribution also applies to operations of different sorts. For example, suppose that $f: (\alpha, \beta) \rightarrow \delta$ and $g: (\alpha, \gamma) \rightarrow \delta$. A combination must be formed with enough arguments of enough types to simulate both f and g. The specific form of the combination will depend on implementation factors, but here is one possibility: with parameters $a: \alpha$, $b: \beta$, and $c: \gamma$,

$$FG(i, a, b, c) \stackrel{\text{def}}{=} case\ i\ of\ \textsf{f}: f(a, b)$$
$$\textsf{g}: g(a, c)$$

As before, *sel* distributes to get

$$sel(P, f(A, B), g(A', C)) \equiv FG(sel(P, \textsf{f}, \textsf{g}),$$
$$sel(P, A, A'),$$
$$sel(P, B, \texttt{\#}),$$
$$sel(P, \texttt{\#}, C))$$

This is one way in which don't-care values (#s) are safely introduced to system descriptions. Depending on P the c input to FG does not matter, so long as it is a γ. Another way of introducing #s comes from replicating selections, according to rewriting rules like

$$sel(P, S, T) \quad \equiv \quad sel(P, sel(P, S, \#), T)$$

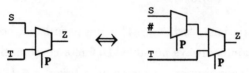

So long as it is assured that # really means "don't care," and not "don't know," selections simplify according to

$$sel(P, S, \#) \quad \rightarrow \quad S$$
$$sel(P, \#, T) \quad \rightarrow \quad T$$

On the other hand, there are many occasions when it is preferable to instantiate #s as suggested by

This kind of transformation is the subject of the final law for rewriting system descriptions.

COLLATION. *If signal expressions S and T are of the same type, then X and Y can be combined*

$$\begin{array}{c} \vdots \\ X = sel(P, S, \#) \\ Y = sel(P, \#, T) \\ \vdots \end{array} \quad \xRightarrow{S, T;\tau} \quad \begin{array}{c} \vdots \\ X = sel(P, S, T) \\ Y = X \\ \vdots \end{array}$$

In the next section, collating is done by introducing a distinct new identifier, $XY = sel(P, S, T)$ and using it in place of X and Y throughout the system.

4. System Factorizations – Four Examples

In essence, the result of a factorization is simply the introduction of a combination. The transformation problem is to isolate the expression(s) to be combined. Four examples illustrate the tactical issues. The first three deal with purely combinational terms; the last encapsulates a sequential combination. Figures 1 and 2 show schematics for the the source and target descriptions in each of the four examples.

Derivation of hardware centers on the dependent tasks of control synthesis, refinement of architecture, and structuring for physical realization. System factorization addresses the second of these, but must interact with the others. Often, it is not possible to obtain a desired architecture without refinement to control; sometimes, the intended physical organization, the 'target technology', influences the conceptual hierarchy of modules. The examples are intended to give a sense of this interplay.

4.1. Example One

The names of the base operations do not matter but are chosen to be evocative. Assume a single type int, with operations $add: (\text{int}, \text{int}) \rightarrow \text{int}$ and $dn, up: \text{int} \rightarrow \text{int}$, and consider the system description fragment

$$\vdots$$

$$\begin{aligned} U &= sel(P, add(A, dn(B)), up(C)) \\ X &= sel(P, dn(D), add(E, F)) \end{aligned} \tag{1.0}$$

$$\vdots$$

The first derivation goal is to combine all applications of add. This is specified by a set of patterns in which caligraphic variables a matched with subexpressions. The instances of these abstractions are called the *subject terms* of the factorization. In this case, the specification set is $\{add(\mathcal{U}, \mathcal{V})\}$ and the subject terms are $add(E, F)$ and $add(A, \mathcal{V})$, where $\mathcal{V} = dn(B)$. First, subject terms are isolated from the surrounding equations. After replicating selection in signals U and X, the isolated terms are identified as signals V and Y.

$$\begin{aligned} U &= sel(P, V, up(C)) \\ W &= sel(P, dn(B), \#) \\ X &= sel(P, dn(D), Y) \\ V &= sel(P, add(A, W), \#) \\ Y &= sel(P, \#, add(E, F)) \end{aligned} \tag{1.2}$$

It is important to keep the surrounding selections, as in V and Y above. These two signals are now collated into a single signal, VY.

$$U = sel(P, VY, up(C))$$
$$W = sel(P, dn(B), \#)$$
$$X = sel(P, dn(D), VY) \tag{1.3}$$
$$VY = sel(P, add(A, W), add(E, F))$$

Using distribution the defining expression for VY is reduced to obtain a single add component.

$$U = sel(P, VY, up(C))$$
$$W = sel(P, dn(B), \#) \tag{1.4}$$
$$X = sel(P, dn(D), VY) \tag{2.0}$$
$$VY = add(sel(P, A, E), sel(P, W, F))$$

The schematic for (1.4) in Figure 1 simplifies W to $dn(B)$. However, W is left as above for the next example.

As this example illustrates, the factorization process has three phases. Subject terms are isolated and, if necessary, identified. Then, the subject terms are collated into a reduced collection of signals. Finally, tests are distributed to arguments. Example Two shows one way that things can go wrong.

4.2. Example Two

System (1.4) is used as a starting point for this example. Since selection tests, P, never change, it makes things a bit clearer to use an abbreviation. Henceforth, the term $sel(P, S, T)$ is written instead as $sel_P(S, T)$ Let us now attempt to factor applications of dn and up from system (2.0). The subject terms are instances of the pattern set $\{dn(\mathcal{X}), up(\mathcal{X})\}$. As before, they are isolated as signals Z and T:

$$U = sel_P(VY, T)$$
$$X = sel_P(Z, VY)$$

$$W = sel_P(dn(B), \#)$$
$$Z = sel_P(dn(D), \#) \tag{2.1}$$
$$T = sel_P(\#, up(C))$$

$$VY = add(sel_P(A, E), sel_P(W, F))$$

The intended factorization fails because it is impossible to collate the signals W, Z, and T. There is a clash of $dn(B)$ and $dn(D)$. However, these signals can be partitioned into groups that can be collated. With the partition $\{W, T\}$ and $\{Z\}$ we get

$$
\begin{aligned}
U &= sel_P(VY, WT) \\
X &= sel_P(Z, VY) \\
Z &= sel_P(dn(D), \#) \\
WT &= sel_P(dn(B), up(C)) \\
VY &= add(sel_P(A, E), sel_P(WT, F))
\end{aligned}
\tag{2.2}
$$

After introducing instruction tokens $\{dn, up\}$, selection distributes over the combination of dn and up. Define

$$
UPDN(i, v) \stackrel{\text{def}}{=} \begin{array}{l} case\ i\ of\ \textsf{dn}\colon\ dn(v) \\ \qquad\qquad\quad\ \textsf{up}\colon\ up(v) \end{array}
$$

Replace the defining equation for WT by an instance of $UPDN$. In (2.3), signal Z is also simplified.

$$
\begin{aligned}
U &= sel_P(VY, WT) \\
X &= sel_P(Z, VY) \\
Z &= dn(D) \\
I &= sel_P(\textsf{dn}, \textsf{up}) \\
WT &= UPDN(I, sel_P(B, C)) \\
VY &= add(sel_P(A, E), sel_P(WT, F))
\end{aligned}
\tag{2.3}
$$

In the $UPDN$ combination, the decisions of the surrounding system are encoded by the instruction signal I. This is the practical essence of a factorization—to introduce components that are independent of the decision making apparatus of a specific design.

Clashes are almost always avoidable by using more specific pattern sets. For example, the set $\{dn(B), up(\mathcal{X})\}$ determines the factorization in (2.3). This technique is used in the remaining examples.

4.3. Example Three

Let us follow an alternative derivation from original system in Example One:

$$
\begin{aligned}
U &= sel_P(add(A, dn(B)), up(C)) \\
X &= sel_P(dn(D), add(E, F))
\end{aligned}
$$

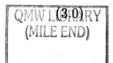

The first subgoal is to factor $\{up(C), add(A,\mathcal{U})\}$. Isolating the instances and identifying subterms yields

$$W = sel_P(dn(B), \#)$$
$$X = sel_P(dn(D), add(E, F)) \tag{3.1}$$
$$U = sel_P(add(A, W), up(C))$$

In order to distribute selection in U, we must first decide how to superimpose the arguments (A, W) and (C). A, C, and W are all ints, so there are many possibilities. Suppose that the following combination is given:

$$XALU(i, a, b) \stackrel{\text{def}}{=} case \ i \ of \ \text{add:} \ add(a, b)$$
$$\text{dn:} \ dn(a)$$
$$\text{up:} \ up(b)$$

With this component as a target, selection distributes in signal U as:

$$U = XALU(U_I, U_A, U_B)$$
$$U_I = sel_P(\text{add}, \text{up})$$
$$U_A = sel_P(A, \#)$$
$$U_B = sel_P(W, C) \tag{3.2}$$
$$W = sel_P(dn(B), \#)$$
$$X = sel_P(dn(D), add(E, F))$$

Similarly, the set $\{dn(B), add(E, F)\}$ factors as signal Z in system (3.3):

$$U = XALU(U_I, U_A, U_B)$$
$$U_I = sel_P(\text{add}, \text{up})$$
$$U_A = sel_P(A, \#)$$
$$U_B = sel_P(Z, C)$$
$$X = sel_P(dn(D), Z) \tag{3.3}$$
$$Z = XALU(Z_I, Z_A, Z_B)$$
$$Z_I = sel_P(\text{dn}, \text{add})$$
$$Z_A = sel_P(\#, E)$$
$$Z_B = sel_P(B, F)$$

Signals U_A and Z_A are reduced to A and E in Figure 1. As a general stratagem, it is better to defer this kind of simplification. Wolf has suggested leaving this kind of optimization entirely to automatic logic synthesizers [23], and our experience bears this out.

4.4. Example Four

This example encapsulates a sequential components. Again the vocabulary is suggestive but arbitrary. Assume three types, mem, addr, and data; with operations $rd: (\text{mem}, \text{addr}) \to \text{data}$ and $wt: (\text{mem}, \text{addr}, \text{data}) \to \text{mem}$; and consider the system

$$\vdots$$
$$
\begin{aligned}
M &= m^0 \ ! \ sel_P(M, wt(M, X, Y), M) \\
N &= sel_P(rd(M, U), V, W)
\end{aligned}
\tag{4.0}
$$
$$\vdots$$

The form $sel_P(\star, \star, \star)$ stands for a three-way selection combination. Since the goal is to hide the abstract signal $M: \text{mem}$ from the surrounding system, this kind of transformation has been called an 'abstract component' factorization in [12, 10], and later a 'signal factorization' in [13]. The pattern set is $\{M, rd(M, \mathcal{U}), wt(M, \mathcal{U}, \mathcal{V})\}$. With knowledge of how arguments to rd and wt should be superimposed, the subject terms in (4.0) are isolated as follows:

$$
\begin{aligned}
M &= m^0 \ ! \ sel_P(M, wt(M, M_A, M_D), M) \\
M_R &= sel_P(rd(M, M_A), \#, \#) \\
M_A &= sel_P(U, X, \#) \\
M_D &= sel_P(\#, X, \#) \\
N &= sel_P(M_R, V, W)
\end{aligned}
\tag{4.1}
$$

With instruction tokens $i \in \{\text{id}, \text{rd}, \text{wt}\}$ a *MEMORY* combination is formed, with definition

$$
MEMORY(m, I, A, D) \stackrel{\text{def}}{=} R
$$
$$
\begin{aligned}
&where \\
(R, M) = \quad &(\#, m^0) \ ! \ case \ i \ of \ \text{id} : (\#, M) \\
&\qquad\qquad\qquad\quad \text{rd} : (rd(M, A), M) \\
&\qquad\qquad\qquad\quad \text{wt} : (\#, wt(M, A, D))
\end{aligned}
$$

Using *MEMORY*, system description (4.1) becomes

$$
\begin{aligned}
M &= MEMORY(m^0, M_I, M_A, M_D) \\
M_I &= sel_P(\text{rd}, \text{wt}, \text{id}) \\
M_A &= sel_P(U, X, \#) \\
M_D &= sel_P(\#, X, \#) \\
N &= sel_P(M, V, W)
\end{aligned}
\tag{4.2}
$$

According to the specification for *MEMORY*, it would be all right in a tightly coupled implementation to use a conventional read/write memory for M, but the id instruction token must be eliminated. One approach is to rewrite the signals M_R in system (4.1) to

$$M_R = sel_P(rd(M, M_A), \texttt{\#}, rd(M, M_A))$$

It follows that only two instructions are needed. Alternatively, one might deduce from the *MEMORY* definition that id can represented by rd in representation. In either case, the derivation that encapsulates M must reflect the implementation intent.

In this example, a sequential combination is encapsulated with the effect of factoring off some of the original description's state. The tactics happen to be specialized for a known component. Supposing that the purpose of the factorization was simply to suppress the type mem, how should we regard *MEMORY* combination? One way of looking at it is to consider *MEMORY* to be an assertion about correct external behavior. If (4.2) is to behave correctly, a *MEMORY* *device* must respond to instructions rd and wt as specified by *MEMORY*. From this point of view, factorization has generated a verification condition from a higher level of description.

5. Conclusions

A semiautomated transformation system has been implemented to explore digital design derivation. Designs are constructed from a restricted class of functional control specifications. Factorizations are applied to the resulting system descriptions in order to develop a logical organization. Then, binary representations are incorporated for symbolic entities, and the description is restructured for logic synthesis. A number of moderate designs have been derived, including several versions of a garbage collector, a prototype computer system based on an SECD processor, and several conventional processor designs. Designs have been realized in MSI and VLSI using programmable target technologies. The examples in Section 4 are distilled from the design of a garbage collector [13]. In that derivation, a series of eight factorizations was needed to develop a logical orgainization. This is typical of designs we have done. Selection combinations, which model controllers, typically have between 30 and 100 alternatives.

A derivation is entered as a sequence of transformation commands, which is applied to the initial design description. The designer looks at intermediate descriptions in order to evaluate the derivation. If things are not going as planned, the derivation script is modified. The factorizations implemented by the transformation system are substantially the same as the examples illustrate, although the treatment in this article is somewhat more general. The factorization algorithm takes a specification of subject terms, isolates them, and then attempts to form a combination. Intervention is required for clashes. The superimposition of arguments is done according to a simple convention—adequate for lower levels of description, A more general approach to this step is under study.

The experimentation establishes that logical organization—modularity—can be developed later in the design process. Factorizations are used to isolate subsystems for compilation to hardware; they sustain correct connectivity as designs are edited for physical realization. In practice, two kinds of problems require intervention. The most common are clashes in collation. Methods for resolving clashes range from trial and error to induced transformations on the control specification. [14, 2]. This interaction is analogous to that of device allocation and operator scheduling in high level synthesis. A more serious kind of problem results from 'information hiding' factorizations of the kind illustrated in Example Four. When the intent is to encapsulate an abstract data type, inference is sometimes needed to determine the subject terms. An example of this problem is discussed in [13].

As a formal method, derivation can be likened to direct proof. Its fundamental laws correspond to the inference mechanisms of a theorem proving system. It is the task of the designer to engineer an 'equational' proof that the implementation has the behavior of its specification. Factorizations correspond to lemmas, which guide the actual proof process, but are reducible to more basic reasoning. As suggested in Section 4.3, factorizations may also be a means of integrating design synthesis and formal verification. A factored combination encapsulates "the rest of the system" stating how the implementation's environment must behave to use the implementation correctly. This appears to be a way to segregate formal reasoning tasks from the mundane processes of a design synthesis. This prospective relationship motivates our study of the underlying algebra.

Acknowledgments

I thank Garaint Jones, Mary Sheeran, and Warren Hunt for their observations and corrections at the work shop. Bhaskar Bose and David Boyer contributed in several ways to the this research and this article, but I claim any errors as my own. I am grateful to the National Science Foundation for funding this research.

References

[1] RAYMOND BOUTE, "Systems Semantics: Principles, Applications, and Implementations," *ACM Transactions on Programming Languages and Systems* **10**(1):188–155 (1988).

[2] C. DAVID BOYER AND STEVEN D. JOHNSON, "A Derived Garbage Collector," in J. Darringer and F. Ramming (eds.) *Computer Hardware Description Languages and their Applications* (Proceedings of the Ninth IFIP WG 10.2 Symposium, CHDL-89), Elsevier, Amsterdam, in preparation.

[3] PAOLO CAMUARATI AND PAOLO PRINETTO, "Formal Verification of Hardware Correctness: Introduction and Survey of Current Research," *Computer* **21**(7):8–19 (1988).

[4] A.L. DAVIS, "What Do Computer Architects Design Anyway?" (Preliminary papers of the 1988 Banff Hardware Verification Workshop).

[5] DANIEL D. GAJSKI, *Silicon Compilation*, Addison-Wesley, Reading, 1987.

[6] GANESH C. GOPALAKRISHNAN, RICHARD M. FUJIMOTO, AND KEVIN SMITH, "Specification Driven Design of Custom Architectures in HOP, (Preliminary papers of the 1988 Banff Hardware Verification Workshop).

[7] J.A. GOGUEN, J.W. THATCHER, AND E.G. WAGNER, "An Initial Algebra Approach to the Specification, Correctness, and Implementation of Abstract Data Types," in R. Yeh (ed.) *Current Trends in Programming Methodology* Vol. IV, Prentice Hall, 1978, 80–145.

[8] H.A. HARMAN AND J.V. TUCKER, "Clocks Retimings, and the Formal Specification of a UART," in G. J. Milne (ed.), *The Fusion of Hardware Design and Verification*, North-Holland, Amsterdam, 1988, 375–396 (Proceedings of the IFIP WG 10.2 Working Conference, Glasgow, 1988).

[9] FREDRICK J. HILL AND GERALD R. PETERSON, *Introduction to Switching Theory and Logical Design*, (3rd ed.) John Wiley and Sons, New York, 1981.

[10] STEVEN D. JOHNSON, "Applicative Programming and Digital Design", *Eleventh Annual ACM Symposium on Principles of Programming Languages* (1984) 218–227.

[11] STEVEN D. JOHNSON, "Digital Design in a Functional Calculus," in: G.J. Milne and P.A. Subrahmanyam (eds.), *Formal Aspects of VLSI Design*, Elsevier Science Publishers B. V. (North-Holland), Amsterdam, 1986 (Proceedings of the 1985 Workshop on VLSI, Edinburgh).

[12] STEVEN D. JOHNSON, *Synthesis of Digital Designs from Recursion Equations*, The MIT Press, Cambridge, 1984.

[13] STEVEN D. JOHNSON, BHASKAR BOSE, AND C. DAVID BOYER, "A Tactical Framework for Digital Design," in *VLSI Specification, Verification and Synthesis,* (eds.) Graham Birtwistle and P.A. Subramanyam, Kluwer Academic Publishers, 1987, 349–384 (proceedings of the 1987 Calgary Hardware Verification Workshop).

[14] STEVEN D. JOHNSON, BHASKAR BOSE AND ROBERT W. WEHRMEISTER, "On the Interplay of Hardware Synthesis and Hardware Verification: Experiments with the FM8501 Microprocessor Description," submitted.

[15] JACQUES LOECKX AND KURT SIEBER, *The Foundations of Program Verification,* John Wiley and Sons, Chichester, 1984.

[16] GEORGE J. MILNE, "CIRCAL and the Representation of Communication, Concurrency, and Time," *ACM Transactions on Programming Languages and Systems* **7**:270–298 (1985).

[18] MARY SHEERAN, "Retiming and Slowdown in Ruby," in G. J. Milne (ed.), *The Fusion of Hardware Design and Verification,* North-Holland, Amsterdam, 1988, 289–308 (Proceedings of the IFIP WG 10.2 Working Conference, Glasgow, 1988).

[19] MARY SHEERAN, *μFP, and Algebraic for VLSI Design,* D. Phil. Thesis, Programming Research Group Monograph PRG–39, Oxford University, 1983.

[20] P.A. SUBRAHMANYAM, "Contextual Constraints, Temporal Abstraction and Observational Equivalence in VLSI Design," in G. J. Milne (ed.), *The Fusion of Hardware Design and Verification,* North-Holland, Amsterdam, 1988, 159–R184 (Proceedings of the IFIP WG 10.2 Working Conference, Glasgow, 1988).

[21] FRANKLIN P. PROSSER AND DAVID E. WINKEL, *The Art of Digital Design* (2nd ed.) Prentice-Hall, Englewood Cliffs, 1987.

[22] GLYNN WINSKEL, "A Compositional Model of MOS Circuits," in *VLSI Specification, Verification and Synthesis,* (eds.) Graham Birtwistle and P.A. Subramanyam, Kluwer Academic Publishers, 1987, 323–347 (proceedings of the 1987 Calgary Hardware Verification Workshop).

[23] WAYNE WOLF, personal communication.

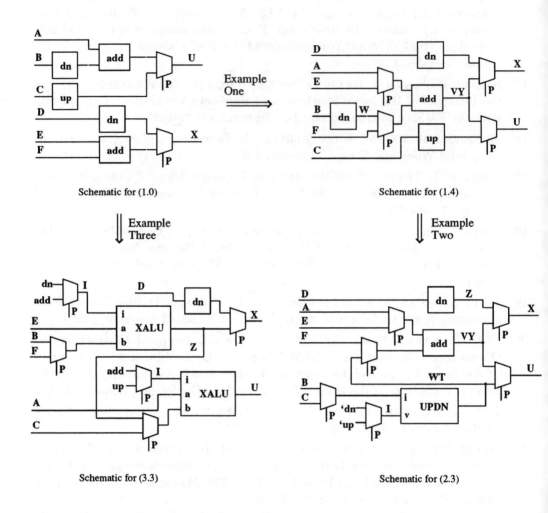

Figure 1   Schematics from Examples One, Two and Three

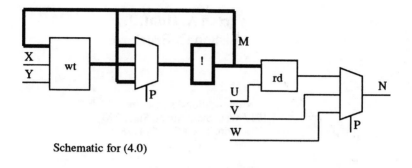

Schematic for (4.0)

Example
Four

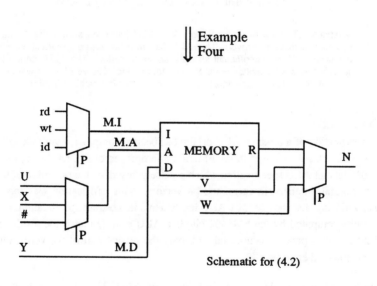

Schematic for (4.2)

Figure 2   Schematics from Examples Four

The Verification of a Bit-slice ALU

Warren A. Hunt, Jr.
Bishop C. Brock

Computational Logic, Inc.
1717 West Sixth Street, Suite 290
Austin, Texas 78703-4776
U.S.A.

Telephone: +1 512 322 9951
E-mail: Hunt@CLI.COM, Brock@CLI.COM

Abstract. The verification of a bit-slice ALU has been accomplished using a mechanical theorem prover. This ALU has an n-bit design specification, which has been verified to implement its top-level specification. The ALU and top-level specifications were written in the Boyer-Moore logic. The verification was carried out with the aid of Boyer-Moore theorem prover in a hierarchical fashion.

1. Introduction

The verification of a bit-slice ALU design has been accomplished with the aid of a mechanical theorem prover. This ALU, used in the FM8502 microprocessor [5], has been proved to implement the FM8501 abstract ALU specification which precisely describes the operation of the FM8501 ALU in terms of natural numbers, integers, and bit vectors. This verification was accomplished in two steps: one, verifying that the FM8501 ALU implements its abstract specification, and two, verifying that the results computed by the FM8502 bit-slice ALU exactly match the results computed by the FM8501 ALU. This paper is concerned with only the second part of the verification; the first part has been documented elsewhere [3].

Here we consider the abstract specification of the FM8502 ALU (henceforth referred to as the bit-slice ALU) to be the FM8501 ALU specification itself. The FM8501 ALU specification describes an n-bit ALU; that is, the specification of the FM8501 ALU describes how to construct an ALU of any size. The bit-slice ALU is also specified as an n-bit ALU, but requires far fewer gates.

The verification of the bit-slice ALU with respect to the FM8501 ALU represents an exhaustive Boolean comparison of the behavior of the two ALUs; i.e., the gate graphs specified by each ALU compute exactly the same results. The verification of Boolean functions with respect to other Boolean functions has recently received much attention. Randal Bryant [2] has described a fast mechanism to compare Boolean circuits. This type of approach works well for many Boolean circuits, but is known to take exponentially increasing time with larger and larger multiplier circuits. Although Bryant's method is very fast, it does not allow specifications to be anything but Boolean functions.

Our approach involves using a general-purpose logic to represent our specifications. This allows the comparison of our Boolean circuits to abstract specifications containing, for example, integers, as well as comparing Boolean circuits to other Boolean circuits. Both ALU specifications are described as functions in the Boyer-Moore logic [1]. The proof time to verify the equivalence of the two *n*-bit Boolean ALU specifications takes constant time. When a particular sized ALU is desired, then the ALU specifications functions are expanded (in linear time) into graphs of gates suitable for implementation.

The remainder of this paper begins with a summary of what we have proved, along with a quick introduction to our methodology. We then proceed in a bottom-up manner until we are able to present the specification of the two ALUs. The verification of the bit-slice ALU with respect to the FM8501 ALU is presented by describing how we organized our proof. This is followed by a comparison of the gate graphs generated from our two specifications.

2. Our Approach

The final theorem we prove is an equality correspondence theorem between the FM8501 and bit-slice ALUs. These two ALUs provide exactly the same functionality; our proof demonstrates their equality. In this section we sketch the ALU (equality) correspondence theorem before introducing our methodology. The proof methodology employed in establishing the ALU correspondence theorem is demonstrated by proving the correctness of two selector implementations.

2.1. A Look at the Final Theorem

The ALU correspondence theorem is presented below, written in the Lisp-style syntax of the Boyer-Moore logic. The FM8501 ALU is named **BV-ALU-CV** and the bit-slice ALU is named **NEW-ALU**. The correspondence theorem simply states that **BV-ALU-CV** and **NEW-ALU** are identical functions when **C** is a Boolean, **A** and **B** are bit vectors of the same length, and **OP-CODE** is a bit vector.[1]

```
(IMPLIES (AND (BOOLP C)
              (BV2P A B)
              (BITVP OP-CODE))

         (EQUAL (NEW-ALU C A B OP-CODE)
                (BV-ALU-CV A B C OP-CODE)))
```

This proof is one of Boolean equivalence; that is, the inputs are constrained to be Boolean or vectors of Booleans and the outputs are Booleans and a vector of Booleans.

An interesting facet of the ALU definitions is that they both describe *n*-bit ALUs. Our proof of their correspondence demonstrates the correctness of the **NEW-ALU** with respect to **BV-ALU-CV** for all word sizes. This type of verification requires induction, which is not found in Boolean decision procedures. To demonstrate our approach we present the verification of two selector implementations by induction.

---

[1]Later we present definitions for **BOOLP**, **BV2P**, **BITVP**, **NEW-ALU**, and **BV-ALU-CV**.

2.2. The Boyer-Moore Logic and Theorem Prover

The Boyer-Moore logic [1] is a quantifier-free, first-order predicate calculus with equality. Logic formulas are written in a prefix-style, Lisp-like notation. Included with the logic are several built-in data types: Booleans, natural numbers, lists, literal atoms, and integers.

The Boyer-Moore logic is unusual in that the logic may be extended by the application of any of the following axiomatic acts: defining conservative functions, adding recursively constructed data types, and adding arbitrary axioms. Adding an arbitrary formula as an axiom does not guarantee the soundness of the logic; we do not use this feature.

The Boyer-Moore theorem prover is a Common Lisp [7] program which provides a user with various commands to extend the logic and to prove theorems. The theorem prover is interactive and users enter commands through the top-level Common Lisp interpreter. The theorem prover manages a database of axioms, definitions, and proved theorems, thus allowing a user to concentrate on the less mundane aspects of proof development. The theorem prover contains decision procedures for tautology checking and linear arithmetic, a simplifier, and a rewriter. It is possible to add decision procedures to the theorem prover after proving their correctness.

We use the Boyer-Moore theorem prover as a proof checker. The theorem prover is led to difficult theorems by giving it a graduated sequence of more and more difficult lemmas until a final result can be obtained.

2.3. Bit Vectors

Bit vectors are axiomatized by adding a new Boyer-Moore data type. Bit vectors are defined recursively, and each bit vector constructor function takes a bit and a bit vector as arguments. We employ the Boyer-Moore Shell Principle to formally define the bit vector data type.

Shell Definition.
Add the shell **BITV** of two arguments, with
base function **BTM**;
recognizer function **BITVP**;
accessor functions **BIT** and **VEC**;
type restrictions **(ONE-OF FALSEP TRUEP)** and **(ONE-OF BITVP)**; and
default functions **FALSE** and **BTM**.

Some of the axioms introduced as a result of this data type definition are below.

```
(NOT (EQUAL (BITV X Y) (BTM)))

(IMPLIES (AND (BITVP X)
              (NOT (EQUAL X (BTM))))
         (EQUAL (BITV (BIT X) (VEC X)) X))

(IMPLIES (OR (FALSEP X) (TRUEP X))
         (EQUAL (BIT (BITV X Y)) X))

(IMPLIES (BITVP Y)
         (EQUAL (VEC (BITV X Y)) Y))
```

We define our bit vectors to have a "little-endian" format; thus the number 6 can be represented by (BITV F (BITV T (BITV T (BTM)))). We define the function **NAT-TO-BV** to convert a natural number **N** into a bit vector of **SIZE** bits.

```
(NAT-TO-BV N SIZE)
=
(IF (ZEROP SIZE)
    (BTM)
    (BITV (NOT (ZEROP (REMAINDER N 2)))
          (NAT-TO-BV (QUOTIENT N 2) (SUB1 SIZE)))))
```

We define several functions which are useful when working with bit vectors. The function **BTMP**, defined below, formalizes our notion of an empty bit vector. If **X** is recognized as a bit vector, then **X** is empty if **X** = (BTM); otherwise, **X** is considered empty.

```
(BTMP X) = (IF (BITVP X)
               (EQUAL X (BTM))
               T))

(SIZE X) = (IF (BTMP X)
               0
               (ADD1 (SIZE (VEC X)))))
```

SIZE computes the size of a bit vector as follows: an empty bit vector has size 0; otherwise, the bit vector has a size one greater than the size of the **VEC** of the bit vector. **SIZE** is a recursive function; we will see many functions which recur on the structure of a bit vector.

Bit vectors are appended with the function **V-APPEND**, which operates in a manner analogous to a list append function. The function **BITN** selects a particular bit from bit vector **X** given an index **N**. **TRUNC** truncates (or extends with **F**'s) bit vector **A** to a size **N**.

```
(V-APPEND X Y) = (IF (BTMP X)
                     Y
                     (BITV (BIT X)
                           (V-APPEND (VEC X) Y)))

(BITN X N) = (IF (ZEROP N)
                 F
                 (IF (EQUAL N 1)
                     (BIT X)
                     (BITN (VEC X) (SUB1 N))))

(TRUNC A N) = (IF (ZEROP N)
                  (BTM)
                  (BITV (BIT A)
                        (TRUNC (VEC A) (SUB1 N))))
```

The function **BOOLP** is defined to recognize Boolean valued objects. We have defined the predicate **BV2P** which recognizes two bit vectors of identical size. This predicate is often used in the hypothesis of theorems which state properties about functions which operate upon two bit vectors simultaneously.

```
(BOOLP X) = (OR (FALSEP X) (TRUEP X)))

(BV2P X Y) = (AND (BITVP X)
                  (BITVP Y)
                  (EQUAL (SIZE X) (SIZE Y))))
```

2.4. Hardware Primitives

We use functions to formalize our notion of combinational logic. We do not formalize registers or memory devices here, as our two ALUs are purely combinational.

```
(B-BUF  X)            =    (IF X T F)
(B-NOT  X)            =    (NOT X)

(B-NAND  A B)         =    (NOT (AND A B))
(B-NAND3 A B C)       =    (NOT (AND A B C))
(B-NAND4 A B C D)     =    (NOT (AND A B C D))

(B-OR   A B)          =    (OR A B)
(B-OR3  A B C)        =    (OR A B C)
(B-OR4  A B C D)      =    (OR A B C D)

(B-EQUV X Y)          =    (IF X (IF Y T F) (IF Y F T))
(B-XOR  X Y)          =    (IF X (IF Y F T) (IF Y T F))

(B-AND  A B)          =    (AND A B)
(B-AND3 A B C)        =    (AND A B C)
(B-AND4 A B C D)      =    (AND A B C D)

(B-NOR  A B)          =    (NOT (OR A B))
(B-NOR3 A B C)        =    (NOT (OR A B C))
(B-NOR4 A B C D)      =    (NOT (OR A B C D))
```

We think of the functions above as representing primitive gates, e.g., gate array macro cells. When we expand circuit implementation specifications, we do not expand the definitions of the above functions.

For convenience we have defined several other gate functions; these functions are not primitives but are defined in terms of gate primitives. These functions are listed below.

```
(B-XOR3 A B C)        =    (B-XOR (B-XOR A B) C)
(B-XOR4 A B C D)      =    (B-XOR (B-XOR A B) (B-XOR C D))

(B-AND5 A B C D E)    =    (B-AND (B-AND3 A B C) (B-AND D E))
(B-AND6 A B C D E G)  =    (B-AND (B-AND3 A B C) (B-AND3 D E G))
```

2.5. A Hardware Verification Methodology

The hardware verification methodology we employ involves using the Boyer-Moore logic to record abstract specifications and design specifications. Abstract specifications represent what we think of as "obviously" correct specifications. Design specifications describe implementations in terms of graphs of gates. Often we use recursive functions to describe *n*-bit implementations. We first present our methodology in general; we later narrow our focus to the comparison of Boolean functions.

To demonstrate our methodology, we consider the specification and verification of a selector. Our hardware selector selects one of two inputs for output. The value of the output is controlled by a third input. Abstractly, we specify a selector with inputs **A** and **B** and control input **C** by the following expression.

```
(IF C A B)
```

This specification is more abstract than combinational hardware implementations permit; for instance, **A** could be **7**.

Before giving the definition of our bit-vector selector, we investigate the Boolean selector defined below.

```
(B-IF C A B)
=
(B-NAND (B-NAND C A)
        (B-NAND (B-NOT C) B))
```

This formal design specification can also be represented schematically as shown in Figure 2-1. The

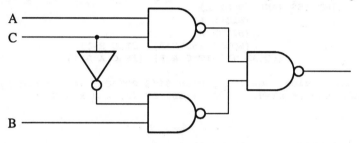

Figure 2-1: One-bit Selector Circuit

proof of correctness of the one-bit selector we state as follows.

```
(IMPLIES (AND (BOOLP A)
              (BOOLP B)
              (BOOLP C))
         (EQUAL (B-IF C A B)
                (IF C A B)))
```

This theorem says the one-bit selector **B-IF** implements our abstract specification when **A**, **B**, and **C** are Boolean.

Our bit-vector selector implementation assumes that **A** and **B** are bit vectors of the same size, and that **C** is a Boolean input. Our bit vector selector is composed of some number of bit selectors. Using a recursive function we specify an *n*-bit selector named **BV-IF**.

```
(BV-IF C A B) = (IF (BTMP A)
                    (BTM)
                    (BITV (B-IF C (BIT A) (BIT B))
                          (BV-IF C (VEC A) (VEC B))))
```

The function **BV-IF** recurs when **A** is not empty. The proof that **BV-IF** implements our abstract specification is stated below.

```
(IMPLIES (AND (BOOLP C)
              (BV2P A B))
         (EQUAL (BV-IF C A B)
                (IF C A B)))
```

This theorem is proved by induction. The proof of this theorem can be carried out by the theorem prover automatically. We present the theorem prover input and its output for this proof. The theorem prover command for a proof attempt is **PROVE-LEMMA**, the name of this event is **BV-IF-WORKS**, and the lemma type is **REWRITE**. We have also given two heuristic hints (**INDUCT** and DISABLE) which are technically unnecessary but make the output more compact.

```
(PROVE-LEMMA BV-IF-WORKS (REWRITE)
   (IMPLIES (BV2P A B)
            (EQUAL (BV-IF C A B)
                   (IF C A B)))
  ((INDUCT (BV-IF C A B))
   (DISABLE SIZE)))
```

This formula can be simplified, using the abbreviations BTMP,
BV2P, IMPLIES, NOT, OR, and AND, to the following two new
formulas:

Case 2. (IMPLIES (AND (BTMP A)
                      (BITVP A)
                      (BITVP B)
                      (EQUAL (SIZE A) (SIZE B)))
                 (EQUAL (BV-IF C A B) (IF C A B))).

This simplifies, rewriting with SIZE-BOTTOM, and unfolding the
definitions of BTMP, BITVP, SIZE, BV-IF, and EQUAL, to:

> T.

Case 1. (IMPLIES (AND (BITVP A)
                      (NOT (EQUAL A (BTM)))
                      (IMPLIES (BV2P (VEC A) (VEC B))
                               (EQUAL (BV-IF C (VEC A) (VEC B))
                                      (IF C (VEC A) (VEC B))))
                      (BITVP B)
                      (EQUAL (SIZE A) (SIZE B)))
                 (EQUAL (BV-IF C A B) (IF C A B))),

which simplifies, appealing to the lemmas BV2P-VEC,
BITV-BIT-VEC, and B-IF-WORKS, and expanding the definitions
of BV2P, IMPLIES, TRUEP, BOOLP, BTMP, and BV-IF, to the goal:

```
(IMPLIES (AND (BITVP A)
              (NOT (EQUAL A (BTM)))
              (NOT C)
              (EQUAL (BV-IF C (VEC A) (VEC B))
                     (VEC B))
              (BITVP B)
              (EQUAL (SIZE A) (SIZE B)))
         (EQUAL (BV-IF F A B) B)).
```

However, this again simplifies, applying the lemmas BITV-BIT-VEC
and B-IF-WORKS, and expanding the definitions of TRUEP, BOOLP,
BTMP, and BV-IF, to:

```
(IMPLIES (AND (BITVP A)
              (NOT (EQUAL A (BTM)))
              (EQUAL (BV-IF F (VEC A) (VEC B))
                     (VEC B))
              (BITVP B)
              (EQUAL (SIZE A) (SIZE B))
              (EQUAL B (BTM)))
         (EQUAL (BITV F (BTM)) B)).
```

This again simplifies, rewriting with the lemma SIZE-BOTTOM, and opening up the functions VEC, BITVP, SIZE, and BTMP, to:

T.

Q.E.D.

[0.1 1.1 0.4]
BV-IF-WORKS

To produce a gate graph from a recursive circuit specification, for instance **BV-IF**, we symbolically expand the circuit specification on symbolic inputs. Before expanding a function we identify any common subexpressions present; each common expression is expanded only once and its output is fanned out.

The function **BV-IF** contains only one common subexpression in its body, namely **C**. We can observe that the input **C** will be fanned out to every call of **B-IF**, because **C** is recursively passed on without being buffered. Let us proceed through the expansion of **BV-IF** into a two-bit selector. Our expansion process assumes that all free variables are constrained to be Boolean; we make this explicit later.

To begin our symbolic expansion of **BV-IF** we instantiate the formal arguments of a call to **BV-IF** with a control input and two, two-bit bit vectors. By replacing the call of **BV-IF** with its definition we obtain the second expression below. The third expression below is a simplification of the second after observing that **(BTMP (BITV A0 (BITV A1 (BTM))))** is false and using facts about **BIT**, **VEC**, and **BITV**.

```
(BV-IF C (BITV A0 (BITV A1 (BTM))) (BITV B1 (BITV B1 (BTM))))
=
(IF (BTMP (BITV A0 (BITV A1 (BTM))))
    (BTM)
    (BITV (B-IF C (BIT (BITV A0 (BITV A1 (BTM))))
                  (BIT (BITV B1 (BITV B1 (BTM)))))
          (BV-IF C (VEC (BITV A0 (BITV A1 (BTM))))
                   (VEC (BITV B1 (BITV B1 (BTM)))))))
=
(BITV (B-IF C A0 B0)
      (BV-IF C (BITV A1 (BTM)) (BITV B1 (BTM))))
```

We now expand **BV-IF** again, simplify, and get the next expression. The remaining call of **BV-IF** is simplified to just **BTM**.

```
(BITV (B-IF C A0 B0)
      (BITV (B-IF C A1 B1)
            (BV-IF C (BTM) (BTM))))
=
(BITV (B-IF C A0 B0)
      (BITV (B-IF C A1 B1)
            (BTM)))
```

We now expand the definition of **B-IF** to obtain the following expression.

```
(BITV (B-NAND (B-NAND C A0)
              (B-NAND (B-NOT C) B0))
      (BITV (B-NAND (B-NAND C A1)
                    (B-NAND (B-NOT C) B1))
            (BTM)))
```

The expansion process presented above is somewhat simplified. We did not need to explicitly identify any common subexpression other than C, thus we did not need to share any active circuitry (gates). Our mechanical expansion process actually produces a theorem where the input variables (C, A0, A1, B0, B1) are constrained to be Boolean. For example, the theorem produced for the two-bit selector is given below.

```
(IMPLIES (AND (AND (OR (FALSEP C)   (TRUEP C))
                   (OR (FALSEP A0)  (TRUEP A0))
                   (OR (FALSEP A1)  (TRUEP A1))
                   (OR (FALSEP B0)  (TRUEP B0))
                   (OR (FALSEP B1)  (TRUEP B1)))
              (AND (EQUAL X-1 (B-NAND C A0))
                   (EQUAL X-2 (B-NOT C))
                   (EQUAL X-3 (B-NAND X-2 B0))
                   (EQUAL X-4 (B-NAND X-1 X-3))
                   (EQUAL X-5 (B-NAND C A1))
                   (EQUAL X-6 (B-NOT C))
                   (EQUAL X-7 (B-NAND X-6 B1))
                   (EQUAL X-8 (B-NAND X-5 X-7))))
         (EQUAL (BV-IF C
                       (BITV A0 (BITV A1 (BTM)))
                       (BITV B0 (BITV B1 (BTM))))
                (BITV X-4 (BITV X-8 (BTM)))))
```

Common subexpressions are named and placed in the hypothesis of the theorem. Note, however, that the term (B-NOT C) occurs twice. The expander only collects the common subexpressions which appear in the body of a function definition and not those which manifest themselves during the expansion process. It is possible to submit this theorem back to theorem prover and have it prove it.

2.6. A Narrow View of Circuit Verification

The abstract specification for our bit-slice ALU is the FM8501 ALU. As mentioned previously, more abstract specifications for the ALUs can be found elsewhere [3, 4]. Here we are interested in demonstrating the precise correspondence of two Boolean functions without concerning ourselves with their more general properties. Both ALU functions produce a Boolean carry output, a Boolean overflow output, and an n-bit bit vector result, and we want to prove the exact correspondence of these two design specifications. Part of the verification is similar to other methods of Boolean function verification; however, proving the correctness of n-bit circuit specifications requires the use of induction.

To demonstrate our ALU verification approach, we define a new selector implementation and verify it with respect to BV-IF. As an aside, once we have verified that our new selector specification is identical to BV-IF, then we know this new selector satisfies our original abstract selector specification.

We begin by presenting the definition of our new selector function **BV4-IF**. This function is more complicated than **BV-IF** for several reasons: the circuit fan-out is limited, it recurs four bits at a time, and it contains a larger case structure. The helper function **B-IF-BAR** is used in **BV4-IF**.

```
(B-IF-BAR C C-BAR A B)
 =
(B-NAND (B-NAND C A)
        (B-NAND C-BAR B))


(BV4-IF C A B)
 =
(LET ((A0 (BIT A))
      (A1 (BIT (VEC A)))
      (A2 (BIT (VEC (VEC A))))
      (A3 (BIT (VEC (VEC (VEC A)))))
      (B0 (BIT B))
      (B1 (BIT (VEC B)))
      (B2 (BIT (VEC (VEC B))))
      (B3 (BIT (VEC (VEC (VEC B)))))
      (C     (B-BUF C))
      (C-BAR (B-NOT C)))

  (COND
   ((BTMP A) (BTM))

   ((BTMP (VEC A))
    (BITV (B-IF-BAR C C-BAR A0 B0) (BTM)))

   ((BTMP (VEC (VEC A)))
    (BITV (B-IF-BAR C C-BAR A0 B0)
          (BITV (B-IF-BAR C C-BAR A1 B1)
                (BTM))))

   ((BTMP (VEC (VEC (VEC A))))
    (BITV (B-IF-BAR C C-BAR A0 B0)
          (BITV (B-IF-BAR C C-BAR A1 B1)
                (BITV (B-IF-BAR C C-BAR A2 B2)
                      (BTM)))))
   (T (BITV
       (B-IF-BAR C C-BAR A0 B0)
       (BITV
        (B-IF-BAR C C-BAR A1 B1)
        (BITV
         (B-IF-BAR C C-BAR A2 B2)
         (BITV
          (B-IF-BAR C C-BAR A3 B3)
          (BV4-IF C
                  (VEC (VEC (VEC (VEC A))))
                  (VEC (VEC (VEC (VEC B)))))))))))))
```

The first part of the **BV4-IF** definition contains abbreviations for the first four bits of the two input vectors and buffered control inputs; these abbreviations are used in the main body of the definition. This definition considers five cases depending on the size of **A**. For the cases where the size of **A** is three bits or less, this definition describes fixed-sized gate graphs. When the size of **A** is greater than four, this function recurs.

To prove the equivalence of these two functions, we prove the following lemma.

```
(IMPLIES (BV2P A B)
         (EQUAL (BV4-IF C A B)
                (BV-IF C A B)))
```

We prove this lemma by first proving the following two lemmas with induction. The first lemma says, if bit vector **A** has size **N**, then **(TRUNC A N)** is just **A**. The second lemma describes the operation of **BV4-IF** on any two bit vectors.

```
(IMPLIES (AND (EQUAL (SIZE A) N)
              (BITVP A))
         (EQUAL (TRUNC A N) A))

(IMPLIES (AND (BITVP A)
              (BITVP B))
         (EQUAL (BV4-IF C A B)
                (IF C A (TRUNC B (SIZE A)))))
```

By chaining these two lemmas together along with our lemma above describing the operation of **BV-IF**, we can prove that the two selectors work identically.

It is interesting to compare the implementations specified by the two different selector functions. The items we compare are gate count, fanout, and delay: gate count is the number of primitive gates required for the circuit; fanout is specified as the maximum number of gate inputs driven by any gate primitive or any input; and delay is the maximum number of gate delays encountered by all input signals where each gate primitive has unit delay. Below is a table comparing three differently sized expansions of our two selectors.

Selector Gate Graph Comparison						
Selector Size in Bits	BV-IF Gate Count	BV-IF Fan-out	BV-IF Delay	BV4-IF Gate Count	BV4-IF Fan-out	BV4-IF Delay
8-bits	32	16	3	28	6	4
16-bits	64	32	3	56	6	6
32-bits	128	64	3	112	6	10

We see **BV-IF** has a delay of three, but has a very large fanout. **BV4-IF** fanout is limited to six, but the delay is longer because of the buffering of the control line.

This concludes the introduction to our method. The remainder of this paper is a presentation of the FM8501 and bit-slice ALUs, the verification of the bit-slice ALU with respect to the FM8501 ALU, and a comparison of the two implementations.

3. The FM8501 ALU Specification

The FM8501 ALU is composed of a number of functional units connected by a large selector. The FM8501 ALU is a 16-function ALU with logical, shift, addition, and subtraction operations which are summarized in Table 3-1. We first present the various functional units and then the ALU definition itself.

Several of the ALU operations are simple logical operations. For each of these logical

OP-CODE	Result	Description
0000	a	Move
0001	$a+1$	Increment
0010	$b+a+c$	Add with carry
0011	$b+a$	Add
0100	$0-a$	Negation
0101	$a-1$	Decrement
0110	$b-a-c$	Subtract with borrow
0111	$b-a$	Subtract
1000	$a>>1$	Rotate right, shifted through carry
1001	$a>>1$	Arithmetic shift right, top bit duplicated
1010	$a>>1$	Logical shift right, top bit zero
1011	$b \veebar a$	Exclusive or
1100	$b \vee a$	Or
1101	$b \wedge a$	And
1110	$\neg a$	Not
1111	a	Move

Table 3-1: FM8501 ALU Operation Summary

operations we have defined a hardware implementation specification. Each of these specifications operate on n-bit inputs. **BV-NOT** provides logical negation. **BV-AND**, **BV-OR**, and **BV-XOR** are the logical and, logical or, and exclusive or functions, respectively.[2]

```
(BV-NOT X) = (IF (BTMP X)
                 (BTM)
                 (BITV (B-NOT (BIT X))
                       (BV-NOT (VEC X))))

(BV-AND X Y) = (IF (BTMP X)
                   (BTM)
                   (BITV (B-AND (BIT X) (BIT Y))
                         (BV-AND (VEC X) (VEC Y))))

(BV-OR X Y) = (IF (BTMP X)
                  (BTM)
                  (BITV (B-OR (BIT X) (BIT Y))
                        (BV-OR (VEC X) (VEC Y))))

(BV-XOR X Y) = (IF (BTMP X)
                   (BTM)
                   (BITV (B-XOR (BIT X) (BIT Y))
                         (BV-XOR (VEC X) (VEC Y))))
```

There are three right shift operations: logical shift right, **BV-LSR**; arithmetic shift right, **BV-ASR**; and rotate right with carry, **BV-ROR**. Left shift operations can be provided by the adder.

---

[2]Note: The definitions presented below for the FM8501 ALU specification are syntactically slightly different than previously presented [3]; however, they are semantically the same.

```
(BV-LSR A) = (IF (BTMP A)
                 (BTM)
                 (V-APPEND (VEC A)
                           (BITV F (BTM))))

(BV-ASR A) = (IF (BTMP A)
                 (BTM)
                 (V-APPEND (VEC A)
                           (BITV (BITN A (SIZE A)) (BTM))))

(BV-ROR A C) = (IF (BTMP A)
                   (BTM)
                   (V-APPEND (VEC A)
                             (BITV C (BTM))))
```

The addition and subtraction functions are all composed from the function **BV-ADDER**. Typically, hardware adders return a bit vector of the same size as their inputs; however, **BV-ADDER** is a specification of a ripple-carry adder which returns a bit vector whose size is one bit longer than its **A** formal parameter. We define three functions for addition and subtraction which, given two n-bit inputs and a carry input, provide an n-bit output, a Boolean overflow output, and a Boolean carry-out output. **BV-ADDER-OUTPUT** truncates the output of **BV-ADDER** to the size of the **A** bit vector. **BV-ADDER-CARRY-OUT** returns the carry-out by selecting the most significant bit of **BV-ADDER**. **BV-ADDER-OVERFLOWP** computes a Boolean result which is true when integer addition does not provide the correct answer.

```
(BV-ADDER C A B)
 =
(IF (BTMP A)
    (BITV C (BTM))
    (BITV (B-XOR C (B-XOR (BIT A) (BIT B)))
          (BV-ADDER (B-OR (B-AND (BIT A) (BIT B))
                          (B-OR (B-AND (BIT A) C)
                                (B-AND (BIT B) C)))
                    (VEC A)
                    (VEC B))))


(BV-ADDER-OUTPUT C A B) = (TRUNC (BV-ADDER C A B) (SIZE A))

(BV-ADDER-CARRY-OUT C A B) = (BITN (BV-ADDER C A B)
                                   (ADD1 (SIZE A)))

(BV-ADDER-OVERFLOWP C A B)
 =
(B-AND (B-EQUV (BITN A (SIZE A)) (BITN B (SIZE B)))
       (B-XOR (BITN A (SIZE A))
              (BITN (BV-ADDER-OUTPUT C A B)
                    (SIZE A))))
```

```
(BV-SUBTRACTER-OUTPUT C A B)
=
(BV-ADDER-OUTPUT (B-NOT C) (BV-NOT A) B)

(BV-SUBTRACTER-CARRY-OUT C A B)
=
(B-NOT (BV-ADDER-CARRY-OUT (B-NOT C) (BV-NOT A) B))

(BV-SUBTRACTER-OVERFLOWP C A B)
=
(BV-ADDER-OVERFLOWP (B-NOT C) (BV-NOT A) B)
```

Similarly, **BV-SUBTRACTER-OUTPUT** defines a subtracter function with an n-bit output given an n-bit input. **BV-SUBTRACTER-CARRY-OUT** outputs **T** when a borrow is required, else **F**. **BV-SUBTRACTER-OVERFLOWP** computes whether an integer subtraction overflowed.

The FM8501 ALU returns three results: a bit vector result, a carry-out, and an overflow. We define a new data type, with constructor **BV-CV**, which simply packages a bit vector and two Booleans into one object. Below is a hardware selector function for objects of this new data type. The **BV-CV-IF** function selects between two **BV-CV** objects, **A** and **B**, by accessing their components, with accessors **BV**, **C**, and **V**; using **B-IF** and **BV-IF**; and recombining the selector results with **BV-CV**.

```
(BV-CV-IF C A B)
=
(BV-CV (BV-IF C (BV A) (BV B))
       (B-IF  C (C  A) (C  B))
       (B-IF  C (V  A) (V  B)))

(IMPLIES
 (BV2P AV BV)
 (EQUAL (BV-CV-IF C (BV-CV AV AC AO) (BV-CV BV BC BO))
        (IF        C (BV-CV AV AC AO) (BV-CV BV BC BO))))
```

The lemma just above gives an abstract view of the **BV-CV-IF** selector function.

With the definitions above, it is now possible to define the FM8501 ALU. It takes a carry input, **C**, two bit vector inputs, **A** and **B**, and a 4-bit operation code, **OP-CODE**. This ALU computes all three outputs, bit vector, carry, and overflow, for every operation code.

```
(BV-ALU-CV A B C OP-CODE)
=
(LET ((BV-ZERO (NAT-TO-BV 0 (SIZE A))))
  (BV-CV-IF (BITN OP-CODE 4)
    (BV-CV-IF (BITN OP-CODE 3)
      (BV-CV-IF (BITN OP-CODE 2)
        (BV-CV-IF (BITN OP-CODE 1)
          (BV-CV A F F)                 ; op-code 15 - move
          (BV-CV (BV-NOT A) F F))       ; op-code 14 - not
        (BV-CV-IF (BITN OP-CODE 1)
          (BV-CV (BV-AND A B) F F)      ; op-code 13 - and
          (BV-CV (BV-OR A B) F F)))     ; op-code 12 - or
```

```
    (BV-CV-IF (BITN OP-CODE 2)
      (BV-CV-IF (BITN OP-CODE 1)
        (BV-CV (BV-XOR A B) F F)                    ; op-code 11 - xor
        (BV-CV (BV-LSR A) (BITN A 1) F))            ; op-code 10 - lsr
      (BV-CV-IF (BITN OP-CODE 1)
        (BV-CV (BV-ASR A) (BITN A 1) F)             ; op-code 9 - asr
        (BV-CV (BV-ROR A C)                         ; op-code 8 - ror
               (IF (ZEROP (SIZE A))
                   C
                   (BITN A 1))
               F))))
    (BV-CV-IF (BITN OP-CODE 3)
      (BV-CV-IF (BITN OP-CODE 2)
        (BV-CV-IF (BITN OP-CODE 1)
          (BV-CV (BV-SUBTRACTER-OUTPUT F A B)    ; op-code 7 - sub
                 (BV-SUBTRACTER-CARRY-OUT F A B)
                 (BV-SUBTRACTER-OVERFLOWP F A B))
          (BV-CV (BV-SUBTRACTER-OUTPUT C A B)    ; op-code 6 - subb
                 (BV-SUBTRACTER-CARRY-OUT C A B)
                 (BV-SUBTRACTER-OVERFLOWP C A B)))
        (BV-CV-IF (BITN OP-CODE 1)               ; op-code 5 - dec
          (BV-CV (BV-SUBTRACTER-OUTPUT T BV-ZERO A)
                 (BV-SUBTRACTER-CARRY-OUT T BV-ZERO A)
                 (BV-SUBTRACTER-OVERFLOWP T BV-ZERO A))
                                                 ; op-code 4 - neg
          (BV-CV (BV-SUBTRACTER-OUTPUT F A BV-ZERO)
                 (BV-SUBTRACTER-CARRY-OUT F A BV-ZERO)
                 (BV-SUBTRACTER-OVERFLOWP F A BV-ZERO))))
      (BV-CV-IF (BITN OP-CODE 2)
        (BV-CV-IF (BITN OP-CODE 1)
          (BV-CV (BV-ADDER-OUTPUT F A B)             ; op-code 3 - add
                 (BV-ADDER-CARRY-OUT F A B)
                 (BV-ADDER-OVERFLOWP F A B))
          (BV-CV (BV-ADDER-OUTPUT C A B)             ; op-code 2 - addc
                 (BV-ADDER-CARRY-OUT C A B)
                 (BV-ADDER-OVERFLOWP C A B)))
        (BV-CV-IF (BITN OP-CODE 1)                   ; op-code 1 - inc
          (BV-CV (BV-ADDER-OUTPUT T A BV-ZERO)
                 (BV-ADDER-CARRY-OUT T A BV-ZERO)
                 (BV-ADDER-OVERFLOWP T A BV-ZERO))
          (BV-CV A F F))))))
```

It is this definition of the FM8501 ALU that we prove equivalent to the bit-slice ALU.

4. The Bit-slice ALU Specification

The bit-slice ALU definition is similar in structure to a conventionally designed ALU. This ALU has a bit-slice implementation and uses a propagate and generate structure for computing carries in each slice. Carry propagation between each 3-bit slice is serial.

Schematically, our new ALU is constructed as shown in Figure 4-1. The **Shift or Buffer** module either buffers the input or performs one of three right shifts, as prescribed by **Decode shift**. The **3-Bit-by-3-bit recursive ALU** is the bit slice ALU which provides the functions besides right shifts. **Carry Help** and **Overflow Help** adjust the output of the ALU to conform with the FM8501 ALU.

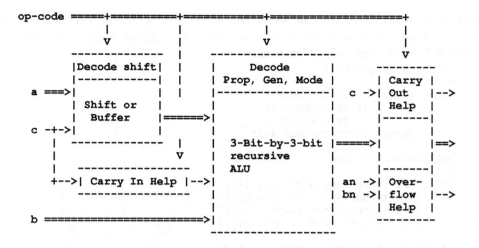

Figure 4-1: Bit-slice ALU Structure

We define the bit-slice ALU in pieces, starting with the shift unit. This shift unit provides three kinds of right shifts or buffers its input. We define **BV-SHIFT-RIGHT** to right shift **A** one bit, with the most significant bit now being **SI**.

```
(BV-SHIFT-RIGHT A SI) = (IF (BTMP A)
                            (BTM)
                            (BV-APP (VEC A)
                                    (BITV SI (BTM)))))
```

```
(BV-SHIFT-OR-BUF C A OP-CODE)
=
(LET ((OP1 (B-BUF (BITN OP-CODE 1)))
      (OP2 (B-BUF (BITN OP-CODE 2)))
      (OP3 (B-BUF (BITN OP-CODE 3)))
      (OP4 (B-BUF (BITN OP-CODE 4))))

  (LET ((DECODE-BUF (B-OR (B-AND OP1 OP2)
                          (B-NAND (B-NOT OP3) OP4)))
        (DECODE-ASR (B-AND4 OP1 (B-NOT OP2) (B-NOT OP3) OP4))
        (DECODE-ROR (B-AND4 (B-NOT OP1) (B-NOT OP2)
                            (B-NOT OP3) OP4)))

    (BV4-IF DECODE-BUF A
            (BV-SHIFT-RIGHT A (B-OR (B-AND DECODE-ASR
                                           (BITN A (SIZE A)))
                                    (B-AND DECODE-ROR C)))))))
```

The function **BV-SHIFT-OR-BUF** provides buffering for the input operation code and decodes when this function should buffer, arithmetic shift right, or rotate right. The decoding logic controls the functions **BV4-IF** and **BV-SHIFT-RIGHT** to provide the desired functionality.

The main part of the bit-slice ALU is a three-bit wide bit-slice which provides most of the ALU functionality. Before defining this bit-slice function, we define three decoding functions, generate, propagate, and mode, which control the bit-slice function. Each of the decoding functions takes only the operation code as an argument; they are all composed of random logic. These next five definitions should be skipped upon a first reading.

```
(DECODE-MODE OP-CODE)
=
(B-AND (B-OR3 (BITN OP-CODE 1)
              (BITN OP-CODE 2)
              (BITN OP-CODE 3))
       (B-NOT (BITN OP-CODE 4)))

(DECODE-PROP OP-CODE)
=
(LET ((OP1 (B-BUF (BITN OP-CODE 1)))
      (OP2 (B-BUF (BITN OP-CODE 2)))
      (OP3 (B-BUF (BITN OP-CODE 3)))
      (OP4 (B-BUF (BITN OP-CODE 4))))

  (BITV (B-OR (B-AND (B-NOT OP4) OP2)
              (B-AND3 (B-NOT OP2) OP3 OP4))
        (BITV (B-NAND3 OP1 (B-NOT OP2) OP3)
              (BITV (B-OR (B-AND3 OP2 (B-NOT OP3) (B-NOT OP4))
                          (B-AND3 OP4 (B-EQUV OP1 OP2)
                                  (B-XOR OP2 OP3)))
                    (BITV (B-AND OP3
                                 (B-OR (B-NOT OP4)
                                       (B-AND (B-NOT OP1) OP2)))
                          (BTM))))))

(DECODE-GEN OP-CODE)
=
(LET ((OP1 (BITN OP-CODE 1))
      (OP2 (B-BUF (BITN OP-CODE 2)))
      (OP3 (B-BUF (BITN OP-CODE 3)))
      (OP4 (BITN OP-CODE 4)))

  (BITV (B-AND OP2 (B-NOT OP4))
        (BITV (B-AND4 OP1 (B-NOT OP2) OP3 (B-NOT OP4))
              (BITV (B-AND3 OP2 OP3 (B-NOT OP4))
                    (BTM)))))

(ALL-8 A B OP-CODE)
=
(B-XOR3 (B-AND3 A B (BITN OP-CODE 1))
        (B-AND A (BITN OP-CODE 2))
        (B-AND B (BITN OP-CODE 3)))

(ALL-16 A B OP-CODE)
=
(B-XOR4 (B-AND3 A B (BITN OP-CODE 1))
        (B-AND A (BITN OP-CODE 2))
        (B-AND B (BITN OP-CODE 3))
        (BITN OP-CODE 4))
```

DECODE-MODE produces a Boolean which is true for additions and subtractions, else false. DECODE-PROP and DECODE-GEN compute bit vectors which control the propagate and generate logic in the ALU. **ALL-8** and **ALL-16** define two combinational logic functions which compute one (either eight or sixteen logical functions.

Function **BV3-ALU-HELP** is the heart of the bit-slice ALU. This function recurs three bits at time providing carry look-ahead over three bits.[3] If three bits do not remain in the input argumen then the result is computed with a size appropriate to the input.

```
(BV3-ALU-HELP C A B MODE OP-PROP OP-GEN)
=
(LET ((A0 (BIT A))
      (B0 (BIT B))
      (A1 (BIT (VEC A)))
      (B1 (BIT (VEC B)))
      (A2 (BIT (VEC (VEC A))))
      (B2 (BIT (VEC (VEC B))))))

  (LET ((PROP0 (ALL-16 A0 B0 OP-PROP))
        (GEN0   (ALL-8  A0 B0 OP-GEN))
        (PROP1 (ALL-16 A1 B1 OP-PROP))
        (GEN1   (ALL-8  A1 B1 OP-GEN))
        (PROP2 (ALL-16 A2 B2 OP-PROP))
        (GEN2   (ALL-8  A2 B2 OP-GEN)))

    (LET ((C0 (B-AND MODE C))
          (C1 (B-AND MODE (B-OR GEN0 (B-AND C PROP0))))
          (C2 (B-AND MODE (B-OR3 GEN1
                                  (B-AND PROP1 GEN0)
                                  (B-AND3 PROP0 PROP1 C))))
          (C-OUT (B-OR4 GEN2
                         (B-AND PROP2 GEN1)
                         (B-AND3 PROP1 PROP2 GEN0)
                         (B-AND4 PROP0 PROP1 PROP2 C))))

      (LET ((F0 (B-XOR C0 (B-XOR PROP0 GEN0)))
            (F1 (B-XOR C1 (B-XOR PROP1 GEN1)))
            (F2 (B-XOR C2 (B-XOR PROP2 GEN2)))))
```

---

[3]Why three bits? To dispell the notion that ALUs must be constructed in 2^N sized slices.

```
(COND
 ((BTMP A) (BITV C0 (BTM)))

 ((BTMP (VEC A))
  (BITV F0 (BITV C1 (BTM))))

 ((BTMP (VEC (VEC A)))
  (BITV F0 (BITV F1 (BITV C2 (BTM)))))

 (T (BITV F0
     (BITV F1
      (BITV F2
       (BV3-ALU-HELP C-OUT
                     (VEC (VEC (VEC A)))
                     (VEC (VEC (VEC B)))
                     (B-BUF MODE)
                     (BV-BUF OP-PROP)
                     (BV-BUF OP-GEN))))))))))))
```

The above definition should be studied in sections. The first LET expression defines a set of names for the first three bits in each bit vector whether these bits exist or not. These bits are only referred to if it makes sense to do so. The second LET defines the propagate and generate components for each of the three bits in a slice. The third LET constructs the carry outs for each bit of the slice. These carry outs provide carry look-ahead for each slice. The fourth LET specifies the three output bits for one slice of the ALU. The body of this function then selects one of four results depending on the size of the input vector. For instance, if (BTMP A), then just the carry-out is produced, and so on. It can be seen by inspection that BV3-ALU-HELP produces a bit vector result which has a size one greater than its A argument. This last bit is the carry out when BV3-ALU-HELP is performing addition and subtraction.

We now define the remaining three helper functions we require to build the bit-slice ALU. They assist in producing the ALU carry-out and overflow outputs and one provides help in providing the correct carry-in to the ALU. These functions were all composed by hand and are constructed from random logic. These next three definitions should be skipped upon a first reading.

```
(CARRY-IN-HELP C OP-CODE)
 =
(LET ((OP1 (B-BUF (BITN OP-CODE 1)))
      (OP2 (B-BUF (BITN OP-CODE 2)))
      (OP3 (B-BUF (BITN OP-CODE 3))))

  (B-OR (B-OR3 (B-AND (B-NOT OP2) (B-NOT OP3))
               (B-AND3 (B-NOT OP1) (B-NOT OP2) OP3)
               (B-AND3 OP1 OP2 OP3))
        (B-OR (B-AND (B-AND (B-NOT OP1) OP2)
                     (B-AND (B-NOT OP3) C))
              (B-AND (B-AND (B-NOT OP1) OP2)
                     (B-AND OP3 (B-NOT C))))))
```

```
(CARRY-OUT-HELP CIN A RESULT OP-CODE)
=
(LET ((OP1 (B-BUF (BITN OP-CODE 1)))
      (OP2 (B-BUF (BITN OP-CODE 2)))
      (OP3 (B-BUF (BITN OP-CODE 3)))
      (OP4 (B-BUF (BITN OP-CODE 4))))

  (B-OR4 (B-AND4 (B-NOT OP4) (B-OR OP1 OP2) (B-NOT OP3) RESULT)
         (B-AND3 (B-NOT OP4) OP3 (B-NOT RESULT))
         (B-AND4 OP4 (B-NOT OP3) (B-XOR OP1 OP2) (BITN A 1))
         (B-AND5 (B-NOT OP1) (B-NOT OP2) (B-NOT OP3) OP4
                 (IF (BTMP A) CIN (BITN A 1))))))

(OVERFLOW-HELP TOP-BIT-RESULT TOP-A TOP-B OP-CODE)
=
(LET ((OP1 (B-BUF (BITN OP-CODE 1)))
      (OP2 (B-BUF (BITN OP-CODE 2)))
      (OP3 (B-BUF (BITN OP-CODE 3)))
      (OP4 (B-BUF (BITN OP-CODE 4)))
      (AN  (B-BUF TOP-A))
      (BN  (B-BUF TOP-B))
      (TOP (B-BUF TOP-BIT-RESULT)))

  (B-OR4 (B-AND5 (B-NOT OP4) OP3 OP2
                 (B-XOR AN BN)
                 (B-XOR BN TOP))
         (B-AND4 (B-NOT OP4) OP3 (B-NOT OP2)
                 (B-OR (B-AND3 OP1 AN (B-NOT TOP))
                       (B-AND3 (B-NOT OP1) AN TOP)))
         (B-AND5 (B-NOT OP4) (B-NOT OP3) OP2
                 (B-EQUV AN BN)
                 (B-XOR BN TOP))
         (B-AND6 (B-NOT OP4) (B-NOT OP3) (B-NOT OP2)
                 OP1 (B-NOT AN) TOP)))
```

The bit-slice ALU is defined by the function **NEW-ALU**. This function just connects together the various functions defined above in a fashion suggested by Figure 4-1.

```
(NEW-ALU C A B OP-CODE)
=
(LET ((OP (BV-BUF OP-CODE))
      (ASIZE (SIZE A)))

  (LET ((MODE (DECODE-MODE OP))
        (PROP (DECODE-PROP OP))
        (GEN  (DECODE-GEN  OP))
        (AX   (BV-SHIFT-OR-BUF C A OP))
        (CX   (CARRY-IN-HELP C OP)))

    (LET ((BV3-ALU (BV3-ALU-HELP CX AX B MODE PROP GEN)))

      (BV-CV (TRUNC BV3-ALU ASIZE)
             (CARRY-OUT-HELP C A (BITN BV3-ALU (ADD1 ASIZE)) OP)
             (OVERFLOW-HELP (BITN BV3-ALU ASIZE)
                            (BITN A ASIZE)
                            (BITN B ASIZE)
                            OP)))))
```

This completes the definition of the bit-slice ALU.

5. The ALU Correspondence Proof

The proof of correspondence of the bit-slice and FM8502 ALUs is by no means straightforward. We construct a graduated sequence of lemmas which leads the theorem prover to the proof. There were several major steps in this development which we outline here.

The Boyer-Moore theorem prover is used by entering definitions and proof requests. Definitions, if accepted, are stored in its internal database and are used during proofs as needed. Proof requests cause the theorem prover to attempt to establish the validity of a conjecture. Proved conjectures, which we call lemmas, are also stored in the theorem prover database. Previously defined functions and proved lemmas may be used in a current theorem prover request.

Definitions and lemmas for the correspondence proof are entered into the Boyer-Moore theorem prover with a script containing all the necessary commands. The ordering of the commands is important, e.g., a definition cannot be used before it is defined.

The first part of the correspondence proof script is concerned with defining Booleans and bit vectors. We then define several functions which manipulate bit vectors (e.g., **TRUNC**, **BITN**, **SIZE**, etc.) and prove often needed properties of these definitions. We next define our primitive hardware functions (e.g., **B-NOT**, **B-AND**, etc.) and their vector versions. The sizes of these vector hardware functions are noted with a lemma.

We proceed by defining the adder and subtractor functions; these were taken from the original FM8501 proof script. We define the previously described selectors: **BV-IF** and **BV4-IF**. We then define the **BV-CV-IF** selector. These definitions are all proved to implement selectors. The FM8501 ALU is defined next.

The bit-slice ALU definition proceeds in exactly the same fashion as described in the last section, except we prove some lemmas about **BV-SHIFT-OR-BUF** just after its definition.

We are now ready to begin the correspondence proof. This proceeds in two basic steps: the inductive proofs that the bit-slice ALU help function **BV-ALU-HELP** can provide the required logical and arithmetic operations, and the gluing together of these inductive proofs to complete the proof. Let us examine one of the inductive proof statements; below we state that **BV-ALU-HELP**, under certain conditions, operates just like the vector-and function **BV-AND**.

```
(IMPLIES
  (AND (BITVP A)
       (BITVP B)
       (EQUAL MODE F)
       (EQUAL OP-PROP (BITV T (BITV F (BITV F (BITV F (BTM))))))
       (EQUAL OP-GEN  (BITV F (BITV F (BITV F (BTM))))))
  (EQUAL (BV3-ALU-HELP C A B MODE OP-PROP OP-GEN)
         (V-APPEND (BV-AND A B) (BITV F (BTM)))))
```

Notice we append a false Boolean value onto the result of the **BV-AND** function because **BV3-ALU-HELP** produced a vector one bit longer than its input.

After proving lemmas describing the operation of **BV3-ALU-HELP** for the various functions our bit-slice ALU provides, we prove the final theorem below. This final theorem is obtained by examining the cases of the operation code and using the lemmas described just above.

```
(IMPLIES (AND (BOOLP C)
              (BV2P A B)
              (BITVP OP-CODE))

         (EQUAL (NEW-ALU C A B OP-CODE)
                (BV-ALU-CV A B C OP-CODE)))
```

The Boyer-Moore theorem prover requires 15 minutes to process the ALU correspondence proof script on a Sun 3/280. This time includes defining Booleans and bit vectors, processing the ALU definitions, and proving their correspondence. We then may use these definitions in other proofs. In fact, the FM8501 ALU has been verified to have abstract properties with respect to Boolean bit vectors, natural numbers, and integers. In turn, these abstract properties are used in the verification of the Piton assembler [6] for the FM8502.

6. ALU Expansions

The FM8501 and bit-slice ALUs specify very different implementations. The FM8501 ALU design is overly simple for actual hardware use. The bit-slice ALU design specifies an implementation which is comparable in gate count to actual working implementations. In this section we present comparisons of gate counts, fanouts, and delays for each ALU.

Our ALU implementation specifications are blueprints for ALUs of any size. We compare our ALUs by expanding our specifications into a number of fixed-sized ALUs. Gates are required even when the bit-vector portion of the result of the ALUs is empty; these gates compute the carry out and overflow results. The zero-bit, bit-slice ALU requires more gates than the zero-bit, FM8501 ALU because of the greater amount of decoding logic used in the bit-slice ALU.

ALU Gate Graph Comparison						
ALU Size in Bits	FM8501 Gate Count	FM8501 Fanout	FM8501 Delay	Bit-slice Gate Count	Bit-slice Fanout	Bit-slice Delay
0-bits	37	5	10	64	4	11
1-bit	205	39	13	137	7	19
2-bits	345	48	16	157	7	21
4-bits	665	80	22	205	7	21
8-bits	1305	144	34	295	7	25
16-bits	2585	272	58	483	7	29
32-bits	5145	528	106	851	7	41
64-bits	10265	1040	202	1595	7	61
128-bits	20505	2064	394	3075	7	105

We can see how much better the bit-slice ALU is than the FM8501 ALU. The fanouts in the

FM8501 ALU are unrealistic and the delay is too long. The bit-slice ALU benefits from using three and four input gate primitives, whereas the FM8501 ALU only uses two input gate primitives. This does not affect the gate count that much, for instance, the 32-bit version of the bit-slice ALU has 1020 two-input primitive gates instead of the 851 reported in the table above. However, restricting the implementation to one and two input gate primitives affects the delay more dramatically by increasing it from 41 to 64.

The widest primitive gates we used have four inputs. The three-bit wide ALU slice takes best advantage of these primitives as can be observed in the computation of the carry outs in the function BV3-ALU-HELP. With wider primitives it is possible to make faster and faster ALUs by wider slices.

The expansion process just unfolds of definitions, notes common subexpressions, and applys applicable rewrite rules. The 128-bit, bit-slice ALU gate graph takes 100 seconds to generate.

7. Conclusions

The verification of the bit-slice ALU with respect to the FM8501 ALU has been accomplished by using a general-purpose mechanical theorem prover. These ALU specifications demonstrate the use of a functional language as a combinational logic design language. The verification of these ALU specifications represents an exhaustive comparison of Boolean functions without using exhaustive techniques.

The FM8501 ALU specification is too inefficient to be useful as a specification for real hardware; however, it is a useful intermediate specification step on the way to verifying arithmetic properties of the bit-slice ALU. The FM8501 ALU is composed of simple internal functions connected together with selectors. This arrangement provided a straightforward path to verify the arithmetic properties of the FM8501 ALU. Each internal function is studied independently, and its properties identified and verified. Using these properties and our knowledge about selectors, we are able to compose an ALU with known mathematical properties. We still know of no other ALU whose operations are completely verified with respect to Peano and integer arithmetic.

The bit-slice ALU specification has a gate structure comparable in gate count and gate delay to a serially interconnected set of 74181s composed with a right-shift unit. The bit-slice ALU does not have the simple structure of the FM8501 ALU, and thus verifying the arithmetic properties of the FM8502 ALU directly is more difficult than verifying the FM8501 ALU arithmetic properties. The purpose of verifying the bit-slice ALU with respect to the FM8501 ALU is to ensure that the bit-slice ALU has the arithmetic properties we desire.

The bit-slice specification was developed and verified in a hierarchical fashion. The ALU is composed of several modules as pictured in Figure 4-1. Some of these modules are composed of sub-modules. For instance, the Shift or Buffer module is composed of several sub-modules: a selector, a shifter, and some decoding logic. We performed the verification hierarchically also. In the case of the Shift or Buffer module we verified a selector lemma and then used this lemma in the verification of the module. Later, the Shift or Buffer module lemmas were used in the verification of the entire ALU.

We were able to design and verify the bit-slice ALU in several weeks time. Small changes (of which we made many) often only changed a part of the proof, and when we made errors (not quite so many) we found our problems quickly. In fact, the Boyer-Moore theorem prover output was instrumental in the location of errors, in that it often became "stuck" right at the error in question.

The use of a general-purpose logic allows more abstract circuit specifications than Boolean decision procedures allow. For instance, when specifying addition we refer to numbers; these simply do not exist in Boolean decision procedures. Here we did not make use of this generality, but instead demonstrated the Boolean equivalence of two large functions.

We believe recursion is an underutilized method for dealing with large circuits. Hardware by its very nature is quite repetitive, and recursion captures this regularity. Recursively defined hardware can be verified with induction; this ability is lacking from Boolean decision procedures. We expect our recursive techniques to extend directly to multipliers and other more complicated circuits.

8. Acknowledgments

This work was sponsored in part at Computational Logic, Inc., by the Defense Advanced Research Projects Agency, ARPA Orders 6082 and 9151. The views and conclusions contained in this document are those of the authors and should not be interpreted as representing the official policies, either expressed or implied, of Computational Logic, Inc., the Defense Advanced Research Projects Agency or the U.S. Government.

References

[1]   R. S. Boyer and J S. Moore.
        A Computational Logic Handbook.
        Academic Press, Boston, 1988.

[2]   Randal E. Bryant.
        Graph-Based Algorithms for Boolean Function Manipulation.
        IEEE Transactions on Computers C-35(8):677--691, August, 1986.

[3]   Warren A. Hunt, Jr.
        FM8501: A Verified Microprocessor.
        Technical Report ICSCA-CMP-47, University of Texas at Austin, 1985.

[4]   Warren A. Hunt, Jr.
        The Mechanical Verification of a Microprocessor Design.
        In D. Borrione (editor), *From HDL Descriptions to Guaranteed Correct Circuit Designs*,
              pages 89-132. North Holland, 1987.

[5]   Warren A. Hunt, Jr.
        Microprocessor Design Verification.
        Journal of Automated Reasoning (to appear), 1989.

[6]   J S. Moore.
        Piton: A Verified Assembly Level Language.
        Technical Report 22, Computational Logic, Inc., 1717 West Sixth Street, Suite 290 Austin,
              TX 78703, 1988.

[7]   Guy L. Steele Jr.
        Common LISP: The Language.
        Digital Press, 1984.

Verification of a Pipelined Microprocessor Using Clio *

Mark Bickford
Mandayam Srivas
Odyssey Research Associates, Inc.,
301A Harris B. Dates Drive
Ithaca, NY 14850.

Abstract

Clio is a system for verifying properties of expressions written in *Caliban*, a higher-order polymorphic strongly-typed lazy functional language akin to Turner's Miranda. Clio was designed for verifying each step in the implementation of a program: the specification, the high-level language, the assembly language, the microcode, and the hardware. This paper describes the use of Clio for verifying the correctness of an instruction pipelined microprocessor design. The *abstract* and the *realization* levels of behavior of the processor are modeled as *infinite streams*. The abstract specification describes the behavior in terms of a suitably chosen programmer's model of the processor. A *realization* specification gives a description of the design of the processor by describing the activities that happen in the circuit over a single microcycle. We develop a general criterion of correctness to relate the two levels which is verified using a form of fixed-point induction.

1 Introduction

Clio [2] is a system for verifying properties of expressions written in Caliban, a polymorphic strongly-typed functional language similar to Turner's Miranda[1] [18]. Sentences to be proved are expressed in the Clio *assertion language*, a vehicle for

---

*This work was funded by the Air Force Systems Command at Rome Air Development Center under Contract No. F30602-86-C-0115.

[1]Miranda is a trademark of Research Software Limited.

first-order logic in which the terms are Caliban expressions denoting elements of a complete lattice.

Clio was designed for verifying each step in the implementation of a program: the specification, the high-level language, the assembly language, and the hardware. A lazy language with higher-order functions, such as Caliban, is well suited for writing specifications and for expressing the semantics of every level in the hierarchy. In this paper we present the use of Clio for microprocessor verification.

The recent past few years have seen several successful microprocessor verification efforts, some using the HOL system ([7], [14]) and others based on functional calculii ([13], [16], [4]). With the aim of advancing the state of the technology even further we set up the following specific goals for our microprocessor verification project.

- To verify a large, realistic processor that was not designed just for the purpose of verification.

- To formally reason about new aspects in microprocessor design which were not addressed by previous efforts. We chose to investigate the treatment of pipelining and interrupts.

- To set up the correctness model and the verification framework as general and problem-independent as possible. We plan to use the framework as a basis for a general microprocessor verification tool.

The processor, *MiniCayuga*, we have used to illustrate our verification framework is a 3-stage instruction pipelined RISC processor that supports a single interrupt. *MiniCayuga* and its design are based on the machine *Cayuga* being developed by the Cayuga Group [12] at Cornell University as a vehicle for research on RISC architectures. *MiniCayuga* was conceived to serve as a first step in the development of a microprocessor verification framework on Clio. It supports a subset of the functionality of *Cayuga*. In the next phase of our research we plan to extend the design of *MiniCayuga* to support the full instruction set of *Cayuga* including multiple prioritized interrupts. We believe a lot of the verification effort that has been done for *MiniCayuga* can be reused in the next phase.

In our method both the *abstract* and the *realization* levels of behavior of the processor are modeled as *infinite streams*. The stream denotes a trace of the state of the processor over time as the processor executes instructions stored in the memory. The *abstract* specification describes the behavior in terms of a suitably chosen programmer's model of the processor. A *realization* specification gives a description of a design of the processor describing the activities that happen in the circuit over a single microcycle. The components used in the design are at the level of registers, multiplexers, ALU, and register file. The timing is at a *synchronous* level in the sense that actions on the components are triggered by some synchronizing event of an implicit clock which may have multiple phases.

We develop a general criterion of correctness to relate the two levels of behavior of the processor. To use the correctness criterion for a specific design one must, in general, additionally characterize the following information about the design: (1) A function that specifies the desired relationship between the representations of the state of the processor at the two levels. (2) Any useful *invariant* properties that are preserved by the design at the end of every microcycle in which an instruction is completed.

The next section gives an overview of the Clio verification system. Section 3 presents the specification and correctness model. Section 4 gives an informal description of *MiniCayuga*. Section 5 is about the formal specification of the processor. Section 6 describes the main correctness lemmas and how they are proved. The last section presents our concluding remarks.

2   The Clio Verification System

The following is a summary of the Clio system. A more detailed description can be found in [2]. Clio uses two languages, an <u>executable</u> *object language* and an *assertion language*. *Objects* are defined in the object language, and assertions about them are made in the assertion language. An expression denoting an object is executed by reducing it to its irreducible *normal form*.

The object language is Caliban, a functional programming language similar to Miranda. A Caliban program, or a *script*, consists of a sequence of definitions of types and objects, which are elements belonging to a type. The language has several built-in types including NAT, bool, char, tuple, function types (->) and the polymorphic type of lists, [*], which has the constructors "nil" and "cons", written [] and : in Caliban.

Type definitions are introduced with the construct '::='. For example, the following defines bpath to be the type constructed from the atom, Nil, and two *constructor* functions, Left and Right. Such a type is called a *constructed type*.

```
bpath ::= Nil | Left bpath | Right bpath
```

Definitions of function objects are introduced with = and can be made via "pattern matching." For example, the functions map and filter are defined below. If x is a list, then map f x is the result of applying f to each element of x; and filter P x is the sublist of x consisting of those elements, a, such that P a is true. Note that the comma in the definition of filter introduces a guard (this can also be written with an arrow as A -> B;C) and that an expression (such as the P x after the comma) ends whenever the next character is to the left of the beginning of the expression (the "offsides" rule).

```
map f [] = []
map f (a:x) = (f a):(map f x)

filter P [] = []
filter P (a:x) = a:(filter P x) , P x
                filter P x
```

The definitions of map and filter also use recursion. Recursion in Caliban is unrestricted, unlike in HOL [10] and the Boyer-Moore prover [5], and Clio allows one to reason about functions defined with unrestricted recursion. It is also possible to define *infinite* lists since the list constructor (:) is nonstrict in Caliban. For example, the following defines an unbounded search operator least, which returns the least natural number, if any, greater than or equal to x that satisfies P, and a second-order operator trace, which generates the infinite list of iterates of an operation op:

```
least P x = x, P x
            least P (SUCC x)

trace op x = x:(trace op (op x))
```

The semantics of Caliban is provided by a Scott domain [17], D, which is a complete partial order with a *bottom* element denoted by bottom. Symbols (such as least and trace) denote the least fixed point of their definitions, and the least fixed point always exists.

2.1 The Assertion Language

The assertion language is first-order predicate calculus over the language of D. A term of this language is a Caliban expression enclosed in back-quotes. For example, 'least P x' is a term in the language of D. The atomic formulae are of the form term1 = term2 and term1 <= term2, where <= is the partial ordering of the domain D. The formulae are closed under the logical connectives &, V, ~, => and quantifiers (x), (Ex). The set of true assertions is the first order theory of the Caliban domain D. For example, here is a true (and provable!) assertion about least:

```
assertion1 := (x)(P) 'P (least P x)'='true' & 'x <= (least P x)'='true'
                \/ 'least P x'='bottom'
```

Here the left side, assertion1, is an abbreviation, introduced by ':=', of the right side. The back-quotes are necessary for two reasons. The first is that the logical symbols are all overloaded. For example, trace (~) x is a Caliban expression in which (~)

denotes a Caliban function symbol, which is an element of the domain D of type `bool->bool`. In the language of D, however, ~, is logical negation; the back-quotes distinguish between the two uses. For example, in the assertion `~('f (~x)'='g x')` the first ~ is "assertion level not" while the second is "Caliban not." The second reason for the back quotes is that they help us keep in mind the distinction between Caliban expressions like <u>least P x</u> and what they denote, `'least P x'`, and they clearly identify the parts of an assertion that are executable Caliban expressions.

The quantifier `(x)` in `assertion1` does not range over the whole domain D. Clio infers a type for every expression. The quantifiers, `(x)` and `(Ex)` are actually bounded quantifiers `(x :: tau)` and `(Ex :: tau)` ranging over objects whose type unifies with tau. In `assertion1` the quantifiers are `(x :: NAT) (P :: NAT -> bool)`.

2.2   The Theorem Prover

The theorem prover is interactive with several useful automatic strategies built-in. The basic strategy used by the prover is to reduce the assertion being proved to a conjunction of atomic sentences and then to prove each atomic sentence by rewriting its left and right sides to the same normal form.

To prove an implication, A `=>` B, the hypothesis, A, is added to the *rule-base* and B is proved. If the proof succeeds, the previous state of the rule-base is restored and A `=>` B is added to the rule-base.

To prove a universally quantified sentence, `(x) P x`, there are two strategies, *generalization* and *induction*. To prove it by generalization, a new symbol, `@x`, is created and P `@x` is proved. The assertion can be proved by (structural) induction only when the type of x is a constructed type. In this case we prove, for example when x is a `NAT`, `(P bottom) & (P ZERO) & (P $x => P (SUCC $x))`. The `@` and `$` signs are used to make the generic constants and induction variables distinctive.

When presented with an atomic sentence `'E'='F'`, the prover reduces E and F to their normal forms using the built-in reduction rules and the rewrite rules in the rule-base. During reduction, symbols in the two expressions can also be *expanded*, i.e., replaced by their definitions.

Another strategy which is often used is to "case split" on some expression, A, that has a constructed type. Since the object, A, must be in the range of one of the constructors of its type, we may prove the assertion in each case. For example, if A is a `bool` we may prove an assertion `assert` by proving: `('A'='true' => assert) & ('A'='false'=>assert) & ('A'='bottom' => assert)`.

The prover supports the principle of *fixed-point induction*, which can be used to prove an assertion about an object defined by an unrestricted recursion. Such an object is the least fixed-point of its defining equation `ob = F ob`. To prove P ob (under suitable restrictions on P) we prove (P bottom) & (P \$ob => P (F \$ob)). For example, `assertion1` is proved by fixed-point induction on `least`, and assertions about infinite traces may be proved by fixed-point induction on `trace`.

2.3 The Rule Manager

Assertions that have been proved or assumed are made into *rules*. These rules are used in two ways, as *conditional rewrite rules* and in a limited form of *resolution*. For example, suppose that `f`, `g` and `h` are some Caliban functions for which we have proved the following assertion. (In the assertion language the comma separates a rewrite rule from its condition and is equivalent to an implication, i.e., **A,B** means **B=>A**).

```
assertion2 := (x)'f x'='g x' , 'h x'='true'
```

The rule made from `assertion2` will be used as a conditional rewrite rule by the reducer. For example, when reducing (p (f a)), the reducer will match (f a) with the left-hand side of the rule and attempt to prove the condition 'h a'='true'. If it succeeds, it rewrites (p (f a)) to (p (g a)).

The rule is used in resolution by the rule manager itself. If asked to add the rule 'h a'='true' (which it will make into an unconditional rewrite rule), the rule manager will notice that this *positive literal* unifies with the *negative literal*, 'h x'='true' from `assertion2`. It will then also add the rule, 'f a'='g a' to the rule-base. This kind of resolution is done only when one of the rules involved is a *single literal* to avoid an explosion in the number of rules.

The rule manager also allows the user, interactively, to *instantiate* existing rules and to *expand* them (replace symbols by their definitions).

3 The Correctness Model

We use a functional approach for modeling hardware components and designs. The specifications are expressed in Caliban with data types, (higher-order) functions, and *streams*, i.e., infinite lists, playing a central role. The correctness assertions and the lemmas are expressed and proved in the assertion language of Clio. This approach should be contrasted with the HOL approach [6] in which predicates play a central role, and the specifications and assertions are expressed at the same level in the same formalism. Although it is possible to mimick the HOL approach in Clio, we decided to use the two-tier approach to keep the specifications of the processor executable.

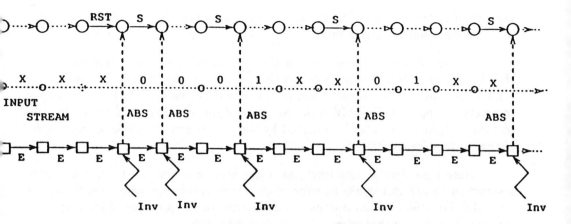

Figure 1: The Correctness Relationship

The behavior of a microprocessor at both the levels of specification is modeled as an *infinite trace*, shown in Figure 1, of the state of the microprocessor and its environment, i.e., its inputs, as the microprocessor executes a stream of instructions stored in the memory. Every transition in the trace denotes an advancement of a cycle on the clock. The trace at both the levels consume the same input stream which is shown between the two traces in the figure. For *MiniCayuga* the input stream denotes the interrupt signal over time.

The outputs produced by the processor are also most naturally represented as a separate stream. For convenience, in our model we assume that they are accumulated as part of the state. In the *MiniCayuga* design the memory is assumed to have a fixed response time, and to be under the exclusive control of the processor. In this case it is more convenient to include the state of the memory as one of the externally visible components of the state of the processor. This eliminates the need to model the outputs of the processor explicitly.

3.1   The Instruction Level Model

The *abstract specification* describes the (macro)instruction level behavior of the processor. This presents a view of the processor which is intended to be useful for some one programming the processor or specifying the behavior of a larger system, eg., an operating system kernel, of which the processor is a component. At this level, most of the details about pipelining except the prefetching behavior is abstracted away. The *abstract state* of the processor includes only those items which are relevant externally. The advancement of the state is performed by means of the actions abs_reset and step (denoted RST and S, respectively, in Figure 1) that are suitable at this level. abs_reset defines the effect of the initializing sequence that the processor must go through after "power-up." The function **step** defines the effect on the abstract state of executing a single instruction in memory.

The number of cycles needed for the completion of an instruction depends on the class of the instruction and whether there is an interrupt during the execution of teh instruction. At the abstract level, we take the view that the effect of executing an instruction happens indivisibly in the last cycle of the instruction. In the cycles prior to that the processor "idles," indicated by the dotted arrows in the figure, without changing its abstract state.

Note that time at this level has deliberately not been abstracted to macro-instruction boundaries unlike in some of the previous microprocessor verification efforts [13], [7], [16]. The instruction level behavior in the presence of interrupts and pipelining cannot be characterized accurately otherwise.

3.2 The Design Level Model

The *realization specification* describes the circuit design level behavior of the processor. The *realization state* of the processor is represented in terms of the (abstract) states of the components. The trace at this level advances the state of the processor at every instant of the clock as specified by the function **execute** (denoted by E in Figure 1). The function **execute** specifies the effect of the actions that happen on the circuit components over the four phases of a single clock cycle.

The circuit design of the processor is partitioned into a *controller* component and a set of *data path* components. Every component, including the controller, supports a collection of *actions*. An action may cause a change in the internal state and/or the state of the signals at the outputs of a component. The controller, which is a finite state machine, determines the schedule of actions to be performed on the components.

The specification models the design at a *synchronous level* of timing. The actions are assumed to be triggered by some synchronizing events, eg., the rising edge, of an implicit clock which may have multiple phases. The actions on the components may introduce different amounts of delay measured as integral numbers of phases of a clock cycle. If an action, with a delay of δ (≥ 0) units, is triggered on a component in phase t of a cycle, then the effect of the action is guaranteed to be completed and the "results," i.e., state and outputs, available for use in phase $t+\delta$; between t and $t+\delta-1$ the state is "undefined" and the outputs may or may not be "undefined." We assume that all the input data signals needed for an action must be stable in the phase in which the action is triggered. We do not model "set up" and "hold" times on the data signals needed for an action.

Some actions may have "zero" delay. This means that the delay introduced by an action on such a component is negligible, and its outputs are available in the same phase as the action is triggered for use by other actions scheduled in the same phase.

As a component the behavior of the controller is more constrained than the rest of the components. The action on the controller that causes a state transition must have a unit delay since every state transition denotes a single phase on the clock.

3.3 The Correctness Criterion

The abstract model differs from the realization model in two ways. Firstly, the state at the abstract level is an abstraction, i.e., it contains only the externally visible parts, of the state at the realization level. Secondly, the abstract trace uses the function step to update the state of the processor, while at the realization level the state is updated using execute.

To formulate the correctness statement we must first define the desired correspondence between the representations of the state at the two levels. This is done by defining an *abstraction function* ABS from the realization state to the abstract state. Assuming S is a valid realization state, ABS(S) gives the abstract state denoted by S. A realization specification *correctly implements* an abstract specification if every trace generated by the latter is an *abstraction* (as defined by ABS) of the trace generated by the former assuming both the specifications are subjected to identical input streams. More precisely, suppose the abstract and the realization models are "initialized" so that the memory is in an identical state at both levels, and the processor is in a certain predetermined "power up" state. Suppose the two models are then subjected to identical input streams to generate the traces as described in the specification. Then, the state in the abstract trace at every instant of time must be an abstraction (ABS) of the state in the realization trace at the corresponding instant of time.

In some situations, it may be sufficient to ensure that the realization trace corresponds with the abstract one only at selected points in the trace. For *MiniCayuga*, for instance, it is possible to specify the time instants at which an instruction gets completed as a function of abstract state and the inputs. Soon after power up it takes takes 3 cycles; after that the processor takes at most four cycles to complete an instruction depending on the class of the current instruction, and whether there is an interrupt. Then, from a certain perspective, it is not important that the states at the two levels must correspond at every point in time, just as long as they correspond at those instants when an instruction is completed.

We set up the verification condition to reflect this weaker correspondence, which is depicted by the vertical arrows (labeled ABS) in Figure 1. Note that even if the number of cycles for an instruction is indefinite, which can be the case, for instance, if the memory has an indefinite response time, as long as the instruction completion time can be expressed as a condition on the abstract state and the external inputs it is possible to use the weaker form of the criterion. In the present case this information is expressed by means of a function (`completion_point`) that gives the number of cycles to be advanced on the clock before the next instruction gets completed.

The correctness statement is proved by the prover using a form of *fixed-point induction* on the trace generating functions. To carry out the proof by induction it is, in general, necessary to define an *invariant* condition (indicated by `Inv` in Figure 1) on the realization state which must be shown to be preserved in every cycle in which an instruction execution is completed. The invariant expresses certain critical properties about the hidden parts of the realization state.

The correctness statement for the *MiniCayuga* design expressed in the Clio assertion language is given below. The `RESET_THEOREM` states the initial part of the requirement shown in Figure 1, namely that upon power up the two traces get into corresponding states after 3 cycles. The `MAIN_THEOREM` states the general relationship on the traces. Note that a precondition of the theorem requires the input stream to be infinite, expressed by requiring a finite prefix of the list to be always well-defined, since the correctness statement is a relation on two infinite traces. The trace generating functions themselves are defined later as part of the specification. In the following `s` ranges over the realization state and `l` ranges over the input stream; `Next` applies `Execute` repeatedly until it exhausts the finite fragment of the input stream that it gets as the second argument.

```
MAIN_THEOREM := (s)(l)( Invariant 's' & infinite 'l') =>
                    'map ABS (Real_trace s l)'
                          ='Abs_trace (ABS s) l'
RESET_THEOREM := (s)(l)( powered_up 's' & 'length l' = '#3' &
                    '!!l' = 'true' ) => Reset_ok 's' 'l'
Reset_ok 's' 'x' := Invariant 'Next s x'
                    & 'ABS(Next s x)'='abs_reset (ABS s) x'
```

4 The MiniCayuga Processor

MiniCayuga and its design are based on the experimental machine *Cayuga* being developed by the Cayuga Group [12] at Cornell University as a vehicle for research on RISC architectures. *MiniCayuga* was conceived to serve as a first step in investigating the use of Clio [2] in the verification of large and realistic pipelined microprocessor designs. It supports only a subset of the functionality of *Cayuga*. In the next phase of our research we plan to extend the design of *MiniCayuga* to support the full instruction set of *Cayuga* including multiple interrupts and traps.

MiniCayuga is a 3-stage instruction pipelined RISC processor. It consists of 32 general purpose registers (each 32-bit wide) organized into a register file (`REGFILE`), and several special purpose registers including PC and NXPC (next PC). It supports a (32-bit wide) word at a time transfer between the memory and the cpu. We assume that the memory is dedicated to the cpu and has a fixed response time. *MiniCayuga* assumes that the cache is off-chip. It supports just one kind of interrupt request, **reset**, which forces the processor to start executing instructions beginning at a given location in memory.

4.1 MiniCayuga Instructions

MiniCayuga supports only a subset of the instructions of *Cayuga*, but its instructions are chosen such that every instruction class - arithmetic, load, store, jump - of *Cayuga* is represented. Instructions belonging to the load/store class are the only ones that move data between memory and registers. The instructions are of fixed length (32-bit) and use a fixed format: '*Opcode i? dst src1 src2*', where *dst* and *src1* always denote (5-bit) indexes into REGFILE, and *src2* can be either a register index or a 16-bit immediate constant depending on the bit *i?*. In the following 'R_i' denotes the ith register in the register file; $oprnd_1$ denotes the contents of R_{src1}; $oprnd_2$ denotes 'if *i?* then *src2* else the contents of R_{src2}'; and, $msb[R_i]$ denotes the most significant bit of R_i.

Arithmetic Class (ACLASS)
This includes add (ADD), subtract (SUB), and compare (CNE) instructions.
'*ADD src1 src2 dst*' has the effect '$R_{dst} \leftarrow oprnd_1 + oprnd_2$'.

'*CNE src1 src2 dst*' has the effect '$msb[R_{dst}] \leftarrow$ if $oprnd_1 = oprnd_2$ then 0 else 1'.

Load Class (LCLASS)
'*LOAD src1 src2 dst*' has the effect '$R_{dst} \leftarrow mem[oprnd_1 + oprnd_2]$'.

Store Class (SCLASS)
'*STR src1 src2 dst*' has the effect '$mem[oprnd_1 + oprnd_2] \leftarrow R_{dst}$'.

Jump Class (JCLASS)
This includes unconditional (JMP) and conditional (JIT, JIF) jump instructions.
'*JMP src1 src2 dst*' has the effect '$NXPC \leftarrow oprnd_1 + oprnd_2$'.

'*JIT src1 src2 dst*' has the effect '$NXPC \leftarrow$ if $msb[R_{dst}]=1$ then $oprnd_1 + oprnd_2$'.

'*JIN src1 src2 dst*' has the effect '$NXPC \leftarrow$ if $msb[R_{dst}]=0$ then $oprnd_1 + oprnd_2$'.

4.2 The MiniCayuga Pipeline

The actions involved in the execution of every instruction of *MiniCayuga* can be partitioned into three stages: *instruction-fetch*, *compute*, and *write-back*. The instruction-fetch stage consists of the actions involved in fetching the instruction. The compute stage includes all the actions necessary to compute the "result" of the instruction including the ones on the ALU and REGFILE. For load/store instructions the result denotes the memory address of the destination/source operand. The write-back stage consists of the actions necessary to "move the result of the instruction to its destination." For load/store class instructions this involves a memory access, for others it only involves register operations.

MiniCayuga uses a 3-stage instruction pipeline with one stage corresponding to each of the instruction execution stages described above. In any given clock cycle the processor can potentially be executing in parallel the actions involved in three different stages of three distinct instructions in a program. For example, writing back the results of the *current* instruction; performing the compute stage of instruction at NXPC; and fetching the instruction at NXPC+1. Note that the existence of jump instructions implies that the three instructions being executed in the pipeline do not have to be stored contiguously in the memory.

The *MiniCayuga* pipeline is designed on the assumption that a memory operation requires roughly the same amount of time as it takes to complete the compute stage of an instruction. This means instruction fetch and compute stage can go on at the same time. Write back, which does not take as long as a compute stage, can also be scheduled during the latter part of the compute stage so as to avoid clashing with the reading of the register file.

But, what about those instructions, such as load/store, which require a memory operation as part of their write-back ? It is not possible to schedule the memory operation in parallel with instruction-fetch because the memory, which has only one set of data and address pins, is being used for an instruction fetch. The solution adopted in *MiniCayuga* is to perform the instruction-fetch in the following cycle by *suspending* (or introducing a *bubble* in) the pipeline, i.e., not executing any other stages, for that cycle. (The pipeline is said to be *active* in a cycle if it is performing all three stages in the cycle.)

4.3   Implications of Pipelining

The use of pipelining has two implications on the design and programming of *MiniCayuga* which must be noted. Suppose there are two consecutive instructions (A and B) in a program so that a source register of the second instruction B is identical to the destination register of A. In this case B may not get the result of A since the compute stage of B is executed in parallel with the write-back stage of A. The *MiniCayuga* design resolves this situation by using *internal forwarding*. That is, there is a special piece of hardware in the design which checks if internal forwarding is necessary, and if so, the saved intermediate result of the previous compute stage is used to perform the current write-back.

The second implication concerns the effect of "delayed jump." The instruction following a jump instruction in a program will get executed by the processor whether the logic of the program requires it or not since the instruction is prefetched. The programmer, and hence our abstract specification, must take this into account in formalizing the instruction level behavior of the processor.

4.4 Interrupts

MiniCayuga is designed to support asynchronous interrupts. In the event of an interrupt the processor, in general, goes through the following "complete-clean-up-handler-fetch" sequence of actions:
Complete: complete the instruction, if any, in the pipeline that has advanced to the write-back stage;
Clean-up: abort the execution of the other instructions in the pipeline, possibly saving some part of the processor state;
Handler-fetch: use the interrupt input as an index into a table to determine the starting address of the interrupt handler corresponding to the interrupt and begin executing it.

The processor takes 3 or 4 cycles to complete the complete-clean-up-handler-fetch sequence depending upon the state the processor is upon the arrival of an interrupt: 3 if it is in a bubble state or if it completed an ACLASS instruction; 4 otherwise. The processor ignores any interrupt it receives when it is in the last two cycles of the complete-clean-up-handler-fetch sequence. Currently, *MiniCayuga* supports only a single kind of interrupt, namely **reset**, which is used to reset the processor to begin executing instructions from a pre-determined location in memory.

5 Specification of MiniCayuga

5.1 Abstract Specification

The abstract specification is intended to present a view of the processor which is useful for some one programming the processor or specifying a larger system, egs., the kernel of an operating system, of which the processor is a component. There are two issues that must be addressed in determining the level of detail of an abstract specification of a pipelined processor with interrupts.

The first one concerns the amount of pipelining information that must be included. From a compiler correctness and a machine level programmer's points of view most of the details of pipelining, except prefetching, is irrelevant. The prefetching aspect must not be hidden because it has a direct consequence on the operational semantics of the macro-instruction level programs. If the abstract view hides prefetching then the two models will not behave the same way on every program. For example, self-modifying programs and programs that are sensitive to the delayed jump effect will not behave the same way.

The second issue concerns the degree to which time can be abstracted at this level. In the absence of interrupts time can be abstracted to macro-instruction boundaries as in [13], [7], [16]. We retain time at a level corresponding the individual cycles of the clock. This allows the capturing of the sensitivity of the instruction level behavior to the arrival time of an interrupt accurately as described informally in section 4.4.

The abstract state is represented by a tuple with four components: the memory state (mem), the "next pc" (nxpc), the state of the registers (regfile), and the current instruction (instrn) to be next completed. Note that retaining a copy of the current instruction in the abstract state, rather than getting it from mem using nxpc, allows the exposing of the effect of prefetching in a simple way.

The memory state is represented by a function of the type [addr -> data], and the state of regfile by a function of type [regaddr -> data]; the other two components are of type data. The types data, addr and regaddr model the kinds of data signals that may appear on the wires. These are treated as abstract data types (*sorts*) with suitable operations defined (axiomatized in the Clio assertion language) on them, without imposing any *a priori* constraints on their sizes. Thus, our specifications and proofs are, in a sense, parameterized with respect to these sorts.

A top level excerpt of the specification of the machine is given below. Abs_trace generates the abstract trace of the processor starting from a given abstract state (s) and a stream (1) of on inputs. It actually generates a "filtered" version of the abstract trace shown in figure 1 in which only the states at the relating points are retained. It uses the function completion_point to determine the number of idle transitions needed to be traversed before arriving at the next relating point. The initial sequence that resets the processor immediately after power up is specified by abs_reset.

The function step, which defines the cumulative effect on the abstract state over an instruction completion cycle, takes the state (s) and a list (1) of inputs the length of which is determined by completion_point. The action taken by step depends on whether there is an interrupt in the list 1.

Note that an alternative (an perhaps a more direct) way of generating the ("unfiltered") abstract trace would be to consume the input stream one at a time deciding "on the fly" whether to idle or step. This method, however, requires maintaining additional information in the abstract state.

```
Abs_trace s l = trace Step completion_point s l

completion_point s l = ((hd l|hd(tl l)) ->#4;#2) , is_ls s
              (hd l ->#3;#1)
is_ls s = load_or_store (opclassof (opof (instrn s)))
```

```
|| Step takes an ABS_STATE and a list of interrupts.
Step s l = <<newmem s, newnxpc s (is_int l), newreg s,
                                        newinstr s (is_int l)>>
newmem s = store_effect s , current_opclass s = SCLASS
          mem s


newreg s  = alu_effect s, current_opclass s = ACLASS
            load_effect s, current_opclass s = LCLASS
            reg s

|| The new current instruction is usually fetched as follows:
prefetch s = mem s (data_to_addr(nxpc s))

|| But when there is an interrupt the instruction isn't prefetched.
handler s = newmem s addr_0

handler_fetch s = newmem s (data_to_addr(handler s))

newinstr s i = handler_fetch s , i
               prefetch s

|| The new next pc.
newnxpc s i =  inc_data(handler s), i
               jump_effect s, current_opclass s = JCLASS
               inc_data(nxpc s)

|| Specification of power-up (which includes a reset)
reset_addr s = mem s addr_0
reset_inst s = mem s (data_to_addr (reset_addr s))
abs_reset s l = <<mem s, inc_data (reset_addr s), reg s, reset_inst s >>
```

5.2 Realization Specification

The design of *MiniCayuga* is built from a central *controller*, and several instances of a set of component types, each of which supports several *actions*. The controller implements a finite state machine that schedules actions on the components based on a nonoverlapping 4-phase clock. The actions of the components may have different amounts of delays measured in terms of an integral number of clock phases.

The realization specification is organized into four parts:

1. *Components specification*: this gives a (generic) description of every component type and its actions.

2. *Controller specification*: this specifies the controller component

3. *Structural specification*: this defines the actual components (as instances of a component type), specifies the connectivity among them, and defines the function **execute**.

5.2.1 The Components Specification

Every component instance used in the design is an element of a **component** type, which is itself constructed as a *labeled union* of a finite number of *component class* types. The component class types used in the design are: **latch**, **mux3**, **memory**, **alu**, **incrementer**, **decoder**, and **regfile**.

The actions on the components are organized in a similar fashion. Every action is an element of an **action** type, which is constructed as a labelled union of a finite number of *action class* types, one for every component class. An action class consists of the actions which can be triggered on a component belonging to the corresponding component class.

A component specification specifies the behavior of every component in a component class. It consists of the following: (1) a type defining the state of a component and (2) for every action, three functions which give the new outputs, the new state, and the delay associated with the action. We give below the actions defined on some of the component classes used in our design.

A **latch** has a single action **set**; a **mux3** has three actions **choose1**, **choose2**, and **choose3**; **decoder** has one action **decode** which supplies as output the five fields of an instruction; **alu** supports three actions - **add**, **subtract**, **compare** - corresponding to the three operations we need on the **alu**.

The **regfile**, which is one of the most functionally complex components used in the design, supports three actions: **load**, **unload**, and **d_unload** to read and write into the individual registers using the data signals at its input ports **src1**, **src2**, and **dst** as indexes.

5.2.2 The Structural Specification

A block schematic of the *MiniCayuga* design is shown in Figure 2. The major blocks of the design are the REGFILE, ALU, CONTROLLER, DECODER, and INC, which is an instance of the **incrementer**. IREG, NXPC, PC, RESULT, and DST are instances of **latch**. MUX1, ... , MUX6 are instances of the multiplexor type **mux3**.

In any given cycle when the pipeline is active, IREG contains the instruction whose compute stage is being performed; NXPC contains the address of the instruc-

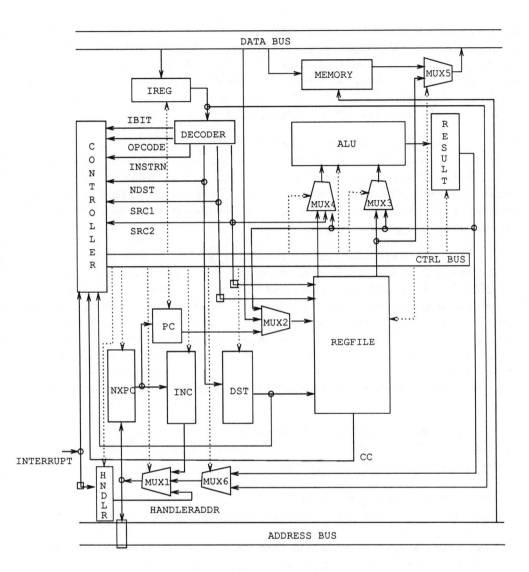

Figure 2: MiniCayuga Design Schematic

tion being fetched; RESULT contains the result of the compute stage performed in the previous cycle which will be used for the write-back; DST contains the destination for performing the write-back stage. The sources of the operands for the ALU are normally obtained from the REGFILE indexed by the appropriate field of the DECODE output except when the CONTROLLER detects that internal forwarding is needed. In the latter case, the contents of RESULT are used as instead.

The state of the design in a given phase within a clock cycle is represented as a function state, which maps every component instance in the design to its local_state. The local_state of a component is a tuple which contains its internal state and the state of the signals at its outputs in a phase. A function process (from time, i.e., clock phases, to state) is used to keep track of the progression of the state of the design over the phases.

The function execute is defined hierarchically in terms of do_phases, do_actions, and do_act. The function do_act actually performs actions specified by the CONTROLLER. Note that if the schedule determined by the CONTROLLER attempts to trigger a new action on a component before another action on it is completed do_act returns bottom. A top level specification of the realization trace generation and execute is given below. Real_trace generates a filtered version of the actual trace using the function completion_point specified in the abstract specification. At the realization level the trace does not have any idle transitions, the trace is generated simply by applying execute the number of times specified by completion_point.

```
|| A process is a function :: time->state
process ::~ NUM -> state
state ::~ component -> local_state

|| realization trace generation
Real_trace s l = trace Next (completion_point.ABS) s l

|| Next takes a real state and a list of inputs. It iterates Execute
|| once for each input on the list.
Next s [] = s
Next s (a:x) = Next (Execute s a) x

|| execute :: state -> state
execute s b = do_phases 0 (make_process (Set_ext b s))
make_process s t = s

|| do_phases :: process -> state
do_phases t p = p t , t = 4
                do_phases (t+1) (do_phase t p)
do_phase t p = do_actions t (scheduler t (CONTROLSTATE p t)
                                         (CONTROL_IN p t)) p
```

```
|| do_actions :: time -> list -> process -> process
do_actions t [] p = p
do_actions t (a:x) p = do_actions t x (do_act a t p)

do_act a t p newt c = p newt c , c ~= ( component a)
                      p newt c , newt < t
                      bottom , newt < (t + (delay a))
                      effect a t p c
```

5.2.3   The Controller Specification

Figure 3 shows an abstracted version of the finite state machine implemented by the CONTROLLER component. Every transition in the diagram, which may be conditioned upon the arrival of an interrupt, corresponds to a single cycle on the clock. The possible states that the CONTROLLER may assume when the pipeline is active appear enclosed within the dotted box. These states are partitioned into four kinds, one for every possible class to which the instruction whose write-back stage was done belongs. DLD_FETCH (read "delayed fetch") corresponds to the state in which the processor is processing a bubble in the pipeline. The rest of the states correspond to the points where the processor is performing the "complete-clean_up-handler_fetch" sequence necessitated by an interrupt.

Every transition of the state diagram of figure 3 can be "blown up" into a more detailed state machine in which a transition corresponds to a single phase of the clock. Figure 4 shows a blow up of the state diagram corresponding to the transition leading out of WBACLASS state when there is no interrupt. The four way branching corresponds to the four cases possible for internal forwarding. A transition in the detailed machine is labelled with the set of actions generated by the CONTROLLER in that phase. We have shown the actions generated for one of the paths through the machine.

The controller is specified as a component with three actions: match, and advance advance the state of the controller; schedule outputs the set of actions to be scheduled in each of the four phases.

The controller state is represented as a tuple with four components. The first is a history, which maintains some information about the actions of the controller in the previous cycle, and the second is used to implement the internal forwarding mechanism.

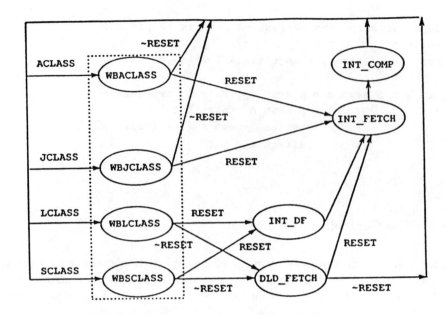

Figure 3: The Controller State Diagram

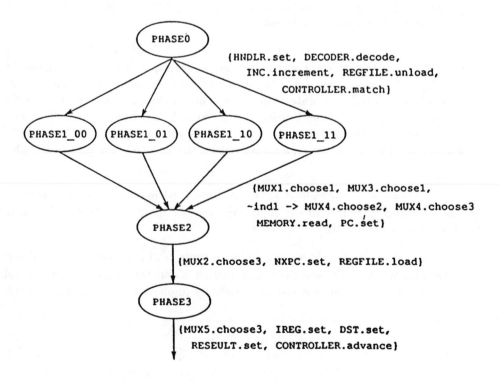

Figure 4: A Detailed Controller State Diagram

6 Verification of MiniCayuga

In the following we give an outline of the main steps involved in the verification of
MiniCayuga. Full details of the verification can be found in [3]. We first specify the
information - the abstraction function and the invariant - that must be formulated
for formulating the verification conditions.

The abstraction function (*ABS*) extracts from the realization state the externally visible components, which for *MiniCayuga* consists of the memory state, the
next pc, the state of the register file, and the current instruction, i.e., the instruction
to be next completed. A Caliban definition of ABS is given below.

```
ABS s = <<getmemstate (s (M MEMORY)),
        getlatchval (s (L NXPC)),
        getregstate (s (R REGFILE)),
        curr_op s >>
```

6.1 The Invariant

Note that due to pipelining the realization model "looks ahead" of the abstract model
by two instructions. While performing the write-back stage of the current instruction
kept in the abstract state, the processor would be performing the compute stage of
the instruction at nxpc, and fetching the instruction one step even further ahead.
Some of the hidden registers (IREG, RESULT, DST) maintain information about
the instructions that have already been partially executed. The invariant expresses
the connection that must exist in a correct design between the abstract level state
and these hidden registers of the realization state. This connection (given below)
must hold in every cycle in which an instruction gets completed.

1. The contents of IREG is the instruction at nxpc.

2. The contents of RESULT is the "result" of the current instruction.

3. The contents of DST is the destination of the current instruction.

4. The pipeline is active, i.e., the controller is in one of the four possible active
   states.

The invariant will only hold in those cycles in which the processor is in one
of the four states enclosed within the dotted box in the controller state diagram
of figure 3. The Caliban definition of the invariant is given below. The predicate
Pipe_inv characterizes the conditions listed above. We also include as part of the
Invariant the Proper_state conditions, which ensure that no part of the realization
state can be bottom. In the realization model, some part of the state can become

bottom iff either an external input is bottom, or if the schedule of actions generated by the controller is such that there are timing-related inconsistencies.

```
Invariant 's' :== Proper_state 's' & Pipe_inv 's'
Pipe_inv 's' := 'prefetch(ABS s)'='ireg_latch s'
              & 'writeback_class s'= 'current_opclass(ABS s)'
              & 'current_dst (ABS s)'='dst_latch s'
              & 'current_result(ABS s)'='result_latch s'
```

6.2   The Verification Conditions

The MAIN_THEOREM asserts that for any state satisfying the Invariant, the infinite traces of the behavior at the two levels correspond (for any input stream). The RESET_THEOREM asserts that it takes, soon after power-up 3 cycles for the processor to attain a desired "initial" realization state in which instruction execution will begin. The initial state must satisfy the invariant, and abstract to the corresponding initial state (defined by abs_reset) in the abstract model.

```
MAIN_THEOREM := (s)(l)( Invariant 's' & infinite 'l') =>          .
                        'map ABS (Real_trace s l)' = 'Abs_trace (ABS s) l'

Reset_ok 's' 'x' := Invariant 'Next s x'
                  & 'ABS(Next s x)' = 'abs_reset (ABS s) x'

RESET_THEOREM := (s)(l)( powered_up 's' & 'length l' = '#3' &
                        '!!l' = 'true' ) => Reset_ok 's' 'x'
```

6.3   Proof of the Verification Conditions

The proof of the RESET_THEOREM is fairly routine, so let us consider the MAIN_THEOREM. In this assertion, both of the infinite traces Real_trace and Abs_trace are defined (as shown in sections 5.1 and 5.2) in terms of the trace-generating function trace which is defined by an unrestricted (infinite) recursion. We prove MAIN_THEOREM by fixed-point induction on trace. The induction step of the proof reduces to showing that the Invariant holds and the realization and abstract states "commute" when the traces are advanced by "one box" in Figure 1 shown earlier in section 3. The advancement of the traces by a box is accomplished by the functions Next_real and Next_abs.

The Advance_lemma stated below establishes the commutes condition and part of the Pipe_inv part of the invariant. Since Next_real is an iteration of execute we can show that the Proper_state part of the invariant is preserved by proving the more general Timing_ok_lemma. We call it Timing_ok_lemma because if any of the timing constraints imposed by the delays on the actions are violated, then the resulting state `execute s x` will contain some `bottom` values and will not satisfy `Proper_state`.

```
Timing_ok_lemma :=  Proper_state 'execute s x',
                                    Proper_state 's' & '!x'='true'

Advance_lemma :=  ( Invariant 's' & Input_ok 's' 'l')   => Next_ok 's' 'l'

Next_ok 's' 'l' := 'ABS(Next_real s l)'='Next_abs (ABS s) l'
                    & Pipe_inv 'Next_real s l'

|| The next real state
Next_real s l = Next s (Next_input (ABS s) l)

|| The next abstract state
Next_abs s l = Step s (Next_input s l)

|| num_input is defined in the abstract specification
Next_input s l = take (num_input s l) l
```

The proofs of the `Timing_ok_lemma` and `Advance_lemma` in Clio now follow a standard strategy. From the compiled definitions, Clio can automatically generate conditional rewrite rules; this generates about three hundred rewrite rules. In the proof of the `Advance_lemma`, Clio assumes `Invariant 's'` and tries to prove `Next_ok 's'`. The assumption, `Invariant 's'`, will add rewrites for the clauses of `Pipe_inv 's'` and adds the rule `Proper_state 's'`. In addition to the rewrite rules automatically generated, it was necessary to prove a small number of lemmas which, under the assumption `Proper_state 's'`, cause Clio to automatically rewrite the states of the components of `'s'` in terms of new symbolic constants. One of these new constants represents the `opclass` of the current instruction. In the interactive mode, we now ask Clio to "case split"; it will consider the four cases corresponding to the four possible classes of instructions. In each case, the rewrite rules will eventually reduce the commutes condition and invariant to true (after a few more case splits on whether internal forwarding was necessary).

Thus, after a small number of preparatory lemmas are proved, the proof can be done essentially automatically. In fact, the same proof strategy was used to verify several earlier versions of *MiniCayuga*.

7 Concluding Remarks

In conclusion, we compare our work with some of the other significant microprocessor verification efforts. In [11] Gordon carried out the verification of a small microprogrammed computer using the LCF [9] system. His computer was later re-verified on the VERIFY system [1] and using HOL [10] in [15]. The verification of FM8501 by Hunt [13] was the first exercise in verifying a large realistic processor. It was done on the Boyer-Moore theorem prover [5] using the semantic foundations used in [11]. Recently, in an effort chartered by the Defense Ministry of UK, Cohn [7] used HOL to verify the design of another large processor called Viper.

Our work is similar to the above in that it also addresses the functional correctness of microprocessor designs described at a synchronous level. The features that distinguish our work are the following. We have shown for the first time the treatment of the correctness of a microprocessor design that uses instruction pipelining and multi-phase clocking discipline with user-specified (heterogeneous) propagation delays for components. Recently, [8] has shown a formal treatment of pipelining actions in hardware using a process model. [8] illustrates the method on a stack and memory example. In addition to the *MiniCayuga* example discussed in the paper, the framework has also been used for the formal analysis of another large microprogrammed machine *MiniLilith* discussed in [16]. The work reported in [16] shows the treatment of correctness of handshake interactions between the processor and memory.

Our experience of microprocessor verification using Clio has been quite positive. The verification of *MiniCayuga* took about 4 manmonths of effort by an expert user of Clio. Including the time spent on developing the specification techniques, the correctness model, and the verification of an earlier version of the processor which did not support interrupt, the total effort amounted to about one manyear. The overall complexity of the design of *MiniCayuga* is comparable to that of FM8501 and the second level of Viper. It is less complex because it supports a smaller instruction set, and also some of its blocks, such as ALU, are not decomposed to the same level as in the others. On the other hand instruction pipelining makes ours more complex. In contrast, the second level verification of VIPER took about 12 manmonths of effort, and that of FM8501 must have taken at least as much. We plan to extend our effort to the verification of an extended design of *MiniCayuga* that supports the full functionality of *Cayuga*.

Acknowledgements

We thank Profs. Keshav Pingali, Lov Grover and the rest of the members of the Cayuga Group at Cornell University for helping us understand the basics of pipelining and the details of the *Cayuga* design.

References

[1] Harry G. Barrow. "Verify: A Program for Proving Correctness of Digital Hardware Designs". *Artificial Intelligence*, 24:437–491, 1984.

[2] M. Bickford, C. Mills, and E.A. Schneider. "Clio: An Applicative Language-Based Verification System". Technical Report TR 15-7, Odyssey Research Associates, Inc., 301A Harris B. Dates Drive, Ithaca, NY 14850, March 1989.

[3] Mark Bickford and Mandayam Srivas. "The Verification of MiniCayuga Using Clio". Technical Report TR 15-11, Odyssey Research Associates, Inc., 301A Harris B. Dates Drive, Ithaca, NY 14850, September 1989.

[4] D. Borrione, P. Camurati, J.L. Paillet, and P. Prinetto. "A Functional Approach to Formal Hardware Verification". In *ICCD-88*, pages 592–595, Rye Brook, NY, Oct 1988.

[5] Robert S. Boyer and J Strother Moore. *ACM Monograph Series: A Computational Logic*. Academic Press, Inc., 1979.

[6] Albert Camilleri, Mike Gordon, and Tom Melham. "Hardware Verification using Higher-Order Logic". In *IFIP WG 10.2 Workshop, From HDL to Guaranteed Correct Circuit Designs*, pages 85–114. North-Holland Publishing Co., 1986.

[7] Avra Cohn. "Correctness Properties of the Viper Block Model: The Second Level". Technical Report 134, Computer Laboratory, University of Cambridge, Cambridge, U.K., May 1988.

[8] Ganesh Gopalakrishnan. "Specification and Verification of Pipelined Hardware in HOP". In *Computer Hardware Description Languages and their Applications*, pages 117–132, Washington, DC, June 19-21, 1989.

[9] Michael J.C. Gordon. "LCF-LSM". Technical report, Computer Laboratory, University of Cambridge, Cambridge, UK, 1983.

[10] Mike Gordon. "A Machine Oriented Formulation of Higher Order Logic". Technical Report 68, Computer Laboratory, University of Cambridge, Cambridge, U.K., July 1985.

[11] M.J. Gordon. "Proving a Computer Correct". Technical Report 42, Computer Laboratory, University of Cambridge, Cambridge, UK, 1983.

[12] The Cayuga Group. "Cayuga Chip Specification: Release 2.2". Technical report, Departments of Computer Science and Electrical Engineering, Cornell University, Ithaca, NY 14853, December 1988.

[13] Warren A. Hunt. "FM8501: A Verified Microprocessor". In *IFIP WG 10.2 Workshop, From HDL to Guaranteed Correct Circuit Designs*, pages 85–114. North-Holland Publishing Co., 1986.

[14] J. Joyce. "Formal Specification and Verification of Microprocessor Systems". In *Proceedings of the 14th Symposium on Microprocessing and Microprogramming (EUROMICRO 88)*, Zurich, Switzerland, August 29 - September 1, 1988. North-Holland Publishing Co.

[15] J. Joyce, G. Birtwistle, and M.J. Gordon. "Proving a Computer Correct in Higher Order Logic". Technical Report Research Report No. 85/208/21, Department of Computer Science, University of Calgary, 2500 University Drive, Calgary, Canada T2N 1N4, August 1985.

[16] R.C. Sekar and M.K. Srivas. "Formal Verification of a Microprocessor Using Equational Techniques". In *Banff Hardware Verification Workshop*, Banff, Canada, June 12-18 1988.

[17] Joseph E. Stoy. *Denotational Semantics: A Scott-Strachey Approach*. MIT Press, Cambridge, MA 02139, 1977.

[18] D.A. Turner. "An overview of Miranda". *ACM SIGPLAN Notices*, 21(12):158–166, December 1986.

Verification of Combinational Logic in Nuprl

David A. Basin[*]

Peter Del Vecchio[†]

Abstract

We present a case study of hardware specification and verification in the Nuprl Proof Development System. Within Nuprl we have built a specialized environment consisting of tactics, definitions, and theorems for specifying and reasoning about hardware. Such reasoning typically consists of term-rewriting, case-analysis, induction, and arithmetic reasoning. We have built tools that provide high-level assistance for these tasks.

The hardware component that we have proven is the front end of a floating-point adder/subtractor. This component, the MAEC (Mantissa Adjuster and Exponent Calculator), has 5459 transistors and has been proven down to the transistor level. As the circuit has 116 inputs and 107 outputs, verification by traditional methods such as case analysis would have been a practical impossibility.

1 Introduction

Over the last decade there has been a growing interest in applying formal methods to the design of real-world circuits. Some of the best known examples of work in this field are the verification of the VIPER microprocessor by the British Royal Radar Establishment [6], and the verification of the FM8501 by Warren Hunt [10]. In addition, using the results of Barrett [1], INMOS Corporation formally verified the floating-point unit of their IMS T800 microprocessor [11].

The increasing application of formal design methods has been motivated primarily by two factors. First, when specifications are given in a language with well-understood semantics, the behavior and structure of devices can be precisely defined. Second, once the devices have been formally specified, they are subject to analysis by proof

---

[*]Dept. of Computer Science, Cornell University, Ithaca NY, 14853. Supported in part by an IBM Fellowship.

[†]Dept. of Electrical Engineering, Cornell University, Ithaca, NY 14853. Supported in part by NSF grant CCR8616552 and ONR grant N00014-88-K-0409.

in a formal system; one can rigorously demonstrate that their structural descriptions meet their behavioral specifications.

We have recently begun a study, at Cornell, of formalizing floating-point hardware. Our goal is to specify and prove properties of general-purpose parameterized components such as shifters, multiplexers, and adders. Our hope is that by building a general collection of proven devices, we can then build circuits such as floating point adders and multipliers simply by gluing together the appropriate specifications; specifics such as exponent and mantissa length are specified by instantiating subcomponent parameters. Moreover, the proofs of correctness for these new devices should follow simply from the proven behavioral specifications of their components.

The Nuprl proof development system [7] provides the formal basis for our research. Nuprl's logic is a higher-order constructive type theory, well-suited for formalizing mathematical arguments, especially those with computational significance. The system itself features: sophisticated editors that support the interactive development of definitions and proofs; a high-level meta-language that facilitates the development of tactics; and powerful decision procedures for arithmetic reasoning.

Within Nuprl we have designed an environment that has been tailored for specifying and reasoning about hardware. The basis of this environment is an encoding of quantified boolean logic, and a set of decision procedures and tactics that aid in reasoning about boolean formulas. To date we have used the environment for specifying and verifying combinational logic. It should serve equally well as a foundation for sequential logic.

We have used our environment to verify a number of hardware components. In this report we show how these components can be combined to specify and verify the MAEC (Mantissa Adjuster and Exponent Calculator). The MAEC is a section of a floating-point adder used in a systolic array FFT processor. This processor is being developed under a contract for NASA and will be used to process images from large ground-based telescopes. The MAEC inputs the mantissas and exponents for two floating-point numbers and adjusts the two mantissas so that bits with equal weight are aligned in the two mantissas. Each of the mantissas has 49 bits. Each exponent has 9 bits. Thus, since the circuit has 116 inputs and 107 outputs, verification by traditional methods such as case analysis would have been a practical impossibility.

Our paper is organized as follows. Section 2 contains an informal account of Nuprl. Section 3 describes our hardware environment. Section 4 provides an overview of the MAEC and the structural descriptions and behavioral specifications of its major components. The final section draws conclusions and suggests future research directions.

2 Nuprl

Nuprl's logic is a descendent of Martin-Löf's constructive type theory [12]. It is an extremely expressive logic; sufficiently rich, for example, to act as a foundation for constructive mathematics. Types are stratified in an unbounded hierarchy of universes. U_1 is the first universe and contains all small types. Small types include data-types common to programmers and mathematicians such as integers, lists, pairing, disjoint union, function space, equality (e.g., $a = b$ in int), and first order propositions. Higher-order logic is defined within the theory via the propositions-as-types correspondence: a proposition is true if and only if the type associated with it is inhabited. Hence, when we speak of "formulas" or "propositions" we mean these defined notions.

The rules of Nuprl deal with *sequents*, objects of the form

$$x_1{:}H_1, x_2{:}H_2, \ldots, x_n{:}H_n \gg P. \tag{1}$$

The H_i are referred to as *hypotheses* and the proposition P the *goal* or *conclusion*. ">>" is Nuprl's equivalent of a turnstile. A sequent is true if the conclusion follows from the hypotheses. Constructively, this means that given members x_i of the types H_i, we can construct a member of the type P. Nuprl contains facilities to extract the computational content of theorems and execute this content in its *evaluator*. This ability to execute the computational content of proofs gives rise to the proofs-as-programs paradigm [7].

Nuprl's proofs are trees containing sequents and inference rules and are built in a top-down fashion. The root sequent is the goal to be proved. The user applies inference rules which refine the goal into subgoals such that the truth of the goal may be established by the truth of the subgoals. The following, for example, might be a node in a proof tree where &-introduction occurs.

$$
\begin{array}{ll}
\gg \quad P \ \& \ Q & \text{By Intro} \\
\quad \gg P & \\
\quad \gg Q &
\end{array}
\tag{2}
$$

Here the goal $P \ \& \ Q$ has been refined to the subgoals P and Q.

Inference rules in Nuprl may either be primitive rules or ML programs called tactics. Nuprl tactics are similar to those in LCF [8]: given a sequent as input, they apply primitive inference rules and other tactics to the proof tree. The unproven leaves of the resulting tree become the subgoals resulting from the tactic's application. Tactics, then, act as derived inference rules; their correctness is justified by the way the type structure of ML is used. This mechanism provides a powerful method of raising the level of inference in Nuprl proofs. Ideally, users supply only the main proof ideas and tactics fill in the details. Moreover, as the tactic calls are themselves part of Nuprl proof trees, the proofs can serve as high-level explanations of formal arguments.

Theorem proving takes place within the context of a Nuprl *library*: an ordered collection of tactics, theorems, and definitions. Objects are created and modified using window-oriented structure editors. Nuprl contains a definition mechanism which is essentially a macro facility. Nuprl's text editor, together with this definition facility, permits easily readable notations for objects in Nuprl's type theory. A proof editor is used to construct proofs in a top-down manner, and to view or modify previously constructed proofs. Proofs are retained by the system and can be referred to by either the user or by tactics.

3   The Hardware Environment

A large amount of research at Cornell has been dedicated to designing *environments* in Nuprl [2,3,9]. An environment is a collection of definitions, theorems, and tactics for reasoning about a specific problem domain. Our belief is that it is better to start with a general logic and build specific environments than to work in logics specifically tailored around problem domains or to use proof systems with fixed problem solving strategies. In hardware verification, reasoning typically consists of term-rewriting, case analysis, induction, and arithmetic reasoning. We have built tools that provide high-level assistance for these tasks.

This section contains an overview of our environment. Our emphasis is on device specification and reasoning paradigms. The specifics concerning the MAEC will be covered in the following section. The definitions, theorems, and proof steps that we present appear much as they would on the screen of a Nuprl session.

3.1   Quantified Boolean Logic

Reasoning about combinational logic, whether at the gate or transistor level, requires reasoning about bits and functions that operate on bits. Hence, our environment begins with an encoding of boolean logic. We define the type **bool** to be the two element set containing only the integers zero and one.

$$\text{bool} \doteq \{ \text{ i:int} \mid \text{i} = 0 \text{ in int} \lor \text{i} = 1 \text{ in int} \}$$

Truth and falsity (**tt** and **ff**) are defined as one and zero respectively. We say that a boolean formula **p** is true when it satisfies the predicate **tr(p)** defined by

$$\text{tr(p)} \doteq \text{p} = \text{tt in bool}.$$

These initial definitions are somewhat arbitrary, as booleans can be defined in terms of any two element set, but they have far reaching consequences. We can now efficiently define other boolean connectives taking advantage of special properties of arithmetic. For **p** and **q** booleans, we define the following operators of type **bool→bool→bool** (i.e., the operators take two boolean arguments and return a boolean):

$$p \wedge_B q \;\doteq\; p^*q$$
$$p \vee_B q \;\doteq\; p{+}q{-}(p^*q)$$
$$p \Rightarrow_B q \;\doteq\; (1{-}p) + p^*q$$
$$\neg_B p \;\doteq\; (1{-}p)$$

Other binary operators such as $\Leftrightarrow_B$ (boolean iff) and **xor** (exclusive or) are defined similarly. These operations are only sensible on booleans. However, there is a correspondence between these operators and operators defined on propositions. Specifically, we proved

$$\text{tr}(p \wedge_B q) \;=\; \text{tr}(p) \;\&\; \text{tr}(q) \text{ in } U_1 \tag{3}$$
$$\text{tr}(p \vee_B q) \;=\; \text{tr}(p) \vee \text{tr}(q) \text{ in } U_1 \tag{4}$$
$$\text{tr}(p \Rightarrow_B q) \;=\; \text{tr}(p) \Rightarrow \text{tr}(q) \text{ in } U_1 \tag{5}$$
$$\text{tr}(\neg_B p) \;=\; \neg\text{tr}(p) \text{ in } U_1 \tag{6}$$

where the connectives $\&$, $\vee$, $\Rightarrow$, and $\neg$ represent the propositional connectives **and, or, implies,** and **negation.** We shall generally leave off the boolean B subscripts that label the connectives, leaving context to clarify whether the symbols in question are boolean or propositional operators.

Boolean quantifiers are now directly definable in terms of boolean conjunction and disjunction. Specifically, we define the operators $\forall_B$ and $\exists_B$ of type $(\textbf{bool}{\to}\textbf{bool}){\to}\textbf{bool}$:

$$\forall_B x.P(x) \;\doteq\; P(\text{tt}) \wedge P(\text{ff})$$
$$\exists_B x.P(x) \;\doteq\; P(\text{tt}) \vee P(\text{ff})$$

As before, we can establish the following correspondences between these boolean formulas and their associated propositions.

$$\text{tr}(\forall_B x.P(x)) \;\Longleftrightarrow\; \forall x{:}\textbf{bool}.\ \text{tr}(P(x)) \tag{7}$$
$$\text{tr}(\exists_B x.P(x)) \;\Longleftrightarrow\; \exists x{:}\textbf{bool}.\ \text{tr}(P(x)) \tag{8}$$

It is worth noting that the underlying constructivity of Nuprl's type theory poses no barriers to reasoning about boolean logic. As integer equality is decidable, it follows that for all booleans p, $p \vee \neg p$ is provable. Moreover as our logic is constructive, the correspondences given in Equations 7 and 8 allow us to extract functions from true AE ($\forall/\exists$) boolean formulas. That is, if we can prove

$$\texttt{>>}\text{tr}(\forall_B x_1, ..., \forall_B x_n.\ \exists_B y_1, ..., \exists_B y_m.\ p),$$

then we can automatically (via rewriting) prove

$$\texttt{>>}\forall x_1, ..., \forall x_n.\ \exists y_1, ..., \exists y_m.\ \text{tr}(p).$$

From this second sequent, Nuprl's extractor can produce a function such that given as input $x_1, ..., x_n$ the extracted function returns values $y_1, ..., y_m$ such that p is true when the x_i and the y_i are bound to these values.

3.2 Circuit Representation

We represent hardware circuits as relations; the methodology we use is similar to that employed by Mike Gordon's HOL group [5]. A circuit is specified by an n-ary relation $R(a_0, ..., a_{n-1})$ that is built from logical connectives, constants, simpler relations, and recursion. The a_i represent inputs and outputs and we may think of them as external connections or ports of the circuit. The simpler relations may be basic logic gates (e.g., nand or xor), transistors, or previously defined relations. If we view each relation as specifying a constraint on the ports a_i, then anding together the various components gives a constraint for the entire circuit. Wires are represented by names; internal wires are hidden by existentially quantifying their names.

Our circuits are specified at the transistor level. We consider two types of transistors, n-type and p-type MOS, which we model as switches.

$$\text{ntran(g,a,b)} \;\dot{=}\; g \Rightarrow (a \Leftrightarrow b)$$
$$\text{ptran(g,a,b)} \;\dot{=}\; \neg g \Rightarrow (a \Leftrightarrow b)$$

Power is a constraint that the value on a line p is always tt. Similarly, ground constrains p to ff.

$$\text{pwr(p)} \;\dot{=}\; p \Leftrightarrow tt$$
$$\text{gnd(p)} \;\dot{=}\; p \Leftrightarrow ff$$

As a simple example, consider the circuit shown in Figure 1. This circuit generates the carry_out bit of a one-bit full-adder and is defined as follows:

$$
\begin{aligned}
&\text{Carry\_ckt(a,b,carry\_in,carry\_out)} \;\dot{=} \\
&\quad \exists \text{p0, p1a, p1b, p2, n0, n1a, n1b, n2, carry\_outb : bool.} \\
&\quad \text{Pwr(p0)} \wedge \text{Gnd(n0)} \wedge \\
&\quad \text{ptran(b,p0,p1a)} \wedge \text{ntran(b,n0,n1a)} \wedge \\
&\quad \text{ptran(a,p0,p1a)} \wedge \text{ntran(a,n0,n1a)} \wedge \\
&\quad \text{ptran(carry\_in,p1a,carry\_outb)} \wedge \text{ntran(carry\_in,n1a,carry\_outb)} \wedge \\
&\quad \text{ptran(a,p0,p1b)} \wedge \text{ntran(a,n0,n1b)} \wedge \\
&\quad \text{ptran(b,p1b,carry\_outb)} \wedge \text{ntran(b,n1b,carry\_out)} \wedge \\
&\quad \text{Pwr(p2)} \wedge \text{ptran(carry\_outb,p2,carry\_out)} \wedge \\
&\quad \text{Gnd(n2)} \wedge \text{ntran(carry\_outb,n2,carry\_out)}
\end{aligned}
\tag{9}
$$

If we define a relation Sum_ckt for the sum port of the adder, we may then define a one-bit full-adder constructed as follows:

$$
\begin{aligned}
&\text{add\_1(a,b,carry\_in,sum,carry\_out)} \;\dot{=} \\
&\quad \text{Carry\_ckt(a,b,carry\_in,carry\_out)} \wedge \text{Sum\_ckt(a,b,carry\_in,sum)}
\end{aligned}
\tag{10}
$$

Many of the circuits in the MAEC are defined by primitive recursion. These include an n-bit adder, shifters, multiplexers, and other devices that take bit-vectors

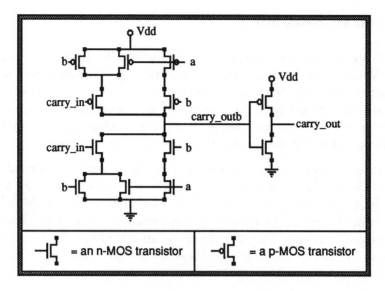

Figure 1: Schematic of the Carry_ckt

for arguments. For example, it is straight-forward to use the relation add_1 to define an n-bit ripple-carry adder using Nuprl's combinator for primitive recursion on higher types. Thus, we can recursively define an n-bit adder where:

$$\begin{aligned}
&\text{add\_n(0,avec,bvec,carry\_in,outvec,carry\_out)} = \\
&\quad \text{carry\_in} \Leftrightarrow \text{carry\_out} \\
&\text{add\_n(n+1,avec,bvec,carry\_in,outvec,carry\_out)} = \\
&\quad \exists \text{cn. add\_n(n,avec,bvec,carry\_in,outvec,cn)} \wedge \\
&\quad \text{add\_1(a(n),b(n),cn,out(n),carry\_out)}
\end{aligned} \tag{11}$$

In the above circuit, avec, bvec, and outvec are elements of a defined type called vector, a vector being a function from integers (the bit position) to booleans (the value of that bit). We often take the view that vectors represent unsigned integers. That is, given an n-bit vector, we define a function vec_val where:

$$\begin{aligned}
\text{vec\_val(0,vec)} &= 0 \\
\text{vec\_val(n+1,vec)} &= 2^n * \text{Bitval(vec(n))} + \text{vec\_val(n,vec)}
\end{aligned} \tag{12}$$

Here Bitval is the identity function of type bool $\rightarrow$ int.

The adder used in the MAEC is somewhat more sophisticated than the adder presented here. The MAEC's adder does have a rippling-carry, but the Carry_ckt we used produces an inverted carry_out. This saves us from one inversion per full-adder block and thus reduces propagation delay. However, having the carry_out inverted means that every other stage in the adder has to use negative logic. The MAEC's adder thus had to be constructed from pairs of full-adder blocks.

3.3 Boolean Reasoning

Our encoding of boolean logic gives us several methods for reasoning about boolean formulas. We can view boolean formulas as arithmetic expressions and prove them by arithmetic evaluation. We can also reason on the propositional level by refining the propositions that the formulas correspond to. Sometimes, though, we reason somewhere in between, refining a sequent until the conclusion follows by evaluating some small part of it. Let us examine these options in more detail.

If **p** is a closed term, we can invoke Nuprl's evaluator which will normalize **p** down to a ground term: either 0 or 1. When **p** is true it evaluates to 1 and **>> tr(p)** follows immediately. Hence, our encoding permits a reasonably efficient decision procedure for determining the truth of quantified boolean formulas (given the intractable nature of the underlying problem). This decision procedure is sufficient, for example, to prove that any non-inductively specified circuit is equivalent to its arithmetic, gate-level, or transistor-level specification.

When a goal **tr(p)** contains variables bound in the hypothesis list $\mathcal{H}$ rather than the term itself, we prove $\mathcal{H}$ **>> tr(p)** by combining case analysis with evaluation. Specifically, we have proved the following lemma which justifies case analysis on propositional valued boolean functions:

$$\forall P\text{:bool} \to U_1.\, P(\text{tt}) \lor P(\text{ff}) \Rightarrow \forall b\text{: bool}.\, P(b) \tag{13}$$

Now, given a sequent where **b** is bound to **bool** in the hypothesis list and the conclusion is P(b), a (U_1) proposition where **b** occurs free, we can backchain through Equation 13. This results in the two new goals: $\mathcal{H}$ **>>** P(tt) and $\mathcal{H}$ **>>** P(ff). When P(b) is **tr(p)** we can repeat this case analysis until the subgoals are closed terms which can be proved or disproved by evaluation.

We have constructed a number of tactics for combining case-analysis and evaluation. One of our simpler tactics, **BoolCaseEval**, works as described above; it repeatedly (second-order) matches the conclusion against Equation 13 and completes the proof by evaluation. Others, such as **BoolCaseAnalyze**, are stronger and take added measures such as bringing over to the conclusion any hypotheses upon which the truth of the conclusion might depend and unfolding definitions to expose boolean subterms to match against **b** in Equation 13. These tactics have worked well in practice.

As in the case of the MAEC, many combinational circuits are too large to prove by evaluation or case-analysis. Also, when proving behavioral specifications for parameterized hardware blocks such as an n-bit adder, case analysis is impossible. In these situations, we reason directly about properties of the propositions using the correspondence theorems given in Equations 3 through 8. We may use these equations directly as rewrite rules to convert boolean formulas to propositions about booleans. However, in practice we have found it convenient to create tactics that use these equations to implement derived introduction and elimination inference rules for these defined operators. For example, the &-introduction shown in Equation 2 can be recast as

```
>>  tr(P ∧ Q)    By BoolIntro
  >> tr(P)
  >> tr(Q)
```

where the tactic **BoolIntro** backchains through Equation 3 and then applies the propositional **Intro** tactic. This approach of rewriting boolean formulas to propositions allows us to reason at the level of predicate calculus and apply Nuprl's powerful standard tactic collection to the rewritten sequent.

3.4 Tactics

In addition to our tactics that support boolean evaluation, case analysis, and derived boolean inference rules, we have created a number of other special purpose tactics for use in hardware verification. Many of these are built around a general rewrite package. Our rewrite package is similar to Paulson's [13] which provides the basis for rewriting in LCF and HOL. It provides procedures for creating rewrite functions from theorems (such as Equations 3-8) and provides higher-order operators for sequencing and composing rewrites. We have used it to implement a number of term normalizers and simplifiers that operate on boolean, arithmetic, and propositional expressions. These are described in detail elsewhere [2].

The design and application of Nuprl's standard tactic collection is one of the subjects of Howe's thesis [9]. This collection is substantial and includes components that support common forms of inference, arithmetic and other decision procedures, term and sequent manipulation functions, and many other general purpose programs. Many of these tactics find direct use in hardware verification. The most important tactic is **Autotactic**, which is usually applied after refinement steps to prove resultant subgoals. This tactic succeeds in proving subgoals that follow from certain kinds of arithmetic reasoning and has a component which attempts to prove membership goals, i.e., that some term is a member of some type. Such subgoals arise constantly. For example, demonstrating formula well-formedness takes the form of a membership goal. In general, membership is undecidable as it is equivalent to proving that a program meets a specification. However, **Autotactic** usually succeeds in proving well-formedness.

An Example

We conclude this section by returning to the relations **add_1** and **add_n** given in Equations 10 and 11. It is straightforward to prove that these basic low-level relations are equivalent to arithmetic specifications. Once these behavioral specifications are proved, further reasoning about these devices is abstract to their implementation.

That is, it no longer matters whether they were implemented on the transistor or gate level, or how they were specified. Instead, their behavioral specification is used as a rewrite rule that lifts the level of reasoning up to arithmetic.

The behavioral specification for **add_1** is:

>>∀a,b,carry_in,sum,carry_out: bool.
tr(add_1(a,b,carry_in,sum,carry_out)) ⇒
2 * Bitval(carry_out) + Bitval(sum) =
Bitval(a) + Bitval(b) + Bitval(carry_in) in int

This and other theorems for non-recursively specified devices are usually proved directly with **BoolCaseEval**; the single refinement step

(IntroAlls THEN BoolCaseEval ...)

serves as the proof. **IntroAlls** does five ∀-introduction steps. **THEN** is a tactical which applies **BoolCaseEval** to the subgoals produced after the ∀-introductions. The "..." indicates that a definition was invoked that runs **Autotactic** on all unproven subgoals. In this proof, **Autotactic**'s only task is to prove that the theorem statement is well-formed.

Similarly, the behavioral specification for **add_n** is:

>>∀n: N.∀avec, bvec, outvec: vector.∀carry_in, carry_out: bool.
tr(add_n(n+1,avec,bvec,carry_in,outvec,carry_out)) ⇒
2^{n+1} * Bitval(carry_out) + vec_val(n,outvec) =
vec_val(n,avec) + vec_val(n,bvec) + Bitval(carry_in) in int

Correctness proofs for recursively specified circuits require induction. In this example, induction is performed on **n**. The base case is proved automatically by **BoolCaseAnalyze**. The inductive case consists of unfolding the definition of the n-bit adder given in Equation 11. The resulting sequent is then reduced to simple arithmetic reasoning by backchaining through the inductive hypothesis, **add_1**'s behavioral specification, and the definition of **vec_val**. The entire proof takes 9 steps and is presented in [2].

4   MAEC — Case Study

4.1   Introduction

The hardware component that we have verified is known to us as the MAEC (Mantissa Adjuster and Exponent Calculator). The MAEC is the front-end to a floating-point adder/subtractor that will be used in a systolic array FFT processor. Briefly, the function performed by the MAEC is:

1. it inputs the exponents and mantissas for two floating-point numbers,

2. it right-shifts one of the two mantissas so that bits with equal weight are aligned in the two mantissas, and

3. it outputs:

    (a) the mantissa that was shifted,
    (b) the mantissa that was not shifted, and
    (c) the larger of the two exponents.

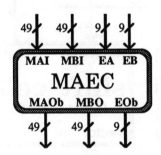

Figure 2: Block Symbol for the MAEC

The inputs to the MAEC are:

$$
\begin{aligned}
\text{MAI} &= \{\text{mai48}, \ldots, \text{mai0}\} \\
\text{MBI} &= \{\text{mbi48}, \ldots, \text{mbi0}\} \\
\text{EA} &= \{\text{ea8}, \ldots, \text{ea0}\} \\
\text{EB} &= \{\text{eb8}, \ldots, \text{eb0}\}
\end{aligned}
$$

The vector **EA** is the exponent for mantissa **MAI**. **EB** is the exponent for mantissa **MBI**.

The outputs from the MAEC are:

$$
\begin{aligned}
\text{MAOb} &= \{\text{mao48b}, \ldots, \text{mao0b}\} \\
\text{MBO} &= \{\text{mbo48}, \ldots, \text{mbo0}\} \\
\text{EOb} &= \{\text{eo8b}, \ldots, \text{eo0b}\}
\end{aligned}
$$

The vector **MAOb** is a shifted and inverted copy of **MAI**[1]. **MBO** is a non-inverted, shifted copy of **MBI**. **EOb** is the inverse of the larger of **EA** and **EB**. Each of the input and output mantissas has 49 bits. The exponents have 9 bits.

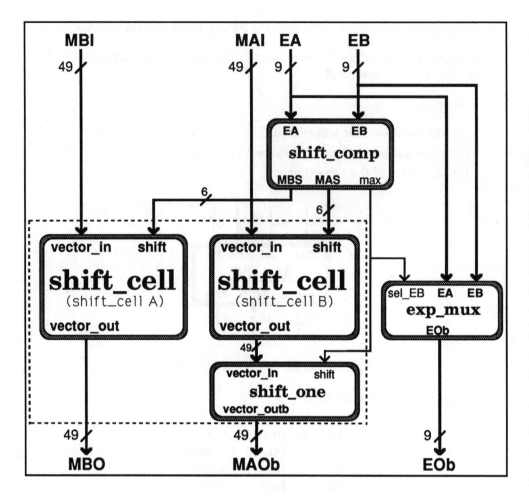

Figure 3: Top-Level Schematic for the MAEC

4.2 MAEC Schematic

As shown in Figure 3, the MAEC has 5 major subcomponents: one shift computer (**shift_comp**), two shifters (**shift_cell A** and **shift_cell B**), one exponent multiplexer (**exp_mux**), and one shift-by-one block (**shift_one**).

The **shift_comp** block inputs the exponents **EA** and **EB**, decides which of the two is larger, and computes the amount that mantissa A (**MAI**) and mantissa B (**MBI**) are to be shifted. The amount that we need to shift mantissa A is output by the **shift_comp** at **MAS**. Similarly, the amount that we need to shift mantissa B is output at **MBS**. The output **max** is high when **vec_val(9,EB)>vec_val(9,EA)**.

---

[1] We use the convention that a lower-case "b" at the end the name of a boolean or vector indicates that the boolean or vector is inverted. Thus, **MAOb** is an inverted vector.

The shift_cells take two bit-vectors as input: vector_in and shift. The output, vector_out, is a copy of vector_in, right-shifted by vec_val(6,shift) positions.

The exponent multiplexer (exp_mux) copies the inverse of either EA or EB to the output EOb. When the input sel_EB is high, the inverse of EB is copied to EOb. When sel_EB is low, the inverse of EA is copied to EOb.

Finally, the shift_one block right-shifts its input, vector_in, by either one or zero positions, depending on the state of shift. When shift is low, vector_outb is simply the inverse of vector_in. When shift is high, vector_in is right-shifted by one position and then inverted to produce vector_outb.

4.3 Behavioral Specification of the MAEC

```
∀  MAI, EA, MBI, EB, MAOb, MBO, EOb:vector.
 MAEC(MAI, EA, MBI, EB, MAOb, MBO, EOb)  =>
  if vec_val(9,EA)≥vec_val(9,EB)

   then ∀ i: {0..8}.  EOb(i)   =¬(EA(i))   in bool    &
        ∀ j: {0..48}. MAOb(j) =¬(MAI(j))  in bool    &
        ∀ k: {0..48}.
            let offset  = vec_val(9,EA)-vec_val(9,EB)          in
            MBO(k)   = ( (k+offset<49) => MBI(k+offset)   | 0 )  in bool
   else ∀ i: {0..8}.  EOb(i)   = ¬(EB(i))  in bool    &
        ∀ j: {0..48}. MBO(j)   =     MBI(j)  in bool    &
        ∀ k: {0..48}.
            let offset = vec_val(9,EB)-vec_val(9,EA)           in
            MAOb(k) = ( (k+offset<49) => ¬(MAI(k+offset)) | 1 )  in bool
```

Figure 4: Behavioral Specification for the MAEC

The behavioral specification the MAEC, as encoded in Nuprl, is shown in Figure 4. This specification tells us that when the value of exponent EA is greater than or equal to the value of exponent EB, then:

1. the output exponent, EOb, is an inverted copy of EA,

2. the output A mantissa, MAOb, is an inverted copy of the input A mantissa, MAI, and

3. the output B mantissa, MBO, is a copy of the input B mantissa, MBI, right-shifted by vec_val(9,EA)−vec_val(9,EB) positions.

When **EB** is greater than **EA**, the situation is analogous.

As can be seen from the description of Figure 4, when right-shifting is done in the MAEC we drop any bits that are right-shifted past bit number zero. Also, non-inverted vectors (e.g., **MBO**) are left-filled with zeros, while inverted vectors (e.g., **MAOb**) are left-filled with ones.

It is interesting to note that the MAEC's behavioral specification is natural and understandable. This results from the flexibility of Nuprl's definition facility and the expressiveness of Nuprl's underlying logic. **If-then-else** constructs are not included in the constructive logic upon which Nuprl is based. Neither are the **let ... in** or (**a ⇒ b | c**) forms. However, since Nuprl lets the user custom-define how propositions are displayed, we were able to use very natural constructs to form the goals in our hardware proofs.

4.4 Proof of the MAEC in Nuprl

4.4.1 Introduction

In the following section we will try to give the reader a feel for the capabilities of the Nuprl hardware environment by presenting the behavioral descriptions that were developed and proven for each of the main subcomponents of the MAEC. We will also present sample proof steps which illustrate some of the tactics that have been developed.

The first subcomponent that we will consider is the **shift_cell**. This was proven as a specific case of a general, parameterized linear shifter called the **shifter**.

The next component we'll look at is the **shift_one**. This cell was constructed and proven as a specific case of one of the subcomponents of the **shifter**.

Following the **shift_one** we'll look at the **shift_comp**. This cell was perhaps the most interesting component of the MAEC to prove because it is constructed from blocks that were defined in very different manners (parameterized/non-parameterized and recursively/non-recursively). Also, since this cell performs an arithmetic function, a good deal of arithmetic reasoning was needed in its proof.

Finally, the last cell we'll look at is the **exp_mux**. The **exp_mux** is a simple cell — it contains only one string of multiplexers. The proof of the **exp_mux**'s behavioral specification was thus concise and straightforward.

4.4.2 The shift_cell

The **shift_cell** is a linear shifter that takes as input one 49-bit vector named **vector_in**, and one 6-bit vector named **shift**. The output, **vector_out**, is a copy of **vector_in**, right-shifted by vec_val(6,shift) positions. Like vector_in, vector_out has 49 bits.

```
∀ vector_in, shift, vector_out:vector.
   shift_cell(vector_in, shift, vector_out) =>
    ∀ i:{0..48}.
      let index = i+vec_val(6,shift) in
      vector_out(i) = ( (index<49) => vector_in(index) | 0 ) in bool
```

Figure 5: Behavioral Specification of the shift_cell

The behavioral specification for the shift_cell is given in Figure 5. The proof of this specification is interesting for two reasons: first because we have shown that the shift_cell used in the layout of the MAEC is logically correct, and second because the shift_cell is merely a specific case of a more general hardware block that was proven in Nuprl called the shifter.

The shifter is a general-purpose vector shifter that is parameterized by:

1. the number of bits in the vector that is to be shifted, and
2. the number of "shift blocks" that it contains.

The "shift blocks" are subcomponents of the shifter that, when activated, shift their input by some integral power of 2 positions. A shifter composed of n shift blocks will have blocks that shift by 2^0 positions, 2^1 positions, 2^2 positions, and so on up to 2^{n-1} positions. Thus, by turning its subcomponents on and off, a shifter with n blocks can implement any shift between 0 and $\sum_{i=0}^{n-1} 2^i = 2^n - 1$ positions. The structure of the shifter is defined recursively as follows:

```
shifter(0, num_bits, vector_in, shift, vector_out) =
         shift_block_pair(num_bits, 1, vector_in, shift(1), shift(0), vector_out)
shifter(num_blk_pairs, num_bits, vector_in, shift, vector_out) =
         ∃ mid_vec:vector.
            shift_block_pair(num_bits, -1+2*num_blk_pairs, vector_in,
                shift(-1+2*num_blk_pairs),shift(2*(num_blk_pairs-1)), vector_out) &
            shifter(num_blk_pairs-1, num_bits, mid_vec, shift, vector_out)
```

The cell shift_block_pair used in the above definition of the shifter contains one pair of shift blocks. The first parameter for this cell (given the value num_bits above) specifies the number of bits in the vector that is to be shifted. The second parameter (assigned the value 1 for the base case of the shifter, and 2*num_blk_pairs for the inductive case) is the $\log_2$ of the number of positions that the upper shift block in the pair shifts its input. The lower block shifts by $2^{2*num\_blk\_pairs-1}$ positions.

The behavioral specification that was proven for the shifter is:

>> ∀ num_bits:{i:Int|3≤i}. ∀ num_blk_pairs:{j:Int|0<j & 2^(2*j-1)<num_bits}.   (14)
    ∀ vector_in, shift, vector_out:vector.
      shifter(num_blk_pairs, num_bits, vector_in, shift, vector_out) ⇒
        ∀ i:{0..num_bits-1}.
          let index = i+vec_val(2*num_blk_pairs,shift) in
          vector_out(i) = ((index<num_bits) ⇒vector_in(index) | 0) in bool

This specification tells us that **vector_out** is a copy of **vector_in**, right-shifted by vec_val(2*num_blk_pairs, shift) positions.

By comparison with Figure 5, we can see that the **shift_cell** is indeed just a specific case of the **shifter**: shift_cell(vector_in, shift, vector_out) performs the same function as shifter(49, 3, vector_in, shift, vector_out). In fact, in our proof of the MAEC, a shifter(49, 3, ...) was used whenever a shift_cell(...) was needed.

As our first example of a proof in Nuprl, we will discuss briefly how the **shifter** was proven. Since the structure of the **shifter** is defined recursively, an inductive proof was required, where we induct on the variable **num_blk_pairs**. In the base case we have only one pair of shift blocks, i.e., one **shift_block_pair**. This case was proven by expanding the definitions of **shifter** and **vec_val**, and then instantiating the following lemma that was proven for the **shift_block_pair** cell:

>> ∀ num_bits:N+. ∀ shift_power:{j:Int|0<j & 2^j<num_bits}.   (15)
    ∀ vector_in:vector. ∀ shift1,shift0:bool. ∀ vector_out:vector.
      shifter_block(num_bits, shift_power, vector_in, shift1, shift0, vector_out) ⇒
        ∀ i:{0..num_bits-1}.
          let index = i + 2^n*shift1 + 2^(n-1)*shift0
          vector_out(i) = ((index < num_bits) ⇒vector_in(index) | 0) in bool

This lemma tells us that the **shift_block_pair** cell will right-shift **vector_in** by 2^n*shift1 + 2^{n-1}*shift0 positions to produce **vector_out**.

The inductive case of the proof was done by unrolling the shifter(num_blk_pairs, ...) into a shifter(num_blk_pairs-1,...) and a shift_blk_pair, instantiating (15) above, and then forward-chaining through the inductive hypothesis. The step in which the unrolling was done is interesting because it is a good example of both rewriting and arithmetic reasoning in Nuprl. The section of the proof relevant to this step is reproduced in Figure 6.

At the top of Figure 6 we have the initial set of hypotheses and the goal to be proven. In the middle we have the tactic that is being executed: (**RewriteHyp ShifterUnroll 10...tmono**). On the bottom we have the hypotheses that were changed and the new goal. (Here only hypothesis number ten changed.)

```
1. bits:{i:Int|i≥3}
2. blk_pairs:int
3. 1<blk_pairs
 ⋮ {omitted hypotheses}
10. shifter(bits, blk_pairs, vector_in, shift, vector_out)
>> let index = i+ vec_val(2*blk_pairs, shift) in
     vector_out(i) = ( index<bits => vector_in(index) | 0 )

BY (RewriteHyp ShifterUnroll 10...tmono)

10. ∃ mid_vec:vector.
     shifter_block_pair(bits, blk_pairs-1, vector_in,
          shift(-1+2*blk_pairs), shift(-2+2*blk_pairs), mid_vec) &
     shifter(bits, blk_pairs-1, mid_vec, shift, vector_out)
>> let index = i+ vec_val(2*blk_pairs, shift) in
     vector_out(i) = ( index<bits => vector_in(index) | 0 )
```

Figure 6: Snapshot of a Rewrite Step in the Proof of the **shifter**

The rewrite that was used in Figure 6, **ShifterUnroll**, was created from a shifter-unrolling theorem which proves that an unrolling is always valid when **num_blk_pairs**>1. The "...tmono" in the refinement rule in Figure 6 indicates that Nuprl's **Autotactic** was run after the unrolling was finished, and that the tactic **MonoTac** was run on any monotonicity goals that arose. **MonoTac** is a general-purpose tactic that proves most of the monotonicity goals that arise in our hardware proofs. In this case, the following two monotonicity goals arose:

1. num_blk_pairs:Int, 1<num_blk_pairs >> 2*num_blk_pairs-1$\geq$0
2. j:Int, 0<j >> 2*j-1$\geq$0

In 2. above, **j** is an arbitrary integer. These goals came up because, as we see in (14), we must to prove that **num_blk_pairs** is within the set {j:Int|0<j & 2^(2*j-1)<num_bits}. Both of these monotonicity goals were proven automatically by **MonoTac**.

4.4.3 The shift_one

The **shift_one** cell has two inputs: one vector, 49-bits long named **vector_in**, and one boolean named **shift**. When **shift** is high, **vector_in** is right-shifted by one position and inverted to produce the **shift_one**'s output, **vector_outb**. Like **vector_in**, **vector_out** has 49 bits. When **shift** is low, **vector_outb** is simply an inverted copy of **vector_in**. The behavior of the **shift_one**, as encoded in Nuprl, is given in Figure 7.

Since the **shifter** that was used to construct the **shift_cell** is composed of blocks which shift their input by 2^n positions, where **n** is any natural number, we were able

```
∀ vector_in:vector. ∀ shift:bool. ∀ vector_outb:vector.
  shift_one(vector_in, shift, vector_outb) =>
    ∀ i:{0..48}.
      let index = i+shift in
      vector_outb(i) = ( (index<49) => ¬(vector_in(index)) | 1 ) in bool
```

Figure 7: Behavioral Specification for the shift_one

to implement the shift_one cell by using one of these same shift blocks, setting n equal to zero. The block that we used is named the two_to_n_bit_shifter. The behavioral specification of the two_to_n_bit_shifter appears in Figure 8. As can be seen from this specification, the two_to_n_bit_shifter is parameterized by the number of bits in the input vector (num_bits) and the $\log_2$ of the number of positions that the block will shift (n). Thus, the shift_one cell is just a two_to_n_bit_shifter with num_bits=49 and n=0.

```
∀ bits:N+. ∀ n:{i:Int|0≤i & 2^i<bits}.
  ∀ a:vector. ∀ shift:bool. ∀ yb:vector.
    two_to_n_bit_shifter(bits, n, a, shift, yb) =>
      ∀i:{0..bits-1}.
        let index = i+2^n*shift in
        yb(i) = ( (index<bits) => ¬(a(index)) | 1 ) in bool
```

Figure 8: Behavioral Specification for the two_to_n_bit_shifter

Verifying the shift_one consisted of instantiating num_bits and n in the proven behavioral specification of the two_to_n_bit_shifter. The proof of the two_to_n_bit_shifter was accomplished by doing a case split on the variable shift, substituting shift into the boolean logic specifications of the multiplexers that make up the two_to_n_bit_shifter, and then using a rewrite tactic called BoolSimp to reduce the resulting expressions. An example of BoolSimp in action is shown in Figure 9. In this figure, our intent is to simplify the expressions shown after the "⟷" signs shown in hypotheses 7 and 8. BoolSimp simplifies these expressions to those in the new hypotheses 7 and 8 (at the bottom of the figure).

4.4.4 The shift_comp

The shift_comp has two responsibilities:

1. it computes the amount to shift the two mantissas which are input to the MAEC and

2. it determines what the MAEC's output exponent will be.

```
⋮ {omitted hypothses}
6. i:{0..bits-1}
7. ∀ x.{0.._bits-(2^n)-1}. vector_outb(x) ⇔ (ff∧¬(vector_in(x+2^n))) ∨
     (¬(ff)∧¬(vector_in(x)))
8. ∀ y.{bits-2^n..bits-1}. vector_outb(y) ⇔ (¬(ff)∧¬(vector_in(x))) ∨ ¬(¬(ff))
>> vector_outb(i) = ¬(vector_in(i)) in bool

BY (BoolSimpHyp 8...) THEN (BoolSimpHyp 7...)

7. ∀ x.{0..bits-(2^n)-1}. vector_outb(x) ⇔ ¬(vector_in(x))
8. ∀ y.{bits-2^n..bits-1}. vector_outb(y) ⇔ ¬(vector_in(y))
>> vector_outb(i) = ¬(vector_in(i)) in bool
```

Figure 9: Example of the **BoolSimp** Tactic

This block has two inputs — the 9-bit vectors **EA** and **EB** — and has 3 outputs — two 6-bit vectors named **MAS** and **MBS**, and one boolean named **max**. **EA** is the exponent for mantissa A (**MAI**); **EB** is the exponent for mantissa B (**MBI**). The value of **MBS**, i.e., **vec_val(6,MBS)**, is the amount that mantissa B must be shifted. Mantissa A must be shifted by **vec_val(6,MAS)+1** positions. The output **max** (Mantissa A eXtra) is a flag that goes high when the shift for mantissa A is non-zero. (Equivalently, it goes high when **EA<EB**.) The **vec_val(6,MAS)** part of mantissa A's shift is implemented by **shift_cell** A. The extra "+1" is implemented by the **shift_one** cell.

```
∀ EA,EB,MAS,MBS:vector. ∀ max:bool.
  if shift_comp(EA,EB,MAS,MBS,max)
    then if vec_val(9,EA)≥vec_val(9,EB)
      then
        vec_val(6,MAS)=0 in N &
        max=0 in bool &
        if (shift_needed_for_mantissa_B(9,EA,EB) > max_shift_for_n_shift_blocks(6))
          then (vec_val(6,MBS) > shift_needed_to_zero_mantissa(49))
          else (vec_val(6,MBS) = shift_needed_for_mantissa_B(9,EA,EB) in Int)
      else
        vec_val(6,MBS)=0 in N &
        max=1 in bool &
        if (shift_needed_for_mantissa_A(9,EA,EB)-1 > max_shift_for_n_shift_blocks(6))
          then (vec_val(6,MAS) > shift_needed_to_zero_mantissa(49))
          else (vec_val(6,MAS) = shift_needed_for_mantissa_A(9,EA,EB)-1 in Int)
```

Figure 10: Behavioral Specification of the **shift_comp**

The behavioral specification for the **shift_comp** is given in Figure 10. Before we can fully understand this specification, we must first define the following functions which are used therein:

$$\text{shift\_needed\_for\_mantissa\_A(n, EA, EB),}$$
$$\text{shift\_needed\_for\_mantissa\_B(n, EA, EB),}$$
$$\text{max\_shift\_for\_n\_shift\_blocks(n), and}$$
$$\text{shift\_needed\_to\_zero\_mantissa(n).}$$

The function **shift_needed_for_mantissa_A**, as its name implies, returns the amount of shift needed for mantissa A. By definition, mantissa A must be right-shifted by 0 positions if $EA \geq EB$, and $EB-EA$ positions otherwise. So, by definition:

shift_for_mantissa_A(n, EA, EB) $\equiv$

$$\begin{cases} 0 & \text{if vec\_val(n,EA)} \geq \text{vec\_val(n,EB)} \\ \text{vec\_val(n,EB)-vec\_val(n,EA)} & \text{otherwise} \end{cases}$$

shift_needed_for_mantissa_B is analogous:

shift_for_mantissa_B(n, EA, EB) $\equiv$

$$\begin{cases} \text{vec\_val(n,EA)-vec\_val(n,EB)} & \text{if vec\_val(n,EB)} \geq \text{vec\_val(n,EA)} \\ 0 & \text{otherwise} \end{cases}$$

The function **max_shift_for_n_shift_blocks(n)** inputs a natural number, n, and returns the maximum amount of shift that n shift blocks can produce. As discussed in the **shift_cell** section of this paper, assuming that the blocks shift by 2^0, 2^1, ..., 2^{n-1} positions respectively, the maximum shift is 2^n-1 positions.

Finally, the function **shift_needed_to_zero_mantissa(n)** tells us how many positions we must right-shift a vector of length n before all of the bits in the vector become left-filled with zeros. This function is the identity function — if you right-shift an n-bit vector by n positions while left filling with zeros, the vector will be completely zeroed.

Now that we have defined all of the functions that are used in the specification of the **shift_comp**, we can interpret what the specification is telling us. For the condition that $EA \geq EB$:

1. **MAS**, the vector that tells **shift_cell A** how much to shift mantissa A, is zero,

2. **max**, the Mantissa A eXtra flag, is zero,

3. if the shift needed for mantissa B is greater than the maximum amount that a **shift_cell** can implement, then **MBS** is set to a value that will cause **shift_cell B** to zero mantissa B, and

4. if the shift needed for mantissa B is less than or equal to the maximum amount that a **shift_cell** can implement, then **MBS** is equal to the amount that we want to shift mantissa B.

For the condition that **EA<EB**, the situation is analogous.

The proof of the **shift_comp** is interesting because it combines many different styles of reasoning. The subcomponents of the **shift_comp** — a ripple-carry adder, a pair of multiplexers, and an "overflow" detector — were defined in very different manners and thus required different styles of proof. Also, since this cell performs an arithmetic function, a good deal of arithmetic reasoning was required in its proof.

The adder, for example, was parameterized by the number of bits in the input vectors and was defined recursively. The proof of this block required the use of induction and arithmetic reasoning.

The pair of multiplexers in the **shift_comp** is named the **shift_mux**. This cell is responsible for sending either zero or **shift_needed_for_mantissa_A−1** into **MAS**, and either zero or **shift_needed_for_mantissa_B** into **MBS**. This cell is constructed from basic multiplexer cells which are grouped into two separate strings. Each string is constructed by universally quantifying over the bits in the input and output vectors. For example, the multiplexer-string used for the **MAS** vector is represented by

$$\forall x[0..5].\text{smuxc}(\text{MASIb}(x),\text{A\_select},\text{MAS}(x)).$$

If **A_select** is high, the cell **smuxc** sends the inverse of **MASIb(x)**, an internal signal, to **MAS(x)**. If **A_select** is low, **MAS(x)** is set equal to zero. Due to the non-recursive structure of the **shift_mux**, no unrolling or induction was necessary in its proof — the proof consisted mainly of expanding cell definitions, case splits, substitutions, and boolean simplifications.

The **shift_comp**'s **overflow_detector** is a specific, non-parameterized component designed specifically to deal with the MAEC's 49-bit mantissas and 9-bit exponents. It was not, therefore, defined using recursion or universal quantification, but rather as a flat circuit, with all of its components on one level. Because of its "flatness", this block was verified through rewriting boolean equations and case analysis.

Finally, at the top level of the **shift_comp**'s proof (the point where we glued together the subcomponents), somewhat sophisticated arithmetic reasoning was needed. For example, this cell computes either **EA−EB** or **EB−EA**, whichever is positive. The **shift_comp** computes only **EA−EB**. This is the subtraction needed when **EA≥EB**. If it turns out that **EA−EB** is negative, then **EA≱EB** and we actually wanted to compute **EB−EA**. Rather than now calculating **EB−EA** directly, the **shift_comp** simply inverts the result of (**EA−EB**) and uses the property, which we proved, that if **EB>EA** then (**EB−EA**) = ¬(**EA−EB**) + 1. Thus, the **shift_comp** calculates either **EA−EB** when **EA≥EB**, or **EB−EA−1** when **EA<EB**.

Another complication in this proof stems from the fact that in the shift_comp, as in most hardware subtractors, subtraction is implemented by adding the inverse of the subtrahend to the minuend. Since the functions shift_needed_for_mantissa_A and shift_needed_for_mantissa_B were defined in terms of subtraction and not inverted addition, we had to prove that one's complement subtraction is valid.

4.4.5 The exp_mux

The exp_mux has three inputs: the two 9-bit exponents EA and EB, and one boolean named sel_EB. This cell performs a very simple function — when sel_EB is high, the inverse of EB is output at EOb; when sel_EB is low, the inverse of EA is copied to EOb. The behavioral specification for the exp_mux is given in Figure 11. Since the exp_mux is such a simple cell, its proof was also very simple. The complete proof consisted only of the following steps (each of these steps corresponds directly to a tactic used in the proof):

1. introducing the universally quantified variables,

2. performing a case split on the boolean variable shift,

3. expanding the exp_mux down to quantified boolean logic equations,

4. substituting the value of shift into the logic equations,

5. performing a boolean simplification on the equations,

6. performing an elimination, and

7. rewriting a boolean iff into an equality (i.e., transforming an expression of the form a⇔b into a=b in bool).

Total time to define the structure of the exp_mux and to create and prove the behavioral specification: approximately 45 minutes.

$$
\begin{array}{l}
\forall \text{ EA,EB:vector. } \forall \text{ easb:bool. } \forall \text{ EOb:vector.} \\
\quad \text{exp\_mux(EA,EB,easb,EOb)} => \\
\quad\quad \text{if easb=tt in bool} \\
\quad\quad\quad \text{then} \forall \text{ i:\{0..8\}. EOb(i)=}\neg\text{(EB(i)) in bool} \\
\quad\quad\quad \text{else} \forall \text{ j:\{0..8\}. EOb(j)=}\neg\text{(EA(j)) in bool}
\end{array}
$$

Figure 11: Behavioral Specification for the exp_mux

4.4.6 The MAEC

The behavioral specification of the MAEC was presented in Section 1.4.3. The structural specification is:

```
MAEC (MAI, EA, MBI, EB, MAOb, MBO, EOb) =
    ∀ MAS, MBS:vector. ∀ max:bool.
        shift_comp(EA, EB, MAS, MBS, max)  &  exp_mux(EA, EB, max, EOb)  &
        shift_cell(MBI, MBS, MBO)  &
        ∃ temp:vector.
            shift_cell(MAI, MAS, temp)  &  shift_one(temp, max, MAOb)
```

The proof of the MAEC's behavioral specification was quite straightforward. Once the predicate logic specifications of its subcomponents were verified, the proof of the MAEC consisted mainly of instantiating the theorems developed for the subcomponents, performing case splits, introductions, eliminations, arithmetic simplifications, and substitutions.

5 Conclusion

The specification and verification of the MAEC took approximately three man-months. The final library contains approximately 500 objects, 154 of which are theorems, the remainder definitions. Most of the time was spent building preliminaries such as the basic hardware tactic collection, theories for reasoning about bit-vectors, theorems and tactics centered around monotonicity reasoning, and extensions to our rewrite package.

Almost all of the MAEC was built from parameterized subcomponents or components that could easily be generalized. The proof of the MAEC's behavioral specification combined the behavioral specifications of its components in a straight-forward way. This gives us some confidence that we can attain our goal of building a floating-point tool kit where users can build customized floating-point circuits from components that come with proven behavioral specifications. The library we have built is a large step in that direction.

Our effort was the first application of Nuprl to hardware verification. On the whole we are pleased with the results. One of the authors (DelVecchio) had created a behavioral specification for the MAEC in predicate calculus before he knew Nuprl. Due to the expressiveness of Nuprl's logic and its flexible definition facility, the behavioral specification of the MAEC in Nuprl (Figure 4) is essentially identical to his original predicate calculus specification. Another extremely useful feature of Nuprl is its computation system. All terms in Nuprl can be evaluated. In particular closed quantified boolean formulas evaluate to true or false. This property gives us a decision procedure for verifying non-inductively specified devices. If we had to rely on some alternative procedure, such as one based on rewriting, execution would be many orders of magnitude slower. Finally, Nuprl's tree-structured proof editor helps manage the complexity of editing large proofs. Proofs are retained by the system and can be viewed and modified at a later date. Moreover, sections of proofs can be saved and re-executed on different sequents. This ability to mark and copy proofs saved us much effort in reproving theorems after making minor changes to definitions and theorem statements. It also found repeated use as a simple analogy tactic.

There is, of course, room for improvement. On the system side, a major bottleneck is well-formedness reasoning. As previously mentioned Nuprl propositions must be proved well-formed and in general this is recursively undecidable. However, the well-formedness of the propositions that are used to specify device structures and and their behaviors is decidable; **Autotactic** will always succeed in constructing the appropriate well-formedness proof. However, this is time consuming; a single rewrite step can generate dozens of well-formedness goals. Several solutions to this problem are under consideration. The simplest is a scheme to cache well-formedness proofs.

Another area for future work is improving our tactic collection. Heuristics to automate induction similar to those used by Boyer and Moore [4] would be tremendously valuable. Arithmetic and equality reasoning is still time consuming and tactics for algorithms such as congruence closure could offer much assistance. Such reasoning is especially tedious when it involves division and remainders. There are plans to build up a library of basic number theory facts and related tactics.

Acknowledgements

The authors wish to thank Professors Miriam Leeser and Geoffrey Brown for discussions and careful proof-reading of this document. Also, DelVecchio gives special thanks to Suzanne Nobrega for her inspiration in this effort.

References

[1] G. Barrett. Formal methods applied to a floating point number system. *IEEE Transactions on Software Engineering*, 15(5):611–621, May 1989.

[2] David A. Basin. *Implementing Problem Solving Environments In Constructive Type Theory*. PhD thesis, Cornell University, 1990. To appear.

[3] David A. Basin. Building theories in Nuprl. In *Logic At Botik, '89*, 1989. To Appear.

[4] Robert S. Boyer and J. Strother Moore. *A Computational Logic*. Academic Press, 1979.

[5] A. J. Camillieri, M. J. C. Gordon, and T. F. Melham. Hardware verification using higher-order logic. In D. Borrione, editor, *From HDL Descriptions to Guaranteed Correct Circuit Designs*. North Holland, September 1986.

[6] A. Cohn. A proof of correctness of the VIPER microprocessor: The first level. In G. Birtwistle and P.A. Subrahmanyam, editors, *VLSI Specification, Verification, and Synthesis*, pages 27–72. Kluwer, 1988.

[7] R.L. Constable et al. *Implementing Mathematics with the Nuprl Proof Development System*. Prentice Hall, 1986.

[8] Michael J. Gordon, Robin Milner, and Christopher P. Wadsworth. *Edinburgh LCF: A Mechanized Logic of Computation*, volume 78 of *Lecture Notes in Computer Science*. Springer-Verlag, 1979.

[9] Douglas J. Howe. *Automating Reasoning in an Implementation of Constructive Type Theory*. PhD thesis, Cornell University, 1988.

[10] Warren J. Hunt. The mechanical verification of a microprocessor design. In D. Borrione, editor, *From HDL Descriptions to Guaranteed Correct Circuit Designs*, pages 89–129. Elsevier Science Publishers B. V. (North-Holland), 1987.

[11] INMOS. T800 architecture. INMOS Technical note 6.

[12] Per Martin-Löf. Constructive mathematics and computer programming. In *Sixth International Congress for Logic, Methodology, and Philosophy of Science*, pages 153–175, Amsterdam, 1982. North Holland.

[13] Lawrence C. Paulson. A higher-order implementation of rewriting. *Science of Computer Programming*, 3:119–149, 1983.

VERITAS+: A SPECIFICATION LANGUAGE BASED ON TYPE THEORY

F K Hanna, N Daeche and M Longley

Keywords   Specification languages, Type theory, Formal verification.

Abstract   A specification language, VERITAS+, based on type theory, is proposed as being an ideal notation for specifying and reasoning about digital systems. The development, within VERITAS+, of a formal theory of arithmetic and numerals is outlined and its application to the specification, at differing levels of abstraction, of arithmetic devices is illustrated. A significant theorem is established within this theory that describes the relationship between specifications and iterative implementations of arithmetic functions and thus provides a general approach to the synthesis and formal verification of arithmetic circuits.

A brief account is given of the computational implementation of the VERITAS+ logic.

1 Introduction

The features that an ideal specification language, intended for supporting the formal verification of digital systems, should possess include expressiveness, generality, naturalness, inferential power, credibility and ease of implementation.

- The language should be sufficiently *expressive* to capture not just descriptions of digital systems, but also descriptions of a large part of mathematics, since the latter will be required in reasoning about the former.

- The language should allow specifications to be written in a very *generic* way, so that a single specification can cover many instances.

- The language should allow specifications to be expressed in as *direct and natural* way as possible, so as to allow the intuitive concepts and informal modes of reasoning of the digital engineer to be easily related to their formal counterparts.

- The inferential calculus associated with the specification language should be as *powerful* as possible, so as to allow as much as possible of what is true to be formally deduced.

- The specification language should be *credible* in the sense that it has a well-established mathematical pedigree; there must be no room for doubt about the soundness of the associated inferential calculus.

- The specification language and its logic should be amenable to efficient *computational implementation* in a way which demonstrably preserves the soundness of the underlying mathematical formalism.

1.1 The VERITAS⁺ specification language

In this paper we describe a specification language, VERITAS⁺, that we believe comes close to satisfying the criteria outlined above. It is a hybrid of a conventional higher-order logic and Martin-Löf's INTUITIONISTIC TYPE THEORY (ITT) [ML84]. Its name reflects the fact that it is a further development of an earlier polymorphic higher-order logic, VERITAS, that was developed for formal verification of digital systems [H83, HD86a]. The main features of VERITAS⁺ are:

- It is an extension of a classical (ie, non-constructive) typed higher-order logic. Unlike ordinary typed logics, however, it allows the types to be manipulated in the same way as ordinary terms.

- It includes a *datatype* construction that allows both simple enumerated types (eg, *colour* = *R* | *G* | *B*) or recursive types (eg, *nat* = *0* | *suc nat*) to be introduced, and a construction that allow functions to be defined on such types by primitive recursion.

- It includes *dependent types* (the Π and Σ types from ITT, a generalisation of the function space (→) and cartesian product (×) operators of ordinary typed languages) that allow very *fine* type distinctions to be made and allow polymorphism to be encompassed.

- It allows *subtypes* to be defined (for example, *bit*, a subtype of *nat*). Combined with datatypes, this also allows *non-free* algebraic types (for example, the integers) to be defined.

- It exploits the 'Propositions as Types' principle; that is, it treats *derivations* (or proofs) in a similar way to terms (this results in a considerable conceptual economy).

- Metalinguistically, the overall logic appears as a *partial, many-sorted algebra* [HD86b, HD88]. The logic is thus a relatively simple and well-founded mathematical entity in its own right.

- It is computationally implemented in a EDINBURGH LCF-like fashion [GMW79]. This means that the associated computational tools (including parsers, unparsers and interactive proof editors) used for manipulating the logic cannot compromise its soundness.

Contents   In the remainder of this paper, we cover three main topics. Firstly, we give a tutorial overview of VERITAS⁺ by illustrating how the theories of elementary arithmetic and of the positional system of numeration may be defined, and then how, within these theories, the specification of a typical digital device may be expressed.

Secondly, and with the motivation of demonstrating the advantages gained by the use of type theory, we describe the formulation and proof (in VERITAS⁺) of the 'Factorisation Principle', a theorem that allows the correctness of a wide class of iteratively defined arithmetic circuits for arbitrary length words comprising digits of an arbitrary base (or possibly, sequence of bases) to be established simply by showing that the underlying arithmetic function possesses a simple property.

Thirdly, we give a brief overview of the metalinguistic techniques used to define VERITAS⁺ and briefly describe the computational implementation of the logic and its associated toolset.

2 A Theory for Reasoning about Digital Systems

In this section, we will outline the development of a theory suitable for describing and reasoning about digital systems at the 'binary arithmetic' level of abstraction. The concepts introduced in this section are not, of course, new; what is, we believe, new is the clarity and precision with which VERITAS⁺ allow them to be defined. The description is in two parts: first, the development of elementary number theory, and then, the development of a theory of numerals.

Throughout this account, the syntax used is, with only minor exceptions, the syntax used by the computational implementation of the system.

2.1 Number theory

We begin by introducing the type *nat* of natural numbers $\{0, 1, 2, \ldots\}$. This type is defined as a *recursive datatype*:

datatype $nat = 0 \mid suc\ nat$

This specifies that *nat* is defined inductively from two *constructors* (the constant 0, and the *successor* function $suc: nat \rightarrow nat$). Given this datatype definition, we can start to introduce definitions over *nat*, as for example

$$1 \stackrel{\wedge}{=} suc\ 0; \qquad 2 \stackrel{\wedge}{=} suc\ 1 \qquad \text{etc.}$$

Functions over datatypes may be defined using **case** expressions. For example, *addition* may be defined by

$$\{plus\ +\} \stackrel{\wedge}{=} \lambda n, m: nat.$$
$$\text{case } m \text{ of}$$
$$0 \mapsto n \mid$$
$$suc\ i \mapsto suc\ (\textbf{rec } i)$$
$$\textbf{endcase}: nat$$

This introduces and defines a new symbol, *plus* (or, in operator form, $+$), giving it the type $nat \times nat \rightarrow nat$. In order to shorten such definitions, we will in future omit the type information and present them in the abbreviated form

$$n + m \stackrel{\wedge}{=} \text{case } m \text{ of } 0 \mapsto n \mid suc\ i \mapsto suc\ (\textbf{rec } i) \textbf{ endcase}$$

This definition states that the value of $n + 0$ is n, and that the value of $n + suc\ i$ is the successor of the value of this same case expression **recursively** evaluated with i replacing the m in the discriminant (that is, the subterm **rec** i stands for **case** i **of** ...).

The above definition will be recognised as being a *primitive recursive* one; VERITAS$^+$ allows such definitions over any datatype. The advantage of being able to define functions in this way (as distinct from by introducing axioms that assert their properties) is that it allows theories to be entirely *definitional*, and thus guarantees their consistency.

The rules of inference of the logic allow **case** expressions to be used for case-analysis, and they allow the **rec** components of such statements to be unfolded. From the two main definitions introduced so far, all of the elementary properties of the natural numbers can be deduced including, for example, Peano's axioms and the commutativity and associativity of addition.

Here are some further examples of definition by primitive recursion. First, the *predecessor* function (ie, the left-inverse of suc) is:

$$pred\ n\ \triangleq\ \textbf{case } n \textbf{ of } 0 \mapsto 0 \mid suc\ i \mapsto i\ \textbf{endcase}$$

The *proper subtraction* function (a version of integer subtraction which yields 0 in place of negative integers, so that, for example $5 \overset{\cdot}{-} 3 = 2$ but $3 \overset{\cdot}{-} 5 = 0$) is:

$$n \overset{\cdot}{-} m\ \triangleq\ \textbf{case } m \textbf{ of }\ 0 \mapsto n \mid suc\ i \mapsto pred\ (\textbf{rec } i)\ \textbf{endcase}$$

The multiplication and exponentiation functions are:

$$n \times m\ \triangleq\ \textbf{case } m \textbf{ of }\ 0 \mapsto 0 \mid suc\ i \mapsto n + (\textbf{rec } i)\ \textbf{endcase} \qquad \text{and}$$

$$n \uparrow m\ \triangleq\ \textbf{case } m \textbf{ of }\ 0 \mapsto 1 \mid suc\ i \mapsto n \times (\textbf{rec } i)\ \textbf{endcase}$$

The usual ordering operators on nat are easily defined in terms of proper subtraction; for example $n \geq m\ \triangleq\ (m \overset{\cdot}{-} n = 0)$.

Subtypes   A *subtype* of a type may be defined by specifying the characteristic predicate of the subtype. For example, the subtype consisting of the positive natural numbers, nat^+, may be defined as:

$$nat^+\ \triangleq\ \{n: nat \mid n > 0\}$$

There are two inference rules associated with subtypes. One, used to inject a term into a subtype, takes a theorem asserting that the term satisfies the characteristic predicate of the subtype; the other, given an element of a subtype, yields the theorem asserting that the term satisfies the characteristic predicate.

An important example of subtype construction is presented by

$$N\ \triangleq\ \lambda n: nat.\ \{m: nat \mid m < n\}$$

Here, N is a *type-constructing* function; it takes a number n and specifies a subtype corresponding to the subrange $0\ ..\ (n-1)$. For example, the subtype *bit* can be defined as $bit\ \triangleq\ N\ 2$. The type of N itself is $nat \rightarrow I\!\!P\ nat$; that is, it maps from nat to the powerset of nat.

Dependent types   Dependent types [ML84] are generalisations of the ordinary '$\times$' and '$\rightarrow$' types which allow the *type* of a term to depend upon the *value* of its component subterms. Dependent types allow *finer* type distinctions to be made than do ordinary types, and thus they are invaluable in writing clear and concise specifications.

A good illustration of dependent types is provided by the *mod* function (that yields the remainder when one number is divided by another non-zero one). It *could* be given the ordinary (ie, non-dependent) type

$$mod: nat \times nat^+ \to nat$$

However, we know that an application of this function will always yield a number belonging to the subtype $N\ m$, where m is the value of the divisor. This useful information can be captured by giving *mod* instead the finer, dependent type:

$$mod: [n: nat;\ m: nat^+] \to N\ m$$

(Read as: "*mod* is a function that takes a pair of arguments, n of type *nat* and m of type nat^+, and yields a result of type $N\ m$.") For example, the type of the term $x\ mod\ 2$ is $N\ 2$, and thus, from its type alone, it may be inferred that the value of the term is 0 or 1.

We shall be using both the *mod* and the closely related *div* functions extensively in this paper. It turns out that, rather than define them separately, it is better to pair the two functions together, forming one function which we shall name *divide* (or, as an operator, $//$), of type

$$\{divide\ //\}: [n: nat;\ m: nat^+] \to nat \times N\ m$$

defined so that the value of $a//b$ is a pair consisting of the quotient and the remainder (for example, $23//6\ =\ 3, 5$). The definition of this function is an interesting one:

$$
\begin{aligned}
n//m\ &\overset{\wedge}{=}\ \textbf{case } n \textbf{ of}\\
&\quad 0 \mapsto 0, 0\ |\\
&\quad suc\ i \mapsto \textbf{let } q, r\ =\ (\textbf{rec } i)\ \textbf{in}\\
&\qquad\qquad \textbf{if } suc\ r\ =\ m \textbf{ then } (suc\ q, 0) \textbf{ else } (q, suc\ r)\\
&\quad \textbf{endcase}: nat \times N\ m
\end{aligned}
$$

It can be seen how, using primitive recursion, the value of $(i+1)//m$ is defined in terms of $i//m$ and ultimately in terms of $0//m$. Notice that the **case** expression is tagged with a subtype. This indicates that the desired type of the expression is $nat \times N\ m$; without it, the expression would be taken as having its natural type, $nat \times nat$.

2.2 Theory of numerals

Numbers are represented by numerals. There are many different systems of numeration; the commonest one is the *positional* (or *radix*) notation in which a sequence of ℓ digits, each a number in the range $0\ ..\ (m-1)$, represents a number in the range $0\ ..\ (m^\ell - 1)$.

There are several ways in which such numerals may themselves be represented within a logic. One frequently employed way is to represent them as *lists*. For example, binary numerals might be represented using the datatype

$$\textbf{datatype } numeral\ =\ nil\ |\ cons\ bit\ numeral$$

This is a natural form of representation for numerals of arbitrary length, but it turns out to be quite awkward for the representation of the fixed-length numerals generally used in digital systems.

We have found that a good representation for fixed-length numerals is obtained by using subtypes and treating a base-m, length-ℓ numeral as a mapping from an indexing type $N\ \ell$ to a digit type $N\ m$. To this end, we introduce a type-constructing function

$$V \stackrel{\wedge}{=} \lambda m: nat^+; \ell: nat.\ N\ \ell \to N\ m$$

so that $V\ (m, \ell)$ is the type of base-m, length-ℓ numerals. For instance, the type *byte* (ie, an 8-bit word) may be defined as $byte \stackrel{\wedge}{=} V\ (2, 8)$.

The component digits of a numeral are obtained by application. For example, given a declaration $B: byte$ (which is equivalent to stating that B is of type $N\ 8 \to bit$), the component digits of the byte B are $B\ 0$, $B\ 1, \ldots$, $B\ 7$. Notice that the type discipline of the logic prevents any reference to non-existent digits; for instance, the notion "*the 8th digit of byte B*" would be inexpressible since the term $B\ 8$ is not well-typed.

It will often be convenient to adopt the convention that application may be denoted by subscripting, so that an application like $f\ x$ may equivalently be written as f_x. Using this abbreviation (which is not, at present, supported by the computational implementation of the logic) allows the component digits of B to be written as B_0, B_1, $\ldots$, B_7.

In order to describe the relation between a fixed-length numeral and the number it represents, we introduce a valuation function *val*. This function may be thought of an *abstraction* function, mapping from the concrete domain of base-m, length-ℓ numerals to the abstract domain of numbers in the subrange $0 \ . \ . \ (m^\ell - 1)$. This useful information about the range type of *val* may be captured by giving it a dependent type:

$$val: [m: nat^+; \ell: nat] \to V\ (m, \ell) \to N\ (m \uparrow \ell)$$

That is, it takes a non-zero number m and a number ℓ, and yields a function that maps base-m, length-ℓ numerals to the subtype $N\ (m \uparrow \ell)$. For instance, the term $val_{(2,8)}\ B$ is of type $N\ 256$ and denotes the number corresponding to the byte B. The function *val* may be defined using primitive recursion

$$val_{(m,\ell)}\ A \stackrel{\wedge}{=} \textbf{case } \ell \textbf{ of}$$
$$0 \mapsto 0\ |$$
$$suc\ i \mapsto A_i \times (m \uparrow i) + (\textbf{rec } i)$$
$$\textbf{endcase}: N\ (m \uparrow \ell)$$

(In practice, definitions like this need to be framed in a slightly different way in order to satisfy the rules for type checking.)

If, in addition to fixed-length numerals, we also wished to be able to deal with variable-length ones (as might, for instance, be used for arbitrary-precision arithmetic) this can easily be accommodated within the same framework, simply by defining a *dependent pair* type constructing function

$$W\ m \stackrel{\wedge}{=} [\ell: nat] \times V\ (m, \ell)$$

Using this type, a base-m numeral is represented as an element of type W m, that is, as an ordered pair whose first component is a number ℓ that represents the length of the numeral and whose second component is a (fixed-length) numeral of length ℓ. For instance, the type W 2 (of binary numerals) contains the pair $(8, B)$ as one of its elements. The type-discipline of the logic (specifically, the rule for pair-formation) ensures that the two components of the pair are guaranteed to be mutually consistent.

3 Specification, Implementation and Correctness

Having now captured the concepts of number theory and numerals within VERITAS^{+}, we can move on to illustrate the techniques that may be used from formulating specifications for digital devices, for describing possible implementations, and for expressing the notion of correctness.

General principles   The overall approach we use, introduced in [H83, HD85, G86] within the context of *ordinary* typed higher-order logic, is to use predicates (ie, *bool*-valued functions) to describe the possible, externally-observable behaviour of devices or systems. In more detail:-

- We treat a *behavioural specification* of a device as a predicate ϕ on the tuple ν of signals at the ports of the device. This predicate defines the signal tuples that are deemed to be allowable.

- We describe a possible *implementation* of this specification by a predicate ψ of the same type. The *intension* (or form) of this predicate reflects the structure of the implementation. Its *extension* (or value) represents the set of signal tuples that (by virtue of satisfying all the constraints imposed by the component parts of the implementation) might actually occur at the ports of the device, on the assumption that the implementation is electrically *well-formed* with respect to its intended environment.

- An implementation ψ is said to be *correct* with respect to a specification ϕ if any tuple ν of signals that might occur at the ports of the implementation satisfy the specification. This relation may be expressed as $\vdash \forall \nu.\ \psi\ \nu \Rightarrow \phi\ \nu$, or, using the combinator $\sqsupseteq$ ('is as strong a predicate as'), as $\vdash \psi \sqsupseteq \phi$.

In the following account, we shall be aiming to highlight:

- How the techniques of data abstraction may be used to build up a complex specification in a structured way.

- How the use of type theory facilitates writing highly *generic* specifications (and thus leads towards *reusability* of specifications).

- The techniques used in writing specifications that are no stronger (in the sense of overspecification) than necessary.

The particular example we choose concerns the specification of a *comparator*, that is, a device that accepts two numerals and determines their relative magnitude.

The first specification we give of the comparator is an *abstract* one, in the sense that the types involved are chosen to be those best suited to defining the underlying operation. Later, we will *elaborate* these types so as to obtain what we term a 'Level I' specification involving types that are more concrete, and then further elaborate these types to obtain a 'Level II' specification involving the actual concrete types required.

3.1 Abstract specification of a comparator

To describe the result of comparing two numbers, we introduce a 3-valued enumerated type

$$\textbf{datatype } \textit{order } = \ G \mid E \mid L \qquad \text{(ie, } \textit{greater than, equal to, less than)}$$

Using this datatype, we can then introduce a 'comparison' operator $\sim: nat^2 \to order$ defined by

$$a \sim b \ \triangleq \ \textbf{if } a > b \textbf{ then } G \textbf{ else if } a < b \textbf{ then } L \textbf{ else } E$$

(So that, for example, $5 \sim 3$ has the value G.)

The first definition of a comparator we give is at an abstract level. We shall assume (Fig 1) that the comparator has four ports. Two of these ports accept the pair of numbers a and b that are to be compared. Since our concern will be with *finite* arithmetic, we assume that these numbers are restricted to a subrange $0 \,.\,.\, (n-1)$, for some positive number n. The other two ports carry incoming and outgoing comparison values c and d. The reason for defining the specification to have an incoming comparison value will become apparent later; for the present, we will assume it takes the value E. We give the specification the dependent type

$$comp: [n: nat^+] \to N\ n \times N\ n \times order \times order \to bool$$

and define it as

$$comp_n\ (a, b, c, d) \ \triangleq \ (d \ = \ \textbf{case } c \textbf{ of}$$
$$G \mapsto G \mid$$
$$E \mapsto (a \sim b) \mid$$
$$L \mapsto L \mid$$
$$\textbf{endcase})$$

This, for the case $c = E$, is equivalent to the specification $d = (a \sim b)$, as required.

3.2 Level I specification of the comparator

The actual comparator specification that we seek requires to be defined on concrete types rather than the abstract ones that *comp* was defined on. We tackle this transformation from abstract to concrete (a process we term *elaboration*) in two stages. In the first, dealt with here, we replace the numbers (ie, elements of $N\ n$) that occur in the abstract specification by base-m length-ℓ numerals — that is, by elements of $V_{(m,\ell)}$. We name this new more concrete specification, *Comp*, giving it (see Fig 2) the type

$$Comp: [m: nat^+; \ell: nat] \to V\ (m, \ell) \times V\ (m, \ell) \times order \times order \to bool$$

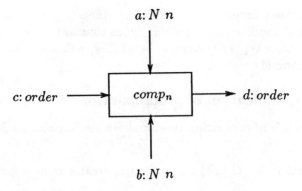

Fig 1. $comp_n$ is the abstract specification of a comparator.

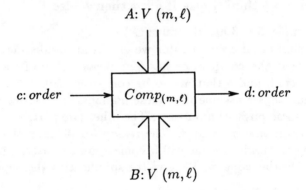

Fig 2. $Comp_{(m,\ell)}$ is the Level I concrete specification of a comparator.

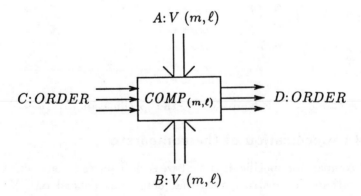

Fig 3. $COMP_{(m,\ell)}$ is the Level II concrete specification of a comparator.

It is defined in terms of the abstract specification *comp*, using the abstraction function *val*, to relate the numerals A and B to their values $val_{(m,\ell)}\ A$ and $val_{(m,\ell)}\ B$ (both of type $N\ (m \uparrow \ell)$)

$$Comp_{(m,\ell)}\ (A, B, c, d) \;\stackrel{\Delta}{=}\; comp_{(m\uparrow\ell)}\ (val_{(m,\ell)}\ A,\ val_{(m,\ell)}\ B,\ c,\ d)$$

3.3 Level II specification of the comparator

The final stage in defining the fully concrete specification of the comparator involves elaborating the abstract type *order*. We choose to represent it (see Fig 3) with a type $ORDER$, defined as

$$ORDER \;\stackrel{\Delta}{=}\; bit \times bit \times bit$$

and with an abstraction function chosen in such a way that the abstract value G (signifying $a > b$) is represented by $(1, 0, 0)$, E by $(0, 1, 0)$ and L by $(0, 0, 1)$.

We are then faced with the question of how to deal with the remaining 5 possible bit patterns. These could, of course, be arbitrarily mapped into *order*; for instance, the bit pattern $(1, 1, 0)$ could be treated as an alternative representation for G, and the bit patterns $(0, 0, 0)$, $(1, 1, 1)$ and $(1, 0, 1)$ as alternative representations for E, etc. Whilst this approach would not be incorrect, it would not be ideal, since it would constitute an arbitrary *overspecification* of the comparator. It would, quite unnecessarily, restrict the choice of implementation open to a designer.

In order to avoid this problem, we shall adjoin an extra element, an error element, to the abstract type *order*, and arrange that the abstraction function maps invalid bit patterns to this error element. This will then allow the concrete specification to be formulated in such a way that it is trivially satisfied (ie, any behaviour is allowed) if an invalid bit pattern is present at the input ports.

We obtain the effect outlined above by introducing a datatype

datatype *Order* $=$ *Valid order* | *Invalid*

and an abstraction function *abs* of type *abs*: $ORDER \rightarrow Order$ defined as

$abs\ X \;\stackrel{\Delta}{=}\;$ **if** $X = (1, 0, 0)$ **then** *Valid G* **else**
$\qquad\quad$ **if** $X = (0, 1, 0)$ **then** *Valid E* **else**
$\qquad\quad$ **if** $X = (0, 0, 1)$ **then** *Valid L* **else** *Invalid*

Thus, the three valid bit patterns are mapped to the *Valid* elements of the datatype, and the remaining ones to the *Invalid* element. We can now formulate the totally concrete version, $COMP$, of the comparator specification. We give it the type

$$COMP \colon [m\colon nat^+; \ell\colon nat] \rightarrow V\ (m, \ell) \times V\ (m, \ell) \times ORDER \times ORDER \rightarrow bool$$

and define it by

$COMP_{(m,\ell)}\ (A, B, C, D) \;\stackrel{\Delta}{=}\;$ **case** *abs C* **of**
$\qquad\qquad\qquad\qquad$ *Valid c* $\mapsto$ **case** *abs D* **of**
$\qquad\qquad\qquad\qquad\qquad\qquad$ *Valid D* $\mapsto$ $Comp_{(m,\ell)}\ (A, B, c, d)$ |
$\qquad\qquad\qquad\qquad\qquad\qquad$ *Invalid* $\mapsto$ *false*
$\qquad\qquad\qquad\qquad\qquad$ **endcase** |
$\qquad\qquad\qquad\qquad$ *Invalid* $\mapsto$ *true*
$\qquad\qquad\qquad$ **endcase**

Notice the asymmetry between the treatment of the input bit pattern C and the output one D. If C is invalid, then the specification is trivially satisfied, otherwise if D is invalid, the specification is not satisfied. If both C and D are valid, then the comparator specification $COMP$ is defined in terms of the Level I comparator specification, $Comp$.

3.4 Implementation of a comparator

Many arithmetic operations can be implemented by one-dimensional iterative structures (Fig 4), in which the operands, represented as base-m, length-ℓ numerals, are digit-wise applied to a row of identical cells that are interconnected by a 'carry' line. We can define a combinator $fold$ that takes the behavioural predicate satisfied by an individual cell and *lifts* it to yield the behavioural predicate satisfied by the corresponding iterative structure. The type of $fold$ is

$$fold: [t: U0; m: nat^+; \ell: nat] \rightarrow$$
$$(N \ m \times N \ m \times t \times t) \rightarrow V \ (m, \ell) \times V \ (m, \ell) \times t \times t \rightarrow bool$$

and its definition is

$$fold_{(t,m,\ell)} \ P \ \triangleq \ \textbf{case} \ \ell \ \textbf{of}$$
$$0 \mapsto \lambda A, B, c, d. \quad c = d \ |$$
$$suc \ i \mapsto \lambda A, B, c, d.$$
$$\exists e. \ P \ (A_j, B_j, c, e) \ \wedge \ (\textbf{rec} \ j) \ (A, B, e, d)$$
$$\textbf{endcase}$$

For example (Fig 4), if $cell$ is a predicate of type $cell: N \ m \times N \ m \times t \times t \rightarrow bool$ (for some carry type t and digit-base m), then the predicate obeyed by the overall iterative structure is simply $fold_{(t,m,\ell)} \ cell$.

Correctness   Let us now consider the correctness of an implementation of this form for the comparator specifiction defined above. To allow us to focus on the essentials, we will work from the Level I specification, $Comp_{(m,\ell)}$, the one in which the numbers are represented by the concrete type of base-m, length-ℓ numerals, but the carries are represented by the abstract type $order = G \mid E \mid L$.

Suppose that the behavioural predicate for an individual 'comparator cell' were $P: [m: nat^+] \rightarrow N \ m \times N \ m \times order \times order \rightarrow bool$. Then, the behavioural predicate for the overall comparator (similar in form to Fig 4) would be $fold_{(order,m,\ell)} \ P_m$. This implementation would be *correct* if this predicate were as strong as the comparator specification, $Comp_{(m,\ell)}$. Expressed formally, this correctness criterion is

$$\forall m: nat^+; \ \ell: nat.$$
$$\forall A, B: V \ (m, \ell); \ c, d: order.$$
$$fold_{(order,m,\ell)} \ P_m \ (A, B, c, d) \Rightarrow Comp_{(m,\ell)} \ (A, B, c, d)$$

or, expressed in higher-order form

$$\forall m: nat^+; \ell: nat. \ fold_{(order,m,\ell)} \ P_m \ \sqsupseteq \ Comp_{(m,\ell)}$$

Viewed theoretically, this statement is fine, but in practical terms it immediately raises two questions:

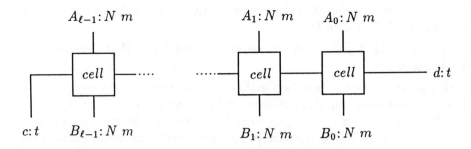

Fig 4. The iterative structure yielded by $fold_{(m,\ell)}$ cell.

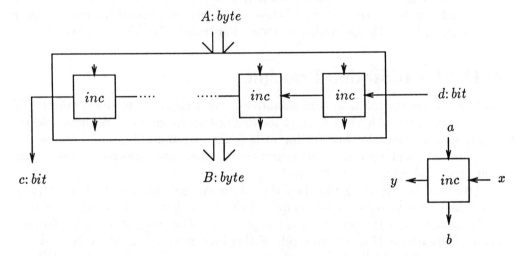

Fig 5. An 8-bit incrementor. Each cell of the incrementor implements the relation $(y, b) = (x + a)//2$.

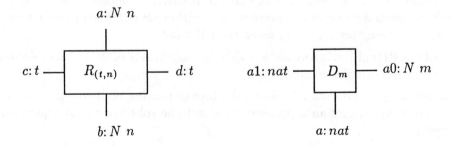

Fig 6. Representations of the relations $R_{(t,n)}$ and D_m.

- How does one decide what the actual behavioural predicate P_m for an individual comparator cell should be?

- Given a proposed P_m, how does one set about establishing that the correctness criterion holds?

A plausible answer to the first question is that one uses informal reasoning to come up with a likely candidate for P_m, validating it by trying it out on a few test cases. The second question is not so easily answered. Experience shows that creating a formal proof of the correctness criterion is not easy. There are many lemmas that require to be proven and a large amount of detail to be kept under control; without very careful planning, it is all too easy to lose sight of the woods for the trees.

In the next section, we shall formulate and prove a principle that provides a direct and simple answer to both of these questions, and that deals not just with comparators, but with the implementation of arithmetic functions in general.

4 The Factorisation Principle

Our aim in this section is to demonstrate a general approach to the synthesis and formal verification of iteratively implemented arithmetic circuits. We have selected this task as an example, both for its intrinsic interest and utility and because it it provides a particularly convincing example of the benefits conferred by the dependent types and subtypes of VERITAS$^+$.

We start by observing that in a typical one-dimensional iterative circuit, it is often the case that each cell of the overall circuit implements a modulo-m version of the relation that the overall circuit implements. For example, consider an 8-bit binary incrementor (Fig 5); each cell of this incrementor behaves as a modulo-2 incrementor. Specifically, the overall circuit implements the relation $(c, val\ B) = (d + val\ A)//(2 \uparrow 8)$ whilst each individual cell implements the relation $(c, b) = (d + a)//2$. We shall say that an arithmetic relation that displays this property is *iteratively implementable*.

Of course, not all arithmetic relations are iteratively implementable. However, we have identified two simple properties of arithmetic relations, namely being *factorisable* and being *proper*, and proven the following

Factorisation Principle: *Any arithmetic relation which is both factorisable and proper is iteratively implementable.*

This is a significant result, since it allows the task of proving the correctness of an iterative implementation of an arithmetic relation to be split into two independent components:

- A proof of the Factorisation Principle, that is, a proof showing the correctness of an iterative implementation of *any* relation that is factorisable and proper. (Since this proof is carried out at a level of abstraction where it is not cluttered up with the irrelevant detail pertaining to any particular relation, it is relatively easy to establish.)

- A proof showing that the particular relation under consideration is factorisable and proper. (Since this proof does not involve numerals, it too is relatively easy to establish.)

Thus, assuming the Factorisation Principle has been proven (a task that only requires to be undertaken once), the task of verifying the correctness of, for example, the base-m, length-ℓ implementation of the comparator discussed in the last section (a relatively complex undertaking), reduces to the relatively simple task of proving that the comparison relation *comp* is factorisable and proper.

4.1 The Factorisation Principle

In explaining the Factorisation Principle, we will state the main definitions and the theorem formally, but we will rely upon informal arguments and diagrams for conveying the spirit of the proof. We start with a relation $R_{(t,n)}$, the *abstract specification* of the behaviour we wish to implement. We take $R_{(t,n)}$ as being of type

$$R: [t: U0; n: nat^+] \rightarrow N\ n \times N\ n \times t \times t \rightarrow bool$$

where t describes the type of the carry signal. In diagrams, we shall represent ths relation as shown in Fig 6. Notice that, since the approach to verification that we are using abstracts away from causality, there is no requirement to distinguish input ports from output ones. A typical instance of the relation $R_{(t,n)}$ is the abstract specification of the comparator, $comp_n$, defined earlier.

Next, in order to describe the relation between a number a and its quotient $a1$ and remainder $a0$ on division by m, we introduce a relation $D: [m: nat^+] \rightarrow nat \times nat \times N\ m \rightarrow bool$ defined by

$$D_m\ (a, a1, a0) \triangleq (a1, a0) = a//m$$

(a relation that may be equivalently stated as $a = a0 + a1 \times m$). Fig 6 also shows the way that this relation is depicted.

We are now able to introduce the notion of *factorisable* and *proper* relations. Basically, a relation $R_{(t,n)}$ is said to be factorisable if (see Fig 7) it can always be 'factored' into two instances of itself, $R_{(t,m)}$ and $R_{(t,k)}$ (with $m \times k = n$). Formally, the property of factorisability is defined as

$$
\begin{aligned}
&factorisable_t\ R \triangleq \\
&\quad \forall m, k: nat^+. \\
&\quad\quad \forall a0, b0: N\ m;\ a1, b1: N\ k;\ c, d: t. \\
&\quad\quad\quad \textbf{let } a\ =\ a0 + a1 \times m \textbf{ in} \\
&\quad\quad\quad \textbf{let } b\ =\ b0 + b1 \times m \textbf{ in} \\
&\quad\quad\quad \big(\exists e: t.\ R_k(a1, b1, c, e) \wedge R_m(a0, b0, e, d)\big) \Rightarrow R_{(m \times k)}(a, b, c, d)
\end{aligned}
$$

A relation $R_{(t,n)}$ is said to be proper if the relation $R_{(t,1)}$ behaves as the identity relation; that is

$$proper_t\ R \triangleq \forall c: t.\ R_1(0, 0, c, c)$$

The motivation behind the introduction of these properties will become clear shortly.

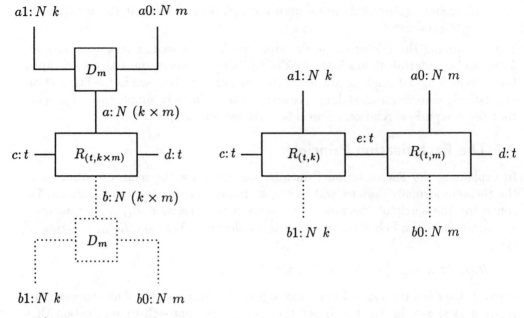

Fig 7. A relation R is said to be *factorisable* if these two relations are equal.

(Note: In order to save space, the lower half of such diagrams, here shown dotted, is omitted in subsequent diagrams.)

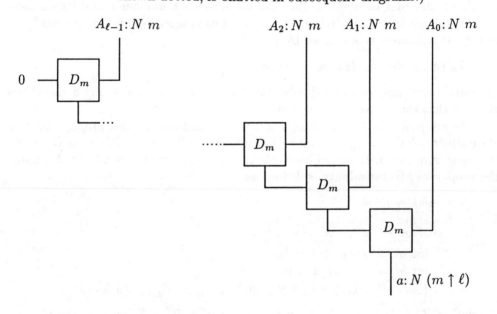

Fig 8. Illustration of how the relation $a = val_{(m,\ell)} A$ may be defined in relational form by folding D_m over the base-m length-ℓ numeral A.

Using the relation D_m defined above, the numeral-to-number abstraction function $val_{(m,\ell)}$ can be defined as a relation

$$a \;=\; val_{(m,\ell)} \; A \qquad\qquad \text{for } a\colon N \;(m \uparrow \ell) \text{ and } A\colon V \;(m, \ell).$$

simply by *folding* the relation D_m over A, as shown in Fig 8.

We shall assume that the concrete specification, *Spec*, will be expressed in terms of base-m, length-ℓ numerals, and related to the abstract specification R by means of the abstraction function $val_{(m,\ell)}$. Thus *Spec*, will be of type

$$Spec\colon [m\colon nat^+; \ell\colon nat] \to V\;(m, \ell) \times V\;(m, \ell) \times t \times t \to bool$$

and defined by

$$Spec_{(m,\ell)}\;(A, B, x, y) \;\triangleq\; R_{(m \uparrow \ell)}\;(val_{(m,\ell)}\;A,\; val_{(m,\ell)}\;B,\; c, d)$$

Using the relational form of the abstraction function $val_{(m,\ell)}$ just defined, this specification can be represented as shown in Fig 9a. The Level I specification of the comparator, $Comp_{(m,\ell)}$, defined earlier, is a typical instance of a concrete specification.

So far, all we have done is to introduce a series of definitions. Now, however, if we assume that the relation R is factorisable and proper, we can incrementally strengthen the specification of Fig 9a to that of 9b, and finally to that of 9c, with the knowledge that the latter relation will be no weaker than the former one. This last form which the specification has been shown to imply can, using the *fold* combinator introduced earlier, be expressed as

$$fold_{(t,m,\ell)}\; R_m\;(A, B, c, d)$$

and it is immediately clear that it describes an *iterative implementation* of the concrete specification $Spec_{(m,\ell)}$.

Stated formally, the theorem whose proof we have (in a very informal way!) outlined is

$$\forall t\colon U0.$$
$$\forall R\colon [n\colon nat^+] \to N\; n \times N\; n \times t \times t \to bool.$$
$$\forall m\colon nat^+; \ell\colon nat.$$
$$A, B\colon V\;(m, \ell);\; c, d\colon t.$$
$$factorisable_t\; R \Rightarrow$$
$$proper_t\; R \Rightarrow$$
$$fold_{(t,m,\ell)}\; R_m\;(A, B, c, d) \Rightarrow$$
$$R_{(m \uparrow \ell)}\;(val_{(m,\ell)}\;A,\; val_{(m,\ell)}\;B,\; c,\; d)$$

In words: "For any type t, for any relation R, for any base m and word-length ℓ, for any numerals A and B and carry values c and d, if R is factorisable and proper, then an *iterative implementation* of it (with each cell implementing the relation R_m) will satisfy the given concrete behavioural specification $R_{(m \uparrow \ell)}$."

4.2 An example

As an example of the application of the Factorisation principle, consider the synthesis and formal verification of the comparator discussed earlier.

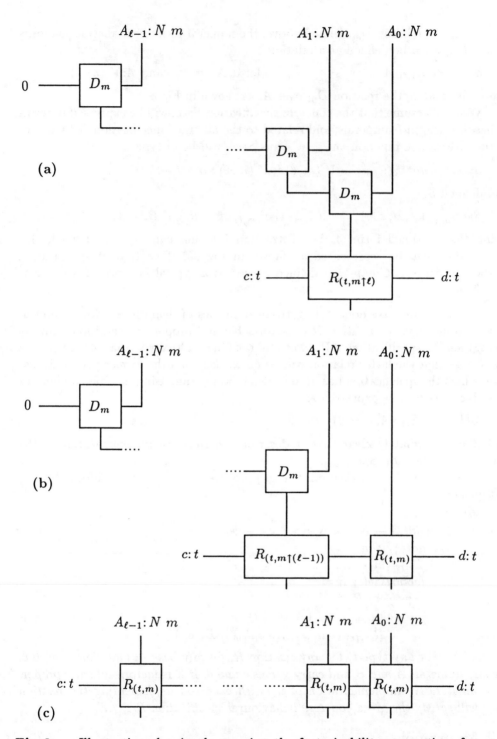

Fig 9. Illustration showing how, using the factorisability properties of R, the concrete specification (a) can be transformed to (b), and ultimately to (c), where it has the form of an iterative implementation.

To make use of this principle, we need to prove that the relation *comp*, the abstract specification of a comparator, is *proper* and that it is *factorisable*.

Proving that it is *proper* means establishing the theorem

$$\vdash \forall c\colon order.\ comp_1(0, 0, c, c)$$

or, after substitution of the definition for *comp*, the theorem

$$\vdash \forall c\colon order.$$
$$c\ =\ \textbf{case}\ c\ \textbf{of}\ G \mapsto G\ |\quad E \mapsto (0 \sim 0)\ |\quad L \mapsto L\ \textbf{endcase}$$

The proof, which follows immediately from $(0 \sim 0) = E$, is trivial.

Proving that *comp* is *factorisable* means establishing the theorem

$$\vdash \forall m, k\colon nat^+.$$
$$\forall a0, b0\colon N\ m;\ a1, b1\colon N\ k;\ c, d\colon order.$$
$$\textbf{let}\ a\ =\ a0 + a1 \times m\ \textbf{in}$$
$$\textbf{let}\ b\ =\ b0 + b1 \times m\ \textbf{in}$$
$$(\exists e\colon order.\ comp_k(a1, b1, c, e) \wedge comp_m(a0, b0, e, d)) \Rightarrow$$
$$comp_{(m \times k)}(a, b, c, d)$$

Althougth this theorem may look complicated, it is an easy consequence of the lemma

$$\vdash (a0 + a1 \times m) \sim (b0 + b1 \times m)\ =\ \textbf{case}\ (a1 \sim b1)\ \textbf{of}$$
$$G \mapsto G\ |$$
$$E \mapsto (a0 \sim b0)\ |$$
$$L \mapsto L$$
$$\textbf{endcase}$$

This lemma is the quintessential justification for the validity of an iterative implementation of a comparator. The lemma itself depends on the elementary theorem

$$\vdash \forall a, b\colon nat.\ (a < b) \vee (a = b) \vee (a > b)$$

an easily proven property of inequalities. Thus, given a proof that the relation *comp* is indeed proper and factorisable, the Factorisation Principle immediately:

- States that this relation may be iteratively implemented and that each cell of the implementation should realise the relation $comp_m$ (where m is the base of the numerals).

- Yields a formal proof that this implementation, $fold_{(order, m, \ell)}\ comp_m$ is correct with respect to the Level I concrete specification $Comp_{(m, \ell)}$ given earlier.

Other examples   Each cell of the comparator implementation just described had two 'digit' input ports and a carry signal going from right to left. However, the Factorisation Principle as presented is (since the direction of causality, as implied by the I/O port labelling, is irrelevant) equally applicable to other kinds of one-dimensional circuit. For example, it may be applied to the synthesis/verification of circuits like incrementors or decrementors (as in Fig 5) where each cell has one 'digit' input port and one 'digit' output port, and the carry signal goes from right to left, or to a divide-by-k circuit (for fixed k) where the carry signal goes from left to right, etc. Of course, related versions of the Factorisation Principle may also be derived for cells having a greater or lesser number of ports.

Finally, we mention that the Factorisation Principle easily extends to more general systems of numeration, such as, for instance, systems where successive digits are to different bases (for example: *hours, minutes, seconds*), and also (we hypothesise) to *dependent* systems of numeration, where the base of each digit may depend upon the value of more significant digits (as for example, in calendar dates). We believe also that a version of the principle may be formulated that encompasses two-dimensional (and higher) iterative circuits.

5 Computational Implementation

In order to support theorem proving in VERITAS$^+$, the logic is computationally implemented. This means that:

- The well-formedness of all terms and the validity of all inferences are computationally checked.

- Large parts of the process of constructing proofs may be automated, with the user only being required to provide high-level guidance to the system.

- A secure database of theorems may be maintained

The VERITAS$^+$ logic is implemented using the ALGEBRAIC approach, a development of the EDINBURGH LCF approach [GMW79]. As with LCF, the type discipline of the meta language is used to guarantee the integrity of object-level entities (terms, theorems, etc). The distinctive features of the ALGEBRAIC approach [HD86c] are that:

- The *object logic* (ie, VERITAS$^+$) is represented as a partial, many-sorted algebra (in computational terms, as a *partial datatype*).

- Signatures (ie, 'theory presentations', or, informally, sequences of definitions) are explicitly represented as *values* (rather than as components of the state of the meta language, as in LCF).

- The meta language (named META) is a purely functional one; it has no imperative features of any kind.

The net effect of these features is that the definition of the object logic is both relatively concise and reasonably clear in its intent; both of these factors contribute towards assuring the soundness of the implementation of the logic.

Overall, the VERITAS$^+$ logic includes about 25 term-formation rules and about 35 derivation-formation rules.

Concrete notation In order to translate between the abstract algebraic representation of the logic and a human-readable concrete notation, *parsing* and *unparsing* functions (written in META) are used. The concrete notation is expressed in an extended character set (that includes mathematical and logical operators, Greek characters, superscripts and subscripts, and several fonts). This allows a very close approximation to be obtained to conventional mathematical and logical notation; this is an important feature, since it greatly increases the readability of complex specifications. For printing, the notation is converted to POSTSCRIPT; apart from the minor exceptions noted in the text, the output from the system is very similar to the form used throughout this paper.

The concrete notation allows VERITAS$^+$ signatures, terms and derivations (ie, 'proofs') to be expressed. There are two notations employed for terms: an *input notation* and an *output notation*. In many cases, these two notations coincide; they differ mainly where is is necessary (since the type system is not fully decidable) to provide extra information in order to *rewrite* the type of a term (as, for example, in going from the term $A: byte$ to $A: N\ 8 \rightarrow N\ 2$) or to *inject* a term into a subtype (as, for example, in going from the term $0: nat$ to the term $0: N\ 2$) in order to make it compatible with its context.

5.1 Goal-directed proof editing

In order to allow the user to interact with the primitive, very low-level, rules of inference of VERITAS$^+$ in reasonably high-level terms, theorem-proving is carried out using an interactive, goal-directed proof editor. This editor provides the user with an environment specially tailored to support theorem proving; like all the other support tools, it is a function written in META, and any flaws in its implementation cannot compromise the soundness of the underlying logic. The main features the editor provides are:

- It supports goal-directed construction of derivations, using *tactics* (broadly as defined in EDINBURGH LCF).

- It supports *interactive* parsing of terms for which non-trivial type-changing operations are required to establish their well-typing.

- It allows *browsing* of through the proof trees (that is, the trees induced by the user's choice of tactics — in effect, high-level representations of the actual derivations.)

- It contains a database mechanism whereby lemmas can be stored and subsequently referenced (in effect, by anti-quotation) within terms and derivations by the parsers.

- It allows editing activity on a proof tree to be suspended (maybe in order to create another proof tree for establishing a lemma, or to devise a new tactic) and to be resumed later.

- It can generate a listing that summarises the structures of the proofs in a readable form, or a representation of the proofs that allows the entire set of proofs to be rebuilt *ab initio*.

Present status   The VERITAS$^+$ logic and its toolset have been implemented on SUN-3 and MIPS machines, and have been in active use for some months. The sizes of the various components, expressed in lines of META, are about:

The primitive VERITAS$^+$ *logic*	*2000*
The parser and unparser functions	*1300*

The interactive goal-directed proof editor   *2600*
The present collection of tactics (about 40 in all)   *1000*

A variety of proofs relating to formal verification of digital systems have been carried through on the system; in particular, a proof of the Factorisation Principle described earlier has been completed.

It is our intention to make the system (including its database of signatures and proofs) available to interested parties in the near future.

6 Conclusions

At the beginning of this paper, we listed the features that an ideal specification language should possess; we believe that VERITAS$^+$ approaches this ideal quite closely. The distinctive feature of VERITAS$^+$ is in its use of the dependent types and subtypes of ITT. These finer, more expressive types allow specifications to be written that are both clearer and more concise. The price that is paid for dependent types is the loss of fully decidable type checking. In our experience, however, this turns out not to be a problem; in practice, software tools (tactics, etc) deployed within a suitable support environment enable the great majority of type checking to be carried out automatically. By and large, those instances of type checking that cannot easily be automated represent formal reasoning that would have to be dealt with explicitly in any logic.

The rules of inference of VERITAS$^+$ are rather more numerous and more complex than those of an ordinary higher-order logic, and this means that a greater degree of expertise is required on the part of a user in guiding the construction of proofs. On the other hand, we believe that the reading or the writing of specifications that containing dependent types comes easily to anyone already familiar with ordinary higher-order logic.

Formal synthesis   Finally, we mention that, in addition to using VERITAS$^+$ for formal verification, we are also using it for *formal synthesis*, a term we have coined to describe an interactive, goal-directed process that allows a designer to start with a behavioural specification and to finish with a structured description of the design (in our case, expressed in the MODEL VLSI design language), a formal proof in VERITAS$^+$ that asserts the correctness of the design, and a structured description of the process by which the design was evolved. We hope to be reporting on this work shortly.

Acknowledgments   Our interest in type theory derives mainly from Martin-Löf's ITT [ML84] and from Constable's NUPRL language [C86]. The decision that VERITAS$^+$ theories should be purely definitional in nature was motivated by Gordon's HOL [G85]. The idea that specifications can usefully abstract away from directionality is due to Sheeran [S86].

Work on the VERITAS$^+$ project is funded by the UK Science and Engineering Research Council under grant GR/D84733.

7 References

[C86]   Constable, R.L., et al., "Implementing Mathematics with the Nuprl Proof Development System", Prentice-Hall, 1986

[G85]   Gordon, M.J., "A Machine Oriented Formulation of Higher-Order Logic" Technical Report 68, Computer Laboratory, University of Cambridge, 1985.

[G86]   Gordon, M.J., "Why Higher-Order Logic is a Good Formalism for Specifying and Verifying Hardware" in "Formal Aspects of VLSI Design", ed. G.J. Milne and P.A. Subrahmanyam, North Holland, 1986.

[GMW79]   Gordon, M.J., Milner, A.J., Wadsworth, C.P., "Edinburgh LCF — a Mechanised Logic of Computation", Vol 78, LNCS, Springer-Verlag, 1979.

[H83]   Hanna, F.K., "Overview of the Veritas Project", Technical Report, University of Kent, 1983.

[HD85]   Hanna, F.K., Daeche, N., "Specification and Verification using Higher-Order Logic", in Proc CHDL, ed. Koomen and Moto-oka, North Holland, 1985.

[HD86a]   Hanna, F.K., Daeche, N., "Specification and Verification using Higher-Order Logic: A Case Study", in "Formal Aspects of VLSI Design", ed. G.J. Milne and P.A. Subrahmanyam, North Holland, 1986.

[HD86b]   Hanna, F.K., Daeche, N., "Purely Functional Implementation of a Logic" 8th Intnl Conf on Automated Deduction, pp598-607, Vol 230, LNCS, Springer-Verlag, 1986.

[HD88]   Hanna, F.K., Daeche, N., "Computational Logic: An Algebraic Approach", Technical Report (3 vols), University of Kent, 1988

[ML84]   Martin-Löf, P. "Constructive mathematics and computer programming", pp501-518, Phil Trans R. Soc. London, A 312, 1984.

[S86]   Sheeran, M., "Describing and Reasoning about Circuits using Relations", in Proc 1986 Leeds workshop on Theoretical Aspects of VLSI Design.

Categories for the Working Hardware Designer

Mary Sheeran
Computing Science Dept.
Glasgow University
Glasgow G12 8QQ, Scotland.

Abstract. *We show how standard results from category theory can be used to derive useful theorems about a hardware description language. The theorems correspond to behaviour preserving circuit transformations. We also show how a categorical viewpoint can help in the design of a formally based hardware description language. All necessary category theory is introduced.*

1. Introduction

Our approach to VLSI design is to use a special purpose design language with a simple formal semantics [5,6]. Higher order functions capture common circuit forms and algebraic laws capture common design steps, or transformations. This approach is particularly well suited to the design of cellular and systolic arrays, which form an important subset of VLSI circuits. Typical algebraic laws describe either spatial or temporal transformations. These algebraic laws, which are theorems about the language, are central to the approach. One of the jobs of the language designer is to find a useful set of theorems, and to verify them. Category theory provides a way of generating many of these theorems directly from the types of the expressions that describe circuit behaviour. The theorems are not difficult to prove, but avoiding the need to prove them should still save considerable time and effort.

The first part of the paper introduces all necessary category theory. Next, we show how the types of expressions in a formal hardware description language can be used to generate theorems. The category theoretic approach can also give some guidance in the choice of higher order functions with nice algebraic properties. It can, therefore, help in language design. The latter part of the paper takes some first steps in this direction. This work is in its early stages. Comments are welcome.

2. Basic Category Theory

What is a category? A category is made up of three parts :-

(i)   A collection of objects

(ii)   A collection of arrows each of which points from an object to an object.
An arrow points from its domain object to its codomain object. We write

$$f : A \to B$$

to indicate that *f* has domain A and codomain B. A and B need not be distinct. Indeed,
every object is equipped with an identity arrow such that

$$id_A : A \to A$$

(iii)   An associative composition operator on arrows.
If $f : A \to B$ and $g : B \to C$, their composition $f ; g : A \to C$. The codomain of f and the
domain of g must be equal. For any arrows $f : A \to B$, $g : B \to C$ and $h : C \to D$

$$(f ; g) ; h = f ; (g ; h).$$

The identities for composition are identity arrows of the appropriate types. For any arrow
$f : A \to B$,

$$f ; id_B = f \quad \text{and} \quad id_A ; f = f$$

In the categories that we need, objects will always be sets, and arrows will always be
either functions or relations between sets. Categories will be indicated by boldface
uppercase letters. It is standard to show categories or parts of categories as diagrams.

Commuting diagrams. An assertion can be made graphically using a commuting diagram.
A diagram is said to commute if for every pair of objects A and B in the diagram, all paths
between A and B are equal. A path between A and B corresponds to the composite arrow
that is made by composing all the arrows along the path. The most common form of

commuting diagram is the commuting square. Asserting that the following square commutes

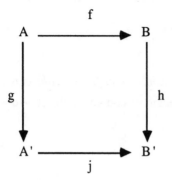

is the same as saying that g ; j = f ; h.

Two important categories. **SET** is the category that has sets as objects and total functions between sets as arrows. The composition operator is function composition. Clearly, the composition of two total functions is a total function, and function composition is associative. The reader might like to check that the identity functions have the required properties. **SET** is the archetypal example of a category.

REL is the category that has sets as objects and binary relations between sets as arrows. If p : A → B in **REL** then p is a binary relation from A to B. We write

$a\,p\,b$

to assert that *a* in A is related by p to *b* in B. The composition operator is ordinary relational composition.

$$a\,(p\,;q)\,c \qquad =_{\text{def}} \qquad \exists b.\ a\,p\,b\ \&\ b\,q\,c.$$

If p : A → B and q : B → C, then p ; q : A → C. The reader should check that relational composition has the properties required to make **REL** a category.

Products of categories. The product of two categories **C** and **D** is a category **C×D** whose objects are pairs of objects, one each from **C** and **D**, and whose arrows are pairs of arrows from **C** and **D**. For example, if p : A → B and q : A' → B' in **REL**, then we will draw the arrow (p, q) : (A, A') → (B, B') in **REL×REL** as

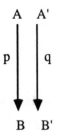

A   A'

p   q

B   B'

Having seen what a category is, we are now ready to build two important ideas on top - functors and natural transformations.

What is a functor? A functor is an arrow between *categories*, with special properties. The arrow must preserve the structure of those categories. We write F : **C** → **D** to indicate that F is a functor from category **C** to category **D**. F maps each object in **C** to an object in **D**, and each arrow in **C** to an arrow in **D** so that if p : A → B in **C** then F(p) : F(A) → F(B) in **D**. If F is to be structure preserving, then it must behave properly with respect to the identity arrows and composition operators in **C** and **D**. To be a functor, F : **C** → **D** must obey these two rules for each object A and pair of composable arrows p and q in **C**.

1. $F(id_A)$ = $id_{F(A)}$
2. $F(p) ; F(q)$ = $F(p ; q)$

(Note: in rule 2, the ';' on the left is the composition operator in the category **D**, while that on the right is in **C**.)

The most instructive examples of functors come from type systems. The functor _* is familiar to functional programmers. It is from **SET** to **SET**.

_* : **SET** → **SET**

The underscore indicates where the argument will go, so _* is postfix. If A is a set (i.e. an object of **SET**), then A* is the set of finite lists (or sequences) of elements of A. If f is a function from set A to set B, then f* is the function from A* to B* that *maps* f over a list, that is applies f to each element of the list. The reader should check that _* is a functor from **SET** to **SET**. We can also adapt _* to relations, to make it a functor from **REL** to

REL. The relation r* relates the list $(x_0, x_1, .. x_n)$ to the list $(y_0, y_1, .. y_n)$ if and only if r relates x_i to y_i for each i in 0..n. Again, the rules for a functor are obeyed.

1. $(id_A)^*$ $=$ id_{A^*}
2. $f^* ; g^*$ $=$ $(f ; g)^*$

Both are well known to be true. A useful way to think of a functor is as a parameterised type constructor with an associated operation. So, the example just given constructed lists from elements, and constructed relations on lists from relations on elements.

Another familiar functor is the cross product operator $\_\times\_$. If A and B are sets, then $A \times B$ is the set of pairs of elements, drawn one from A and one from B. Let us consider $\_\times\_$ as a functor from **REL×REL** to **REL**. (Such functors are called bifunctors.) We have already defined what it does to objects. What does it do to arrows? If $p : A \to B$ and $q : A' \to B'$ in **REL**, then $p \times q : A \times A' \to B \times B'$ in **REL**.

$$(a, b) \ p \times q \ (a', b') \quad =_{def} \quad a \ p \ a' \ \& \ b \ q \ b'.$$

Here (a,b) is the pair containing a and b. On the other hand, $p \times q$ is not a pair of relations, but a single relation from pairs to pairs. It is an arrow in **REL** and should be distinguished from (p, q) which is a pair of relations and therefore an arrow in **REL×REL**. We must check that $\_\times\_$ is a proper functor.

1. $id_A \times id_B$ $=$ $id_{A \times B}$
2. $(f \times g) ; (h \times j)$ $=$ $(f ; h) \times (g ; j)$

Again, both of these are well known to be true. $\_\times\_$ can be generalised to form a tupling operator. Later, we will use $\_\times\_$ as a combining form in our simple hardware description language. Note that $\_\times\_$ is overloaded so that it operates on categories as well as on objects and arrows within a category.

The type constructors $\_^*$ and $\_\times\_$ are both *covariant* functors. Next, we give an example of a *contravariant* functor. A contravariant functor from **C** to **D** maps every object in **C** to an object in **D**, as in the covariant case. The difference is that it maps every arrow in **C** to an arrow *pointing in the opposite direction* in **D**. If $p : A \to B$ then $F(p) : F(B) \to F(A)$. The second rule for a contravariant functor is therefore

2. $F(f) ; F(g)$ = $F(g ; f)$.

Note the reversal of g and f on the right hand side. Perhaps the simplest example of a contravariant functor is relational inverse, which is defined by

$$a \, R^{-1} b \ =_{def} \ b \, R \, a.$$

The functor $\_^{-1}$ maps objects in **REL** to themselves, and arrows in **REL** to arrows pointing in the opposite direction. If $f : A \to B$, then $f^{-1} : B^{-1} \to A^{-1}$. $A^{-1} = A$ and $B^{-1} = B$. The two rules for contravariant functors are well known to be true.

1. $(id_A)^{-1}$ = $id_{(A^{-1})}$ = id_A
2. $f^{-1} ; g^{-1}$ = $(g ; f)^{-1}$

Another way to think of a contravariant functor is as *a covariant functor in the opposite category*. We get the opposite category by reversing the directions of all the arrows in a category.

What is a natural transformation? In keeping with the category theorists' hierarchical view of the world, a natural transformation is a structure preserving arrow between *functors*. Given two functors of the same type, $F : C \to D$ and $G : C \to D$, we say that n is a natural transformation from F to G if for each arrow in **C** (shown on the left) the diagram on the right commutes in **D**. We can also think of a natural transformation $n : F \to G$ as a collection of arrows in **D**, one for each of the objects in **C**. We subscript n with the object at which it is applied, so $n_A : F(A) \to G(A)$ is the A instance of n..

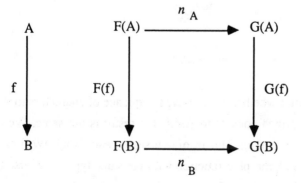

Reading off the diagram, this means that

$$F(f) ; n_B = n_A ; G(f).$$

The important thing to notice is the uniformity of the diagram. It has F applied all down the left hand side, and G applied all down the right hand side. We must always be careful to match this pattern exactly.

Natural transformations abound in programming! As an example, consider the polymorphic function that reverses a list (of anything). Its type is

$$rev : \_^* \to \_^*.$$

The function reverse is in fact a natural transformation from the functor _* to the functor _*. Take the (non-polymorphic) function Ascii that maps a character to an integer.

$$Ascii : Char \to Int \qquad (in\ \mathbf{SET})$$

Now, simply copy down the diagram for natural transformations.

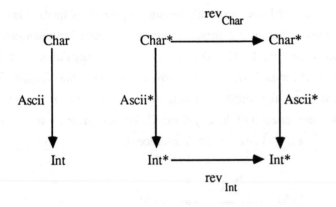

$$Ascii^* ; rev \quad = \quad rev ; Ascii^*$$

This says that it doesn't matter whether we convert a sequence of characters to Ascii and then reverse, or reverse and then convert to Ascii; the result is the same. We can also substitute any other function for Ascii. This is, of course, not surprising. What might be a little surprising is that **any** polymorphic function with the same type as reverse (i.e. any permuting function) is also a natural transformation.

A polymorphic function is one that can be applied to arguments of many different types. For example, the reverse function mentioned above reverses lists of integers, lists of characters, lists of lists of booleans and so on. For any given type *a*, reverse maps a list of *a*s to a list of *a*s. The type can be thought of as a hidden parameter of the function. When we say that a function is polymorphic, we also imply that it *does the same thing* to its arguments, independent of their types. We cannot catch out a polymorphic function by coding up (i.e changing the type of) its arguments. The function should act in the same way on the coded arguments as on the uncoded ones. We can check this by comparing the results of applying the function to coded arguments with the results of coding the output of the function. If these are the same, then we say that the function is polymorphic. Put another way, a first order function is polymorphic if and only if it is a natural transformation.

The term polymorphic is often used quite loosely. Some functions that are traditionally called polymorphic do not pass this test. The most striking example is polymorphic equality as it appears in some functional languages. However, the semantic characterisation of polymorphic functions as natural transformations is both appealingly general and practically useful. Hughes has used it to show how first order polymorphic functions can be analysed (during compilation) using techniques that have previously only applied to monomorphic functions [1]. It is possible to design languages in which every well formed expression is a natural transformation; an example is the polymorphic lambda calculus. Wadler has used this idea to generate theorems from the types of both first order and higher order functions [7]. In the remainder of the paper, we discuss the properties of a simple *relational* hardware description language in terms of functors and natural transformations. Our aim is to show that one can also generate theorems from types in a relational setting.

3. Theorems from types in a simple relational hardware description language

We give a categorical view of a very simple hardware description language. The language closely resembles Ruby, which is described in detail elsewhere [5,6]. We have deliberately chosen a small subset to simplify the presentation. In Ruby, all higher order functions used to build circuit descriptions have both geometric and behavioural interpretation. Here, we consider only the behavioural interpretation, placing greater emphasis on the type system.

Signals. The behaviour of a circuit is described as a binary relation between sets of signals. A signal is a homogeneous stream of data values over time. A data value is either atomic or is a tuple of data values. We represent tupling of data values by round brackets (). s(n) is the nth element of signal s, where n can be thought of as a time index. We represent the construction of signals using angle brackets. <> is the empty signal. If a and b are signals, <a,b> is a signal whose elements are pairs.

$$<a,b>(n) \quad = \quad (a(n),b(n))$$

The append operation for signals is ^. For example,

$$<a,b>^<c,d> \quad = \quad <a,b,c,d>$$

We always construct compound signals using the <_> operator. So, when we make a list of signals (or a bus) using <_>, we get a signal whose elements are lists. This means that complex circuits can still be described as relations between single signals.

If we are to describe the language categorically, we must work in a category whose objects are sets of signals, and whose arrows are binary relations between sets of signals. We will call this stream version of **REL SREL**. The composition operator in **SREL** is defined in exactly the same way as that in **REL**. The basic objects in **SREL** are the set of all integer signals and the set of all boolean signals. For convenience, we will call these two sets Int and Bool. We make compound types using the $\_ \times \_$ and $\_^*$ type constructors.

$$A \times B \quad =_{def} \quad \{<a,b> \mid a \in A \ \& \ b \in B\} \qquad (p1)$$
$$A^* \quad =_{def} \quad \{<a_0, .. \ a_n> \mid \forall i:0..n. \ a_i \in A\} \qquad (m1)$$

Note that because we have used <_> in these definitions, $A \times B$ is a set of signals carrying pairs. So, for example, Int $\times$ Int is the set of integer-pair signals, and Int* is the set of integer-list signals. Once we have made this move from single data values to signals, we can describe and reason about sequential circuits in almost exactly the way that we would for combinational circuits (cf. [3] for further discussion of this point).

The language: primitives. A set of combinational primitives is assumed. None of these combinational primitives is polymorphic. Each has a fixed (monomorphic) type. For example, an integer adder has type

Add : Int × Int → Int   (in **SREL**)

meaning that Add relates streams of pairs of integers to streams of integers. This statement says that Add is an arrow in the category **SREL**. (We will assume from now on that we are working in **SREL**.) Add happens to be a function, as well as a relation, between its domain and its range. This will not always be the case. For example, we might also choose to include

Add' : Int → Int × Int

an adder whose inputs are in its range, and output is in its domain. Some of our relations happen to be functions, but many are not. (Of course, Add is a rather abstract primitive element. We would probably also want to include more concrete primitives, such as full adders, gates, etc. As far as the theory is concerned, it doesn't matter what combinational primitives we choose.)

The only sequential primitive in Ruby is the delay element, D.

$$a\,D\,b \quad =_{\text{def}} \quad a(t-1) = b(t)$$

It is truly polymorphic, meaning that it will delay any stream. We can think of a polymorphic relation as the set of its instances. Those instances are arrows in **SREL**. For example, the instance of D that delays integer-pair streams is an arrow of the form

$$D_{\text{Int} \times \text{Int}} : \text{Int} \times \text{Int} \to \text{Int} \times \text{Int}.$$

As well as the combinational primitives and the delay element, a set of primitive polymorphic wiring relations is assumed. Some typical examples of wiring primitives are

zip, which interleaves two buses to give a bus of pairs

$$\text{zip}_{AB} : A^* \times B^* \to (A \times B)^* \hspace{3cm} \text{(z-type)}$$

e.g.   <<a,b,c>,<x,y,z>> zip <<a,x>, <b,y>, <c, z>>

halve, which divides a bus into its two halves

$$\text{halve}_A : A^* \to A^* \times A^* \hspace{3.5cm} \text{(h-type 1)}$$

e.g.   <a,b,c,d,e,f,g,h> halve <<a,b,c,d>, <e,f,g,h>>

pair, which divides a bus up into pairs (giving a bus of half the length)

$$pair_A : A* \to (A \times A)* \qquad\qquad\qquad \text{(p-type 1)}$$

e.g. $<a,b,c,d,e,f,g,h>$ pair $<<a,b>, <c,d>, <e,f>, <g,h>>$

first and *second*, which select from a pair of signals

$$first\ _{AB} : A \times B \to A \qquad\qquad <a, b>\ first\ a$$
$$second_{AB} : A \times B \to B \qquad\qquad <a, b>\ second\ b$$

join, which acts as a T junction or duplicator

$$join_A : A \to A \times A \qquad\qquad a\ join\ <a, a>$$

The language: higher order functions. Circuit descriptions are built from primitives (combinational elements, wiring or delay) and a small set of higher order functions. The most obvious way to combine circuits described as relations between signals is to use relational composition. This is defined in **SREL** exactly as it is in **REL**. (a, b, c are signals.) We use the standard notation for repeated composition (e.g. $R^3 = R ; R ; R$).

composition. $a\ R ; S\ c$ $\qquad =_{def} \qquad \exists b.\ a\ R\ b\ \&\ b\ S\ c$

Relational inverse is useful, particularly when we give a geometric interpretation to our higher order functions.

inverse. $a\ R^{-1}\ b$ $\qquad =_{def} \qquad b\ R\ a$

Inverse allows us to express such things as the unzipping of a bus of pairs to form a pair of buses, by using zip^{-1}. Because we are using a relational language, equipped with inverse, we can also express and manipulate data abstraction and representation relations, without having to move to a different formalism.

The next two higher order functions give ways of building relations over complex signals. They correspond to our two ways of constructing sets of signals.

pair. $<a, b>\ R \times S\ <c, d>$ $\qquad =_{def} \qquad a\ R\ c\ \&\ b\ S\ d \qquad \text{(p2)}$
map. $<a_0, ..a_n>\ R*\ <b_0, ..b_n>$ $\qquad =_{def} \qquad \forall i{:}0..n.\ a_i\ R\ b_i \qquad \text{(m2)}$

We have defined two functors, $\_\times\_$ and $\_*$. Definition (p1) above gives the action of $\_\times\_$

on objects and definition (p2) gives its actions on arrows in **SREL**. Similarly, definitions (m1) and (m2) define _* as a functor in **SREL**. This way of designing functors based on the type constructors gives us higher order functions with nice algebraic properties. For example, we know, because _×_ is a functor, that

$$(r \times s) ; (t \times v) \quad = \quad (r ; t) \times (s ; v).$$

The way to extend the repertoire of higher order functions is to define new ones recursively (or indeed non-recursively) in terms of these. For example, a triangle higher order function that places increasing numbers of its parameter on the signals in a bus is defined as

$$
\begin{array}{llll}
<> \ R\Delta \quad <> & =_{\text{def}} & \text{true} \\
<a>^{\wedge}b \ R\Delta \quad <c>^{\wedge}d & =_{\text{def}} & a \ R \ c \ \& \ b \ (R^* ; R\Delta) \ d
\end{array}
$$

e.g. $<a,b,c,d> R\Delta <e,f,g,h> = (a \ R \ e) \& (b \ R^2 f) \& (c \ R^3 g) \& (d \ R^4 h)$

To describe this kind of recursion formally, we should introduce μ, the fixed point operator, and show that μ is a functor. However, this construction is beyond the scope of this paper. Here, we discuss, in a relatively informal way, the properties of our small language, concentrating on how the categorical view can help to expose useful properties of the language.

Properties of the language: polymorphic circuits are natural transformations. The first interesting property of this language is that all polymorphic circuits are natural transformations. We do not prove this formally here, but give examples and indicate why it is so. In some cases, we have to place restrictions on the coding relations (that is the downward arrows in the natural transformation diagram). We explain why these restrictions ar required.

We have shown elsewhere that for any Ruby circuit R, D commutes with R [5]. This allows us to push delays around in our circuit descriptions, and corresponds to retiming as discussed in [4]. It is another way of saying that the polymorphic primitive D is a natural transformation.

The wiring primitives are also natural transformations. The diagram for zip is

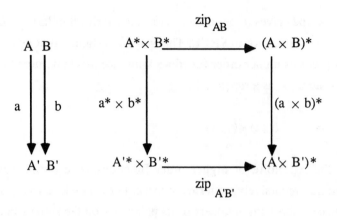

$$a^* \times b^* \; ; \; zip \quad = \quad zip \; ; \; (a \times b)^*$$

is a known theorem of Ruby, so the diagram commutes. Halve and pair are natural transformations since we know that

$$a^* \; ; \; halve \quad = \quad halve \; ; \; (a^* \times a^*) \qquad \text{and}$$
$$a^* \; ; \; pair \quad = \quad pair \; ; \; (a \times a)^*.$$

The close match between these theorems and the types of halve and pair should be obvious. In these examples, there are no restrictions on the coding relations (a and b). When we consider the selectors, first and second, we find that we need restrictions on the coding relations. Let us draw the diagram for first.

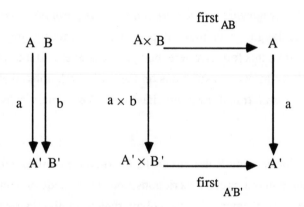

It is the case that

$$a \times b \; ; \; \text{first}_{A'B'} \quad = \quad \text{first}_{AB} \; ; \; a$$

only if b is a total relation. That is, b must relate every element of B to something in B'. If it does not, then the relation on the left is strictly smaller than that on the right, and so the equation does not hold.The problem is caused by the fact that we are throwing away information (by selecting only the first of a pair). To preserve our commuting diagrams, we must make sure to operate on information that may be thrown away using only total relations. The problem did not arise with halve, pair or zip because they are all *linear*. Each piece of information in the domain appears *exactly once* in the range (and vice versa). Linear relations require no restrictions on the coding relations in the natural transformation diagram. Selectors, in which information may be used either zero times, or once, require some of the coding relations to be total.

Join, which performs duplication, causes information to be used more than once. Again, it is only a natural transformation under certain conditions. We would like

$$r \; ; \; \text{join} \quad = \quad \text{join} \; ; \; r \times r$$

In fact, this is only true if r is a function (from its domain to its range). Any pair in the range of the left hand expression must contain equal values, because of the definition of join. The only way to guarantee that pairs in the range of the right hand expression contain equal values is to make r a function.

Clearly, having primitives that are natural transformations is not much use unless the higher order functions used to build circuit descriptions preserve this naturality. In fact, all of our higher order functions do. If their arguments are natural transformations, then so are their results. This is trivially true for composition because we know that the composition of two natural transformations is a natural transformation. For the other higher order functions, we can take advantage of the fact that they are functors, and that functors preserve naturality. If n is a natural transformation from functor F to functor G, then $H(n)$ is a natural transformation from $H(F)$ to $H(G)$. This is best confirmed by drawing the natural transformation diagram for n and then applying H everywhere. This nice property of functors is another reason why defining higher order functions as functors is a good idea.

So, when we compose primitives to make a more complex wiring relation, the result must also be a natural transformation. This immediately gives us a theorem about what commutes with this new wiring relation. For example, riffle, the wiring relation that does a perfect shuffle on the bus in its domain, is defined as

$$\text{riffle} \quad =_{\text{def}} \quad \text{halve ; zip ; pair}^{-1.}$$

$$\text{riffle} : \_^* \to \_^*$$

From the type of riffle, we can conclude that

$$\text{r}^* \text{ ; riffle} \quad = \quad \text{riffle ; r}^*.$$

Such theorems are rather tedious to prove otherwise. Halve, zip and pair are all linear, so riffle is also linear. This means that there are no restrictions on the coding relation r. Clearly, restrictions on the coding relations for parameters to higher order functions will be translated into restrictions for the resulting circuit. So, the theorems generated by the type of a circuit containing both join and selectors will be subject to more restrictions than those for a linear circuit.

This approach gives us a large number of shallow but useful theorems about poymorphic circuits. It must be said, however, that most of our circuits are not polymorphic. How can we generate useful theorems about non-polymorphic circuits? The best way seems to be to move up a level and consider the properties of the higher order functions themselves.

Properties of the language: the higher order functions are natural transformations. Our four primitive higher order functions are themselves natural transformations. To show this, we must express them as arrows between functors. Let us write down the type of composition in standard type notation. A $\leftrightarrow$ B is the set of relations between A and B. Composition takes two relations and gives a relation.

$$;_{\text{ABC}} : (A \leftrightarrow B) \times (B \leftrightarrow C) \to (A \leftrightarrow C)$$

If we are to view this as an arrow between functors, then $\_\leftrightarrow\_$ must be a functor, just as $\_\times\_$ and $\_^*$ are. We must therefore define the action of $\_\leftrightarrow\_$ on *relations*. From the definiton of a functor, we know that if $r : R \to R'$ and $s : S \to S'$, then

$$r \leftrightarrow s : (R \leftrightarrow S) \to (R' \leftrightarrow S')$$

Thus, we must make a relation between R' and S' given a relation, a, between R and S, and the relations r and s. The most obvious way to do this is to invert r, to give $r^{-1} : R' \to R$ and then compose with a and s.

$$a \ (r \leftrightarrow s) \ b \qquad =_{\text{def}} \qquad b = r^{-1} ; a ; s$$

We must check that $\_\leftrightarrow\_$ is a proper functor.

1. $\quad id_A \leftrightarrow id_B \qquad\qquad = \qquad id_{A \leftrightarrow B}$

proof: let $a : A \leftrightarrow B$

$\quad a \ (id_A \leftrightarrow id_B) \ b \qquad\qquad = \{\text{def.} \leftrightarrow\}$

$\quad b = id_A^{-1} ; a ; id_B \qquad\qquad = \{a : A \leftrightarrow B\}$

$\quad b = a \qquad\qquad\qquad\qquad\quad = \{\text{prop. id.}\}$

$\quad a \ (id_{A \leftrightarrow B}) \ b$

2. $\quad (r \leftrightarrow s) ; (t \leftrightarrow v) \qquad = \qquad (r ; t) \leftrightarrow (s ; v)$

proof:

$\quad a \ (r \leftrightarrow s) ; (t \leftrightarrow v) \ c \qquad\qquad\qquad\qquad = \{\text{def.} ;\}$

$\quad \exists b. \ a \ (r \leftrightarrow s) \ b \ \& \ b \ (t \leftrightarrow v) \ c \qquad\qquad = \{\text{def.} \leftrightarrow\}$

$\quad \exists b. \ b = r^{-1} ; a ; s \ \& \ c = t^{-1} ; b ; v \qquad = \{\text{pred. calc.}\}$

$\quad c = t^{-1} ; r^{-1} ; a ; s ; v \qquad\qquad\qquad\qquad = \{\text{def.} \leftrightarrow\}$

$\quad a \ ((r ; t) \leftrightarrow (s ; v)) \ c$

Our next step is to check that composition is a natural transformation, by drawing the diagram and checking that it commutes.

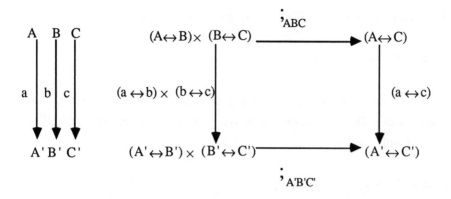

We can read the diagram by imagining a pair of relations (p,q) as an element of the set at the top left hand corner of the square, and then following both paths. The diagram commutes if

$$(a^{-1} ; p ; b) ; (b^{-1} ; q ; c) \qquad = \qquad a^{-1} ; (p ; q) ; c$$

that is if

$$b ; b^{-1} = id.$$

One of the coding relations, b, must be restricted. Saying that a higher order function for circuit construction is a natural transformation is the same as saying that if we apply a transformation of the form $(a^{-1} ; \_ ; b)$ to each parameter (or cell) of the circuit, we get the same result as if we apply a similar transformation to the whole circuit. This means that if there are any internal arcs in the circuit, then we must be able to cancel any relations that appear on those arcs when we transform each cell. Thus, we needed to cancel the $b ; b^{-1}$ that appeared between p and q in the example above. Inverse, $\_\times\_$ and $\_*$ all turn out to be natural transformations without any restrictions on the coding relations, because they don't have any internal connections.

Because natural transformations are closed under composition and substitution, our compound higher order functions are also natural transformations. This again allows us to generate theorems from types. For example, knowing that the type of the higher order function Δ is

$$\Delta : (\_\leftrightarrow\_) \rightarrow (\_^* \leftrightarrow \_^*),$$

we can conclude that

$$(a^{-1} ; r ; a) \Delta \qquad = \qquad (a^{-1})* ; r \Delta ; a* \qquad \text{if } a ; a^{-1} = \text{id.}$$

The restriction on the coding relation again allows cancellation on internal arcs. In fact, any higher order function of the same type obeys the same theorem. To make this statement more precise, we would have to explain formally how new higher order functions are defined, and perform a structural induction. We should really be more explicit about the base cases in recursions, and this may lead to further restrictions on the coding relations. A subsequent paper will tackle these problems. Here, instead, we will consider ways in which the categorical viewpoint just given helps us to extend the language in a methodical way.

4. Category theory as a guide to language design

We would like to extend the language in a way that increases the number of theorems that we can deduce from types. We have already advocated higher order functions that are functors, both because this guarantees nice algebraic properties and because functors preserve the natural transformation property. Thus, the choice of higher order functions is closely bound up with the choice of a type system. The way forward is to extend the type system and to add new higher order functions corresponding to the new type constructors. At present, our type constructors for sets of signals are $\_\times\_$ and $\_*$. We propose two novel type constructors, and show how they allow us to deduce more precise theorems from types.

Repeating sequences. A 2-repeating sequence of signals (a 2r-sequence) is of the form

$$<a_0, b_0, a_1, b_1, a_2, b_2, . . .>$$

where all the a_is have the same type, A, and all the b_is have the same type, B, and A may be different from B. We will use the notation $\_^{2*}$ for this new type constructor. The signal above is of type $(A \times B)^{2*}$. We have deliberately chosen not to make $\_^{2*}$ take two arguments, for reasons that we will explain later. The argument to $\_^{2*}$ must, however, provide a source of both the odd-numbered and the even-numbered elements in the resulting sequence. So, it must be a set of signals that are pairs. Similarly, $\_^{2*}$ operates only on arrows that relate pairs to pairs. This means that $\_^{2*}$ is a partial functor that must be applied to objects and arrows of the correct type. We can also view $\_^{2*}$ as a total functor from the subcategory of **SREL** that contains only the required objects and arrows of **SREL**. This category, **SREL**^{pair}, is certainly different from **SREL**×**SREL**. The arrows in **SREL**^{pair} are relations between signals carrying pairs and we want to discuss the properties of these kinds of relations. (The arrows in **SREL**×**SREL** are pairs of relations.) If r is a relation of type $(A \times B) \to (C \times D)$, then $r^{2*} : (A \times B)^{2*} \to (C \times D)^{2*}$. It can be thought of as dividing its domain and range sequences into pairs, and relating those pairs by r. That is

$$r^{2*} \quad =_{def} \quad pair \; ; r^* \; ; pair^{-1}.$$

Note that $(A \times A)^{2*}$ is the set of even length elements of A^*, so we have certainly added more structure to the type system. A functor for n-repeating sequences is also quite useful, though we will not use it here.

Now that we have introduced more structure into the type system, we can give more precise types to some of the wiring relations. For example,

$$pair_X : X^{2*} \to X^* \qquad\qquad\qquad \text{(p-type 2)}$$

where X must be an object in **SREL**^{pair}. (Strictly speaking we should map the object X in **SREL**^{pair} into the same object in **SREL** before applying the functor $\_^*$ to it.) This type expresses the fact that pair does not disturb certain adjacent elements in the domain sequence, since those elements form pairs in the range sequence. Pairs of adjacent signals are referred to in this type simply as elements of X. They are lumped together as single units and so cannot be separated. If, on the other hand, we had made $\_^{2*}$ a bifunctor, then the type would have been

$$pair_{AB} : (A , B)^{2*} \to (A \times B)^*$$

which admits many more relations, and no longer contains any information about adjacency of signals. This is why we did not make $\_^{2*}$ a bifunctor. Knowing that adjacent signals remain adjacent is important when using relations that work on pairs of signals. Making the type more precise reduces the number of relations that have that type and makes the theorems generated from it more precise.

E-sequences. An e-sequence is of the form

$$\langle a0, a1, a2, .. an, b0, b1, b2, .. bn \rangle.$$

It is an even-length sequence whose first and second halves have possibly different types. Here, if $\langle a0, a1, a2, .. an \rangle$ is in A, and $\langle b0, b1, b2, .. bn \rangle$ is in B, then the sequence shown is in A | B. Only sequences of equal length can be appended in this way. On relations, r | s relates two e-sequences if r relates their first halves, and s relates their second halves. So, r and s must be relations on sequences, and again we need to define a special subcategory of **SREL**, **SREL**^{list}, though we omit the details. The two rules for a functor are obeyed.

1. $\quad id_{(A|B)} \qquad = \qquad id_A \mid id_B$
2. $\quad (f \mid g) ; (h \mid j) \quad = \qquad (f ; h) \mid (g ; j)$

We have introduced yet more structure into the type system. $(A* \mid A*)$ is the set of even length sequences of A. We noted earlier that $(A \times A)^{2*}$ is the same set of even length sequences of A. We have introduced a form of sub-typing and this may cause problems when we try to do type inference. Our type system is certainly powerful. For example, $((A* \mid B*) \mid (C* \mid D*))$ is the set of sequences composed of equal numbers of As, Bs, Cs and Ds. We can now give a better type to halve

$$\text{halve}_{AB} : (A \mid B) \to (A \times B) \qquad\qquad \text{(h-type 2)}$$

and can conclude that

$$(a \mid b) ; \text{halve} \qquad = \qquad \text{halve} ; (a \times b).$$

The new type conveys the information that for a given pair of sequences in the range of halve, the first sequence contains elements drawn only from the first half of the corresponding e-sequence in the domain. A more precise theorem about halve results.

Having more informative types for the primitive wiring relations gives us more informative types for the compound ones. For example, knowing that

$$halve_{A*B*} : (A* \mid B*) \to (A* \times B*) \qquad \text{(inst.h-type 2)}$$
$$zip_{AB} : A* \times B* \to (A \times B)* \qquad \text{(z-type)}$$
$$pair^{-1}_{A \times B} : (A \times B)* \to (A \times B)^{2*} \qquad \text{(by p-type 2)}$$

we can conclude that

$$riffle_{AB} : (A* \mid B*) \to (A \times B)^{2*}.$$

This gives

$$(f* \mid g*) ; riffle \qquad = \qquad riffle ; (f \times g)^{2*}.$$

What we have shown here is that making the types of the wiring relations more and more precise allows more and more precise theorems to be derived about their behaviour. In the limit, the most precise type of riffle, say, says that the type of its domain is related by riffle to the type of its range! The trick seems to be to make the types informative, without having to give too much detail. Much more work needs to be done on this, but it looks promising.

In fact, the theorem about riffle that we have derived is exactly the kind of theorem that one uses when reasoning about butterfly algorithms such as Batcher's bitonic sort [6] and the Fast Fourier Transform [2]. It is our experience in describing and reasoning about such algorithms that has prompted the introduction of the new functors, $\_^{2*}$ and $\_\mid\_$. Ruby already had a higher order function, pmap, corresponding to $\_^{2*}$. However, we had not considered extending the type system in this way. At present, Ruby only has the special case of $\_\mid\_$ in which both parameters are the same. Now that we are aware of its nice algebraic properties, we will use the more general $\_\mid\_$. We have generally added new higher order functions to Ruby in a rather ad hoc way, as they became necessary in examples. It is very useful to be able to extend the language in a more methodical way, using the notion of *type constructor + higher order function = functor* as a guide. We plan to investigate the application of these ideas to functional programming languages, as well as to relational languages. The question of how much type inference can be retained in this richer type system remains to be answered.

5. Conclusion

Studying category theory was worth the effort. When designing μFP, we used FP as a source of free theorems. Now, we use category theory. It seems to be a natural progression. We are not using any deep theorems of category theory, but rather we are using it as a useful notation, and as a way of organising our thoughts. It was interesting to discover that Ruby was already a rather categorical language.

We expect the ability to derive theorems directly from the types of expressions in our relational language to be of practical use. Our aim is to build a transformation system for the language and it should be possible to exploit the close link between types and allowable transformations.

Acknowledgement

Many thanks to Phil Wadler, whose work on and enthusiasm for applications of category theory provided the inspiration for this paper. Wayne Luk and Phil Wadler provided constructive criticism of an earlier draft. The remaining errors are all mine.

References

[1] R.J.M. Hughes, Projections for Polymorphic Strictness Analysis, Proc. Int. Conf. on Category Theory in Computer Science, Manchester, Springer-Verlag, 1989.

[2] G. Jones, Fast Fourier transform by program transformation of the discrete Fourier transform, (submitted for publication).

[3] G. Jones & M. Sheeran, Timeless Truths about Sequential Circuits, Chapter 14 in S.K. Tewksbury et al (eds.) Concurrent Computations: Algorithms, Architecture and Technology, Plenum Press, 1988.

[4] C.E. Leiserson & J.B. Saxe, Retiming Synchronous Circuitry, Tech. Report 13, Digital Systems Research Center, Palo Alto, California 94301, 1986.

[5] M. Sheeran, Retiming and Slowdown in Ruby, in G. Milne (ed.) The Fusion of Hardware Design and Verification, North-Holland, 1988.

[6] M. Sheeran, Describing Hardware Algorithms in Ruby, to appear in Proc. IFIP WG10.1 Int. Workshop on Concepts and Characteristics of Declarative Systems, North-Holland, 1989.

[7] P.L. Wadler, Theorems for Free!, to appear in Proc. Int. Conf. on Functional Programming Languages and Computer Architecture, London, Springer-Verlag, 1989.

Lecture Notes in Computer Science 676

Edited by G. Goos and J. Hartmanis

Advisory Board: W. Brauer D. Gries J. Stoer

DATE DUE FOR RETURN

NEW ACCESSION
CANCELLED

Thomas H. Reiss

Recognizing Planar Objects Using Invariant Image Features

Springer-Verlag

Berlin Heidelberg New York
London Paris Tokyo
Hong Kong Barcelona
Budapest

Series Editors

Gerhard Goos
Universität Karlsruhe
Postfach 69 80
Vincenz-Priessnitz-Straße 1
W-7500 Karlsruhe, FRG

Juris Hartmanis
Cornell University
Department of Computer Science
4130 Upson Hall
Ithaca, NY 14853, USA

Author

Thomas H. Reiss
Engineering Department, Cambridge University
Trumpington Street, Cambridge CB2 1PZ, U.K.

CR Subject Classification (1991): I.3-5

ISBN 3-540-56713-5 Springer-Verlag Berlin Heidelberg New York
ISBN 0-387-56713-5 Springer-Verlag New York Berlin Heidelberg

© Springer-Verlag Berlin Heidelberg 1993
Printed in Germany

Typesetting: Camera ready by author/editor
45/3140-543210 - Printed on acid-free paper